NEW DIRECTIONS IN GERMAN STUDIES
Vol. 16

Series Editor:
Imke Meyer

Editorial Board:
Katherine Arens, Roswitha Burwick, Richard Eldridge,
Erika Fischer-Lichte, Catriona MacLeod, Stephan
Schindler, Heidi Schlipphacke, Ulrich Schönherr, James
A. Schultz, Silke-Maria Weineck, David Wellbery, Sabine
Wilke, John Zilcosky.

Volumes in the series:

Vol. 1. *Improvisation as Art: Conceptual Challenges, Historical Perspectives*
by Edgar Landgraf

Vol. 2. *The German Pícaro and Modernity: Between Underdog and Shape-Shifter*
by Bernhard Malkmus

Vol. 3. *Citation and Precedent: Conjunctions and Disjunctions of German Law and Literature*
by Thomas O. Beebee

Vol. 4. *Beyond Discontent: 'Sublimation' from Goethe to Lacan*
by Eckart Goebel

Vol. 5. *From Kafka to Sebald: Modernism and Narrative Form*
edited by Sabine Wilke

Vol. 6. *Image in Outline: Reading Lou Andreas-Salomé*
by Gisela Brinker-Gabler

Vol. 7. *Out of Place: German Realism, Displacement, and Modernity*
by John B. Lyon

Vol. 8. *Thomas Mann in English: A Study in Literary Translation*
by David Horton

Vol. 9. *The Tragedy of Fatherhood: King Laius and the Politics of Paternity in the West*
by Silke-Maria Weineck

Vol. 10. *The Poet as Phenomenologist: Rilke and the New Poems*
by Luke Fischer

Vol. 11. *The Laughter of the Thracian Woman: A Protohistory of Theory*
by Hans Blumenberg, translated by Spencer Hawkins

Vol. 12. *Roma Voices in the German-Speaking World*
by Lorely French

Vol. 13. *Vienna's Dreams of Europe: Culture and Identity beyond the Nation-State*
by Katherine Arens

Vol. 14. *Thomas Mann and Shakespeare: Something Rich and Strange*
edited by Tobias Döring and Ewan Fernie

Vol. 15. *Goethe's Families of the Heart*
by Susan E. Gustafson

German Aesthetics

Fundamental Concepts from Baumgarten to Adorno

Edited by
J. D. Mininger
and Jason Michael Peck

Bloomsbury Academic
An imprint of Bloomsbury Publishing Inc

BLOOMSBURY ACADEMIC
LONDON • NEW YORK • OXFORD • NEW DELHI • SYDNEY

BLOOMSBURY ACADEMIC
Bloomsbury Publishing Plc
50 Bedford Square, London, WC1B 3DP, UK
1385 Broadway, New York, NY 10018, USA
29 Earlsfort Terrace, Dublin 2, Ireland

BLOOMSBURY, BLOOMSBURY ACADEMIC and the Diana logo are trademarks of
Bloomsbury Publishing Plc

First published in 2016

Copyright © J. D. Mininger, Jason Michael Peck, and Contributors 2016

For legal purposes the Acknowledgements on p.x constitute an extension of this copyright page.

Cover design: Andrea F. Busci

All rights reserved. No part of this publication may be reproduced or transmitted in any form or by any means, electronic or mechanical, including photocopying, recording, or any information storage or retrieval system, without prior permission in writing from the publishers.

Bloomsbury Publishing Plc does not have any control over, or responsibility for, any third-party websites referred to or in this book. All internet addresses given in this book were correct at the time of going to press. The author and publisher regret any inconvenience caused if addresses have changed or sites have ceased to exist, but can accept no responsibility for any such changes.

Library of Congress Cataloging-in-Publication Data
Names: Mininger, J. D., editor. | Peck, Jason Michael, editor.
Title: German Aesthetics : fundamental concepts from Baumgarten to Adorno /
Edited by J.D. Mininger and Jason Michael Peck.
Description: New York : Bloomsbury Academic, 2016. | Includes bibliographical references and index.
Identifiers: LCCN 2016009027 (print) | LCCN 2016017863 (ebook) | ISBN 9781501321481 (hardcover : alk. paper) | ISBN 9781501321498 (ePDF) | ISBN 9781501321504 (Epub)
Subjects: LCSH: Aesthetics, German.
Classification: LCC BH221.G33 G47 2016 (print) | LCC BH221.G33 (ebook) | DDC 111/.850943--dc23
LC record available at https://lccn.loc.gov/2016009027

ISBN: HB: 978-1-5013-2148-1
PB: 978-1-5013-2147-4
Epub: 978-1-5013-2150-4
ePDF: 978-1-5013-2149-8

Series: New Directions in German Studies

Typeset by Fakenham Prepress Solutions, Fakenham Norfolk, NR21 8NN
To find out more about our authors and books visit www.bloomsbury.com
and sign up for our newsletters.

In memory of Jochen

Contents

Acknowledgments		x
Introduction *J. D. Mininger and Jason Michael Peck*		1
1	Imagination *Jochen Schulte-Sasse*	5
2	Judgment *Vivasvan Soni*	14
3	Beauty *Paul Guyer*	25
4	Sublime *David Martyn*	34
5	Mimesis *Christian Sieg*	43
6	Feeling: On *Werther* *Stanley Corngold*	51
7	Irony *Michel Chaouli*	60
8	Listening *Mirko M. Hall*	68
9	Ethics *Jason Michael Peck*	76
10	Absolute Music *Sanna Pederson*	84

Contents

11　The End of Art　　91
　　Eva Geulen

12　Allegory　　100
　　J. D. Mininger

13　Value　　109
　　A. Kiarina Kordela

14　God is Dead　　119
　　Silke-Maria Weineck

15　Tragedy/*Trauerspiel*　　127
　　Ian Balfour

16　Saying/Showing　　136
　　Fabian Goppelsröder

17　Nothingness　　145
　　Kenneth Haynes

18　Messianism　　155
　　Peter Fenves

19　Mediation/Medium　　163
　　James A. Steintrager and Rey Chow

20　Truth　　174
　　Kai Hammermeister

21　Uncanny　　181
　　Thomas Pepper

22　Mood/Attunement　　188
　　Darío González

23　Film　　196
　　Johannes von Moltke

24　Montage/Collage　　204
　　Patrizia McBride

25　Normality　　210
　　Jürgen Link

26　Ugly　　219
　　Richard Leppert

Contents ix

27 Shudder   227
   Karyn Ball

28 Committed Art   236
   Andrew Lyndon Knighton

   Bibliography   245

   Notes on Contributors   257

   Index   263

Acknowledgments

The idea for this book arose well over ten years ago, based largely on the impulse to produce a volume to honor our mentor, Jochen Schulte-Sasse. Mirko Hall—our friend, a contributor to this volume, and a fellow student of Jochen's—provided crucial support in the early stages. Three others—Richard Leppert, Thomas Pepper, and Jack Zipes, all close friends and colleagues of Jochen, and our teachers—gave decisive counsel and encouragement. From its incipience to its publication, Silke-Maria Weineck has given us invaluable guidance—thank you, Silke! We are grateful to all of the volume's contributors for their patience and commitment to the book. We thank Lindsay Waters for helping us to develop the project. We would also like to thank the team at Bloomsbury: Haaris Naqvi, Mary Al-Sayed, and especially *New Directions in German Studies* series editor Imke Meyer. We are grateful to the book's anonymous reviewers, whose insights and suggestions improved the volume.

Jason would like to thank Leslie Morris, Jack Zipes, Susan Gustafson, Jennifer Creech, Marynel Ryan Van Zee, Jason Middleton, Joshua Dubler, Lisa Cerami, Nora Rubel, and Aaron Hughes for their advice and friendship during the gestation of the project. I would like to dedicate this volume to my parents and to Sy, Vi, and Hal, who prove to me every day the existence of the beautiful and the sublime.

For their patience, friendship, and encouragement, J.D. wishes to thank: Tomas Berkmanas, Gintautas Mažeikis, Jurga Jonutytė, Leonidas Donskis, Marlene Wall, Niels Jørgen Cappelørn, Jon Stewart, Thomas Pepper, Richard Leppert, Bartholomew Ryan, Benjamin Olivares Bøgeskov, Christian Møller, Darío González, Christian Sieg, Fabian Goppelsröder, Andrew Knighton, and Brynnar Swenson. I am especially grateful to my parents for their constant support, and to Elijus, Nojus, and Vilma for their laughter, joy, and patience.

It is heartbreaking for us that the person we would most like to thank—Jochen Schulte-Sasse—died in December, 2012. We are proud to dedicate this book to his memory. Words from an obituary written by Mirko Hall best express our own thoughts and feelings:

[Jochen] provided his students with an unwavering model of academic excellence, while exuding those qualities of *Allgemeinmenschlichkeit* that were valorized by the eighteenth-century German thinkers whom he so deeply admired: compassion, humility, kindness, and patience. One is reminded here of that wonderful passage from Lessing's *Emilia Galotti*, a text that he loved: possessing "das Ideal hier (*mit dem Finger auf die Stirne*)—oder vielmehr hier (*mit dem Finger auf das Herz*)," Jochen will always be remembered for this beautiful synergy of intellect and heart.

Thank you, Jochen.

Introduction
J. D. Mininger and Jason Michael Peck

The German-speaking intellectual world has played a unique role in the history of philosophical aesthetics. Many of the foundational concepts and texts of aesthetic theory come from the German-speaking tradition—for instance: the notions of aesthetic autonomy and disinterestedness developed in Immanuel Kant's landmark *Critique of Judgment*; Friedrich Schiller's writings on grace and dignity as well as the aesthetic state in the 1790s; Hegel's provocative claims about the end of art; Friedrich Nietzsche's seminal theories of artistic form and motivation in *The Birth of Tragedy*; or Adorno's dense, powerful *Aesthetic Theory*. The names of German thinkers inundate nearly every canonical account of the history and field of aesthetics, including such figures as Lessing, Schlegel, Schelling, Schopenhauer, Heidegger, Brecht, Benjamin, and Gadamer, just to name a prominent few. Indeed, it is fair to say that without Kant's *Critique of Judgment*, modern aesthetics as we know it would be inconceivable.

The term "aesthetics" was coined by a German-speaking writer, Alexander Baumgarten, whose *Meditationes philosophicae de nonullis ad poema pertinentibus* (translated as *Reflections on Poetry*) is both the canonical starting point of the German aesthetic tradition and equally the founding text of modern aesthetics. Baumgarten reorients philosophy away from "genuine" knowledge and self-evident logic, towards sensation and perception: "Philosophers might still find occasion, not without ample reward, to inquire also into those devices of by which they might improve the lower faculties of knowing, and sharpen them, and apply them more happily for the benefit of the whole world."[1] The study of things perceived requires great care on the part of the philosopher in interpreting "sensate subject matter"

---

1   Alexander Gottlieb Baumgarten, *Reflections on Poetry*, trans. Karl Aschenbrenner and William B. Holther (Berkeley: University of California Press, 1954), 78.

2 German Aesthetics

and, therefore, the aesthetic theorist "is expected to take much greater account of terms."[2] Baumgarten's project of aesthetics required a new semiotic constellation—new terminology, new epistemic orientation, and a reassessment of philosophy's definitions and tasks. In the wake of Baumgarten's vision of aesthetics, the German tradition would play a role of unparalleled importance in providing aesthetics with its own intellectual terms and frames of reference.

Inspired in part by the emphasis aesthetics has continually placed on terminology, this volume presents accessible entry points into significant questions and debates of philosophical aesthetics through the broadly influential German aesthetic tradition and its key terms and concepts. Because concepts from the German aesthetic tradition inform diverse perspectives in other language area studies, as well as in continental philosophy and art theory generally, the book both contributes to and exceeds the boundaries of German studies. *German Aesthetics* provides English-speaking audiences—from uninitiated readers to advanced students and scholars alike—with a reference tool containing fundamental terms and conceptual narratives of the German tradition of philosophical aesthetics from Baumgarten to Adorno (roughly 1750–1970).

Each entry is organized around a key concept or related set of terms. The book's keyword organization proceeds from the condition that aesthetic concepts are often highly contested intellectual territory, that these terms have a history, and that their usage and meanings are prone to shifting on the basis of context, especially as these keywords participate in social, cultural, and political debates. The language we use frames our boundaries of interpretation and thus our experience—of art, of beauty, of matters of taste, and of sensate or aesthetic experience more generally. Greater awareness of the terms we lean on means greater awareness of the rhetorical and ideological commitments we make in the course of our choice and deployment of concepts and keywords. For this reason the volume resists mere summaries of schools of thought or hermeneutic approaches to aesthetic theory. There is enough introductory material in each entry to bring the otherwise uninitiated reader into the conversation. However, the volume's contributors equally interpret the information they provide, with the aim of helping the reader better understand the frames of reference upon which the concerns and key concepts of aesthetic theory are built.

The volume's organization is hardly the only productive way of imagining the construction of fundamental concepts in German aesthetics.[3] For example, in *The German Aesthetic Tradition*, Kai

---

2 Ibid.
3 For an outstanding example of how the German tradition belongs to a wider

Hammermeister uses a structure of paradigms to narrate the emergence, critique, and reformulation of German aesthetics. Hammermeister outlines the historical patterns in the German aesthetic tradition, seeing a "patterned progression" in each paradigm.[4] Complementary to Hammermeister's historically organized account, *German Aesthetics* accentuates conceptual distinctions between key concepts, thinkers, and works—distinctions nevertheless made possible by historical and material conditions. Rather than ignoring the multiple potentials within each term and period, the structure encourages connections and constellations that attempt to explain, express, and even re-imagine each concept. Earlier figures and terms become unfettered from their historical specificity, producing greater potential for innovation, critique, and theorizing "otherwise." Yet the historical coordinates of these keywords simultaneously and stubbornly return the aesthetic inquiries to their material contexts and conditions, as the concepts get revisited, refracted, revived, or even rejected in relation to their own critical pasts and futures. In other words, the book also enacts a creative construction of something new out of pre-existing elements. It is as if Walter Benjamin's realm of "tragic time" were operative, where "we cannot conceive of a single empirical event that bears a necessary relation to the time of its occurrence."[5] Crucially, Benjamin adds the all-important term "necessary" here. In justifying this volume's organizational structure, we do not suggest that the conceptual events of the German tradition of philosophical aesthetics bear no relationship to their historical context. Rather, following Benjamin and the notion of a keyword as a constellation, which activates the myriad past ideas and events that comprise it through the perspective of the present, we simply affirm that historical determinism is not the guiding principle in the construction of this volume. Yet, the volume does bear signposts of periodization, albeit with blurred lines. The concepts at the beginning of the book reflect more emphatically on the eighteenth-century context; those concepts positioned in the middle of the book tend to speak more to the thinkers, texts, and concerns associated with the nineteenth century; and those terms toward the end of the volume incline toward a concentration on the twentieth century.

Western tradition of modern philosophical aesthetics from the eighteenth century to the present that includes Britain, France, and the United States, see Paul Guyer's masterful three-volume study, *A History of Modern Aesthetics* (Cambridge: Cambridge University Press, 2014).

4 Kai Hammermeister, *The German Aesthetic Tradition* (Cambridge: Cambridge University Press, 2002), xiii.

5 Walter Benjamin, *The Origin of German Tragic Drama*, trans. John Osborne (London: Verso, 1998), 55.

4   German Aesthetics

This matter of the subtle relations and historical overlap in discourses of philosophical aesthetics raises an important point about semantics and usage of terms: in today's academy what is often labeled "theory" would have been understood by central figures of German intellectual history as belonging to "aesthetics." One of the implicit theses of this volume is that philosophical aesthetics does not belong only to those who put forth treatises on aesthetic theory. This book accords with studies that unmoor aesthetics from the realms of strictly evaluating artworks or patrolling the disciplinary borders of aesthetics to also include larger questions of presentation and representation within politics and theory.[6] In support of the clearly philosophical foundations of aesthetics, this book does not stress the study of art in its practical capacity (i.e. the actual production of art); rather, it follows the German tradition that used a philosophy of aesthetics to work through myriad theoretical concepts. This strategy does not neglect the fact that some of the figures discussed in the volume did make art; but, more importantly, the volume strives to illuminate aesthetics' role in the shaping of philosophical discourse.

Indeed, perhaps some of the entries in the volume may seem "unaesthetic." For example, at quick glance, "God is Dead" and "Messianism" might not speak to the apprehension of art objects as logically as, for instance, "Beauty," "Truth," and "Judgment." Yet, in light of the history of German aesthetics in particular, it is worth remembering that Baumgarten's original use of the term encompassed all sensate experiences, not merely those related to art. As described at the beginning of this Introduction, the contribution of philosophy was critical to the birth of modern aesthetics, which extended aesthetics into a field of inquiry that included new forms and modes of representation and interpretation. Today as then, the possible range of aesthetically relevant categories continues to grow under the pressure of philosophical attention to ever-changing historical and material conditions, shifting interests and values, and new forms of art. Aesthetics is part and parcel of any modernity whatsoever—due in no small part to the rich history and still ripe potential of the concepts, texts, and figures of German aesthetics.

---

6   For example, see Andrew Cole, *The Birth of Theory* (Chicago: University of Chicago Press, 2014), and Nikolas Kompridis, ed., *The Aesthetic Turn in Political Thought* (New York: Bloomsbury, 2014).

One Imagination
Jochen Schulte-Sasse

The ascent of both "imagination" and "imaginary" as keywords in the eighteenth century comes simultaneously with a marked change in their meanings. By the early nineteenth century, "imagination" had become the central term of a theory of subjectivity with far-reaching aesthetic, psychological, and anthropological ramifications. Samuel Taylor Coleridge, for example, regards genius as the effect of a "synthetic and magical power, to which we have exclusively appropriated the name of imagination."[1] It is the imagination, Coleridge contends, that "brings the whole soul of man into activity, with the subordination of its faculties into each other, according to their relative worth of dignity."[2] Such remarks assume the imagination to be a precondition for the psychological and ethical completion of a person; for the "spirit of unity, that blends, and (as it were) fuses, each into each,"[3] is a characteristic both of an artwork and of a subject that experiences itself as unified.

It is no coincidence that authors adhering to the "modern" concept of a creative imagination simultaneously advance a theory of subjectivity that stresses its constructed nature. Again Coleridge states that the subject "becomes a subject by the act of constructing itself objectively to itself; but which never is an object except for itself, and only so far as by the very same act it becomes a subject."[4] He insists that the subject is always already split and that only because of this split can it construct "itself objectively to itself." In other words, a subject can constitute itself as an individual only on the basis of a mirror relationship. This relationship of reflection that the subject establishes to itself as an object

---

1   Samuel Tayler Coleridge, *Biographia Literaria*, Vol. 1, ed. James Engell and W. Jackson Bate (Princeton, NJ: Princeton University Press, 1983), 15.
2   Ibid., 17.
3   Ibid.
4   Ibid., 273.

is a visual one. Thus it follows also that modern notions of subjectivity often make use of visual terms such as eye, mirror, and image, which again land us back in the domain of the imagination, for which these terms are likewise central. The above propositions raise a significant question: what is the relationship between the modern conception of subjectivity as visual and that of the imagination?

Until the concept of imagination or fancy was valorized in the eighteenth century, it had often been excluded from what "really" constituted humanity, because of its supposed corporeal, as opposed to spiritual or intellectual, nature. Indeed, the imagination was not only compromised by its relegation to the body, but condemned as the antithesis of the spirit; it was held responsible for bodily deformations and formlessness in general. Not only was the imagination as a corporeal phenomenon morally suspect, but also its equivalences, images.

The historically overdetermined complex of related terms like body, eye, image, imagination, sensuality, and earth has been investigated predominantly in connection with Christianity's well-known animosity to the image. As a material object, the image is not adequate to represent God. Consequently, Christians are admonished, as by Lactantius around 300, "not to adore images because they are made of earth."[5] A half-century later, the religious pedagogue Ambrose ascribes a pernicious influence to the imagination, because if "deceived by the imagination, [the soul] turns to matter, and is glued to the body,"[6] whereas the perfect soul despises all that is corporeal: "the imagination, opposed to truth, is a matter of our weakness."[7] Gianfrancesco Pico della Mirandola yields to the pressure of this tradition when, in his *Liber de imaginatione* [On the Imagination] of 1500, the first study devoted entirely to the imagination, he feels compelled to vehemently repudiate his subject matter:

> He who strives to dominate phantasy persists in that dignity in which he was created and placed, and by which he is continually urged to direct the eye of the mind towards God, Father of all blessings ... . But he who obeys the dictates of the perverted sense and deceitful imagination, at once loses his dignity, and degenerates to the brute.[8]

---

5 Lactantius, *The Divine Institutes*, trans. Mary Francis McDonald, Vol. 49 of *The Fathers of the Church* (Washington, DC: Catholic University of America Press, 1964), 101.
6 Saint Ambrose, *Seven Exegetical Works*, trans. Michael P. McHugh, Vol. 65 of *The Fathers of the Church* (Washington, DC: Catholic University of America Press, 1972), 14.
7 Ibid., 93.
8 Gianfrancesco Pico della Mirandola, *Liber de imaginatione* [On the Imagination],

These citations may serve as representative for a two thousand-year tradition in which the imagination was not only deemed morally degenerate due to its ontological distance from the origin or center of being, but held responsible for human deviations like malformations, tumors, monstrosities.

However, by the end of the eighteenth century, the imagination is recuperated through an aesthetic discourse that constructs the imagination as the seat of the creative act, or, as Friedrich Schiller writes to Christian Gottfried Körner in a letter dated February 28, 1793: "Language places everything before the understanding, and the poet brings everything before the imagination. Poetry wants intuitions, language only gives [it] concepts."[9] The creative power of the imagination depends, as much as the understanding, on its power of distance. However, whereas the understanding proceeds conceptually, the imagination proceeds intuitively (*anschaulich*). The imagination is no longer a power that can recall "ideas" through mental images, rather it now creates images out of itself. Reflection now bears in imagining a totality. In assessing the transformation the imagination goes through in the late eighteenth century, what becomes apparent for thinkers such as Kant, Fichte, Hegel, and the early Romantics is that the imagination does not merely behold, it also reflects on the relationship of the distance between the subject and (aesthetic) object.

In this new conceptualization of the imagination, Immanuel Kant forms a middle-point between the prohibition of the imagination exhibited by the earlier, predominantly Christian writers and the new aesthetic discourse that develops around the positive qualities of the imagination. The contrast between the older and newer pathologies of the imagination lies in the underlying difference that Kant, in the context of a discussion regarding the poetic imagination, defines as the difference between *imaginatio affinitas* and *imaginatio plastica*. In his polemic against the *imaginatio affinitas*, Kant describes it as "the sensory productive faculty of affinity based on the shared lineage of ideas from each other."[10] Kant uses a comparison which, in the interest of disciplining it, illuminates the history of the imagination's meaning(s):

Latin text with English translation by Harry Caplan (New Haven, CT: Yale University Press, 1930), 44–5.
9   Leonard Simpson, Esq, ed. and trans. *Correspondence of Schiller with Körner*, Vol. 2 (London: Richard Bentley New Burlington Street, 1849), 216–17.
10 Immanuel Kant, *Anthropology from a Pragmatic Point of View*, trans. Victor Lyle Dowdell (Carbondale: Southern Illinois University Press, 1996), 64.

8   German Aesthetics

> In social conversation people sometimes leap from one subject to another, quite different one, following an empirical association of ideas ...This desultoriness is a kind of nonsense in terms of form, which disrupts and destroys a conversation. Only when one subject has been exhausted and a short pause follows can we properly launch another subject, if it is interesting. A lawless, vagrant imagination so disconcerts the mind by a succession of ideas having no objective connection that we leave a gathering of this kind wondering whether we have been dreaming.[11]

Crucially, in this passage Kant discusses this denunciatory example regarding social conversation in a chapter concerning the power of poetizing, i.e. the "poetic imagination." Like so many other aesthetic theorists of the eighteenth century, Kant tends to detect in the poetic imagination a desire for work which comes from a vaguely perceived similarity under signs and things (or between a work of art and its mimetic reality) and possibly endangered by the bourgeois project of logic.

In the *Critique of Pure Reason*, Kant defines the imagination somewhat traditionally, as: "the power of presenting an object in intuition even *without the object's being present.*"[12] He expands this definition, which had been in use since antiquity, through the concept of the productive imagination:

> Now, all our intuition is sensible; and hence the imagination, because of the subjective condition under which alone it can give to the concepts of understanding a corresponding intuition, belongs to *sensibility*. Yet the synthesis of the imagination is an exercise of spontaneity, which is determinative, rather than merely determinable, as is sense; hence this synthesis can *a priori* determine sense in terms of its form in accordance with the unity of apperception.[13]

Kant understands the opposition between reproductive and productive imagination as an opposition between *imaginatio affinitas* and *imaginatio plastica* and underscores this distinction as a cultural-political one.

The concept of the productive imagination is developed to a greater degree in the *Critique of Judgment*. In this work, Kant understands the imagination "not taken as reproductive, where it is subject to the laws

---

11   Kant, *Anthropology*, 67.
12   Immanuel Kant, *Critique of Pure Reason*, trans. Werner S. Pluhar (Indianapolis: Hackett Publishing Co., 1996), B 151.
13   Kant, *Critique of Pure Reason*, B 152.

of association, but as productive and spontaneous [....]"(§22).¹⁴ The most significant transcendental function of the productive imagination is to make possible the experience of the beautiful, which culminates in a feeling of pleasure: "Only where the imagination is free when it arouses the understanding, and the understanding, without using concepts, puts the imagination into a play that is regular [i.e., manifests regularity], does the presentation communicate itself not as a thought but as the inner feeling of a purposive state-of-mind" (§40).¹⁵ The concept of the imagination is less fundamental as a primary aesthetic concept than as a (reflective) judgment, which, in aesthetic judgment, reflects back on its relationship to its own power. Indeed, without the imagination, the power of judgment would not be operative:

> For this apprehension of forms by the imagination could never occur if reflective judgment did not compare them, even if unintentionally, at least with its ability [in general] to refer intuitions to concepts. Now if in this comparison a given presentation unintentionally brings the imagination (the power of *a priori* intuitions) into harmony with the understanding (the power of concepts), and this harmony arouses a feeling of pleasure, then the object must thereupon be regarded as purposive for the reflective power of judgment.¹⁶

Whenever Kant's designation of the imagination switches from the representational relationship between an intuitive subject and an observed object to a relationship between transcendental faculties (i.e. between the imagination and the understanding in the case of the beautiful), his discussion of the imagination remains within the confines of a general visualization of these faculties. This is because the reflective relationship, which the reflective judgment of the I establishes as an object to itself (the relationship of two capacities), is intuitive.

The concept of the imagination is more central for Kant's successor, Fichte, than it is for Kant. Fichte radicalizes the concept as a function of the "spontaneity of the human mind."¹⁷ As he goes on to explain:

---

14 Immanuel Kant, *Critique of Judgment*, trans. Werner S. Pluhar (Indinapolis: Hackett Publishing Co., 1987), 91.
15 Ibid., 162.
16 Ibid., 30.
17 J. G. Fichte, *Science of Knowledge, with the First and Second Introductions*, trans. and ed. Peter Heath and John Lachs (Cambridge: Cambridge University Press, 1982), 141.

the infinite and the finite are unified in one and the same synthetic unity—if the activity of the I did not extend into the infinite, it could not itself set limits to this activity [...] The activity of the I consists in unbounded self-positing: to this there occurs a resistance. If it yielded to this obstacle, then the activity lying beyond the bounds of resistance would be utterly abolished and destroyed; and the I would not posit itself at all. It must limit itself, that is, it must posit itself to that extent as not positing itself [...]."[18] Moreover, "if the I did not limit itself, it would not be infinite—the I is only what it posits itself to be [...] This exchange of the I with itself in positing itself at the same time as finite and infinite [...] is the power of the *imagination*."[19]

This relationship between the I and the imagination sits in contradistinction to the relationship between the imagination and reason since: "[R]eason alone posits anything fixed, in that it first gives fixity to imagination itself."[20] On the other hand, the imagination as a faculty in itself: "wavers in the middle between determination and non-determination, between finite and infinite [...] This wavering is characteristic of imagination even in its product [...] through the imagination, which unites disparity, the [I and the not-I] can be completely unified."[21]

The unproblematic synthesizing faculty of thinking is an action of the consciousness, with which the I can determine something objective outside of itself, but *not* itself. The imagination, however, "by its own nature, wavers in general between object and non-object."[22] At the same time, the reflected imagination (that is, the imagination reflected off an object) implies: "a total destruction of the (reflected) imagination, and this destruction or non-existence of the imagination, is viewed by the imagination itself be intuited by the imagination."[23] In its wavering between the I and the not-I the imagination sublates the alienated consciousness form in favor of an experience of the self. Only on the basis of a (primary) intuition of itself can the I, in the mode of a (secondary) intuition, turn towards the world: "The I is to intuit; now if the intuitant is to be really just an I, this is as much as to say that the *I is to posit itself as intuiting*; for nothing belongs to the I, save insofar as it attributes the same to itself."[24] Or, to formulate it another way, only

---

18 Ibid., 192. Translation modified.
19 Ibid., 193. Translation modified.
20 Ibid., 194.
21 Ibid. Translation modified.
22 Ibid., 215.
23 Ibid.
24 Ibid., 204. Translation modified.

as a self-consciousness can the I have a consciousness. In this respect: "all reality [...] is brought forth solely by the imagination."[25] It becomes clear how the early Romantics could have elevated art as a medium of a disburdened subject's constitution through Fichte's theory of subjectivity. "Art" becomes, through the basic argument of Fichte's first *Wissenschaftslehre* (the role of the imagination which he diminished in subsequent reformulations), for the early Romantics a mode of experience that would be impossible without science and culture.

In the case of Hegel, his criticism of the imagination places its dependence on visual constellations in the foreground. The goal of philosophizing for him cannot place "art and the imagination [...] as the apex" because: "it is [...] just as necessary to remember that neither in content nor in form is art the highest and absolute mode of bringing to our minds the true interests of the spirit [*Geist*]. For precisely on account of its form, art is limited to a specific content."[26] Hegel's critique of the imagination as a relation of intuition pushes him closer to the Romantics than his well-known polemics against them would allow. Both begin with a critique of the imagination (in Kant and Schiller's sense) as a faculty of intuition, insofar as "the manifold [...] is grasped representationally."[27] From the perspective of these critics, the intuiting imagination undermines the openness of all presentation, an openness that is imposed already from the materiality of its medium, language. This has consequences for the concept of the imagination in the Romantic period, which, with Hegel, seeks a critique of aesthetic experience as manifestation of a longing for the coincidence of subject and object, but, against Hegel, abides by an epistemological primacy of art.

The early Romantics can be considered the original representatives of a social and cultural critical movement, which places knowledge dominated by a category of identity and difference (as well as other forms of knowledge) under sharp criticism. They polemicize against the all-encompassing rationalization of life, against a separation of reality into the distinction between identity and difference. Politically, the Romantics turned against the enlightened, centrally administered state, whose privileging of economic-cameralistic thought they experienced as a suppression of a practical-reflexive use of reason. What the rational understanding, due to its obsession to reduce reality to mere causality, cannot categorize, appears as chaotic. However, for the Romantics, the chaotic opens a path towards the absolute: "The

---

25 Ibid.
26 G. W. F. Hegel, *Hegel's Aesthetics: Lectures on Fine Art*, trans. T. M. Knox (Cambridge: Cambridge University Press, 1975), 9.
27 Ibid.

12   German Aesthetics

fundamental intuition of chaos itself lies within the vision or intuition of the absolute."[28]

This program, laid out by Schelling, is the beginning of the Romantic (and idealist) transformation of the imagination. Schelling reframes the imagination accordingly from a faculty of the intuition to differentiated sublated faculty: "The splendid German word 'imagination' [*Einbildungskraft*] actually means the power of *mutual informing into unity* [*Ineinsbildung*]."[29] Among the early Romantics, both Friedrich Schlegel and Novalis in particular, an analogous transformation of the imagination to an unencumbered, creative faculty takes place, which is not restricted by the understanding. Whereas the analytical understanding in the Enlightenment presented the negative effects of the use of the imagination, the Romantics prized the ability of the imagination to dissolve the "confines of distinction." The productive-destructive effect of the imagination should balance out the disadvantages of reason: "We expect for reason as well as the imagination that nothing will be repressed, limited or subordinated. We demand for each thing a particular and free life. Only the understanding subordinates. In reason and the imagination everything is free and move themselves within the same ether without crowding or rubbing against one another."[30] However, the aesthetic program of the Romantics results mostly in a privileging of "fantasy" over the imagination or the I.

The romantic concept of the imagination, through its deconstructive-anarchic potential, distinguishes itself from the creative imagination of the Enlightenment and classical periods dramatically. However, the Romantic conception of the imagination does not completely distance itself from the basic relationship between the concept of the imagination and intuition as manifested in the Englightenment and classical periods: both conceptions begin somewhat from a gazing subject that is dependent upon an object. That becomes apparent through Schelling's concept of the intellectual intuition, which is taken over by a number of Romantics (especially Novalis). In this sense, Hegel reproaches Schelling (and the Romantics in general) thus: the subject must act *as* the intellectual intuition if it wants to philosophize. In Hegel's critique, the "highest form of the objectivization of reason, because in it sensuous conception is united with intellectuality," takes place in the work of art, "which Schelling terms the power of the imagination."[31]

---

28   F. W. J. Schelling, *The Philosophy of Art*, trans. and ed. Douglas W. Stott, Theory and History of Literature, Vol. 58 (Minneapolis: University of Minnesota Press, 1989), 88.
29   Ibid., 32.
30   Ibid., 38.
31   Hegel, *Hegel's Aesthetics*, 433.

In that sense, the Romantics relativize the meaning of an autonomous work, of the enframed concept of the beautiful as a delineated object of intellectual intuition, but retain the reflection on art as the only way to the approximation of the absolute. The aesthetic reflection fractures the frame of the autonomous work, but cannot completely sublate the object from a reflective subject nor an object that is reflected upon. A complete annihilation of this difference would mean an end to all reflection, all experience, all thinking and would mean, ultimately, death.

What was yet to follow suit was a management of the imagination, on the basis of which modern subjects could organize and direct themselves. The transition we know through Michel Foucault, from an external, disciplinary system based in authority to one of internalized discipline represented by the panopticon, was possible only on the basis of a textual culture in which mirror relations permitted an experience of identity that is at once moral and aesthetic. Ultimately, the imagination becomes the capacity permitting this experience. To elaborate Coleridge's statement that the imagination "brings the whole soul of man into activity, with the subordination of its faculties into each other":[32] it does so in order to allow for a heightened experience of the self as self.

SEE ALSO: Judgment; Beauty

---

32 Coleridge, *Biographia Literaria*, 17.

Two Judgment
Vivasvan Soni

If we were looking for a sweeping characterization of the eighteenth century's intellectual ethos, we could do worse than to describe it as the "Age of Judgment." The concern with judgment is ubiquitous in the period, from logic and epistemology to ethics and aesthetics, and cuts across all conventional disciplinary divisions. Many of the period's most distinctive genres and forms of thought expressly constitute themselves as practices of judgment or reflections on judgment: satire, criticism, the periodical essay, aesthetics, critique. Indeed, the defining philosophical project of the period, the project we call "enlightenment," is unthinkable without a strong defense of judgment. Autonomy, the ultimate purpose of enlightenment, is not only the capacity for self-legislation but also the ability and the right to judge for oneself, uncoerced by settled doctrine, received prejudice, or the opinions of others. Autonomous judgment is at once and paradoxically, as Rousseau will note in *Émile*, the precondition for and goal of any enlightenment.[1]

Aesthetics, our most immediate concern here, is a discipline born in the eighteenth century and closely associated from the very beginning with an inquiry into our capacity for judgment. The association is not fortuitous. In the British empiricist context, to have taste meant to be discerning and discriminating, to be able to judge well of cultural products, works of art, and natural beauty. The cultivation of taste, then, is tantamount to the development of good habits for judging beautiful things.[2] In the German tradition, although Baumgarten coins the term "aesthetics" in his *Reflections* (1735) to refer to the science of

---

1 See also, John Locke, *An Essay Concerning Human Understanding*, ed. R. S. Woolhouse (London: Penguin Books, 1997), 106.
2 See Timothy M. Costelloe, "The Faculty of Taste," in *Oxford Handbook of British Philosophy in the Eighteenth Century*, ed. James A. Harris (Oxford: Oxford University Press, 2014), 430–49.

perception and uses it as the title of his treatise *Aesthetica* (1750/58), it is only with Kant that aesthetics becomes an independent area of inquiry,[3] in a treatise fatefully named the *Critique of Judgment* (1790). Aesthetic discourse, then, appears to be constituted as an investigation into how and why we make judgments about the beautiful, and as such, it becomes an account of our capacity to judge under conditions where no rules or algorithms suffice. However, as profound and indissoluble as the connection between aesthetics and judgment appears to be, it turns out when pressed to be fragile and even unsustainable for the period's thinkers.

Before we explore the unstable relation between aesthetics and judgment, it would be well to get a sense of the dizzying array of meanings for the word "judgment" in the period, some intuitive and still familiar, others technical and unexpected. In the context of aesthetic discussions, to judge has the familiar sense of to discern or discriminate or even to perceive the beautiful, with overtones of active evaluation. In other words, to judge is to be able to distinguish the beautiful object from ordinary objects. This gives rise to one of the more important and surprising technical meanings of judgment in the period, namely the ability to discern, perceive, or recognize difference and even to differentiate.[4] In this sense, judgment is conventionally opposed to "wit," which designates the faculty of perceiving similarities and even synthesizing ideas. What is striking about this opposition in Locke, however, is that it is "wit" that appears to constitute the nascent aesthetic attitude, and judgment that refuses the seductions and confusions generated by the "entertainment and pleasantry of wit."[5] To judge is to bring an analytic scrutiny to bear on an object, inappropriate for the witty and lighthearted traits of association whose "beauty appears at first sight, and there is required no labor of thought, to examine what truth or reason there is in it."[6] But of course, to perceive similarity and discern difference are complementary operations often (and perhaps necessarily) working together, making it difficult to distinguish in practice between wit and judgment. Rousseau captures this equivocation perfectly, when he declares that "to compare is to judge," since comparison encompasses both the work of differentiation and assimilation.[7] Additional

---

3   Frederick C. Beiser, *Diotima's Children: German Aesthetic Rationalism from Leibniz to Lessing* (Oxford: Oxford University Press, 2009), 152–4.
4   Locke, *Essay*, 153.
5   Ibid.
6   Ibid.
7   Jean-Jacques Rousseau, *Émile; or, On Education*, trans. Allan Bloom (New York: Basic Books, 1979), 270.

meanings of judgment include the act of predication and, related to this, Kant's understanding of judgments as "determining," that is to say subsuming a particular under a general rule,[8] which appears to be modeled on the practice of legal judgment. Whether as discernment, evaluation, differentiation, predication, comparison, or subsumption, judgment is understood as indispensable to the work of cognition in general, not merely aesthetic cognition. At the same time, we should take note of another meaning of the term that does not fit easily within this constellation but persists alongside it, and is a way of marginalizing, denigrating, and even pathologizing judgment as a cognitive practice. For Locke, judgment is "the faculty, which God has given man to supply the want of clear and certain knowledge, in cases where that cannot be had."[9] Even though this kind of imprecise, probabilistic, and ultimately unreliable knowledge, derived from judgment, accounts in Locke's view for most of what we know, this attests only to the limits of our cognitive capacities. Judgment, rather than being indispensable for cognition, is here conceived as the very pathology of finite cognition. Part of the challenge of understanding judgment in the eighteenth century is making sense of how these two different and even antithetical senses of the word—as indispensable for cognition and as a supplement for the failure of cognition—coexist within the same conceptual configuration.

These proliferating and antithetical meanings are symptoms of a crisis in conceptualizing judgment. The crisis takes many forms, and cannot be fully described here. Its most persistent symptoms include a denigration or elision of the faculty of judgment among the cognitive faculties, evident in Locke or Mandeville, for example: the development of algorithmic procedures for decision making, in order to bypass the need for judgment; and, antithetically, the development of a sense of freedom that requires the suspension of judgment to be properly realized.[10] To understand the genesis of the crisis, we must look to two of the broadest intellectual developments in the period, which together constitute a systematic assault on the legitimacy of judgment as a way of cognizing and acting in the world. The first is the rise of scientific modes of explanation. Within these paradigms, the only permissible way of accounting for change is through efficient causation, a

---

8 Immanuel Kant, *Critique of the Power of Judgment*, trans. Paul Guyer and Eric Matthews, ed. Paul Guyer and Allen W. Wood, *The Cambridge Edition of the Works of Immanuel Kant* (Cambridge: Cambridge University Press, 2000), 66–7.
9 Locke, *Essay*, 576.
10 For a fuller description, see Vivasvan Soni, "Introduction: The Crisis of Judgment," *The Eighteenth-Century: Theory and Interpretation* 51 (3) (2010): 261–88.

Newtonian mechanical causality. This is perfectly fine for explaining natural phenomena, but when extended to the realm of human action, a dogmatic insistence on efficient causation renders even the simplest forms of intentional behavior unintelligible, because there is no way to take account of what Aristotle calls "final causes," an explanation of action as oriented by ends and purposes. Since the work of judgment has a double relation to ends—constituting the ends for which we act as well as discerning and coordinating the means necessary for the attainment of ends—judgment can have no significant role in these theories. Second, and related to this, are the many attempts to account for human motivation solely through self-interest (Hobbes, Locke, Mandeville), so as to make human behavior intelligible and explicable according to scientific paradigms. Not only do such theories envision self-interest and desire as forms of efficient causation in the psyche, thereby eliding judgment, but they also assume that self-interest is a non-negotiable, given entity, not available to a deliberative process of judgment. Human motivation operates immanently, through the restless movement of desire, rather than being able to posit, through acts of judgment, "transcendent" ends for which it strives.

It is against the backdrop of these explanatory paradigms and the crisis of judgment they precipitate that we must understand the singular emergence of aesthetic theory (as well as the distinctive shape of moral theory) in this period. Aesthetic theory is, from its very inception, concerned to combat both these tendencies (namely, the reduction to efficient causation and the explanation of human behavior through self-interest), by restoring/discovering the purposiveness of natural forms along with the orientation toward ends this presupposes, and staking out a realm of human perception and action in which self-interest is definitively not at stake. However, what is most disappointing about the development of aesthetic theory is that, with the notable exception of Kant, it attempts to achieve these objectives largely without recourse to judgment, which is the only way to secure them in the first place. This becomes apparent if we rely provisionally on Kant's division of aesthetic theory into rationalist and empiricist strains. Rationalism, by offering a conceptual criterion for determining when something is to be deemed beautiful (unity in variety), obviates the difficult work of judging in the absence of definitive criteria, which is precisely what the task of judgment demands. Empiricism, by according apodictic priority to the senses and anchoring the perception of the beautiful in the immediate feeling of pleasure experienced upon apprehending the sensuous form of an object, makes any work of judgment not only unnecessary but also undesirable. Hume explains this position without subscribing to it: "All sentiment is right; because sentiment has a reference to nothing beyond itself, and is always real, wherever a man is conscious of it."[11] Indeed, it is one of the commonplaces of eighteenth-century thought that the senses perceive accurately, and only the superfluous and misleading work of judgment introduces error into perception/cognition.[12]

But even if we do not rely on Kant's distinction, the bypassing of judgment is unmistakable in many individual thinkers in the period. Let us take Hutcheson and Baumgarten as examples. In his *Reflections on Poetry*, Baumgarten defines "aesthetic" as "the science of perception,"[13] and whether we place the emphasis on rationalism or empiricism, on science or perception, there is no place for the work of judgment. The details of Baumgarten's account bear this out, since there is little discussion of judgment. For Baumgarten, a poem is "a perfect sensate discourse," and what distinguishes its representations is that they are "clear and confused,"[14] by which he means the object of the representation can be distinguished from others (clear) but its qualities cannot be specified (confused).[15] In fact, poetic representation is most effective when it mimics sensation itself,[16] which is also distinguished by its "extensive clarity." Now, Baumgarten does refer to the perception of extensive clarity (clear but confused) as a kind of judgment: "A confused judgment about the perfection of sensations is called a *judgment of sense*."[17] But if we recall that judgment is precisely the ability to discern differences and distinctions, then a confused judgment in which the qualities of an object are indistinguishably melded together is precisely not a judgment at all, but a perception or sensation associated with a pleasure that we take to be a sign of perfection. Moreover, were we able to make the confused aesthetic "judgment" distinct, as judgment demands, the poetic quality of the object would be lost since it lies in extensive (confused) clarity rather than clarity and distinctness.[18] In other words, the poetic quality of a representation is gleaned not through an act of judgment but from a certain resistance to judgment

---

11 David Hume, "Of the Standard of Taste," in *Essays, Moral, Political, and Literary*, ed. Eugene F. Miller, rev. ed. (Indianapolis: Liberty Fund, 1987), 230.
12 Locke, *Essay*, 250–1; Hume, "Standard of Taste," 230; Rousseau, *Émile*, 169; Frederick C. Beiser, *Diotima's Children: German Aesthetic Rationalism from Leibniz to Lessing* (Oxford: Oxford University Press, 2009), 141; Francis Hutcheson, *An Inquiry into the Original of Our Ideas of Beauty and Virtue in Two Treatises*, ed. Wolfgang Leidhold (Indianapolis: Liberty Fund, 2004), 140.
13 Alexander Gottlieb Baumgarten, *Reflections on Poetry*, trans. Karl Aschenbrenner and William B. Holther (Berkeley: University of California Press, 1954), 79.
14 Ibid., 42.
15 Beiser, *Diotima's Children*, 38.
16 Baumgarten, *Reflections on Poetry*, 52.
17 Ibid., 69.
18 Ibid., 42.

in the representation itself, its principled refusal to resolve itself into a clear and distinct representation. A "confused judgment" means: a judgment that the representation refuses to be judged!

In his *Inquiry*, Hutcheson seeks to secure the autonomy of beauty and morality against reductive accounts that would explain them as mere modulations of self-interest. Hutcheson's remarkable strategy is to argue that we have internal senses, just like our external senses of sight and hearing, that are especially fitted to perceive the qualities of beauty ("unity in variety" just as in the rationalist tradition) and morality (benevolence). When Hutcheson resorts to the language of sense perception to secure the autonomous existence of moral and aesthetic cognition, he does so by eliding the mediation of judgment. One of the things that appears to distinguish the operation of the senses from cognition is the immediacy with which they grasp or apprehend their objects. Fearing that if the senses were to be guided by judgment they would too easily lose their way, the "promise" of Hutcheson's enterprise is lodged in the ability of the senses to bypass judgment and mediation altogether: "This superior Power of Perception is justly called a Sense, because of its Affinity to the other Senses in this, that *the Pleasure does not arise from any Knowledge* of Principles, Proportions, Causes, or of the Usefulness of the Object; *but strikes us at first* with the Idea of Beauty."[19] Despite the commonplace assumption that taste and the discernment of beauty require the operation of judgment, apparent even in the language of aesthetic theorists, early aesthetic theories do their best to write judgment out of the picture. Aesthetic experience becomes a matter of perception, sensation, and feeling rather than a question of judgment. (For a contrasting view, see Nazar's strong, Arendtian defense of reflecting and deliberative judgment in Hume and Adam Smith.)

In the context of the relentless marginalization of the practice of judgment throughout the century, the radicalism and even daring of Kant's critical project, which puts judgment back at the center of cognition and the aesthetic, becomes apparent. Even before Kant, Rousseau recognized the importance of judgment for any project of enlightenment in his *Émile*, though his attempted recuperation of judgment is more revealing of the *aporias* that confront such a project than a successful program for cultivating autonomous judgment. Kant makes an investigation into judgment a key element of his critical enterprise, and not only in the third *Critique* as though it were an afterthought. The guiding question of the first critique, the *Critique of Pure Reason*, was "How are synthetic judgments *a priori* possible?" and judgment is at stake in determining how to act according to the

---

19 Hutcheson, *Inquiry*, 25, my emphasis.

moral law in particular instances. But in both these cases, the kind of judgment under consideration is what Kant calls a "determining judgment," in which a particular is subsumed under a rule which is given in advance. Determining judgments, as Kant came to realize, do not reveal the operation of judgment as autonomous; rather, the faculty of judgment is itself determined, because the rule or law is given *in advance* by another faculty. As Kant explains with regard to the moral law: "where the moral law speaks there is, objectively, no longer any free choice with regard to what is to be done."[20] Judgment is a mediating faculty, and in its regular operation as determining, it is heteronomous, dependent on the laws given to it by other faculties. For a long time, Kant was not even sure that there could be an autonomous operation of judgment, independent of the other faculties, since judgment as mediating needed its material from elsewhere. But in recognizing the strange status of aesthetic judgments, as at once subjective and yet making a claim to universality, and in attempting to explain how such unlikely judgments were possible, Kant realized that aesthetic judgments opened onto a whole new realm where judgment did operate autonomously (heautonomously), as reflecting rather than determining judgment.[21] In a reflecting judgment, only the particular is given, but in such a way that makes it appear to be an instance of a general rule. The task of reflecting judgment, then, is to speculate subjectively on the possibility of such rules (aesthetic) or to offer such rules as ways of making sense of the profusion of natural phenomena (teleological).

Kant's identification of reflecting judgments as a distinct type is at once the most promising development in the theorization of judgment during the century,[22] and yet beset by innumerable problems that exacerbate the crisis of judgment. It is promising both because it seeks to rescue the possibility of autonomous judgment—a judgment not programmed by the world it perceives but able to reflect on it—and because it takes up the problem of judgment at its most interesting and difficult, namely how thought can grasp or engage with particularity in all its intransigence. But although Kant correctly identifies the crucial question about autonomous judgment and its engagement with particularity, his own solution in the account of aesthetic judgment tends to replicate the very problems it is meant

---

20 Kant, *Critique of the Power of Judgment*, 96.
21 Ibid., 27–8.
22 See Hannah Arendt, *Lectures on Kant's Political Philosophy*, ed. Ronald Beiner (Chicago: University of Chicago Press), 1982; and Linda M. G. Zerilli, "'We Feel Our Freedom': Imagination and Judgment in the Thought of Hannah Arendt," *Political Theory* 33 (2) (2005): 158–88.

to resolve. This is evident most clearly and troublingly in that Kant is only able to establish the autonomy of aesthetic judgment by sacrificing any judgment about the beautiful object at all. The so-called "judgment of taste" is actually a *suspension* of judgment with regard to the object. To see why this should be, we begin by noting that the judgment of taste is, for Kant, not a judgment that the object possesses a certain property ("beauty"), but rather a judgment about the condition the subject's cognitive apparatus finds itself in when perceiving a particular object. This characteristic condition is what Kant terms the free play of the faculties of understanding and imagination, which is nothing but a pleasurable suspension of judgment. After all, when the imagination and understanding enter into a *fixed* and determinate relationship, this is precisely a moment of judgment. Free play is when the mind finds itself in "neutral" (a degree zero of cognition, as it were), recognizing its *capacity* to judge in the interplay between understanding and imagination, but not fixing this relation in a determinate judgment. Kant is explicit that the "judgment of taste" must not issue in an actual judgment; to discover a rule under which to subsume the aesthetic object (such as "unity in variety," "symmetry," "harmony," etc.) would be to arrest the specifically aesthetic experience of free play in a judgment that yields some knowledge about the object.[23] In other words, for Kant, an aesthetic "judgment" (which is really an aesthetic *experience*) forces the judging subject to turn inward on itself—when it recognizes its inability to make a judgment about the object—and reflect on the state of its cognitive faculties. What it discovers, then, is that this inability to judge constitutes the pleasurable free play of its cognitive faculties which it then feels authorized to impute to everyone. A judgment of beauty does not attribute a particular property to an object; what it asserts, rather, is that I require that everyone will experience the same inability to judge when confronted by this object, and the specific nature of this inability (the free play of the faculties, rather than simply confusion or the failure to cognize the object adequately) will be pleasurable in the same way for all of us. In judgments about the beautiful, the autonomy of judgment is only achieved when we experience the beautiful object as resisting our judgment.

The loss of the object of judgment is only one symptom of the

---

23 Schiller's "translation" of Kantian aesthetics makes the necessary suspension of judgment even clearer: "If, after enjoyment of this kind, we find ourselves disposed to prefer some one particular mode of feeling or action, but unfitted or disinclined for another, this may serve as infallible proof that we have not had a *purely aesthetic* experience." Friedrich Schiller, *Letters on the Aesthetic Education of Man*, in *Essays*, ed. Walter Hinderer and Daniel O. Dahlstrom (New York: Continuum, 1993), 149.

problems generated by Kant's approach to recuperating autonomous judgment. Another is the nagging suspicion that there may not be an identifiable act of judgment involved in a so-called aesthetic judgment. It is not simply that, in making an aesthetic judgment, we fail and indeed must fail to find a concept that would account for the particular instance; rather, if judgment is fundamentally an act of cognitive mediation, and mediation takes time, it is far from clear that there is any time for this mediation in an experience of the beautiful. Kant sometimes insists that the beautiful pleases immediately, since it proceeds without the mediation of any concepts.[24] In this he resembles Hutcheson, for whom the immediacy of the perception of beauty elides judgment: "the judgment of taste must rest on a mere sensation."[25] It would be more appropriate to say that we "intuit" beauty rather than judge it. But in a section that Kant calls "the key to the critique of taste," he argues that feeling of universal communicability must precede and even generate the feeling of pleasure we take in the object.[26] Presumably an act of judgment is required in order for us to be able to recognize and distinguish such a state and its ability to produce pleasure in us. As Dieter Henrich astutely points out: "the feeling has to be such that there can be no doubt the aesthetic attitude has occurred. Otherwise a distinctively aesthetic judgment could not be based upon it, let alone a judgment claiming universal agreement."[27] But because everything depends on a feeling or sensation, the necessary judgment lies beyond the limit of articulation, although this is where the difficult work of judgment is most called for. A place for judgment does open up here—especially if, despite some indications, the feeling of pleasure is not immediate—but it is more a placeholder than a viable account of judgment.

A final symptom of the difficulties Kant encounters in theorizing judgment: I have said that judgment concerns our relation to ends, meanings, and purposes, and the *Critique of Judgment* is undoubtedly Kant's effort to reintroduce concerns about purposes and final causes into a world that has otherwise been stripped of them. But in relation to judgments about beauty, the failure of Kant's strategy is apparent in his third definition of the beautiful as "the form of the **purposiveness** of an object, insofar as it is perceived in it **without representation of an end**,"[28] *Zweckmässigkeit ohne Zweck*. Beautiful objects are those

---

24 Kant, *Critique of the Power of Judgment*, 93, 166.
25 Ibid., 167.
26 Ibid., 102.
27 Dieter Henrich, *Aesthetic Judgment and the Moral Image of the World: Studies in Kant* (Stanford, CA: Stanford University Press, 1992), 42.
28 Kant, *Critique of the Power of Judgment*, 120.

that appear as though they have a purpose, but we must not be able to specify (judge) such a purpose or we would put an end to the free play of faculties that is the hallmark of the experience of beauty. Put differently, we might say that beautiful objects remind us of our lost relation to purposes and ends produced by the crisis of judgment, without being able to restore our orientation towards ends. In a natural world disenchanted by the laws of physics, and a moral world subjected to the rigorous discipline of the categorical imperative, beautiful objects—by their uselessness, their failure to signify,[29] their very insignificance—provoke an intuition that purpose is ours to make, even as they mock as naive and unaesthetic any effort to specify those ends and purposes concretely. They invite us to imaginatively enter a world animated, through constitutive acts of judgment, by our own purposes and ends, and then slam the door in our faces when we try! In Kant, Hutcheson, or Baumgarten, aesthetic objects do not restore our capacity for judgment or provide a privilege cited for the exercise of judgment. Rather, aesthetic cognition, the last potential refuge for judgment, reveals only our failure or inability to judge.

If Kant saves autonomous judging only by abandoning the object, and making the judgment of beauty a judgment about the arrangement of the subject's perceptual and cognitive apparatus, we find the opposite and equally unsatisfactory rescue of judgment in Hegelian idealism. Although an account of propositional judgments and their dialectical transformation into syllogisms constitutes one moment in the unfolding structure of Hegel's *Logic*, judgment is far more central to dialectical process.[30] Hölderlin's fragment "Judgment and Being" provides us with the crucial clue here.[31] Hölderlin understands judgment (*Urteil*) as *Ur-teil*, the originary partition and differentiation that takes place within Being. If the Hegelian dialectic is a process of increasing differentiation, complexification, and specification, then it is essentially a work of "judgment" in the sense that Hölderlin means it.[32] Thus, when Hegel says "world history is a court of judgment,"[33] this must not be understood in the merely metaphorical sense that the outcome of history constitutes a justification or endorsement of whatever succeeds: "world history is not the verdict of mere might."[34] Rather, the process of history, as it unfolds in ever-increasing difference,

---

29 Ibid., 93, 114.
30 Terry Pinkard, *Hegel: A Biography* (Cambridge: Cambridge University Press, 2000), 343.
31 Ibid., 133–6.
32 See also, Schiller, *Letters*, 140.
33 Georg Wilhelm Friedrich Hegel, *Hegel's Philosophy of Right*, trans. T. M. Knox (London: Oxford University Press, 1967), 216.
34 Ibid.

complexity, and specificity, must be conceived as acts of judgment of the "universal mind," by which is meant something like the entire sphere of collective human endeavor. In conceiving the process of history as one of "judgment," Hegel returns to the conception of judgment we found in Locke, namely the perception of difference, but he transforms it significantly. Judgment is not simply the discernment of differences, but an active process of differentiation: the production of internal difference within a system. Judgments are the very hinges which articulate the system. The advantage of conceiving judgment in this way is that it becomes a completely objective process. But this objectivity comes at the cost of eliding the cognitive work of judgment performed by any individual subject, thereby dispossessing us of the agency that is the promise of judgment. Though we may make many individual and local judgments, it is ultimately not we who judge but judgment that happens to us in the course of history. The purposiveness of history is ultimately an emergent effect rather than a work of judgment, or better, an emergent effect imagined as if it were a work of judgment. (This particular form of the evasion of judgment can be traced back to Mandeville's theorization of the market as a surrogate for judgment and Shaftesbury's dialectical model of sociality, later taken up by Adam Smith and Schiller.)

For all that judgment was an indispensable concept at the inception of aesthetics, it was a deeply problematic if generative one. Although theorists may have wished to establish the aesthetic as a paradigmatic realm for the practice of judgment, they succeeded rather in precipitating a "crisis of judgment" to which we, in our ongoing discomfort with the work of judgment, remain the heirs still today.[35] One challenge bequeathed to us by the aesthetic theory of the eighteenth century, then—a challenge it could not meet—is whether we can imagine and instantiate viable practices of judgment and the communities necessary to sustain them.

SEE ALSO: Beauty; Sublime; Ethics

---

35 See Soni, "Introduction."

Three Beauty
Paul Guyer

Beauty was a central concept in aesthetics long before Alexander Gottlieb Baumgarten gave the discipline its name in 1735. For much of history, it was the central concept: it was assumed that all aesthetic experience is an experience of beauty, and that all art is intentionally aimed at the production of beauty. In the eighteenth century, other categories became important to aesthetics, notably that of the sublime but also those of the novel and the expressive, while later in the nineteenth century and especially in the twentieth whether beauty is essential to art became contested. Most recently, the concept has been rehabilitated, with some philosophers arguing that beauty is essential to human life in general and art in particular.

In a long, generally Neo-Anic tradition, beauty had been considered an objective property of objects, consisting in the harmony of the parts of an object or its unity amidst its variety, or even an objective property of the universe as a whole, its unity amidst its variety, which is perceived, with pleasure, by the human senses but can lead the human mind to a more intellectual grasp of the objective basis of that pleasure. At the beginning of the eighteenth century, this tradition was represented by Christian Wolff. Wolff conceived of beauty as the perfection of an object insofar as it is perceived by the senses. Following Gottfried Wilhelm Leibniz, he understood sense perception as clear but confused cognition, and he also equated the sensory perception of perfection with the feeling of pleasure,[1] so beauty was perfection insofar as it manifests itself to us through a feeling of pleasure. What Wolff meant by perfection was complex: the formal property of unity amidst the variety is one form of perfection; realization of the intended function of an object is another, for example similarity to its object is perfection in

---

1   Christian Wolff, *Vernünftige Gedancken von Gott, der Welt, und der Seele des Menschen*, Neue Auflage (original edition, 1720) (Halle: Renger, 1751), 404.

the case of a painting, for imitation is the function of painting;[2] and an individual object's reflection of the perfection of the world as a whole, which is itself a mirror of the perfection of God,[3] is a third. There is no incompatibility among these three forms of perfection, so an individual work of art could realize perfection in each of these three senses, and the pleasurable experience of its beauty could be an experience of all three forms of perfection. But since sense perception is clear but confused, the three different forms of perfection that might comprise the beauty of a work of art would not be distinguished in the feeling of pleasure in it itself, although they might be in philosophical reflection on that experience.

Baumgarten introduced the term "aesthetics" in his 1735 dissertation concerning poetry, and began to publish the first textbook entitled "Aesthetics" (*Aesthetica*) in 1750. Baumgarten's theoretical innovation was to permute Wolff's definition of the experience of beauty as the sensory cognition of perfection into a definition of beauty as a perfection of sensory cognition, *perfectio cognitionis sensitivae, qua talis*.[4] What this should have meant for the case of beauty in art in particular is that the beauty of a work of art has more to do with the *way* it represents than with *what* it represents, or with the form of representation rather than the represented content. In fact, Baumgarten's detailed explication of the perfections of sensory cognition shows that he assumed that artistic beauty generally consists in the perfection of both the content represented and the representation of it, thus that we take pleasure in both. Baumgarten's categories included aesthetic "wealth," "magnitude," "truth" or verisimilitude, "light" or clarity, "certitude" or convincingness, and "the life of aesthetic cognition" (*vita cognitionis aesthetica*)[5] or what his disciple Georg Friedrich Meier called the "touching," in other words, emotional impact. Some of these categories clearly concern the qualities of an artistic representation—for example, truthfulness, clarity, convincingness—while for example magnitude, Baumgarten's term for the sublime, has more to do with the character of the object represented, natural or moral greatness;[6] and finally "life" or emotional impact can be achieved by both what is represented and how it is represented. Thus beauty in art can consist in different kinds

---

2 Ibid.
3 Ibid., 1045.
4 Alexander Gottlieb Baumgarten, *Aesthetica* (Frankfurt an der Oder: Johann Christian Kleyb, 1750) and *Aesthetica pars altera* (1758); modern edition with facing German translation by Dagmar Mirbach, 2 vols. (Hamburg: Felix Meiner Verlag, 2007), 14.
5 Ibid., "Prolegomena."
6 Ibid., 181.

of perfection insofar as they are pleasurably represented to the senses as well as in the manner of their representation to the senses.

What was implicit in Baumgarten was made more explicit by Moses Mendelssohn, who in an essay "On the main principles of the fine arts and sciences," originally published in 1757, first defined beauty in Wolffian terms as perfection known by the senses, then defined it in Baumgartian terms as "the *sensuously perfect representation*," and then combined the two definitions by stating that "the essence of the fine arts and sciences consists in an artful, sensuously perfect representation or in a sensuous perfection represented by art."[7] But Mendelssohn also added several key innovations. For one, he made it clear that beauty lies not only in the painting or poem, a "representation" in an everyday sense, but also in the *mental* representation of an object, in the case of art mediated by a painting or poem, thus that there is a perfection in the soul of the person experiencing beauty as well as in an object represented and in the work of the artist who has represented it. Second, Mendelssohn stressed that in the experience of beauty the subject experiences the perfection of her body as well as her soul, that "harmonious sentiments in the soul correspond to harmonious movements in the limbs and the senses."[8] And finally, Mendelssohn used his distinctions to explain how we could experience "mixed sentiments," or experience beauty in the beautiful representation of an object that is not beautiful— where, however, the ugliness of a represented object is not simply outweighed by the beauty of its representation, but actually "enhance[s] the taste of pleasure and double[s] its sweetness," like "a few bitter drops ... mixed into the honey-sweet bowl of pleasure."[9] Here Mendelssohn makes a concrete application of the analysis of the multiple sources of beauty to offer his framework for the solution of the paradox of tragedy.

An important figure following these Wolffians is Johann Georg Sulzer. In his encyclopedic *General Theory of the Fine Arts*, originally published as two volumes in 1770–4 and then expanded into four by Friedrich Blankenburg in 1792–4, Sulzer included entries on "The Beautiful" (*Schön*) in the fine arts (*schöne Künste*) as well as on human beauty (*Schönheit*). In his general treatment of artistic beauty, Sulzer emphasized the subjective side of the experience of beauty more than the perfection of the object, and particularly emphasized that the beautiful is that in which the "manifold" or the multiplicity of its parts

---

7 Moses Mendelssohn, *Philosophische Schriften*, 2nd ed. (Berlin: Voss, 1771), 172–3. Translated in ed. Daniel O. Dahlstrom, *Philosophical Writings* (Cambridge: Cambridge University Press, 1997).
8 Ibid., 140.
9 Ibid., 74.

does not "hinder" the "comprehensibility" (*Faßlichkeit*) of the whole,[10] or is that which facilitates the mental activity of taking it in. Here Sulzer was thinking along the same lines as the Scot, Alexander Gerard, whose 1759 *Essay on Taste* had been translated into German in 1766. But Sulzer also distinguished between beauty that "touches the heart only lightly and as it were on the surface"[11] and beauty that moves us more deeply, and particularly in his discussion of human beauty stressed that "every person holds that to be the most beautiful, whose form [*Gestalt*] announces to the eye of the judge the most perfect and best person,"[12] or whose "outer form expresses the inner character of the person."[13] While emphasizing the pleasurable mental activity of taking in the form of something beautiful, Sulzer thus also emphasizes the contribution of the inner worth of the object, particularly of the human being, in the experience of beauty.

Immanuel Kant's famous theory of beauty as that which triggers a "free play" of the imagination and understanding independently of any determinate concept, which has been held by Hans-Georg Gadamer to represent a "subjectivization" of the concept of beauty, is actually only the first stage of a more complex theory in which beauty ultimately consists in the free play-inducing harmony between the form and content, particularly the moral significance, of a work of art or of a human being or even of anything in nature. Kant's final theory thus stresses both the pleasurable mental activity of the experience of beauty and the morally moving content of the beautiful object, and is close to Sulzer's theory. The initial phase of Kant's theory is the simultaneous analysis of beauty and the "judgment of taste": the judgment of taste is the judgment that an object produces a disinterested,[14] universally valid,[15] and necessary[16] feeling of pleasure that is not determined by a concept and thus by a rule; a feeling of pleasure that can license such a judgment can only be produced by a "free play" or "animation" of

---

10 Johann Georg Sulzer, *Allgemeine Theorie der Schönen Künste*, 2nd ed. [by Friedrich Blankenburg], 4 vols. plus index vol. (Leipzig: Weidmann, 1794), Vol. IV, 309a. Facsimile reprint with introduction by Giorgio Tonell (Hildesheim: Georg Olms Verlag, 1994).
11 Ibid., 309b.
12 Ibid., 320a.
13 Ibid., 322a.
14 Immanuel Kant, *Critique of the Power of Judgment*, ed. Paul Guyer, trans. Paul Guyer and Eric Matthews (Cambridge: Cambridge University Press, 2000). Pagination indicated is that of the volume and page in *Kant's gesammelte Schriften*, edited by the Royal Prussian (later German, then Berlin–Brandenburg) Academy of Sciences (Berlin: Georg Reimer, later Walter de Gruyter, 1900–), 2.
15 Ibid., 6–8
16 Ibid., 18.

the two cognitive powers of imagination and understanding "to an activity that is indeterminate but yet, through the stimulus of the given representation, in unison";[17] and what it is in the representation of an object that stimulates such a state is its "subjective" or "merely formal purposiveness,"[18] which Kant equates with "the purposiveness of the form,"[19] thus with the purely spatio-temporal design or structure of a work, as opposed to its color or coloration, to its content, and particularly to any "charms or emotions" that the object might trigger. Paradigmatic examples of such beauty are the beauty of patterns in foliage or wallpaper and that of "fantasias" or music "without a theme."[20] Thus Kant seems to have a purely formal conception of beauty. He therefore seems to adopt Sulzer's account of beauty as that which is readily grasped while rejecting Sulzer's claim that such beauty is superficial if it does not also express some deeper meaning.

But Kant accepts this claim,[21] and his formalistic conception of beauty is just the first stage of his account, the identification of a necessary feature of all beauty but by no means a complete account of beauty, let alone of the most important kinds of beauty. Kant immediately adds to the simple case of beauty, that is, "pure" or "free" beauty, what he calls "adherent" beauty, where the form of an object is compatible with and perhaps also harmonious with its intended function.[22] Then, clearly following Sulzer, he adds the "ideal of beauty," in which the outward beauty of the form of a human being is interpreted — though not in accordance with any rule—as the "expression of the moral" in such a being.[23] When it comes to fine art, Kant argues that its "spirit" lies in its manifestation of an "aesthetic idea," which is an imaginative presentation of a profound idea of reason or morality in a way that "stimulates so much thinking that it can never be grasped in a determinate concept,"[24] and thereby triggers a pleasurable free play of our cognitive powers, now including reason as well as imagination and understanding. Kant now even goes so far as to claim that *all* "beauty (whether it be beauty of nature or of art) can be called the *expression* of aesthetic ideas";[25] apparently our tendency to read human and moral significance into even non-human beauty is inescapable. And finally, Kant claims that all beauty is a symbol of morality, precisely because

---

17 Ibid., 9, 5:219.
18 Ibid., 10, 5:221; 11, 5:222.
19 Ibid., 13, 5:223.
20 Ibid., 16, 5:229.
21 Ibid., 50.
22 Ibid., 16.
23 Ibid., 17, 5:235.
24 Ibid., 49, 5:315.
25 Ibid., 51, 5:320.

the free play without a concept that constitutes our experience of beauty can be taken as analogous to the freedom of our will in morality, although that is governed by a law, namely the moral law.[26] In other words, for Kant the most interesting and important cases of beauty consist in a harmony between the outward form and the moral significance of objects, whether works of art, human beings, or anything in nature, and Kant's conception of beauty is firmly in the tradition of Sulzer after all.

The famous *Letters on the Aesthetic Education of Mankind* (1795) of Friedrich Schiller argue for the moral and political benefits of the experience of beauty without offering an analysis of beauty itself. But in a series of letters two years earlier sketching a book to be entitled *Kallias or Concerning Beauty*, Schiller had attempted to provide a Kantian but objective rather than subjective account of beauty, describing beauty as "nothing less than freedom in appearance,"[27] or "the self-determination of a thing insofar as it is available to intuition."[28] He illustrated this by objects the forms of which do not appear to have been forced on them by anything external,[29] for example a vase which is to be sure "subject to gravity" but in which "the effects of gravity" do not appear "to deny the *nature of the vase*."[30] However, Schiller's theory of beauty remains essentially Kantian, for not only is there still something subjective about the fact that the form of the vase *appears to us* to be self-determined rather than determined by external forces, but, more importantly, the interest of such an appearance of self-determination in something like a vase is clearly that we can take it as a symbol of our own, moral self-determination, about which Schiller cares as deeply as Kant had.

Aesthetics was central in the explosion of philosophy following Kant known as "German Idealism." Here only the opposing tendencies of Arthur Schopenhauer and Georg Wilhelm Friedrich Hegel can be mentioned. Schopenhauer, although the younger, published his views on beauty first. Schopenhauer combined an extreme version of Kant's conception of the response to beauty as disinterested pleasure with his version of the ideas that Kant had ultimately held to be the content of beautiful objects: for Schopenhauer, aesthetic response is a *"pure, will-less, painless, timeless"* contemplation of the essences of things

---

26 Ibid., 59.
27 Friedrich Schiller, *Kallias or Concerning Beauty:* Letters to Gottfried Körner," trans. Stefan Bird-Pollan, in ed. J. M. Bernstein, *Classic and Romantic German Aesthetics* (Cambridge: Cambridge University Press, 2003), 152.
28 Ibid., 154.
29 Ibid., 156.
30 Ibid., 163.

("Platonic Ideas") — things freed of their particularity, the contemplation of which therefore releases us from our own particularity and its travails.[31] Those objects are beautiful that "meet that state"—"pure contemplative intuition"—halfway, while those objects are sublime that have "a hostile relation to the human will in general" and from which the state of contemplation has to be wrung.[32] Artists are geniuses gifted at intuition, and can thus find objects beautiful that would be more difficult for the rest of us and communicate to us their intuition of the essences of those objects, allowing us to find them beautiful too. One further feature of Schopenhauer's theory is that the "Ideas" come at different levels, representing different degrees of "objectification" of the underlying reality of nature, from the most elementary forces to the nature of human desire and will, and the higher the level of the Idea, the more important the art that expresses it—thus tragedy and finally music, which for Schopenhauer represents the will itself, are the highest forms of art. In this way Schopenhauer reconstructs the kind of view of the importance of artistic beauty that represents important themes that we found in Sulzer and Kant—although to be sure Schopenhauer's conception of a morality based on compassion is quite different from either the hedonism of Sulzer or the autonomy-based morality of Kant.

Hegel lectured on the philosophy of art in Heidelberg in 1818 and then in Berlin from 1819 to 1829. His lectures were posthumously edited by his disciple H. G. Hotho in 1835. Hegel's theory of beauty is actually in the German rationalist tradition: "The beautiful has its being in pure appearance," but "spirit alone is the *true*, comprehending everything in itself, so that everything beautiful is truly beautiful only as sharing in this higher sphere and generated by it." In particular, "the beauty of nature appears only as a reflection of the beauty that belongs to spirit," while the beauty of art, created by humans who are themselves part or product of spirit, is "beauty *born of the spirit and born again.*"[33] Thus Hegel regards artistic beauty as more important than natural beauty, and redefines aesthetics as the philosophy of art only. But while Hegel's view that beauty is the sensuous presentation of the truth about spirit or the "Idea" (for him, this is singular) and that "art's vocation is" therefore to unveil the *truth* in the form of sensuous

---

31 Arthur Schopenhauer, *The World as Will and Representation*, trans. and ed. Judith Norman, Alistair Welchman, and Christopher Janaway (Cambridge: Cambridge University Press, 2010), 34, 210–11; 38, 230. Schopenhauer's first edition was dated 1819; this translation is based on the posthumous 1873 edition by Julius Frauenstädt of Schopenhauer's own considerably enlarged second edition.
32 Ibid., 39, 236–7.
33 Georg Wilhelm Friedrich Hegel, *Aesthetics; Lectures on Fine Art*, trans. T. M. Knox, 2 vols. (Oxford: Clarendon Press, 1975), 4, 2.

artistic configuration"³⁴ is in a general way similar to Schopenhauer's, his conclusions are very different. For Hegel, our apprehension of beauty is a form of knowledge, but of an ultimately inadequate, not sufficiently intellectual form of knowledge, and knowledge is what is important; so art must ultimately be superseded by religion, and, since that itself is still too imagistic, by philosophy: thus "art, considered in its highest vocation, is and remains for us a thing of the past."³⁵ This is Hegel's thesis of the "end of art," which is not that it is no longer possible to make beautiful art, but rather that making beautiful art is no longer as important as it once was. For Schopenhauer, art is also a form of knowledge, but what is important to us is not knowledge itself, but the relief that self-less contemplation brings; for him too art must be superseded, but because it only brings temporary relief, and it is not better theoretical knowledge that supersedes art, but a more fundamental transformation of our ethical attitude toward existence.

The first book of Friedrich Nietzsche, *The Birth of Tragedy out of the Spirit of Music*, was in many ways influenced by Schopenhauer, but it arrives at a different conception of the relation between the beautiful and the sublime. For Nietzsche, the traditional conception of the beautiful is replaced by the "Apollonian," clear and lucid images of individual divinities, while the sublime is replaced by the "Dionysian," the terrifying but intoxicating intimation of the oneness that lies beneath the illusion of the *principium individuationis* (Schopenhauer's term).³⁶ The Dionysian is what is revealed when "The Olympic mountain magic now opens up, as it were, and shows us its roots."³⁷ It may seem as if Nietzsche's message is that we need beautiful illusions to protect us from the ultimate fact of life, the utter insignificance of individual life in the grand scheme of things, but actually his argument is that the "Apolline world of beauty" and the terrifying Dionysian sublime are related by "reciprocal necessity":³⁸ we need beautiful images of individuals to be able to grasp anything at all, but at the same time there is actually comfort and not just terror in the sublime realization that we are all just part of something much bigger than any of us. Beauty cannot be our sole aesthetic object, but it remains a part of the "*aesthetic phenomenon*" by which "existence and the world" is "eternally *justified.*"³⁹

---

34 Ibid., 55.
35 Ibid., 11.
36 Friedrich Nietzsche, *The Birth of Tragedy out of the Spirit of Music*, ed. Raymond Geuss and Ronald Speirs, trans. Ronald Speirs (Cambridge: Cambridge University Press, 1999), 1.
37 Ibid., 3, 23.
38 Ibid., 4, 26.
39 Ibid., 5, 33.

The most important thinker about beauty in twentieth-century Germany, Theodor W. Adorno adopted the famous remark of Stendhal that beauty is only a "promise of happiness" into the idea that it is a promise of happiness that cannot be redeemed, because reality itself can never deliver happiness. "Art's *promesse du bonheur* means not only that hitherto praxis has blocked happiness but that happiness is beyond praxis."[40] It is not just that past or present socio-economic arrangements have not delivered happiness to all; happiness is simply beyond human reach. Influenced by the disastrous history of Germany in the first half of the twentieth century, as much as by early twentieth-century movements in the arts that did not strive for beauty in any traditional form, Adorno rejected the even temporarily or partially redemptive promise of beauty that Schopenhauer and Nietzsche had allowed, while also rejecting Nietzsche's view that there is a kind of redemption in the Dionysian worldview too.

In a changed historical context, Adorno's level of pessimism is difficult to sustain. Beauty is again recognized as an essential part of human experience by more recent German aestheticians,[41] and it seems safe to say that it will continue to be so.

SEE ALSO: Judgment; Sublime; Truth; Ugly

---

40 Theodor W. Adorno, *Aesthetic Theory*, ed. Gretel Adorno and Rolf Tiedemann, trans. Robert Hullot-Kentnor (Minneapolis: University of Minnesota Press, 1997), 12.

41 For example, Andrea Kern, *Schöne Lust: Eine Theorie der ästhetischen Erfahrung nach Kant* (Frankfurt am Main: Suhrkamp Verlag, 2000).

Four Sublime
David Martyn

In the course of the eighteenth century, the word "sublime" came to describe a specific kind of aesthetic response to nature for which until then there had been no name, either because no term for it existed or because the response itself was new. Etymologically, sublime (*erhaben*) means raised up or elevated; in the rhetorical tradition, it referred to a grandiloquent style of speech, the *genus grande* or *vehemens*, which a speaker was to employ when addressing matters of great import. The term was now applied not just to verbal artifacts but to natural objects as well: high mountain ranges, the dizzying expanse of the ocean or the heavens, the terrifying force of storms or volcanoes. The transformation of the concept mirrors the shifts that accompanied the rise of the new field of aesthetics: the demise of rhetoric; the move from neoclassical poetics, which postulated objective formal criteria for beauty, to aesthetics, which analyzed the subjective processes involved in the enjoyment of art and nature; the advent of aesthetic judgment as an autonomous sphere, independent of moral judgments, on the one hand, and truth judgments on the other. The development began in France and England, then, in the second half of the century, moved to Germany, where it took on a course of its own that culminated in the aesthetic theory of Immanuel Kant. Kant remains the essential point of reference for all subsequent considerations of the sublime, both in and outside of Germany.

From Boileau's "Longinus" to Mendelssohn
The starting point for the transformation of the sublime from a rhetorical to an aesthetic category was Boileau's 1674 translation into French of *On Sublimity*, a first-century treatise that was long attributed, erroneously, to the third-century rhetorician Kassios Longinos. Boileau's translation introduced to a wider audience a text which, while clearly still within the purview of classical rhetoric, would provide the seeds

for the sublime's displacement from rhetoric to aesthetics. Pseudo-Longinus identified the sublime not only with the kind of ornate and elaborate language that was commonly associated with the sublime style, but with passages whose impact could be attributed precisely to their stylistic simplicity. Among these, the opening of Genesis—"And God said, Let there be light, and there was light"—was singled out by Boileau as exemplifying a sublimity beyond rhetoric and would remain a staple of the discourse on the sublime from then on. This example and others also pointed up what would become the sublime's signature contrast between its formal characteristics and its effect: simplicity or even a total loss of words could signify grandeur. Ajax's silence at the sight of the summoned dead in Book XI of the *Odyssey* "is grand and indeed more sublime than any words could have been."[1] This, too, pointed beyond the sublime style in rhetoric.

In these and other regards, Boileau's Longinus helped to set the stage for reframing the sublime as a mode of aesthetic enjoyment that could no longer be explained in terms of the classical principles of beauty as form. In 1688, the British critic John Dennis wrote of "a delightful Horrour, a terrible Joy"[2] that he had felt when crossing the Alps—a new and paradoxical kind of pleasure in the face of a landscape that had otherwise inspired in voyagers only a repulsive fright and terror.[3] The word "beautiful" would not have suggested itself in the classical age as a suitable description for such an irregular and formless prospect, and in 1688 the term "sublime" was not yet available as a description of natural objects. This would change in the eighteenth century. Edmund Burke's *Philosophical Enquiry into the Origin of our Ideas of the Sublime and the Beautiful* (1757) redefined the sublime as precisely the kind of delightful terror that Dennis had experienced on crossing the Alps. "Sublime" now came to signify a mode of aesthetic enjoyment prompted not by beautiful forms, but by the opposite: formlessness, chaos, the terrifying forces of nature. Sublimity and beauty now designated two contrasting types of aesthetic phenomena.

Burke's *Enquiry*, which Moses Mendelssohn introduced to the German public in a 1758 review, had a decisive influence on German aesthetics, beginning with the development of Mendelssohn's own theories of the sublime. In the first version of "On the Sublime and the Naïve" (1758), Mendelssohn had explained the sublime in accordance

---

1 Longinus, *On Sublimity*, trans. D. A. Russell (Oxford: Oxford University Press, 1965), 9 [9.2].
2 John Dennis, *The Critical Works*, ed. Edward Niles Hooker. Vol. 2 (Baltimore, MD: Johns Hopkins University Press, 1943), 380.
3 Carsten Zelle, *"Angenehmes Grauen": Literaturhistorische Beiträge zur Ästhetik des Schrecklichen im achtzehnten Jahrhundert* (Hamburg: Meiner, 1987), 81.

with classical principles as the admiration produced by sensible expressions of perfection. In the second version (1771), he tied the sublime, following Burke, to the pleasant shudder experienced in the face not just of perfection but of the immense or immeasurable (*das Unermessliche*), be it the immeasurably great or the immeasurably powerful.[4] All of the elements Kant would draw on to create his epoch-making theory of the sublime—the mix of pain and pleasure, the contrast between the sublime object and the response it produced, the opposition between the sublime and the beautiful, the distinction between a sublime of extension and a sublime of force or power, and the tie to the immeasurable or infinite—had by this point been put in place.

Kant

The most salient innovation to the theory of the sublime introduced by Kant in his 1791 *Critique of Judgment* was to locate the sublime not in nature or art, but in the subject experiencing what until then had been called sublimity: "Sublimity is not contained in anything in nature, but only in our mind."[5] By "mind" (*Gemüt*) Kant meant not the "merely subjective" thoughts of an individual, but what is universal to human beings—the faculties that are common to all because they are a condition of possibility of human experience and action in general. Kant calls "sublime" the *use*[6] that the mind makes of certain natural objects by which it can become aware of these faculties—of what it necessarily shares with every other human mind. Hence, the paradoxical result of Kant's subjectivization of the sublime was to give judgments concerning the sublime a basis for claiming universal validity: true not just for the individual observer, but imputable to everyone.

More specifically, the sublime for Kant involves those dimensions of the mind that are not limited by the laws of nature. The ability to rise above natural causality had been a central tenet of Kant's moral philosophy, which held that all moral behavior necessarily predicates certain metaphysical postulates: freedom, the immortality of the soul, God. In the sublime, Kant now saw an aesthetic experience that could make not these postulates themselves, but the "supersensible vocation" (übersinnliche Bestimmung) of practical (i.e. moral) reason "as though perceptible" (*gleichsam anschaulich*).[7] To show this, Kant presents two versions of the mix of terror and delight, pain and pleasure that

---

4   Moses Mendelssohn, *Philosophical Writings*, ed. and trans. Daniel O. Dahlstrom (Cambridge: Cambridge University Press, 1997), 194–5.
5   Immanuel Kant, *Critique of the Power of Judgment*, ed. Paul Guyer, trans. Paul Guyer and Eric Matthews (Cambridge: Cambridge University Press, 2000), 147.
6   Ibid., 130.
7   Ibid., 141, translation modified.

had been a keystone of the sublime since Burke. They correspond to Mendelssohn's immeasurability of extension (greatness) and of force (power). In the "mathematical sublime," the senses are confronted with an object so vast that they can scarcely comprehend it in a single intuition: mountain ranges, the sea, the pyramids. At the same time, the intellectual faculties, unlimited in their ability to arrive at indefinitely large quantities by means of simple multiplication, are aware that there is more to see than the senses can apprehend in a single intuition, producing displeasure at the inadequacy of the senses to keep up with what the mind can think. This very inadequacy, however, also shows the greater power of the intellect, thereby producing a pleasurable feeling for the superiority of our rational faculties over the greatest faculty of the senses.[8] The same sense for the superiority of reason over sensible nature is at play in the "dynamical sublime," the second of its two modalities, which is experienced in the face not of nature's vastness but of its power and violence: tempests, volcanoes, overhanging cliffs, the stormy sea. Such prospects make us aware of our physical powerlessness while at the same time reminding us of our moral destiny, our power to brave physical danger in the service of an autonomously chosen higher good. In both cases, an initial experience of our limits in the sensible world triggers a sense for our "superiority over nature"[9] in the supersensible power of human reason.

The aspect of this conception that would have the greatest influence on later aesthetic theory was that it allowed for the representation of what, because of its supersensible nature, was not representable by the senses at all. God and immortality are not observable, nor is freedom from natural causality, since human actions can potentially all be traced to empirical motives. Instead of attempting to offer a sensible representation of these supersensible ideas, Kant's sublime showed instead the *limits* of sensible representation in general, thereby awakening a sense that there was more to existence than what the senses and the imagination could represent. The sublime could thus be seen as a "negative presentation"[10] of the unrepresentable—a paradox to which future aesthetic theories would return again and again. To be sure, the sublime had always been linked to religious ideas and to the greatness of God, and the contrast between the sensible qualities of the sublime and its deeper significance had been stressed as well. Already in Pseudo-Longinus, the idea of negative representation is implicit in the example of Ajax's sublime wordlessness. Still, never before had the sensual characteristics of the sublime been so thoroughly negated as

---

8 Ibid., 141.
9 Ibid., 145.
10 Ibid., 156.

in Kant. The *greatness* of nature prompted a sublime response precisely because it appeared so *small* as to vanish altogether when compared with the rational calling of man to rise above it.[11]

The implications of this novel theory of the sublime could be construed in very different ways. On the one hand, by awakening a sense for the autonomy of human reason, the sublime could be linked to the idea of political emancipation. Governments, Kant noted, relied on sensual representations of greatness in order to retain power: by means of "images and childish devices," they relieved their subjects of "the bother, but at the same time also of the capacity to extend the powers of their souls beyond the limits that are arbitrarily set for them and by means of which, as merely passive beings, they can more easily be dealt with."[12] This implied that by demonstrating the smallness of all such sensual representations of greatness, the experience of the sublime could help instill the courage to cast off political tutelage. On the other hand, the sublime victory of reason over nature could also be seen in a much less positive light: as a blueprint for the subjection of nature—including man's own sensual nature—by a numbingly impersonal and impassionate rationality. If the sublime expresses "a superiority over nature on which is grounded a self-preservation of quite another kind" than human survival in the face of natural dangers,[13] one may wonder what, exactly, is preserving itself in the sublime. The victory of reason over the imagination and the senses, which is described in explicitly agonistic terms—reason does "violence" (*Gewalt*) to sensuality[14]—may appear in this light as the subjugation of nature by a reason become so pure that it has only its own self-preservation in mind.

After Kant

The contrasting implications of Kant's theory of the sublime are much in evidence in later treatments of the concept, which from this point on will develop with more or less constant reference to Kant. The emancipatory significance of the sublime was immediately recognized and affirmed by Schiller, who incorporated it, reframed for his own particular purposes, into his project for the aesthetic emancipation of man. As a dramatist, Schiller was interested less in the sublime of nature, which had been Kant's focus, than in the depiction of sublime *deeds* in drama and tragedy; this required him to delineate in more concrete terms than Kant what distinguished the sublime as an aesthetic phenomenon from moral actions and judgments. The examples for the

---

11 Ibid., 140.
12 Ibid., 156, translation modified.
13 Ibid., 145.
14 Ibid., 148, translation modified.

"sublimity of action"[15] Schiller gives in "On the Sublime" and "On the Pathetic" (1793) involve morally reprehensible deeds, such as Medea murdering her children to avenge her treacherous husband in Corneille's version of the play. What makes this immoral act sublime is that Medea's motherly love is undiminished even while she carries it out, and in seeing this conflict between sentiment and deed we come to sense the ability in humans to act independently of natural inclinations. While the depiction of heroic deeds would produce only moral admiration for a single individual, the depiction of moral failings in a noble soul shows freedom in the abstract as something that is common to all humans.[16] The effect is a specifically *aesthetic* one—"The same object can displease us in our moral estimation and still be aesthetically pleasing in the highest degree"[17]—that nevertheless helps to develop the sense of freedom from which moral heroism can follow.[18] Such forms of aesthetic response would later form the basis for the "aesthetic education of man" which Schiller, repulsed by the excesses of the French Revolution, saw as a prerequisite to any political emancipation worthy of the name.

Almost as quickly, at least one other reader saw in Kant's narrative of reason's victory over nature not emancipation but only the excesses of rationalism. In *Kalligone* (1800), a caustic critique of the Kantian aesthetic school, Herder attacked Kant for having initiated an aesthetic apotheosis of reason. "I am the single, absolute and all-sublime: for I create sublime feelings for myself beyond nature and all objects, beyond all measure; but I myself stand nowhere": thus Herder characterized the position Kant attributed to the viewer by situating the sublime in the mind of the subject.[19] In the context of Herder's anthropology, which saw the sensual, rational, and imaginative faculties of man as coordinated parts of an inseparable whole, Kant's narrative of the sublime as a conflict between reason and the imagination seemed at best a contrived fiction. Describing sublimity in pre-Kantian terms as admiration for what is above the spectator, not for what is great in him, Herder insisted on the sublime as what is *sensed* in the perceptible forms of natural objects and works of art. Kant's "negative representation" argument thus made no sense: "If the ideas of reason […] cannot be represented, how can their

---

15   Friedrich Schiller, *Essays*, ed. Walter Hinderer and Daniel O. Dahlstrom (New York: Continuum, 1993), 60.
16   Ibid., 64.
17   Ibid., 61, translation modified.
18   Ibid., 67.
19   Johann Gottfried Herder, *Schriften zu Literatur und Philosophie 1792–1800*, ed. Hans Dietrich Irmscher (Frankfurt am Main: Deutscher Klassiker Verlag, 1998), 881.

incommensurability be represented?"[20] To be sure, Herder's restitution of the sensual dimension of the sublime was attained at the cost of many of what had been its most salient and intriguing features, such as the mix of terror and delight and the contrast between the sublime form and its meaning.

Like Herder, Hegel too objected to Kant's locating of the sublime in "the pure subjectivity of the mind,"[21] but he retained the element of negativity while relegating the sublime to a past epoch in the history of art. Hegel sees art as the history of a struggle between meaning and form that reaches a culminating resolution in classical Greece, in which the ideal of beauty is attained. The sublime belongs to a transitional stage in the progress toward this ideal: the symbolic art of India, of the Muslim cultures, and of the Hebrew Bible. In these art forms, the meaning—the Absolute or the Godly—has yet to find an adequate formal expression, but the conflict between meaning and form itself has now become manifest. Drawing on Kant's concept of the sublime as a negative representation of the unrepresentable, Hegel sees sublimity as an "intuition of the being of God as the purely spiritual and imageless, contrasted with the mundane and the natural."[22] The sublime artwork thus signifies by means of its inadequacy to what it represents. Hegel's historical framework makes this structure appear somewhat less paradoxical than it had in Kant: from the perspective of absolute spirit, we can now know what sublime art was trying, and failing, to represent, and the sublime can thus be observed not just from the side of its inadequate form, but from that of its meaning. Kant's abstract victory of reason over nature, which Herder had decried as empty and vain, is replaced by a concrete and substantive resolution between the intellectual and the sensual faculties, the fulfillment of history in absolute spirit. Whether this provides an effective alternative to what Herder saw as Kant's excessive rationalism depends on one's assessment of Hegel's system.

Both Herder and Hegel construed the sublime not in opposition to the beautiful, but as a transition toward it, and after them, the dualism between the sublime and the beautiful that had defined the concept in the eighteenth century would never fully return. Later thinkers grasped the sublime by means of other conceptual configurations, such as the relation of the sublime to the comical or humorous (Jean Paul, Friedrich Theodor Vischer). The meaning of the term became ever more diffuse. It could now be applied to political and historical events:

---

20 Ibid., 875.
21 Georg Wilhelm Friedrich Hegel, *Aesthetics: Lectures on Fine Art*, ed. and trans. T. M. Knox (Oxford: Oxford University Press, 1998), 363.
22 Ibid., 371.

the 1848 revolution (Kuno Fischer) or Prussia's military successes (Eduard von Hartmann). The aesthetic ideology of National Socialism was generally framed in terms of the beautiful, not the sublime, even while its cultural productions—monumental architecture, neoclassical depictions of heroism in art and sculpture—could be seen as aspiring to a sublime aesthetic. Not surprisingly, the term all but disappeared from aesthetic theory after the war—with the remarkable exception of Adorno's *Aesthetic Theory* (1971).

Adorno, to be sure, shared the post-war disdain for sublime subjects in art: sublime content is "usually only the fruit of ideology and of respect for power and magnitude."[23] But the negative representational *structure* invented by Kant clearly suited Adorno's insistence on art's negativity vis-à-vis the "administered world," his term for late capitalist society. In an age in which alternatives to economical and instrumental reason had become almost unthinkable, "the adequate form for the reception of artworks is that of the communication of the incommunicable." Art has thus come to "occupy the position that was once held by the concept of the sublime."[24] On the condition that the sublime absolve its ties to theology and "turn on its head the enduringness that the idea of the sublime intended," Adorno can affirm the sublime's oppositional force: "Kant was profoundly right to define the sublime as the resistance of spirit to power."[25] The emancipatory potential of the sublime that had been implicit in Kant and that Schiller had first made explicit resurfaces in Adorno.

Not until the 1980s, however, did the sublime fully re-emerge as a central interest of German aesthetic theory. Here again, the initial impulse came from France, where Derrida and Jean-Luc Nancy re-explored the Kantian sublime and Jean-François Lyotard used the term to describe the art of the avant-garde. By relating art and literature to the "unrepresentable," the term was useful in delineating the specificity of aesthetic phenomena *vis-à-vis* other modes of representation. The literature of high modernism, for example, could be characterized as sublime in its concern for "the experience of something unspeakable."[26]

As this brief survey shows, what has made the concept of the sublime so useful to aesthetic theory has been above all its ability to name

---

23 Theodor W. Adorno, *Aesthetic Theory*, ed. Gretel Adorno and Rolf Tiedemann, trans. Robert Hullot-Kentor (Minneapolis: University of Minnesota Press, 1997), 149.
24 Ibid., 196, translation modified.
25 Ibid., 199, translation modified.
26 Karl Heinz Bohrer, "Am Ende des Erhabenen: Niedergang und Renaissance einer Kategorie," *Merkur* 43 (1989): 747.

contrary aesthetic responses: the terrifying or the tragic gives pleasure; naïve or simple language elicits admiration; the overwhelming force of nature shows its lack of power over man's autonomous will; the lack or inadequacy of a sensual form expresses more than can be captured by even the most beautiful or ideal of forms. As a discipline, aesthetics established itself in no small part by its ability to account for such paradoxical subjective responses, for which neither theoretical nor moral philosophy could give a satisfactory explanation. For this reason alone, it seems fair to say that few concepts are as closely entwined with the history of aesthetics as that of the sublime.

SEE ALSO: Judgment; Beauty; Uncanny; Shudder

Five Mimesis

Christian Sieg

In its long history, mimesis has been defined in various ways and has proven significant in a variety of fields. Its conceptualization in aesthetics reflects particular philosophical, anthropological, psychological, and semiotic issues. In the poetological and aesthetic discourses from the eighteenth to the twentieth century, the concept addresses fundamental questions concerning the very definition of art, artistic practice as human behavior, the reception and production of artworks, and the ways in which art relates to the world.

The discourse on mimesis in eighteenth-century German aesthetics starts as a dialogue with Aristotle. Although the conversation gradually draws to an end, Aristotle's importance in this matter can hardly be overestimated. Already in Aristotle, mimesis was an ambiguous concept that oscillates between two ways of thinking about art.[1] On the one hand, it defines the relation between reality and artistic representation. On the other hand, mimesis, as a mode of practice and operating structure, refers to the artistic performance and object. Since mimesis has often been translated as imitation of the natural world, the difference can also be outlined according to the concept of nature. Nature can be imitated as *natura naturata* (nature as product) or *natura naturans* (nature as activity). In the latter sense, the concept encompasses a notion of *poesis* that sets it apart from any form of naïve referentialism. In Aristotle's *Poetics*, already the discussion of dance in the first chapter clearly contradicts the notion that art simply mirrors nature, since dance imitates the human emotions in conventional, not naturalistic ways. Along the same lines, Aristotle does not limit mimesis to imitation of the given. Instead, he notes the difference between the task of the historian and the poet—a distinction that has become highly

---

1 Stephen Halliwell, *The Aesthetics of Mimesis. Ancient Texts and Modern Problems* (Princeton, NJ: Princeton University Press, 2002), 23.

stimulating for the discourse on mimesis. Whereas the historian refers to actual events, the poet may also represent unrealized possibilities. Repudiating Plato's verdict on art, Aristotle's differentiation between the actual and the possible offers nothing less than a theory of fiction. Rather than accusing the poets of lying, he understands poetic imagination as art's claim to a higher degree of universality. Similar to philosophy, art allows for cognitive insight by offering models and symbolic renditions of reality. Since mimesis in Aristotle does not simply designate the reproduction of the given and allows to grasp creative artistic production as well, it had been subject to diverse poetological reflections in the eighteenth century and, finally, helped to conceptualize artistic production as the creative work of genius—a line of aesthetic thought which terminates the popularity of mimesis as an aesthetic concept in the eighteenth century.

The importance of mimesis in the poetological discourse of the eighteenth century becomes apparent in the lengthy subtitle of one of the most influential poetological texts of the time. The subtitle of J. Chr. Gottsched's *Critical Poetics* (1729) presents the imitation (*Nachahmung*) of nature as the very essence of poetry. Arguing in geometrical terms that only the completeness and order of nature guarantees perfection in art, Gottsched makes use of the concept in a rationalistic framework. He differentiates between three forms of mimesis on the basis of their respective object. Painting functions as the paradigm for the lowest form of mimesis: the imitation of natural things through descriptions. The art of acting and certain lyric speech-acts exemplify the second form, which focuses on the imitation of dialogue. Finally, he regards the poetic fable (plot) as the highest form of mimesis. True to Aristotle, Gottsched delineates the task of the poet from that of the historian and, from the backdrop of Leibniz's and Wolff's philosophies, claims that the fable (plot) refers not to the actual but to possible worlds. Whereas this turn gives Gottsched the license to include even Aesop's fables into the mimesis principle, Gottsched emphasizes that possible worlds share the principle of reason with the actual world and that every artistic depiction demands verisimilitude. Both categories of verisimilitude and reason constrain the power of the imagination in Gottsched's poetics and restrain the objects of art's imitation. Mimesis in Gottsched is by no means an end in itself but part of art's educational aim. The poet—understood as *poeta doctus*—ought to represent a world that exemplifies a well ordered system of rational rules.

It is at this point that the difference between Gottsched and J. J. Bodmer as well as J. J. Breitinger becomes apparent. While Breitinger's *Critical Poetics* (1740) as a matter of course ascribes a didactic agenda to poetry, it considers aesthetic issues to a far greater degree. Upon first glance, the similarities between Gottsched and Breitinger prevail. Both firmly stick to the mimesis paradigm as established by Aristotle. They even refer to the same sentence of Wolff's that maintains that fiction is the history of another world. Yet, propelled by the tension between the demand to imitate and the inventiveness of fiction, Breitinger gives more credit to the creative task of the poet. Holding the marvelous and fantasy in high esteem, he gives the aesthetic experience of poetry the preference over its moral purpose. Along the same lines, he contests that reason alone is supposed to judge art and suggests that the imagination orients our aesthetic reception as well. Breitinger's thought foreshadows to a certain degree the rehabilitation of the imagination during the second half of the eighteenth century. An important step on this way is made by A. G. Baumgarten whose *Aesthetica* (1750/58) initiates the development of aesthetics as a discipline. While still working within Wolff's conceptual framework, Baumgarten delineates the sensuous as a cognitive field in its own right. Although Baumgarten does not subordinate the aesthetic quality of art to moral teachings, aesthetic cognition builds on the sensuous which belongs to a rational order. Understanding mimesis as analogous to nature's productivity as a practice that produces sensuous objects, Baumgarten renews one of the major aspects of Aristotle's definition of mimesis.

J. E. Schlegel's contribution to the discourse on mimesis can best be understood through the background of an Aristotelian thesis. Considering the epic in *Poetics*, Aristotle grapples with a tension inherent in the theory of mimesis. Ontologically speaking, everything that is possible may become the object of artistic imitation. Yet, considering the reception of art, the question of credibility arises. Is everything that is possible also credible? Aristotle deals with this tension apodictically: "The use of impossible probabilities is preferable to that of unpersuasive possibilities."[2] Whereas Aristotle recognizes here an exception to the rule of mimesis, by placing emphasis on the subjective conditions of reception, Schlegel uses this tension to subordinate mimesis to art's obligation to communicate pleasure. In *On Imitation* (1742) Schlegel claims that likeness pertains not to the relation between art and world but between art and our understanding of the world. In order to arouse pleasure, the poet thus has to keep the worldviews of his contemporaries in mind: the object of mimesis is not nature but our concepts of nature. Schlegel summarizes the consequences for the theory of mimesis as a paradox: imitation needs to be dissimilar to the object that is being imitated.

In *Laocoön: An Essay on the Limits of Painting and Poetry* (1766), G. E. Lessing chooses another way to reconsider some of the central tenets

---

2 *Aristotle's Poetics. A Translation and Commentary for Students of Literature* (Englewood Cliffs, NJ: Prentice-Hall Inc., 1968), 45.

of the theory of mimesis. Lessing questions the equation of poetry and painting, which in the eighteenth century was a neoclassical commonplace usually ascribed to Horace's dictum *ut pictura poesis*. Lessing's reevaluation builds on J.-B. Dubos' essay *Critical Reflections on Poetry, Painting and Music* (1719), which had an enormous impact on German aesthetic thought. Crucial for Lessing was Dubos' use of the differentiation between natural and arbitrary signs that goes back to Plato's *Cratylus*. While painting operates with natural signs that resemble what they denote, Dubos argues that poetry depends on language—an arbitrary sign system in which signifier and signified differ. This semiotic reflection complicates the idea that painting and poetry are mimetic in the very same way. Since linguistic signs are not iconic, Lessing rejects the idea that poetry represents nature similar to painting in sensuous ways. Yet, at the same time, he maintains that, in light of the object of poetic mimesis, the use of language in poetry is by no means arbitrary. Lessing claims that, due to its auditory quality, poetry operates successively and, thus, imitates something that also progresses in time: action. Therefore, he criticizes contemporary tendencies to use poetry first and foremost as a means of description. Rather than aping painting, poetry should focus on action. What the poet mimetically relates is the effect action has on us:

> He wants [...] to make the ideas he awakens in us so vivid that at that moment we believe that we feel the real impressions which the objects of these ideas would produce on us. In this moment of illusion we should cease to be conscious of the means which the poet uses for this purpose, that is, his words.[3]

Lessing reevaluates aesthetic illusion along the lines of the mimesis paradigm. Since the poet aims at the power of his reader's imagination in order to evoke sensuous impressions, not merely to copy the visible elements of the exterior world, Lessing gives poetry preference over painting as the more creative art. He insists on the "autonomous nature of the imagined object,"[4] which does not overcome but fulfills the demand of mimesis.

At the end of the eighteenth century, aesthetic discourse emphasizes the autonomous dimension of poetic creation to such a degree that the concept of genius often displaces that of mimesis. Kant's *Critique of the Power of Judgment* (1781), for example, states this widely

---

3   Gotthold Ephraim Lessing, *Laocoön: An Essay on the Limits of Painting and Poetry* (Baltimore, MD: Johns Hopkins University Press, 1984), 85.
4   David E. Wellbery, *Lessing's Laocoön. Semiotics and Aesthetics in the Age of Reason* (Cambridge: Cambridge University Press, 1984), 108.

shared assumption: "Everyone agrees that genius is entirely opposed to the spirit of imitation."[5] Notwithstanding such general rejections, eighteenth-century poets such as Karl Philip Moritz and Johann Wolfgang von Goethe aim to pay homage to the imaginative power of the genius and at the same time conceptualize artistic production in terms of mimesis. From the backdrop of the creative dimension of mimesis, Moritz's essay *On the Artistic Imitation of the Beautiful* (1788) stretches the mimesis paradigm to its utmost extent. Moritz understands mimesis as the faculty of artistic production and reception that displaces reason in the realm of art. Mimesis alone allows recognition of the beautiful, which Moritz grasps as a whole that is complete in itself: "Each beautiful whole coming from the hand of the artist is thus an impression in miniature of the highest beauty of the whole of nature; mediated through the hands of the artist, it recreates that which does not immediately belong to the great plan."[6] Moritz conceptualizes art as a medium through which natural beauty reveals itself. Genius mimics natural forces, thereby bringing them into the open. The autonomy of artistic creation is key for Moritz, since nothing but the force of genius produces the beautiful which cannot "be recognized but must be brought out—or felt."[7]

This epistemological significance of art as well as its autonomous status is reflected in Goethe's short treatise, published one year later, *Simple Imitation, Manner, Style* (1789), which returns to his discussions with Moritz in Rome. For Goethe, the threefold typology of his title expresses the advancing order of artistic competence. Whereas simple imitation refers to a mere mirroring of the object, and manner characterizes an artistic process which is dominated by subjectively grounded forms of representation, the highest of the three practices, style, can be understood as synthesis. On the one hand, style, as mimetic practice, is true to the object; on the other hand, it finds a language to express the characteristics of things which are not perceivable in the first place. Thus, style "rests on the most fundamental principle of cognition, on the essence of things—to the extent that it is granted us to perceive this essence in visible and tangible form."[8] Similar to Moritz, Goethe places emphasis on the epistemological task of the poet who operates

---

5 Immanuel Kant, *Critique of the Power of Judgment*, ed. Paul Guyer, trans. Paul Guyer and Eric Matthews (Cambridge: Cambridge University Press, 2000), 187.
6 Karl Philipp Moritz, "From: 'On the Artistic Imitation of the Beautiful,'" in *Classic and Romantic German Aesthetics*, ed. J. M. Bernstein (Cambridge: Cambridge University Press, 2003), 139.
7 Ibid., 143.
8 Johann Wolfgang von Goethe, *Essays on Art and Literature*, ed. John Gearey, Goethe's Collected Works, Vol. 3 (Princeton, NJ: Princeton University Press, 1994), 72.

autonomously rather than aiming at likeness. In Goethe's *On Truth and Verisimilitude in Art* (1798), which builds on the thoughts summarized here, it becomes apparent how this reconsideration of mimesis paves the way for an idealist aesthetics. Evoking the story of the ancient painter Zeuxis, whose paintings are said to be so realistic that birds aimed at eating the painted grapes, Goethe polemically emphasizes the difference between animal and human spectators. The demand that art should appear to be natural is postulated by people who want to enjoy art in "primitive and unsophisticated ways."[9] The true connoisseur, instead, "feels that he must rise to the level of the artist in order to enjoy the work, that he must focus his scattered energies on the work of art, that he must live with it, must see it again and again, and thus achieve a higher level of awareness."[10] While Goethe conceives the artwork as a product of nature insofar as it is a product of genius, it also goes beyond nature. By creating a unified whole, the work provides a *telos* for the education of humankind. Even though the autonomous status of the artwork in Goethe and Moritz can hardly be understood within the mimesis paradigm, both artists—unlike Kant—do not completely break with it. To be sure, also for Kant genius is a product of nature. Yet the artistic practice, he maintains, depends on nature only insofar as it uses nature as material, but the imagination transforms this material "into something entirely different, namely into that which steps beyond nature."[11] For Kant, mimesis only pertains to lesser qualified artists who, lacking the power of genius, imitate the artworks of real artists. Finally, on the background of the aesthetics of genius and the valorization of the imaginative, the German Romantics trenchantly criticized the mimesis principle. It may suffice to quote Novalis, who laments that the mimesis principle "still tyrannizes" the theater and claims: "Poetry too must simply be merely sensible—artificial—invented—fantastic!"[12]

In the twentieth century, the most powerful reevaluation of mimesis as a concept in German aesthetics can be found in the work of Theodor W. Adorno. Tracing the anthropological, biological, and historical dimensions of mimesis together with Max Horkheimer already in the *Dialectic of Enlightenment* (1947), the concept becomes a key term in Adorno's *Aesthetic Theory* (1970). According to Adorno, only art as a field of practice that relies on mimetic behavior breaks with the rule of instrumental reason and treats its objects in non-subordinating

---

9   Ibid., 77.
10 Ibid., 78.
11 Kant, *Critique of the Power of Judgment*, 192.
12 Novalis, "Last Fragments," in *Philosophical Writings*, ed. Margaret Mahony Stoljar (New York: State University of New York Press, 1997), 164.

ways. Rather than subsuming the sensuous particular under abstract concepts, mimetic cognition gives prevalence to the object. Adorno's conceptualization of the mimetic is at odds with any form of referentialism. Instead, art inherits the forces of magical and biological mimesis: "Mimetic behavior does not imitate something but assimilates itself to that something."[13] Along these lines, it allows relating to nature (outside and inside human beings) in non-dominating ways. While Adorno strengthens the anthropological dimension of the concept of mimesis in comparison with the aesthetic tradition, he takes as his historical starting point the very autonomy of art, which already in the eighteenth century began to slowly reduce the attractiveness of the idea that art ought to imitate nature. On the one hand, Adorno, in a Kantian pose, holds the autonomy of art in high esteem, since it allows for a disinterested engagement beyond the reign of pure or practical reason. On the other hand, he criticizes art's autonomy insofar as it offers an illusionary wholeness amidst societal fragmentation. In this dialectical setting, mimesis becomes a cognitive capacity through which art in its own idiom responds to the social. While conceptual thought distances the subject from the object, art functions as a medium for experiences that are otherwise silenced. Along these lines, Adorno reads the negation of traditional artistic forms by modernist artists as mimetic expressions of social suffering. Whereas in the eighteenth century the genius becomes a charismatic figure and embodies the sovereign operations of *natura naturans*, Adorno understands mimesis as a "counter-movement to the subject" which opens an intersubjective realm and demands that the artist possess the "capacity to address or recognize what aesthetic objects themselves enunciate and what they conceal."[14] For Adorno, herein lies the utopian promise of mimesis.

In the twentieth century, reflections on mimesis have also been influenced greatly by Erich Auerbach's seminal work *Mimesis: The Representation of Reality in Western Literature* (1946). This study shifts the perspective on the subject. It does not focus on mimesis as a philosophical concept but on the literary techniques which represent reality. Auerbach reads European literature from Homer and the Evangelists to modernist fiction as interpretations of reality. The German subtitle, which more adequately translates into *Represented Reality in Western Literature*, indicates that clearly. For Auerbach, epistemological doubts concerning the very notion of reality are not the issue; instead, he pursues a literary history in which literary representations increasingly

---

13 Theodor W. Adorno, *Aesthetic Theory*, ed. Gretel Adorno and Rolf Tiedemann, trans. Robert Hullot-Kentor (Minneapolis: University of Minnesota Press, 1997), 162.
14 Ibid., 346.

depict the everyday world as an important aspect of human life. Whereas the classical separation of styles limited everyday occurrences to comic representations, these literary works treat them seriously. Auerbach's *Mimesis* also responds to the sociopolitical context of its time. Towards the end of the Second World War, he expresses his hope that literature might point to "the elementary things which men in general have in common."[15] This humanist idea has been radically reevaluated in the wake of poststructuralism. After the linguistic turn, the ways in which literary representations foster commonly shared beliefs about reality have become the object of heavy criticism. Rather than simply reproducing what is already given, mimesis is understood as a persuasive rhetorical practice which takes part in the imaginary construction of "reality." In this perspective, realism reproduces stereotypical worldviews, thereby repressing alternative ways to perceive the world. Christopher Prendergast's *The Order of Mimesis* (1986) has played a key part in this political critique of the concept. Stressing the prescriptive dimension of mimesis, he takes issue with the mimetic "imperative to submit to the set of symbolic arrangements."[16] Pointing to the important communicative function of a collectively shared symbolic medium, Prendergast at the same time aims to rescue the term. Without the aim of a mimetic language game to communicate representations of reality, the social order turns unintelligible, thereby canceling meaningful engagement with that order. By accepting the ambiguity of mimesis, Prendergast demonstrates the unlikely scenario that we have heard the last word on mimesis. In all likelihood, the tensions inherent in the notion of mimesis since Greek antiquity will endure at the heart of aesthetic debates well into the future.

SEE ALSO: Judgment; Feeling

---

15 Erich Auerbach, *Mimesis. The Representation of Reality in Western Literature* (Princeton, NJ: Princeton University Press, 1991), 552.
16 Christopher Prendergast, *The Order of Mimesis. Balzac, Stendhal, Nerval, Flaubert* (Cambridge: Cambridge University Press, 1986), 5.

Six Feeling: On *Werther*

Stanley Corngold

In the mid-eighteenth century, a chief source of art's instruction and delight is "Witz" (wit). This term has a double valence: on the one hand, it corresponds to the French "esprit" (intellectual acuity and speed); on the other hand, it has a narrower focus and refers to the word-play that points up unsuspected correspondences between things, yoking together apparent contrarieties. In his *Hamburg Dramaturgy* (1767–8), the essayist, playwright, and public intellectual G. E. Lessing composed a "Farewell to Wit" in the name of a more rigorous logic, flashing the allure of Enlightenment thought. Henceforth, dramatists must produce sequences of actions held together not by resemblance and coincidence but by an unrelenting logic of psychological cause and effect. But no sooner has this rational psychology usurped the rule of wit than this factor is itself usurped by a darker, more urgent feature of human nature. The third quarter of the century witnesses, under the caption of "Storm and Stress," the explosive entry into this scene of art and culture by Johann Wolfgang von Goethe, the coryphée of all the new, young exponents of the primacy of *feeling*.

At a point midway into Faust's seduction of Gretchen, in *Goethe's Faust*, Gretchen asks Faust the gilt-edged, vexatious question since preserved in German cultural memory as "the Gretchen Question":

"Do you believe in God?" Faust replies: "My darling, who can say: I believe in God? ... Who can give a name to Him? ... Who encompasses everything, Who preserves everything, doesn't He hold and preserve you, me, Himself? ... . And doesn't everything surge into your head and heart and weave in eternal mystery invisibly-visibly around you? Fill up your heart with it, as great as it is, and when you are wholly blissful in that feeling, then call it what you will: Call it Happiness! Heart! Love! God! I have no name for it! *Feeling is everything;* names are noise and smoke, which befog the glow of heaven."[1]

In the wake of the First World War, the proper Bostonian critic of Romanticism Irving Babbitt focused on Faust's reply as the epitome of the very thing he deplored: the inner life of feeling without "an inner check," without "the true voice of conscience,"[2]

> Faust gives himself to the devil in what was, in the time of the youthful Goethe, the newest fashion: he became a Rousseauist ... and so definition yields to indiscriminate feeling .... Faust breaks down the scruples of Marguerite by proclaiming the supremacy of feeling; ... the upshot of this enthusiasm is ... the seduction of a poor peasant girl.[3]

But at the outset of this polemic, the German literary historian O. E. Lessing had a good Rousseauvean reply: Faust's formula is not "immoral emotionalism" (as Babbitt has it) "but a sincere expression of the very best there is in him. 'Gefühl ist alles,' in its proper connection, means the unsophisticated voice of the heart ... "[4] And O. E. Lessing goes on to embed the prompting of the heart, as did Rousseau his celebrated "sentiment of existence," in a "mystic and monistic" context establishing its truth.[5] For Rousseau the condition of "the sentiment of existence, stripped of any other emotion," is that "the heart ... be at peace and no passion come to disturb its calm."[6]

In this quarrel between two twentieth-century disciples of opposing schools, we revisit the conceptual drama of eighteenth-century German aesthetics and moral philosophy. The "Rousseauists" win. For the young Immanuel Kant (1724–1804), and *pace* Babbitt, feeling is ever the path to morality, it is "the consciousness of a feeling" that in its depth

---

1 Johann Wolfgang von Goethe, *Goethe's Faust*, ed. R-M. S. Heffner, Helmut Rehder, and W. F. Twaddell (Boston: Heath, 1954), 281; II: 3426-58, emphasis added.
2 Otto Eduard Lessing, "Irving Babbitt's *Rousseau and Romanticism*," *Journal of English and Germanic Philology* 18 (1919): 630.
3 Irving Babbitt, *Rousseau and Romanticism* (Boston and New York: Houghton-Mifflin, 1919), 181, 170, 287.
4 Lessing, "Irving Babbitt's *Rousseau and Romanticism*," 631.
5 Lessing, "Irving Babbitt's *Rousseau and Romanticism*," 631; Jean-Jacques Rousseau, *Reveries of a Solitary Walker*, trans. Charles Butterworth (Indianapolis and Cambridge: Hackett, 1992), 69.
6 Rousseau, *Reveries*, 69.

releases "the true voice of conscience," enlarging the scope of the self to include other minds and hearts.⁷ Kant writes:

> True virtue can only be grafted upon principles, and it will become the more sublime and noble the more general they are. These principles are not speculative rules, but *the consciousness of a feeling* that lives in every human breast and that extends much further than to the special grounds of sympathy and complaisance. ... And if this feeling had the greatest perfection in any human heart, then this human being would certainly love and value even himself, but only in so far as he is one among all to whom his widespread and noble feeling extends itself. Only when one subordinates one's own particular inclination to such an enlarged one can our kindly drives be proportionally applied and bring about the noble attitude that is the beauty of virtue ... .⁸

This claim arises from a Rousseauvean source as well, a source that runs all throughout Rousseau and which Kant enthusiastically acknowledges in his early remarks in *Observations on the Feeling of the Beautiful and the Sublime*:

> I myself am a researcher by inclination. I feel the entire thirst for knowledge and the eager restlessness to proceed further in it, as well as the satisfaction at every acquisition. There was a time when I believed this alone could constitute the honor of humankind, and I despised the rabble who knows nothing. Rousseau has set me right... . Rousseau discovered for the very first time beneath the manifold of forms adopted by the human being the deeply hidden nature of the same and hidden law, according to which providence is justified ...⁹

This law, a principle leading to moral cultivation, is apprehended in and through feeling. Rousseau had made the point plain: "There is a purely passive physical and organic sensibility which seems to have as its end only the preservation of our bodies and of our species through the direction of pleasure and pain. There is another sensibility that I call

---

7   Immanuel Kant, "Remarks in the *Observations on the Feeling of the Beautiful and Sublime*," in *Observations on the Feeling of the Beautiful and Sublime, and Other Writings*, trans. Thomas Hilgers, Uygar Abaci, Michael Nance, and Paul Guyer (Cambridge: Cambridge University Press, 2011), 24; Lessing, "Irving Babbitt's *Rousseau and Romanticism*," 181.
8   Kant, "Remarks," 24.
9   Kant, "Remarks," 95, 105.

active and moral which is nothing other than the faculty of attaching our affections to beings who are foreign to us."[10] Decades afterwards, Kant's *Critique of Practical Reason* (1788) would systematically organize Rousseau's explicit celebration of conscience in the *Profession of Faith of a Savoyard Vicar* (1782) as an autonomous source of ethical certainty. And crucially for our topic, Kant would claim in his *Critique of Judgment* (1790) that aesthetic judgments are analogous to moral judgments in the way they arise: to the mind that habitually notes the beauty of nature, we attribute "a good moral disposition."[11] "The beautiful is the symbol of the morally good."[12]

What is key for Kant is that a *feeling* called "delight without interest" (*interesseloses Wohlgefallen*) provides the basis of aesthetic judgment. In judging a form to be beautiful, the subject takes pleasure in the felt harmony of the faculties of mind that play with concepts and images. Here, as elsewhere, the term "feeling" informs German poetry and fiction and philosophical writing and in every one of these mediums attains an unarguable, even absolute validity. Higher feelings (call them feelings of "Happiness! Heart! Love! God!") flow into Goethe from records of religious experience by Meister Eckhart, Susannah von Klettenberg, Spinoza, Klopstock, and Herder.[13] From a more immediate source, the claims of feeling fuel the charged rituals of German Protestantism—especially Pietism, which sought to cultivate "the feeling of the effects of grace." From all these sources and insistences it was a short step for persons to aim to feel the secular equivalents of such grace in feeling the effects of erotic love and feeling the effects of art.

Feeling becomes a source of knowledge—a knowledge different from but not inferior to conceptual cognition. Recall that for Kant the delight in beautiful forms proceeds from the felt harmony of the faculties of imagination and conceptuality undergirding every particular cognition. This is a *general* knowledge lost in the cognitive activity of the everyday that knows a table *qua* table but never the underlying attunement of the faculties producing this equation. The precedence of feeling over conceptual cognition is asserted again and again by Goethe's vice-exister Werther, the hero of his massively influential novel *The Sufferings of Young Werther* (1775), written at about the same time that Goethe posed the Gretchen Question. Werther declares, "Oh, anyone can know what I know [such as that the earth is round]; my

---

10 Rousseau, *Reveries*, 112.
11 Immanuel Kant, *Kant's Critique of Judgement*, trans. James Creed Meredith (Oxford: Clarendon, 1964), 160.
12 Ibid., 223.
13 Lessing, "Irving Babbitt's *Rousseau and Romanticism*," 631.

heart belongs to me alone."[14] The feelings of the heart convey the truth of personal being: "This heart of mine, which is the sole object of my pride, the only source of everything, all my strength, all my bliss, and all my wretchedness."[15] More than a metaphor, the "heart" comes to be the term of choice, in the absence of a more rigorous one, to indicate the fullest cooperation of mind and body. When Werther drinks a whole bottle of wine he is reprimanded by Lotte (with whom he is hopelessly in love). "'Don't do it! she said. Think of Lotte!'—'Think!'" replies Werther, "do you need to tell me that? I think!—I don't think! You are always present to my soul."[16] The heart realizes what thought cannot conceive. Contemplating his own death, Werther declares: "No, Lotte, no—How can I pass away? How can you pass away? We are, yes!—pass away!—what does that mean? That is merely another phrase! an empty noise, which my heart cannot feel."[17] And here we might recall Faust's answer to the Gretchen Question: "names are noise and smoke…"— just as we might recall the lament of Byron (1788–1824), Goethe's beloved poet: "Oh! never more on me/ The freshness of the heart can fall like dew/ Which out of all the lovely things we see/ Extracts emotions beautiful and new … ."[18] Considering the work of extraction it has to do, "feeling," wrote the great contemporary poet Friedrich Hölderlin (1770–1843), "is indeed the best sobriety and reflection of the poet, when it is right and warm and clear and powerful."[19]

Writing on Romantic egoism, the critic George Steiner indicts "those generations which derive from Rousseau and *Werther*… . Literature became a continuous autobiography, and the Romantics suffered 'ecstasies of self-revelation.'"[20] But these generations are not ensconced in egoism. Quite the contrary: we have seen the powerful "ecstasies" felt by Rousseau and Goethe's *Werther* emerge as motors of moral cultivation. It is not knowing something, as Werther declares, that develops a feeling for other minds and hearts: "there is another sensibility," an organization of feelings, which—"moral and active"—responds to a "hidden law."[21] And at the root of this inner sense of a common law—in

---

14 Johann Wolfgang von Goethe, *The Sufferings of Young Werther*, trans. Stanley Corngold (New York: Norton, 2011), 95.
15 Ibid.
16 Ibid., 108.
17 Ibid., 140–1.
18 Lord Byron, *Don Juan by Lord Byron*, ed. Leslie A. Marchand (Boston: Houghton Mifflin, 1958), 57.
19 Friedrich Hölderlin, *Sämtliche Werke*, ed. Friedrich Beißner (Stuttgart: Kohlhammer, 1961), IV: 233.
20 F. George Steiner, "Contributions to a Dictionary of Critical Terms: 'Egoism' and Egotism,'" in *Essays in Criticism* II (4) (October 1952): 446.
21 Jean-Jacques Rousseau, *Rousseau, Judge of Jean-Jacques: Dialogues*, trans. Judith R.

a word, of conscience—Rousseau, Goethe, and Kant find a wider sort of self-love—an affectionate "conscience de soi"—that leads beyond the ego to establish genuine social bonds.

To this feeling of self-love, at once aesthetic and moral, both Rousseau and Kant ascribe powers of disclosure unattainable in the hurly-burly of pragmatic social experience. Rousseau's sentiment of existence, a self-love infinitely more productive than "egoism," has an unsurpassable authenticity, exceeding any moral consciousness arising directly from relations between persons, for these tend to decline into that comparison of oneself with others that Rousseau calls "se refléter." It is telling that Werther's critique of Albert, Lotte's husband—"Oh, he is not the man to fulfill all the desires of that heart"—is based on "a certain lack of sensibility, a lack—make of it what you will; that his heart does not beat sympathetically at Oh!—at the passage in a favorite book where my heart and Lotte's beat as one ..."[22]

In the sentiment of existence Rousseau knows a fullness of free play that, if it is to express itself, can do so only in the metaphor of divinity: Rousseau says he "plays" with his own consciousness "comme Dieu."[23] Goethe's Werther knows a comparable ecstasy, in which he enjoys a feeling of full existence; and here, again, as in Rousseau's phrase "we are sufficient unto ourselves, like God," Werther recalls "how I felt like a god among the overflowing abundance, and the glorious shapes of the infinite world entered and quickened my soul."[24] Rousseau supplies this "other sort of enjoyment" with an intellectual dimension: "But, finally, what did I enjoy when I was alone? Myself, the whole universe, everything that is, everything that can be, everything that is beautiful in the perceptible world, and that is imaginable in the intellectual world ... "[25] Kant, too, in the Introduction to his *Critique of Judgment*, awards a radical intellectual power to this aesthetic mood of self-revelation, defining it as the very ground of intelligible existence in the natural world:

> In a Critique of Judgment the part dealing with *aesthetic* judgment is essentially relevant, as it alone contains a principle introduced by judgment completely *a priori* as the basis of its reflection upon nature. This is the principle of nature's formal finality for our cognitive faculties in its particular (empirical) laws—a principle

---

Bush, Christopher Kelly, and Roger D. Masters (Hanover, NH: University Press of New England, 1990), 112. Kant, "Remarks,"105.
22 Goethe, *The Sufferings of Young Werther*, 96.
23 Rousseau, *Reveries*, 69.
24 Rousseau, *Reveries*, 69. Goethe, *The Sufferings of Young Werther*, 69.
25 Rousseau, *Rousseau, Judge of Jean-Jacques*, 579, 577.

without which understanding could not feel itself at home in nature. ... But the transcendental principle by which a finality of nature, in its subjective reference to our cognitive faculties, is represented in the form of a thing as a principle of its estimation ... resigns to *the aesthetic judgment* the task of deciding the conformity of this product (in its form) to our cognitive faculties as a question of taste (*a matter which the aesthetic judgment decides, not by any harmony with concepts, but by feeling*) (emphasis added) ... .[26]

The rational organization of scientific knowledge depends on an initial *feeling of intelligibility*.

We conclude by returning to Goethe's seminal novel *The Sufferings of Young Werther*, a sort of prose music whose rhythm is determined by Werther's feelings of self-loss and self-gain. In this rush of continuous feeling, Werther's sense of self comes to light as one who reports his moods—as for example, "A wonderful gaiety has seized my entire soul."[27] Where there is such immediacy, the element of report is subordinated to the element of felt life. The letter-writer is himself attuned like the hero of his report; they share a mood.

Werther's self is informed by this rhythm of ecstasy and emptiness, mainly flowing from his relation to Lotte, his beloved. Here, in a sequence of passages, are some very rich clues to Werther's original way of experiencing himself. "And how she scolded me ... about my excessive emotional involvement in everything, and how that would lead to my destruction!"[28] "Oh, it is so certain that it is our heart alone that makes for a happiness."[29] "Oh, then, how often did I long to ... feel for even a moment in the confined power of my breast a drop of the bliss of that Being that brings forth everything in and through Itself."[30] "And so I have been strengthened for the past eight days and become one with myself."[31] "I walked through the gate [to my old home town] and found myself at once, wholly and completely."[32] " ... This heart of mine, which is the sole object of my pride, the only source of everything, all my strength, all my bliss, and all my wretchedness."[33]

> Woe is me! I feel all too clearly that I alone bear all the guilt—not guilt! Enough that the source of all misery lies deep within me,

---

26 Kant, *Critique of Judgment*, 35.
27 Goethe, *The Sufferings of Young Werther*, 23.
28 Ibid., 51.
29 Ibid., 61.
30 Ibid., 69.
31 Ibid., 87.
32 Ibid., 93.
33 Ibid., 95.

as formerly the source of all bliss.—Am I not still the same man who at one time floated in a fullness of feeling, who was followed at every step by a paradise, who had a heart to embrace a whole world with love? And this heart is now dead, no ecstasies flow from it, my eyes are dry, and my senses, no longer refreshed by restorative tears, furrow my brow with anxiety.[34]

Once more, because crucial: "She has reproached me for my excesses! ... : that I am sometimes seduced by a glass of wine into drinking a whole bottle. 'Don't do it!' she said, 'think of Lotte!'—'Think!' I said, 'do you need to tell me that? I think!—I don't think! You are always present to my soul.'"[35] "How her image pursues me! Waking and dreaming, it fills my entire soul! Here when I close my eyes, here inside my head, where the lines of my inner vision join, I find her black eyes. Here! I cannot describe it to you. When I close my eyes, they're there; like an ocean, like an abyss, they lie before me, in me, filling the senses inside my head."[36]

Note the key terms in this "argument" for feeling, since they are decisive for young Goethe and for the work of the contemporaries we have named: the seat of consciousness is, for want of a more precise physiological or philosophical term, the "heart." The relation of the self to its intentional object is not that of a concept to a thing but a "heart" to a "presence": the world is "present-to" a type of consciousness other than a conceptual consciousness—"the consciousness of a feeling," a mode of apprehension closer to inner sensation, to "the senses inside my head," than to the brain or mind.[37] Devouring, overwhelming nature concentrates in Lotte's black eyes, which possess Werther entirely. Now there is nothing left over of his heart for himself. An exquisite, premonitory loss concludes the first book: "They went out along the tree-lined avenue, I stood, gazed after them in the moonlight, and threw myself on the ground and wept and wept and jumped up and ran out onto the terrace and still saw below in the shadow of the tall linden trees her white dress shimmering at the garden door, I stretched out my arms, and it vanished."[38] This loss provokes his desperate ending: "It is settled, Lotte, I want to die ... "[39]

The Sufferings of Young Werther displays features characteristic of the literary movements *Empfindsamkeit* (Sentimentalism) and "Sturm

---

34 Ibid., 107.
35 Ibid., 108.
36 Ibid., 115.
37 Ibid., 115.
38 Ibid., 77.
39 Ibid., 128.

und Drang," constituting both their illustration and their critique. Sentimentalism is a discourse of feeling, to which it lends moral dignity, requiring a regime of self-reflection, by which feelings are identified and judged. Werther's felt love for Lotte and its examination, even though the most excessive expense of wit ("ich witzele mich ... herum"[40]), drives the novel forward. The intensity of Werther's friendship for the male addressee is remarkable: "Oh, that I cannot throw my arms around your neck and with a thousand tears and ecstasies, my dear friend, express the feelings that assail my heart,"[41] as is the saturation of Werther's rhetoric, in the Pietistic manner, by diction of the New Testament. Rather more characteristic of Sturm und Drang literature is the awful force of Werther's outbursts of feeling, rooted in the "robust sensuousness and joys of the body";[42] characteristic, too, is Werther's rebellious impatience with the prevailing aristocratic class structure as well as his epiphanic experiences of "God in Nature," which are finally no compensation for the failure of all his enterprises.

SEE ALSO: Mimesis; Mood/Attunement

---

40 Johann Wolfgang von Goethe, *Die Leiden des jungen Werther*, ed. Katharina Mommsen and Richard A. Koc (Frankfurt am Main: Insel Verlag, 2001), 103.
41 Goethe, *The Sufferings of Young Werther*, 73–4.
42 Ekbert Faas, *The Genealogy of Aesthetics* (Cambridge: Cambridge University Press, 2002), 186.

Seven Irony

Michel Chaouli

> Words often understand themselves better than do those who use them.
>
> Friedrich Schlegel

We live in irony, and irony lives in us. We use it, and we are abused by it. Ads wink at us, TV characters all seem to speak in air quotes, and the tone we hear most often in social media is one of mild self-mockery. Yet the experience of being saturated with irony does not appear to prepare us for the conspicuous, almost exalted, place it has come to occupy in aesthetic thinking. It is not clear why irony, of all things, would stand at the core of much of thinking about art since the time of early (or Jena) romanticism. Why does its main theoretical exponent, the young Friedrich Schlegel, elevate it to a position as the very principle of poetic production? How do we make sense of the fact that by the twentieth century irony had become the key category for a large and otherwise disparate swath of cultural production, from the literary craft of high modernism (in the works of, for instance, Thomas Mann, Proust, and Musil) through Dada and Surrealism to conceptual art and finally the late-century work in literature, music, architecture, and visual art we label postmodern? Though we live with irony, we still need to learn to think with it. What intellectual work does it do?

We know, as it were instinctively, that a definition of irony is unlikely to get us far. "To a person who hasn't got it," Schlegel writes about Socratic irony, "it will remain a riddle even after it is openly confessed."[1] In the words of the critic Kenneth Burke, "we cannot use language maturely until we are spontaneously at home in irony."[2]

---

1   Friedrich Schlegel, *Philosophical Fragments*, trans. Peter Firchow (Minneapolis: University of Minnesota Press, 1991), 13.
2   Kenneth Burke, *Language as Symbolic Action: Essays on Life, Literature, and Method*

Irony, then, is a core feature of language, not an add-on, and like other core features, such as metaphor, any attempt at definition ends up going in circles. If to understand an explanation of what irony is we must already know what irony is (an insight that itself follows an ironic logic), then a definition of irony is not so much impossible as it is pointless, for we strive to define what we must already know in order to grasp the definition we are struggling to devise. This is why the self-described "ironologist" D. C. Muecke opens his rich study of the topic with the observation that "since ... Erich Heller ... has already quite adequately not defined irony, there would be little point in not defining it all over again."[3]

Given this state of affairs, we can expect definitions of irony to be revealing for their failures as much as for their successes. Let us begin with the most conventional, which has it that irony is "a figure of speech in which the intended meaning is the opposite of that expressed by the words used" (as in the *Oxford English Dictionary*). We learn four principal things here: irony is (1) a linguistic trope that (2) works intentionally, whose specificity lies in (3) turning the path of meaning by 180 degrees ("trope" derives from a word meaning "turn"), a deviation that is contrasted with (4) the meaning "expressed by the words used," often also called the "actual," "proper," "primary," or "canonical" meaning of the words. This account is by no means incorrect; it does capture some forms of irony, especially in its more flagrant modes (saying "good job" when someone has knocked over a cup of coffee). Yet some of what is most significant about irony emerges only once we attend to what this definition misses and what other accounts—among them the most ancient—capture, if often only tentatively or implicitly.

Quintilian offers the earliest significant codification of irony in the Western tradition in his first-century textbook on rhetoric, the *Institutes of Oratory*. Like the *OED*, Quintilian classifies irony among tropes, and he too identifies its specific effect as saying "something which is the opposite of what is actually said."[4] Yet almost immediately he introduces an ambiguity that profoundly changes our understanding of the phenomenon. Hardly has he asserted that irony produces the *opposite* meaning from "what is actually said" than he adds that an ironic statement "implies something *other* than it says."[5] This has the welcome effect of acknowledging all those forms of irony that do not just involve a simple turn of the manifest meaning of an utterance on

---

(Berkeley: University of California Press, 1966), 12.
3 D. C. Muecke, *The Compass of Irony* (London: Methuen, 1969), 14.
4 Quintilian, *The Institutio Oratoria of Quintilian*, trans. H. E. Butler (Cambridge, MA: Harvard University Press (Loeb Classical Library), 1920), 9, 2, 45.
5 Ibid., my emphasis.

its head, which is to say exactly those forms of irony in literature and other arts that attract the critics' attention. "Edward—so we shall call a wealthy nobleman in the prime of life—had been spending several hours of a fine April morning in his nursery-garden ..." Nothing in this well-known opening of Goethe's *Elective Affinities* inverts the proper meaning of words, yet we would miss a lot—in a way everything—if we did not pick up the gentle tone of irony that permeates it, as it does the novel as a whole. In opening the concept of irony to such instances, Quintilian's qualification introduces a far-reaching shift in relation to our conventional understanding of irony, a shift that initiates an alarming expansion of irony's range. If irony describes the difference in meaning between what words actually say and what they are meant to say, and if a trope is nothing but "the artistic alteration of a word or phrase from its proper meaning to another," as Quintilian notes,[6] does irony not then name the basic operation of tropes *in general*? The consequence of registering more comprehensively the force of irony lies, it seems, in turning it from a *kind* of trope into the operating principle of *all* tropes.

The ambiguity that encourages an inflationary enlargement of irony's field of operation gestures towards another way in which Quintilian complicates our conventional understanding of irony. In his account, irony is not merely a trope, but also something he calls "figure." His first attempt at distinguishing the two does not make the stakes fully apparent: "in the *trope* the conflict is purely verbal, while in the *figure* the meaning, and sometimes the whole aspect of our case, conflicts with the language and the tone of voice adopted."[7] Then, with the mention of a proper name, his meaning suddenly emerges: "nay, a man's whole life may be coloured with irony, as was the case with Socrates, who was called an *ironist* because he assumed the role of an ignorant man lost in wonder at the wisdom of others."[8] If at first irony was confined to a word or a group of words whose meaning had gone awry, if it then extended to *any* operation of words gone awry (verbal "awryness" as such, we might say), now we come across a notion of irony that leaves behind the "purely verbal" and encompasses "the whole aspect of our case," indeed a "whole life." The figure of the figure of irony has a name; it is Socrates. With his appearance, irony no longer remains a matter of turning a word's meaning this way or that, but becomes a way of conducting a life—as it happens, one of the most celebrated of lives. Irony comes to name an exemplary way of being human. With this move, it is no longer confined to the role of a verbal

---

6   Quintilian, *Institutio*, 8, 6, 1.
7   Ibid., 9, 2, 46.
8   Ibid., 9, 2, 46.

tool directed at others, but, as self-irony, also becomes an attitude applied to one's own place in the world.

Socrates is just one of the two ancient sources of the Western conception of irony. The other, not mentioned by Quintilian here, is Aristophanes, whose comedy *The Clouds* is the earliest known document to use a version of the word "irony." It does not offer the most dignified stage for a word that will go on to have such an illustrious career. Irony enters the Western literary tradition in a torrent of insults: "cheat," "knave," "hangdog," someone shouts, and somewhere in his fusillade there is *eiron*, in our contemporary lexicon the "ironist." (Though Socrates, a character modeled on the philosopher, appears in the play, unfortunately he is not the one so labeled.) While Socratic irony, the attitude that generates the truth by insisting on its own ignorance, becomes the cardinal virtue of the philosophical way of living (and, in his case, of dying), the irony we find in Aristophanes retains a tight link to humor, especially to "low" forms of humor such as parody, burlesque, and satire. Both these forms of irony—the comedic and the philosophical—nourish every significant further conceptualization of this idea: one aggressively aimed at an interlocutor who is to be exposed as a buffoon; the other serious and applied to oneself, though perhaps no less aggressive in its effects.

Referring back to Socrates and Aristophanes makes evident that the two-level mode of communication we have noted in irony—saying one thing *while* saying another—requires a theatrical scene, rather than a merely dialogic one. While the dialogue involves two sides (even in the monologue, which can be seen as an "internal" dialogue), a theatrical scene consists of a minimum of three nodes, namely the two parties involved in a dialogue on stage and the audience that witnesses it. The audience may not be involved in the events on stage, yet it is fully implicated in them; its presence shapes everything that occurs there. This essentially triangular structure gives us a better handle on ironic communication, which always implicitly addresses two addressees at once: the one who gets the wink and the one who misses it: the co-conspirator and the naïf. When Burke speaks of the "mature" use of language being spontaneously at home in irony, it is precisely this distinction that is in play, for every use of irony directed at a mature addressee assumes, usually without bothering to state it, another, immature addressee who manages to pick up no more than the straight level of the communication. If we give this insight a slight shift and say that every ironic communication not only assumes the naïf, but also posits, even creates it, then we begin to touch on the dynamic of power at work in irony. Whatever else it does, every ironic communication—every wink—also establishes a place for the clueless, who is thereby consigned to the periphery of the scene of dialogue in order to move those who are clued in closer to the center, nearer to the ironist.

All of the main features of irony that have emerged in our exploration of its terrain come to a head in the first and most significant articulation of irony as an idea of explicitly aesthetic consequence in the German tradition. This occurs in the 1790s, late by European standards, yet the conception put forward by Friedrich Schlegel is among the shrewdest and most influential in the Western aesthetic canon. His mode of presentation is significant in itself, for he does not offer his thoughts on irony in a teutonically systematic treatise, but instead forms them across countless textual snippets spanning multiple genres—fragments, essays, dialogues, notebook entries, and letters. For readers, this can become a source of endless frustration, for as one makes one's way through Schlegel's writings, the feeling gains strength that a new twist, an unforeseen metaphor, or a bizarre association looms around every textual corner, threatening to upend the understanding one has been laboring to construct. It soon becomes clear, though, that the endlessness, and perhaps even the frustration, constitutes part of the logic of irony: that the presentation, rather than recording an entity called "irony" that exists apart from it, brings it about in the first place.

Let us go back to Schlegel's claim that Socratic irony "will remain a riddle" "to a person who hasn't got it." The paradoxical structure we noted in the statement—one must already know irony to understand it—becomes the leitmotif that Schlegel plays with in multiple registers through the remainder of the passage, taken from *Lyceum* Fragment 108:

> In this sort of irony, everything should be playful and serious, guilelessly open and deeply hidden. It originates in the union of savoir vivre and scientific spirit, in the conjunction of a perfectly achieved philosophy of nature and a perfectly achieved philosophy of art. It contains and arouses a feeling of indissoluble antagonism between the absolute and the relative, between the impossibility and the necessity of complete communication. It is the freest of all licenses, for by its means one transcends oneself; and yet is also the most lawful, for it is absolutely necessary. It is a very good sign when the harmonious bores are at a loss about how they should react to this continuous self-parody, when they fluctuate endlessly between belief and disbelief until they get dizzy and take what is meant as a joke seriously and what is meant seriously as a joke ...[9]

---

9 Schlegel, *Philosophical Fragments*, 13, translation modified.

Right away we note that here too the naïf is conjured up. The appearance of the "harmonious bores" is "a very good sign" because when *they* are flummoxed, we know that *we* are not. These are simply the two sides generated by the logic of irony. But Schlegel ups the ante, for while ordinarily the ironist flatters the members of his audience by assuring them that, in contrast with the imaginary naïf, they are in the know, here readers who are not wholly deluded recognize that they will invariably find themselves on the side of the "bores." As suggested in our fragment, "complete communication" is never entirely available to us; intention does not guarantee meaning because, as Schlegel writes in his essay "On Incomprehensibility," "words often understand themselves better than do those who use them."[10] If that is so, if no one, the speaker included, has full control over "what is meant," then it is a foregone conclusion that at least some of the time we will "take what is meant as a joke seriously" and vice versa. We are bound to become bores, then; we just don't know when it will happen to us.

Schlegel raises the stakes of irony in another crucial way as well. While Socrates uses irony to promote his midwifery of thinking, Schlegel relies on it to bring sharply drawn oppositions into the closest proximity, with no further purpose than to expose the tension between them. Here irony is not meant to lead beyond opposites (to truth, harmony, beauty, ...), but rather to "arouse a feeling of indissoluble antagonism" between contrastive terms such as play and seriousness, nature and art, the impossibility of communication and its necessity. As another fragment states: "Irony is the form of paradox."[11] If irony is understood as an attitude, or a way of living, that encourages the clash of differences, rather than a rhetorical technique that pushes meanings off their usual path, then the entire distinction between primary (actual, proper) meaning and ironic meaning becomes superfluous. For Schlegel, the two sides are symmetrical: at times what looks serious is meant as a joke; at other times what looks like a joke is meant seriously. Neither claims primacy over the other.

Some notebook entries push the violence of irony to the breaking point. Thus Schlegel coins the idea that irony is a "permanent parabasis."[12] Aristophanes' audience would have recognized parabasis immediately. It is the rhetorical name for the moment when a character addresses the audience directly, interrupting the dramatic flow and

---

10 Friedrich Schlegel, "On Incomprehensibility," in *Theory as Practice: A Critical Anthology of Early German Romantic Writings*, ed. Jochen Schulte-Sasse et al. (Minneapolis: University of Minnesota Press, 1997), 119.
11 Schlegel, *Philosophical Fragments*, 6.
12 Friedrich Schlegel, *Kritische Friedrich-Schlegel-Ausgabe*, ed. Ernst Behler et al. (Paderborn: Schoeningh, 1958), 18, 85.

compromising the suspension of disbelief. By calling irony a permanent parabasis, Schlegel asks us to think something acutely paradoxical, for an interruption usually occurs against the background of continuity; it is difficult to make sense of it as something permanent. (Paul de Man has worked out some of the implications of this idea in his essay "The Concept of Irony."[13]) Set against the maieutic productivity of Socrates we encounter here a logic of ceaseless disruption. Hegel is among the earliest observers to have recognized the ruinous potential bundled in this conception of irony, and he greets it with withering criticism.[14]

That the disruption wrought by irony need not equal destruction (though it certainly may entail it) is perhaps the key conceptual-poetic achievement here, for it is this idea, utterly ignored by Hegel, that enables Schlegel's reflection on irony to coalesce into something like a principle for a mode of poetic production fit for a world in which the existence of a coherent and meaningful totality can no longer be assumed—what we, for short, call the modern world. To be sure, this is a form of artistic making sharply distinct from the kinds of productivity to which philosophy—indeed all conceptual thinking—gravitates. Instead of shunning them, this form of making embraces moments of interruption, of incomprehension, and of incompletion. What is more, Schlegel asks us to imagine that the work might do so at *every* point of its construction, that it be open to an ironic loop—a parabasis—at *every* moment of its being. This conception of artistic production is so novel and so far-reaching that in one form or another it has found its way into virtually every current of modern aesthetic thought without having been superseded or even equaled by later theories.

There is a tendency to regard Jena romanticism as fueled by a desire to dissolve all distinctions in one vast mystical project, a tendency that relies on passages such as Schlegel's *Athenäum* Fragment 116, which urges that "progressive universal poetry," another name for romantic poetry, "should mix and fuse poetry and prose, inspiration and criticism, the poetry of art and the poetry of nature."[15] But—this is the moment to play the ironic trump card—such a reading is naïve, deaf to the ironic register. Irony, Schlegel reminds us, is not an optional additive to poetry but "absolutely necessary,"[16] so being deaf to it amounts to remaining deaf to the constitutive principle of poetry itself. Irony forces the antithetical entities together *without* dissolving

---

13 Paul de Man, "The Concept of Irony," in *Aesthetic Ideology*, ed. Andrzej Warminski (Minneapolis: University of Minnesota Press, 1996), 163–84.
14 Georg Wilhelm Friedrich Hegel, *Aesthetics: Lectures on Fine Art*, ed. and trans. T. M. Knox (Oxford: Oxford University Press, 1998), 1, 64–9.
15 Schlegel, *Philosophical Fragments*, 31.
16 Ibid., 108.

their differences; on the contrary, it heightens the feeling of their "indissoluble antagonism." It is this that makes it into the very figure of modernity.

SEE ALSO: Allegory

Eight Listening

Mirko M. Hall

A famous painting by Albert Gräfle in 1877 depicts Beethoven playing the piano for his closest friends. Gathered around the instrument, they are deeply moved by the sounds of the music—listening silently with rapt attention and admiration. A young man reclines in his chair, eyes wide open, and gazes up towards the ceiling. It appears as if the music is unlocking the gates of heaven. This reverential contemplation of music continues to represent today's listening ideal in the serious music culture of the Western world.

Listening is a discursive practice that intimately shapes the acoustic contours of human consciousness, subjectivities, and institutions. Since the mid-eighteenth century, close, attentive listening has played a constitutive role in the ideological construction of modern bourgeois identity. Within the framework of serious music culture, it is a cultural-revolutionary activity that is able to harness the aesthetic force of music to help listeners realize their full human potential. This belief in the transformative power of listening to music—and its ability to initiate a process of critical self-formation (*Bildung*)—is the result of significant epistemological changes in the fields of aesthetics, literature, music, and philosophy. These changes, which were influenced by the Enlightenment's reevaluation of textual culture, valorized the inherent aesthetic potentiality of music to expand our cognitive-affective horizons *ad infinitum*.

Between roughly 1750 and 1850, a new kind of listening—active, critical, and self-reflective—emerged and became the proper disposition for an enlightened citizenry and its connoisseurs of music. This disposition, which later became mythologized through early German Romanticism, demanded a "reverential attitude on the part of the listener that previously would have been more appropriate in a place of worship."[1] Only those individuals, who strove

---

1 Matthew Riley, *Musical Listening in the German Enlightenment: Attention, Wonder,*

to listen carefully—without the slightest noise and commotion—could adequately experience the ways in which music expressed the profundities of human thought and emotion. This new emphasis on music as a quasi-religious experience and the need for intense self-reflection, while actively listening to musical performances, was markedly different from the behavior of earlier generations. Prior to the above-mentioned period, audiences were often characterized by their festive exuberance (eating, drinking, smoking, etc.), particularly during operatic performances. The valorization of listening to music in reverential silence first began taking hold within musical circles in French and German-speaking areas around the 1770s. Although disciplinary techniques like reserved seating, paid subscriptions, and rules of decorum contributed to this new orientation, it was largely scholarly discourses in the public sphere—inspired by nascent developments in literature, music, and philosophy—that reinforced the internalization of close, attentive listening.

This new conception of listening must be understood within the context of various cultural activities that were (at times surprisingly) independent of actual musical production and performance. These activities were based on several intellectual currents in the eighteenth and early nineteenth centuries, which elevated music to the privileged status of a philosophical text that was capable of exploring the nexus between aesthetics and subjectivity. This position served as the catalyst for a remarkable epistemic shift in musical aesthetics that reached its theoretical zenith around 1800. By this time, a wide range of enlightened thinkers—from writers to philosophers and musicians—came to value the "identity of the bourgeois subject, the aesthetic autonomy of art, and the intrinsic worth of high culture."[2] In order to adequately experience the hidden meanings of musical works, these thinkers stressed the adoption of "strenuous effort, the discrimination of fine detail on the level of musical form, and, above all, ... a detached, disinterested aesthetic attitude."[3] Although these developments are often understood through the lens of Romantic aesthetics, the importance attributed to close, attentive listening is a direct outcome of the Enlightenment.

Since the mid-seventeenth century, German rationalist philosophy highlighted the importance of arousing, sustaining, and cultivating *attention* (*Aufmerksamkeit*)—a key cognitive faculty of the human mind. The philosophical writings of Alexander Gottlieb Baumgarten,

---

    and Astonishment (Aldershot: Ashgate, 2004), 1.
2 Berthold Hoeckner, *Programming the Absolute: Nineteenth-Century German Music and the Hermeneutics of the Moment* (Princeton, NJ: Princeton University Press, 2002), 3.
3 Riley, *Musical Listening*, 2.

Gottfried Wilhelm Leibniz, Christian Wolff, Georg Friedrich Meier, and Johann Georg Sulzer (1720–79) investigated (to varying degrees) the intellectual intuition afforded by attention with its special ability to discern the clear and distinct ideas of reason. Although he expressed some ambivalence toward music, Sulzer's articulation of the important relationship between attention and aesthetic perception is valuable for understanding these new listening practices. His encyclopedic *General Theory of the Fine Arts* (2 vols, 1771–4) provided much of the conceptual framework for the era's aesthetic debates. Sulzer believed that the fine arts have a civilizing force, which develops the critical faculties of the general public and cultivates its moral character. To ensure that their aesthetic perception always remains dynamically engaged (and, thereby, encouraging beautiful and moral thought), individuals need to fine-tune their cognition through informed judgment. The faculty of attention supports this judgment by providing extensive and unified clarity, through the human mind's innate capacity for representation, to the multiplicity of aesthetic features within an artwork. Following Sulzer's paradigm, then, close, attentive listening to music—i.e. the ability to completely understand a musical work's compositional structure—energizes one's pleasurable drive to activity, by elevating the human heart and mind. To quote music critic Johann Friedrich Reichardt, an older contemporary of Sulzer: music, thus, "enraptures the entirety of sensible nature with irresistible power and raises it heavenward."[4] This process, however, is not automatic; listening requires careful practice and promotion.

The need to cultivate listening was a key pedagogical project of the music historian Johann Nicolaus Forkel (1749–1818), who sought to improve the listening skills and practices of the general public. He was troubled with the rise of musical amateurs, who—despite their unbridled enthusiasm—lacked the prerequisite technical knowledge to fully appreciate the universality of aesthetic principles that underlie music. To remedy this situation, Forkel organized his now renowned concert series at the University of Göttingen in the 1770s. In the pre-concert lectures, Forkel advocated the "proper exercise and cultivation of the organ of hearing"[5] in order to understand the connection between music's compositional techniques and their intended aesthetic effects. This hermeneutic activity, which follows the temporal unfolding of the musical work, is based not only on the rules of reason and good

---

4 Quoted in: David Gramit, *Cultivating Music: The Aspirations, Interests, and Limits of German Musical Culture, 1770–1848* (Berkeley: University of California Press, 2002), 4.
5 Johann Nicolaus Forkel, *Allgemeine Geschichte der Musik*, 2 vols (Leipzig: Schwickertschen, 1788–1801), 2:8.

taste, but also on close, attentive listening. Forkel believed that amateur listeners were only concerned with the pleasurable external effects of music and did not make a concentrated effort to penetrate its internal workings. To achieve the ideal state of listening, they needed to move beyond simply understanding musical-rhetorical devises or absorbing the aesthetic force of sonorities and, instead, engage the musical work's inner beauty and moral purpose through "effort, deliberate concentration and acuity of perception."[6] For Forkel, individuals need to consciously and deliberately listen—an assertion that will anticipate Romanticism's emphasis on the reverential contemplation of music.

Forkel's interest in educating the general public to recognize the aesthetic universality of music coincides with the establishment of a public sphere for serious music. By the late-eighteenth century, music had become a topic worthy of critical attention and support within a cultivated and enlightened community.[7] No longer a privileged medium for aristocratic patronage or heavenly devotion, music was now capable of realizing the Enlightenment's project of human self-actualization. To harness this potentiality, middle-class men (and some women) actively participated in an ever-expanding public sphere centered around music. They attended symphony concerts, read books about music history and theory, and discussed the virtues of musical life in salons and coffeehouses. This atmosphere was greatly enhanced by a sudden boom in music journalism, which was centered in Leipzig. In a variety of publications (including fashion magazines, intelligence gazettes, and specialized music journals), enthusiasts could read about the entire gamut of contemporary musical life: from biographies of composers to reviews of concert performances and essays on musical aesthetics. Additionally, detailed musical criticism in journals—such as the authoritative *General Musical Newspaper*, published by Breitkopf & Härtel in Leipzig—attempted to help amateur listeners become genuine connoisseurs.

During this same period, instrumental music—i.e. music without accompanying words—became the celebrated medium for the aesthetic expression of close, attentive listening. This position was not always the case. From the seventeenth to the mid-eighteenth century, music theorists had argued (through the so-called Doctrine of Affects) that music aroused human emotions through imitation. But because sound's semantic force could still remain indeterminable, music's stylistic unity and intention needed to be illustrated and clarified through the mediation of language. In the late eighteenth century, however, many post-rationalist thinkers came to believe that instrumental music—as

---

6   Riley, *Musical Listening*, 88.
7   Gramit, *Cultivating Music*, 20–1.

exemplified by the expansive sonoric architectonics of symphonies, concertos, and sonatas—represented a productive emancipation of music from the strictures of language. While recognizing music's sensuous expressiveness and its uncanny affective ability, this new musical aesthetic conceived of music as wholly autonomous—or absolute—because of "its very lack of concept, object, and purpose."[8] The now emerging ideology of absolute music insisted that the musical work was, in fact, the artwork *par excellence*. Because sonoric signifiers are hermeneutically inexhaustible, music could now express what mere human language fails to adequately describe: the endlessly boundless and the utterly infinite. Music's lack of any verbal specificity, which was previously criticized as a deficiency, is now religiously praised.

The notion of absolute music was canonized by E. T. A. Hoffmann's landmark review of Beethoven's Fifth Symphony, published in the *General Musical Newspaper* in 1810. Setting a new standard for musical criticism, which combined philosophical insights with notational analysis, Hoffmann wrote how Beethoven's music opens up "the realm of the colossal and immeasurable" and carries the listener away into "the wonderful spiritual realm of the infinite."[9] The symphony's massed forces and striking movements of sound overwhelm the listener with unpredictable, awe-inspiring music. In this way, music embodies Kant's notion of "aesthetic ideas"—those concepts, ideas, and representations that are beyond the grasp of conventional language.

The valorization of absolute music found an early proponent in Friedrich Schlegel (1772–1829), the key theoretician of early German Romanticism. His writings in the 1790s—especially, the scribbled fragments about music in his literary and philosophical notebooks—insisted that music is the most universal of all artforms. Although he was familiar with contemporary debates on music, Schlegel never developed these fragments into a comprehensive theory of musical aesthetics. In these notebooks, though, Schlegel wrote about the critical-revolutionary nature of instrumental music as an ideal medium for transcendental reflection. He claimed that music's temporal unfolding epitomizes the process of philosophical inquiry itself. Through their infinite perfectibility and hermeneutic inexhaustibility, both media exceed any attempts at finite comprehensibility: they engender critical self-reflection through the continuous generation of new avenues of meaning.

Despite the significant influence that aesthetics, philosophy, and

---

8 Carl Dahlhaus, *The Idea of Absolute Music*, trans. Roger Lustig (Chicago: University of Chicago Press, 1989), 7.
9 E. T. A. Hoffmann, *Sämtliche Werke*, ed. Hartmut Steinecke and Wulf Segebrecht. 6 vols (Frankfurt am Main: Deutscher Klassiker, 2003), 1:535, 534.

musical criticism exerted on listening practices in the late-eighteenth century, it was the field of literature (as a central mechanism for *Bildung* in the public sphere) that most clearly described the aesthetic power of both absolute music and close, attentive listening. The reciprocal effectivity that occurred between literature and music was absolutely critical here. Indeed, many of the ideas associated with absolute music—such as the aesthetic potentiality of sonoric signifiers or the symphony as the foundation of serious musical culture—first appeared in (or were popularized through) the literary works of early German Romanticism. Schlegel's friends like Clemens Brentano, Friedrich von Hardenberg or Novalis, Ludwig Tieck (1773–1853), and Heinrich Wilhelm Wackenroder (1773–98) all expressed the sublime power of music in their writings. These authors and poets believed that music—as represented by the symphonies of Haydn, Mozart, and, later, Beethoven—conveyed a multitude of sensations and representations that surpassed the mere conventions of language: the ineffable, the infinite, and the insurmountable. This newly found reverence for music is beautifully illustrated in Tieck and Wackenroder's two collaborative literary projects, *Outpourings of an Art-Loving Friar* (1797) and *Fantasies on Art for Friends of Art* (1799), which quickly captured the public imagination. However, this particular interpretation of instrumental music did "not find [a truly] adequate object until E. T. A. Hoffmann borrowed [Wackenroder and Tieck's] language in order to do justice to Beethoven."[10]

Quite remarkably, the immense prestige given to instrumental music can be traced to this relatively small group of authors, who were not strictly musicians, but who were still "convinced of the moral superiority of serious music."[11] Besides writing about the quasi-religious qualities of absolute music (or attacking the manipulative affectation and sterile virtuosity of other musical forms), they also outlined—to use Wackenroder's own word—the "true" way of listening.[12] In describing the aesthetic contours of close, attentive listening, Wackenroder was "the single most important figure" in its articulation.[13] He was artistically gifted and even attended Forkel's lectures as a university student in Göttingen. In his literary texts about music, some of which were co-authored with Tieck, Wackenroder (paradoxically) harnessed the

---

10 Dahlhaus, *The Idea of Absolute Music*, 90.
11 Gramit, *Cultivating Music*, 6.
12 Wilhelm Heinrich Wackenroder, *Sämtliche Werke und Briefe. Historisch-Kritische Ausgabe*, ed. Silvio Vietta and Richard Littlejohns. 2 vols (Heidelberg: Winter, 1991), 2:29.
13 Mark Evan Bonds, *Music as Thought: Listening to the Symphony in the Age of Beethoven* (Princeton: Princeton University Press, 2006), 22.

power of poetic language to illustrate the ideal mode of listening. Individuals were to listen with "just the kind of reverence that [one] would in church—just as calmly and motionless, with ... eyes cast down to the ground," and experience the music through "the most attentive observation of the notes and their progression."[14]

It was Schlegel, again, who defined the epistemological stakes involved in close, attentive listening. For him, listening unpacks the musical work as a perpetually dynamic and self-actualizing totality.[15] It closely follows the interactive relationship between a work's sonoric details and its overall compositional structure. Schlegel and his friends argued that the sonata-allegro form was an ideal catalyst for this type of listening. This form, as masterfully exemplified by Beethoven, was characterized by the extensive recontextualization of the musical materials through the striking—and often unexpected—juxtaposition of different harmonic resources. By paying careful attention to the music, listeners are able to understand how its motivic-thematic components undergo continuous development (i.e. variation, juxtaposition, and repetition) through the sonata's temporal unfolding. They discern the inner workings of the composition and are not overwhelmed by its macro-organizational force. But, more importantly, this self-reflective enunciation of the listener reinforces music's privileged status as a medium of reflection, which draws out the signifying potentialities of the musical work itself. In other words, there exists a crucial synchronic dialogue between listeners, whose faculty of attention engages them in pleasurable critical activity, and the musical work, whose meanings constantly self-actualize by guiding listeners toward correlatives in their real and imagined lives.

By the late-eighteenth century and beyond, many thinkers were deeply concerned that musical works—which were intentionally produced as emotionally exploitative trash—would destroy the spontaneous subjectivity that was afforded by listening to serious music. The antidote to this danger was close, attentive listening, which could clearly see through these attempts at rhetorical manipulation. (Because of the later work of Theodor W. Adorno, this approach is now commonly referred to as "structural listening.") In this way, listening became a transformative, cognitive-affective strategy that participates in the public's critical self-formation. It actively influences human subjectivity by drawing its interpretive power from the reciprocal effectivity of music's infinite perfectibility, the composer's reasoned intentionality, the listener's careful discernment, and the critic's insightful mediation.

---

14 Wackenroder, *Sämtliche Werke*, 1:133, 2:29.
15 Mirko M. Hall, "Friedrich Schlegel's Romanticization of Music," *Eighteenth-Century Studies* 42 (2009): 421–5.

The act of listening shapes the thought-processes of listeners through aesthetic experience and develops their acoustic consciousness through a new capacity for individual self-determination. The members of an enlightened citizenry can now achieve intellectual autonomy through music and have the courage to listen for themselves!

SEE ALSO: Absolute Music

Nine Ethics
Jason Michael Peck

Plato's warnings regarding the ethical dangers of poetry in the *Republic* cast a long shadow. Despite coming half a century after Alexander Baumgarten's re-imagining of philosophical aesthetics, Schelling still refers to Plato's critique of art in his *Philosophy of Art*:

> [W]hat is Plato's rejection of the poetic arts—compared particularly with what he says in other works in praise of enthusiastic poesy—other than a polemic against poetic realism, a foreboding of that later inclination of the spirit in general and of poesy in particular? That judgment could be applied least of all to Christian poesy, which on the whole just as decisively displays the character of the infinite as the poesy of antiquity as a whole displays that of the finite [...] For just that reason we are able to elevate ourselves to a more comprehensive understanding and construction of poesy than he.[1]

For philosophy, there is still something that must be defended in conjoining philosophy and aesthetics: the true commingling with the merely apparent. Schelling's assertion that we "modern" philosophers have improved upon Plato's understanding of aesthetics is symptomatic of the re-emergence of aesthetic discourse in the eighteenth century. That is to say: to justify the inclusion of aesthetics as a worthy object of philosophy, there must be a concomitant ethical discourse that secures the legitimacy of aesthetics for philosophy.

This already begins with the figure generally regarded as the originator of German literary criticism and an early proponent of aesthetics: Johann Christian Gottsched. For Gottsched, the pursuit of aesthetic

---

1   Friedrich Wilhelm Joseph von Schelling, *Philosophy of Art*, ed. and trans. Douglas W. Stott (Minneapolis: University of Minnesota, 1989), 5.

perfection mirrors the perfection of natural beauty, which is a manifestation of God's order in the world: "The beauty of an artwork rests not on vain presumption, but rather has its firm and necessary basis in the nature of things [...] Natural things are beautiful in themselves, and so if art also wants to produce something beautiful, it must imitate the pattern of nature."[2] Aesthetics has as its regulatory principle this striving towards natural perfection, whereas: "deviation from its pattern will always give rise to something formless and tasteless."[3] Aesthetic qualities are philosophically judged not in terms of veracity but in terms of beauty's perfection in relation to nature's regulatory beauty.

Fredrick C. Beiser in his study of rationalist aesthetics, *Diotima's Children*, analyzes the connection between Gottsched's aesthetic project and his ethical project:

"[G]ottsched assures us that it [the aesthetic attitude] is entirely compatible with, indeed complementary to, the fundamental principle of ethics itself: 'Do everything to make yourself and others more perfect'[...] the greater the perfection, the greater the pleasure we derive from perceiving it."[4] This increased notion of perfection—tying it to the qualitative and quantitative increase of the beautiful—has its roots in the Leibnizian/Wolfian metaphysics that understood sensory perception as a *lower* faculty of cognition. Aesthetics—derived from the Greek αἰσθάνομαι ("I perceive or I sense")—beyond serving as the study of poetics and art in general, would be the science of sensory perception. To rehabilitate sensory perception from the debased state in which metaphysics had placed it hitherto, the philosophical study of aesthetics would have to contain an ethical demand, one in which sensory perception might "perfect" itself beyond the realm of "mere" appearance.

This becomes the chief concern of the earliest aesthetic practitioners, most notably the founder of modern aesthetics (as well as inventor of the term "aesthetics") Alexander Baumgarten. Again, quoting from Beiser:

> Aesthetics is not only a practical but also an ethical discipline for Baumgarten. The purpose of aesthetics is not simply to create beautiful things but to educate human beings, to create what

---

2   Johann Christoph Gottsched, "Critical Poetics," trans. Timothy J. Chamberlain, *Eighteenth Century German Criticism*. German Library v. 11 (New York: Continuum, 1992), 5.
3   Ibid., 5.
4   Frederick C. Beiser, *Diomima's Children: German Aesthetic Rationalism from Leibniz to Lessing* (Oxford: Oxford University Press, 2009), 78.

Baumgarten calls the 'beautiful spirit' (*schöner Geist, ingenium venustum*). This will be someone who develops not only his reason, but also his powers of imagination, attention, memory, and sensitivity.[5]

In his *Reflections on Poetry* [*Meditationes philosophicae de nonnullis ad poema pertinentibus*] Baumgarten suggests:

> Philosophers might still find occasion, not without ample reward, to inquire also into those devices by which they might improve the lower faculties of knowing, and sharpen them, and apply them more happily for the benefit of the whole world [...] As our definition is at hand, a precise designation can easily be devised [...] *things known* are to be known by the superior faculty as the object of logic; *things perceived* of the science of perception, or **aesthetic**.[6]

According to Baumgarten, general poetics will be "the science which treats generally of the *perfected* presentation of sensate representations."[7] The task of the philosopher, in studying and disseminating the field of aesthetics, is to perfect the lower faculties through the study of poetics.

Baumgarten develops this line of thought to a greater extent in his later *Aesthetica*. Although he still retains the strict division between logic and aesthetics, his work offers a complete method of using aesthetics to attain moral perfection: "The beauty of sensual cognition and the refinement of the aesthetic object presents [*darstellen*] an assemblage of perfection that is universally valid as well."[8] Baumgarten refers to the outcome of this process as "aesthetic truth." Although this truth may not reach the same certainty and perfection as logical truth for the philosopher, aesthetic truth can better account for individual psychology.[9] This recourse to individual psychology, or the bridge between the objective content of the work of art and its analogy in the subject, is the space wherein the ethics of the aesthetic take place: "The possibility of morality belongs to aesthetic truth in [...] the most narrow sense not only in the cognitive subject but also in the object itself which must be examined by the subject in her reflection to be

---

5 Ibid., 121.
6 Alexander Gottlieb Baumgarten, *Reflections on Poetry*, trans. Karl Aschenbrenner and William B. Holther (Berkeley: University of California Press, 1954), 78.
7 Ibid., 78, emphasis added.
8 Alexander Gottlieb Baumgarten, *Theoretische Ästhetik. Die grundlegenden Abschnitte aus der 'Aesthetica' (1750/58)*, ed. and trans. Hans Rudolf Schweizer (Hamburg: Felix Meiner, 1983), §24, my translation.
9 Ibid., §433.

clear and precise in its given presentation."[10] For aesthetics to become moral, a coincidence between the cognitive subject's judgment of the clarity of the beautiful object and the perfection of the object itself must take place. Although there is a greater subjective autonomy in aesthetic cognition, Baumgarten still adheres to an older, metaphysical system wherein aesthetic judgment moves from the imperfection of the sensual world towards the perfect world of logic and truth.

Immanuel Kant's *Critique of Judgment* radically alters the discussion of aesthetics and ethics after its appearance in 1790. In the third Critique, Kant defines taste for the aesthetic object as "the ability to judge an object, or a way of presenting it, by means of a liking or disliking *devoid of all interest*. The object of such a liking is called *beautiful*."[11] Or, additionally, "*Beauty* is an object's form of *purposiveness* insofar as it is perceived in the object *without the presentation of a purpose*."[12] Whereas Gottsched and Baumgarten imagined the ethical recuperation of aesthetics as being primarily didactic in nature (i.e. contemplation of beautiful objects generally lead to moral betterment), Kant argues that: "In order to consider something good, I must always know what sort of thing the object is [meant] to be, i.e., I must have a [determinate] concept of it. But I do not need this in order to find beauty in something."[13] The liking for the good is divorced from a liking for the beautiful.

Kant, however, still feels the need to connect the beautiful with the morally good in the third Critique, ending the "Critique of Aesthetic Judgment" with such a discussion. Yet, in keeping with his desire to eclipse the object in favor of the subject's reflection upon the assent towards aesthetic judgment, he writes: "The morally good is the *intelligible* that taste has in view [...] for it is with this intelligible that even our higher cognitive powers harmonize, and without this intelligible contradictions would continually arise from the contrast between the nature of these powers and the claims that taste makes."[14] The morally good is not the ideal that the beautiful object strives towards; rather it is the regulative concept that allows any judgment of taste whatsoever. According to Kant: "judgment finds itself referred to something that is both in the subject himself and outside him, something that is neither

---

10 Ibid., §435, my translation.
11 Immanuel Kant, *Critique of Judgment*, trans. Werner S. Pluhar (Hackett Publishing Company, Inc., 1987), 211. Pagination indicated is that of the page in *Kant's gesammelte Schriften*, edited by the Royal Prussian (later German, then Berlin-Brandenburg) Academy of Sciences (Berlin: Georg Reimer, later Walter de Gruyter, 1900–).
12 Ibid., 236.
13 Ibid., 207.
14 Ibid., 353.

nature nor freedom and yet is linked with the basis of freedom, the supersensible [...]."[15] Furthermore, "[i]n judging the beautiful, we present the *freedom* of the imagination [...] as harmonizing with the lawfulness of the understanding."[16] The word "harmonizing" here is crucial: to make a determinate connection between the morally good and the beautiful would call into question the very subjective freedom Kant establishes through the lack of interest within aesthetic judgment. He concludes the final section of part one with the following:

> [T]aste is basically an ability to judge the [way in which] moral ideas are made sensible ([it judges this] by means of a certain analogy in our reflection about [these ideas and their renderings in sensibility]); the pleasure that taste declares valid for mankind as such and not just for each person's private feeling must indeed derive from this [link] and from the resulting increase in our receptivity for the feeling that arises from moral ideas (and is called moral feeling).[17]

In order for aesthetic judgments to be valid—our determining something as either evoking feelings of the sublime or beautiful *and* demanding assent from others—these judgments must have an analogy in the supersensible realm of moral ideas. Though Kant goes through great pains to demonstrate how a liking for the morally good and a liking for the beautiful are different,[18] the morally good offers a regulatory principle for judging the beautiful—by appealing to the subject's freedom, which is guaranteed by a supersensible connection.

After Kant's third Critique, the connection between aesthetics and ethics shifts from the notion of perfection cultivated through the contemplation of beautiful objects to a reflection on the subject's freedom afforded by aesthetic contemplation. Friedrich Schiller uses Kant's aesthetic theory as his basis for the aesthetic state in the *Aesthetic Letters on the Education of Man*. Here, Schiller understands the aesthetic condition as the only mode in which man is given his freedom: neither as something granted, as in nature, nor something legislated, as with reason, but as a middle term that allows for free contemplation outside of both: "As our nature finds itself, in the contemplation of the Beautiful, in a happy midway point between law and exigency, so, just because it is divided between the two, it is withdrawn from the

---

15 Ibid., 353.
16 Ibid., 354.
17 Ibid., 356.
18 Ibid., 354.

constraint of both alike."[19] The lack of constraint within the realm of the aesthetic, the ability of the subject to reflect autonomously using both the material of nature and the laws of reason, is precisely where the moral register lies: "[T]he aesthetic alone is a whole in itself, as it combines in itself all the conditions of its origin and of its continued existence. Here alone do we feel ourselves snatched outside time, and our humanity expresses itself with a purity and integrity as though it had not yet experienced any detriment from the influence of external forces."[20]

In a complete reversal of Plato's assessment of art and artists in the *Republic*, Schiller finds the appearance of the moral precisely *in* the realm of the aesthetic: "To the question *how far appearance may exist in the moral world*, the answer is short and concise: *insofar as it is aesthetic appearance*, that is, appearance which neither seeks to take the place of reality nor needs to have its place taken by reality. Aesthetic appearance can never become a danger to moral truth [...]."[21] Because the aesthetic is neither content to eclipse the raw material of nature nor is it content to force reason to submit to facile reality, it presents subjective freedom as the final arbiter of the moral world—much in the same way that Kant's assent to the supersensible presents the judging subject's structural connection to the morally good.

Schiller additionally suggests that not only does the aesthetic produce a regulative connection with the moral and morally good, but that a future state may be based upon this connection:

> If in the *dynamic* state of rights man encounters man as force and restricts his activity, if in the *ethical* state of duties he opposes him with the majesty of law and fetters his will, in the sphere of cultivated society, in the *aesthetic* state, he need appear to him only as shape, confront him only as an object of free play. *To grant freedom by means of freedom* is the fundamental law of this kingdom.[22]

The aesthetic state is the only state in which the subject may be truly free, because it is a state in which the freedoms afforded the subject are granted through a process without constraint (*"To grant freedom by means of freedom"*). Thus: "Everything in the aesthetic State, even the subservient tool, is a free citizen having equal rights with the noblest;

---

19 Friedrich Schiller, *Letters on the Aesthetic Education of Man*, ed. and trans. Reginald Snell (New Haven, CT: Yale University Press, 1954), 78.
20 Ibid., 103.
21 Ibid., 129.
22 Ibid., 137.

and the intellect, which forcibly moulds the passive multitude to its designs, must here ask for assent."[23]

Freedom of the subject is the new ethical position within the realm of the aesthetic. Whereas the ethical description of the aesthetic for Gottsched and Baumgarten is prescriptive (i.e. aesthetics' connection with the moral world resides in its ability to instruct from example), for Kant and Schiller the ethical moment in the aesthetic is descriptive (i.e. aesthetics' connection with the moral world *is* the very freedom it affords the subject).

The text that exemplifies the new ethical register of aesthetics, while critiquing (specifically with regard to Schiller's aesthetic state) the more practically determined use of the aesthetic mode, is the so-called "Earliest Program for the System of German Idealism." This text was most likely written by Hegel, Schelling, and Hölderlin collectively with theology students in Jena in 1796. In it, the question is raised: "How must a world for a moral being be constituted?"[24] The answer, much like Schiller and Kant, is to find morality in the realm of the aesthetic: "I am now convinced that the highest act of reason is an aesthetic act, in that reason embraces all ideas, and that *in beauty alone are truth and goodness joined together*. The philosopher must possess as much aesthetic power as the poet. [T]he philosophy of the spirit is an aesthetic philosophy."[25] Indeed, philosophy becomes subservient to the realm of the aesthetic in this new conception of ethics. It is worth noting that the piece begins with the fragmentary subtitle "—an ethics," confirming that the author(s) of the text imagined their reconceptualization of both philosophy and aesthetics as a new ethics.

The text continues: "In this way, poesy attains a higher level of dignity, it becomes again what it was in the beginning—*the teacher of humanity*, for there is no more philosophy, no more history—the art of poesy [*Dichtkunst*] alone will outlive all other sciences and arts."[26] Again, we are not so far off from the tradition of the ethical discourse within the aesthetic: by making poesy the "teacher of humanity," it seems to serve a practical purpose. Yet, no longer does this practical application of aesthetics have a component of metaphysical perfection. It is not that the work of art, poetry, etc., moves us closer to an *eidos* of truth or beauty outside of ourselves, rather it is as if, immanently, the

---

23 Ibid., 140.
24 Friedrich Hegel et al., "Earliest Program for a System of German Idealism," in *Theory as Practice: A Critical Anthology of Early German Romantic Writings*, ed. Jochen Schulte-Sasse et al. (Minneapolis: University of Minnesota Press, 1997), 72.
25 Ibid., 73.
26 Ibid., 73.

aesthetic improves humanity by simply being thus: "At last the ideas of a moral world, divinity, immortality are developing—overthrow of all superstition, persecution of the priesthood that recently has been feigning reason, through reason itself, and the absolute freedom of all spirits that carry the intellectual world within themselves and must seek neither God nor immortality *outside of themselves.*"[27] To seek "absolute freedom" not in a metaphysical concept outside, but rather through the aesthetic register is the greatest ethical good of the aesthetic. Yet, this immanent use of the aesthetic does not, as in Schiller, extend itself to a new moral and political reality: "[I] want to show that there is no idea of the *state*, because the state is something *mechanical*, just as there is no idea of a *machine*. Only that which is a matter of *freedom* can be called an *idea*. Thus we must transcend the state as well."[28] If Schiller privileged the aesthetic due to its ideal connection with human freedom, then placing it in the service of the state only "fetters" the ethical moment of the aesthetic all over again.

At the end of the "Oldest System Program of German Idealism" essay, the entire relationship between philosophy, ethics, and aesthetics has been reversed. Rather than understanding the aesthetic as either inferior to philosophy or, at best, capable of improving humanity by mimicking philosophy's pedagogical imperative, it is the aesthetic that now improves philosophy through a dissembling discourse:

> Until we make ideas aesthetic, that is, mythological, they are of no interest to the *people* and, conversely, until mythology is reasonable, the philosopher must be ashamed of it. Thus, in the end, enlightened and unenlightened must shake hands, mythology must become philosophical, and the people reasonable, and philosophy must become mythological in order to make the philosophers sensuous.[29]

The aesthetic is no longer that which must be banished from the republic of philosophy in order for truth to dominate; rather, the aesthetic becomes the whole through which philosophy becomes "sensuous" and, therefore, ethical.

SEE ALSO: Imagination; Judgment; Beauty

---

27 Ibid., 72.
28 Ibid., 72.
29 Ibid., 73.

Ten Absolute Music
Sanna Pederson

Is there any phrase that encapsulates the whole of German aesthetics better than "absolute music"? The Absolute invokes the grand tradition of German Idealist philosophy, above all that of Kant and Hegel; "music" encompasses the great flowering of German/Austrian instrumental music in the eighteenth and nineteenth centuries. Together, the phrase "absolute music" conveys the impressively abstract and metaphysical foundation of German aesthetics, while music, the most immaterial of the arts, triumphantly realizes its theoretically ineffable formulations. It would probably be best to leave it at that, because any closer examination exposes too many contradictions and paradoxes. But those unsatisfied with something so abstract and perfect can find a more substantial story by trying to unravel the difficult conceptual knots and chronological tangles that make up the history of absolute music.

Wagner/Beethoven

The first paradox is that Richard Wagner, who coined and disseminated the term "absolute music," did not use it with reference to his own music, but rather to Beethoven's. In his Zürich writings (1849–51), Wagner's reference point was always Beethoven's Ninth Symphony, which he characterized as signaling the end of absolute music. He interpreted the entrance of words and voices in the final "Ode to Joy" movement as acting out the historical transition from the instrumental symphonic tradition that culminated in Beethoven's music to Wagner's artwork (i.e., opera) of the future.

Hanslick

The most respected music reference works (*New Grove Dictionary of Music, Die Musik in Geschichte und Gegenwart, New Harvard Dictionary of Music*) acknowledge that Wagner coined the term, but they all associate it predominantly with the nineteenth-century music critic, Eduard Hanslick. They overlook the fact that Hanslick used the term only once in the book that made him famous, *Vom Musikalisch-Schönen* from 1854: "It can never be said that music can do what instrumental music cannot, because only instrumental music is pure, absolute music."[1] This closely reasoned work, a product of Hanslick's training in philosophy and legal argumentation, remains to this day the most frequently cited text that advocates a formalist understanding of music, often summed up by using his definition of music as *tönend bewegte Formen* ("sounding forms in motion"). But Hanslick did not pursue the analysis of form with any further theoretical writings. Instead, he became Vienna's most important music critic with reviews and essays for the *Neue freie Presse* almost up until his death in 1904. In these writings the phrase "absolute music" is extremely scarce, even after he had become associated with it around 1880. He used it only once (in 1900) with regard to Johannes Brahms, the composer he championed in opposition to Wagner and Liszt. As the 1854 quotation indicates, he seems to have equated absolute music with instrumental music, which is compatible up to a point with Wagner's definition. These two enemies did not disagree so much about the concept, but rather how to evaluate it. For Wagner, instrumental music unto itself was nothing much, but for Hanslick, it was music itself in all its glory.

Terminology

Is this a simple matter of terminology? It is a matter of terminology, but there is not a simple solution. The use of the term has always been marked by uneasiness. From the beginning, absolute music has been used with quotation marks, with the qualifier "so-called," and prefaced by the apology "for lack of a better term." Absolute music, because of its elusiveness, can mean "abstract," "autonomous," "detached," "independent," "pure," "for its own sake," and many other non-equivalent things, such as instrumental music or concert music. Hanslick preferred the term "reine" or "pure" music. Like "absolute," it can be used as an adverb to indicate "only" or "one hundred percent": something is *absolutely* correct or *purely* a matter of semantics. To speak of the purity of music and music that is purified brings up moral, ethical, and religious values that can be different from absolute values, which connotatively shade more into philosophy and science.

---

1 Quoted in Carl Dahlhaus, *The Idea of Absolute Music*, trans. Roger Lustig (Chicago: University of Chicago Press, 1989), 27. Original: Carl Dahlhaus, *Die Idee der absoluten Musik* (Munich and Kassel: Deutscher Taschenbuch Verlag and Barenreiter Verlag, 1978).

Dahlhaus

Terminology was not an issue for the pre-eminent German musicologist Carl Dahlhaus, who finessed the problem by calling his book from 1978 *Die Idee der absoluten Musik* (translated in 1989 as *The Idea of Absolute Music*). According to Dahlhaus's influential, frequently referenced, account, the "idea" of absolute music originated with the early Romantics and became so widespread that it formed the basis of a general aesthetic stance toward art music up to the present. Dahlhaus begins by defining the idea of absolute music as the assumption that music does not need to be supplemented by any kind of paratext, such as a program, a libretto, or the words of a song. Music is best understood on its own terms without reference to anything else. Here, absolute music appears to be equivalent to the autonomous musical artwork. Dahlhaus cites, far more frequently than Wagner or Hanslick, the early Romantic writings of W. H. Wackenroder and Ludwig Tieck from around 1800, despite the fact that none of the early Romantics used the phrase "absolute music." References to the Absolute in a philosophical sense can be found, but to elide it with absolute music as Dahlhaus and others (most egregiously Roger Scruton[2]) does cause difficulties.

Romanticism

The temptation to make absolute music an invention of the early Romantics is understandable. Though he did not use the term, E. T. A. Hoffmann began his review of Beethoven's Fifth Symphony from 1810 by asking: "when we speak of music as an independent art, should we not always restrict our meaning to instrumental music, which ... gives pure expression to music's specific nature, recognizable in this form alone? It is the most romantic of the arts—one might almost say, the only genuinely romantic one—for its sole subject is the infinite."[3] While that declaration is clear enough, the review as a whole, with its combination of bizarre imagery and detailed technical musical analysis, cannot be made to represent a general Romantic understanding of music.

Once Dahlhaus goes into any kind of detail regarding the views of Wackenroder, Tieck, Herder, Karl Philipp Moritz, Friedrich Schleiermacher, and Hoffmann, he acknowledges that their Romantic exaltation of instrumental music usually occurred within the context of

---

2   Roger Scruton. "Absolute Music," in *The New Grove Dictionary of Music*, revised ed., Vol. 1 (London: Macmillan, 2001), 36–7.
3   E. T. A. Hoffmann, *E. T. A. Hoffmann's Musical Writings: Kreisleriana, The Poet and the Composer, Music Criticism*, ed. David Charlton (Cambridge: Cambridge University Press, 2004), 96.

religion. Dahlhaus proceeds to explain that according to the Romantics, absolute music as opposed to other kinds of music is not determined by the music itself but by what the listener hears; music initiates a religious or quasi-religious experience. Therefore the status "absolute" is not inherent in any particular music; any music could potentially act as the catalyst. When a musical work is named— a symphony by Reichardt or Beethoven, a mass by Palestrina—it complicates the definition rather than clarifying it. Dahlhaus never admits that defining absolute music as a type of attitude of the listener contradicts his earlier equivalence of absolute music with the autonomous artwork. Furthermore, there is a chronological issue: if absolute music was an invention of the early Romantics, it was short-lived, unsustainable, and ultimately self-destructive, as Daniel Chua argues in his Adorno-influenced book *Absolute Music and the Construction of Meaning*.[4] It would have ended with late Beethoven, twenty years before the term was coined.

Feuerbach

It is thought that Wagner borrowed the term "absolute" specifically from Ludwig Feuerbach's critique of Hegel. Feuerbach focused on breaking down the logic of the Absolute as absolute identity. As an alternative to absolute spirit (*Geist*) as a creation of philosophical thought, Feuerbach proposed a more anthropological approach based on the immediacy of sensuous experience. Instead of taking thought (*Geist*) as the point of departure, he suggested starting with the materiality of being. When Wagner began using the term, then, it was going through a re-evaluation, falling from the unassailable limit of thought to the problematic basis of idealist philosophy. Wagner may have appropriated it in the broadest sense to make the parallel between Feuerbach's radical critique of the venerable Hegelian tradition and his own critique of the Beethovenian heritage. Wagner argued that the dialectic of history had made absolute music a thing of the past, and that now the time had come to envision an "artwork of the future," a phrase that echoes Feuerbach's call for a "philosophy of the future."

Absolute versus Program Music

In the time period in which absolute versus program music eventually became the prevailing debate in musical aesthetics and musical politics (c. 1880–1914), the antagonism was clear, but what was meant by both terms was not. Some, following Wagner, considered absolute music the opposite of Wagner's operas. But after Franz Liszt, Wagner's closest ally at the time, entered the debate advocating the genre of program

---

4   Daniel K. L. Chua, *Absolute Music and the Construction of Meaning* (New York: Cambridge University Press, 1999).

music (as exemplified by his own symphonic poems), absolute music also came to be understood as instrumental music without a program. Furthermore, absolute and program music may have been seen as opposites in the abstract, but in practice they had a more accommodating relationship: individual musical works could be called absolute music by one critic and program music by another. As program music became predominant towards the end of the century, even Hanslick conceded that a descriptive title to an instrumental work was desirable so that the composer could steer the listener's imagination in the intended direction.

Wagner, Schopenhauer, and Nietzsche

More famously, Wagner also changed his mind. As is well known, Wagner came under the influence of Arthur Schopenhauer's metaphysics of music just a few years after his bout of enthusiasm for Feuerbach. Whereas before he insisted that absolute music was useless on its own and could only have an effect by underscoring the drama, he now reversed his own formulation: the drama was now merely to realize externally the profoundly immaterial and inner truth of music. In sum, Wagner abandoned a short but very public period of anti-romanticism and took up the kind of romanticism that considered music the highest of the arts. Of course it is ironic that Schopenhauer, who went metaphysically further than anyone in claiming that music would exist even if the world did not, never used the term absolute music, first because it had not yet been coined, and second because he categorically rejected the concept of the Absolute as formulated by his archenemy Hegel.

No one was more influenced by the Schopenhauerian Wagner than Friedrich Nietzsche, at least in the beginning. But over the course of his subsequent writings, he furiously renounced romanticism, metaphysics, and above all Wagner. Nietzsche used the term absolute music mostly during his pro-Wagner period that culminated in *The Birth of Tragedy* in 1871, when he understood absolute music in Wagner's sense as an insufficient thing, a separate art unto itself. But this was also the time in which he was most intoxicated by the idea of a romantic, metaphysical, "absolute" music. In any case, by the time of *Human, All-Too-Human* in 1878 (see especially Aphorism 215), Nietzsche had rejected both the positive and negative senses of absolute music in favor of a "genealogy" (i.e., more historical and materialist account) of music.

Metaphysics

Wagner did not make use of the term in his later writings because he had already used it in his earlier publications as a negative concept. It fell to his disciples to recast absolute music in a positive light. In the extraordinary period of Wagnerism after the composer's death and before the First World War, Wagnerians produced endless glosses on his writings that smoothed over contradictions and reinterpreted Wagner's life and works with spectacular hindsight. In 1893, for instance, Friederich von Hausegger's "Richard Wagner und Schopenhauer" claimed to find Schopenhauer's theories manifesting themselves in all of Wagner's works, including those that came before Wagner had even heard of Schopenhauer. These writers fashioned a new, positive definition for absolute music rather than inventing a new term—surely because the term had exactly the kind of grand metaphysical resonance that these writers were looking to confer on Wagner and the Wagnerian composer of symphonies, Anton Bruckner. The term was too valuable to be left to the enemies Hanslick and Brahms. (It should be noted that this philosophical connotation did not transfer completely to another language and culture; English-language publications have always used the term absolute music more casually than the German ones.)

The term came to be defined in a much more esoteric way by the next generation. The music theorists August Halm (1869–1929) and Ernst Kurth (1886–1946) developed ideas that are not to be found in any previous writers on absolute music. These figures are also much more obscure than any of the other writers cited here. However, they are crucial to Dahlhaus and others who have assembled "the idea of absolute music." Halm was strongly influenced by the education reformer Gustav Wyneken and taught at his school at Wickersdorf. His writings on music blend German theology and philosophy, selectively combining parts of the Bible, Hegel, Schopenhauer, and Nietzsche. Halm's younger friend Ernst Kurth brought together psychology, romanticism, and religious feeling inspired by the devoutly Catholic Bruckner to form the basis of his books on Wagner and Bruckner. Halm and Kurt made three striking changes to the definition of absolute music. First, they made a radical break with the listening subject. Absolute music exists whether or not there are listeners, or even humans in general. Halm compared absolute music to a remote star in the universe, indifferent to humanity on earth. Kurth made the pithy assertion: "we can see clearly that the word 'absolute' has a double meaning. In a technical sense, it means dissolved from song; in a spiritual sense, dissolved from man."[5] The second change was just as drastic: absolute music is not, strictly speaking, sounding music. It is pre-music, pre-materiality, that which exists throughout the universe, and in the mind of the genius composer. For Kurth, "absolute music does not have any concrete aspect (*Gegenständlichkeit*); rather, its only

---

5 Quoted in Dahlhaus, *The Idea of Absolute Music*, 40.

law, on which it rests, is that it is only force (*Kraft*) and the radiating out of that force in sound material."[6] The third contention of Halm and Kurth alienates them even more from others: the only sounding music that exists that can give an intimation of absolute music is to be found in the symphonies of Anton Bruckner.

These theories were shaped by the growing popularization of art music at the beginning of the twentieth century. They carved out absolute music as a space for something truly precious that was not accessible to the masses. This version of absolute music expresses a deep anti-modernism and cultural pessimism that cannot be found in the early Romantics, Hanslick, or anyone else in the nineteenth century. Finally, this early twentieth-century understanding is not compatible with more recent, late twentieth-century uses of the term, which do not find absolute music in the echoes of the universe but rather in the rationally interpretable choices of the composer in creating an autonomous musical work.

Conclusion

In his 1997 book *Die Musik und das Schöne*, the German musicologist Hans Heinrich Eggebrecht made the distinction between absolute and autonomous music sound simple: the first is an aesthetic category while the second is a sociological concept.[7] Eggebrecht and Dahlhaus adhered to the traditional understanding of aesthetics as being strictly about music itself. They took on the big aesthetic questions posed by the great philosophers and answered them in a generalized and speculative way. In this information age, we inevitably look at things differently. Now that we have increasing access to a greater range of materials, both aesthetics and music can be seen as categories shaped by ever-changing forces that make the generalizations of the past seem too easy. Absolute music has been understood to mean many different things for many different reasons—and that makes it all the more interesting and important for the history of German aesthetics.

SEE ALSO: Listening

---

6   Ibid.
7   Hans Heinrich Eggebrecht, *Die Musik und das Schöne* (Munich and Zurich: Piper, 1997).

Eleven The End of Art
Eva Geulen

Speculating about an end of art is a profoundly modern obsession that appears to have survived even the presumed end of "grand narratives" (J. F. Lyotard). Rumors about an end of art persist even today, in the era variously designated as postmodern, post-historical, and post-ideological. The particular purposes motivating the rhetoric of the end of art can be just as diverse as occasions for its enunciation. However, every enunciation of an end of art rests on two minimal and interrelated presuppositions, a sense of historicity and a non-normative conception of art. Both conditions are met only in modernity as it began to emerge in Germany in the second half of the eighteenth century, which also saw the rise of aesthetics as a philosophical discipline. While artists from earlier époques may well have complained about the declining quality of artistic production, they never conceived of this as an end of art. By contrast, moderns do and they have done so frequently with considerable pathos and in many different ways.

Two recent examples suffice to indicate the remarkable range of interpretive options available to the end of art. In 2004, art historian Donald Kuspit published a scathing attack (not the first, to be sure) on contemporary art, identifying Marcel Duchamp as the main culprit responsible for initiating the ongoing transition from art to post-art.[1] Post-art in Kuspit's sense may be compared to postmodernism in that all options are open to the artist but such freedom is indeed just another word for nothing left to lose. Accordingly Kuspit's diagnosis is accompanied by nostalgic longing for a past whose unattainable glow indirectly depends on the very shadow cast by the supposed demise of art. In a very different vein, philosopher and art critic Arthur Danto had reached a similar conclusion, though he maintained

---

1 Donald Kuspit, *The End of Art* (Cambridge: Cambridge University Press, 2004).

a thoroughly positive view of the matter.[2] What Kuspit conceives as disastrous relativism, appears on Danto's account as the liberation of artists—and art viewers—from the burden of history. According to Danto, all of us are finally free to determine our individual artistic likes and dislikes. Kuspit and Danto represent two versions of what has repeated itself with such frequency that one may cynically conclude that art is alive only when and so long as people are still debating its end(s). Indeed, the end of art is, paradoxically, the last vestige of a (negative) normativity. The end of art enjoys a similarly canonical status within aesthetic discourse as the problem of aesthetic judgments (pre- and post-Kantian) or aesthetic experience. This is not to say that the end of art belongs exclusively within the domain of aesthetics. On the contrary, it frequently has more to do with political ends than with art or aesthetics (as in 1968 in Paris when the slogan circulated 'Art is dead. Do not consume its corpse'). However, in what follows the end of art will be considered only to the extent that it is a recognizable feature of the German aesthetic tradition since Hegel and that it includes the tradition of anti-aesthetic philosophy of art.

Hegel's double-take on the end of art

Hegel must indeed be credited for having given the motif its enduringly provocative formulation. However, the formulaic death or end of art is not to be found in the posthumously published "Lectures on Aesthetics" (1835) nor in Hegel's most famous work, the "Phenomenology of Spirit" (1807). What came to be known as "Hegel's thesis about the end of art" refers to a passage from the "Lectures" where Hegel notes that art is with respect to its highest vocation for us, artists and recipients alike, a thing of the past and will remain so. According to Hegel, the times when a particular content required a particular form are over. Art has now become "a free instrument," at the disposal of each artist according to his or her subjective preferences. Hegel does not claim that artistic production will cease. In fact, virtually all historical forms and materials are now at the artist's disposal, but nothing produced under these conditions will ever rise above the general relativity to achieve the significance or originality enjoyed by the great art of the past. What Hegel saw coming is the historicist age Danto and Kuspit rediscovered in the late twentieth century. And they could do so because paradoxically, and ironically, Hegel's dictum predates the achievements of modernism still to come. With hindsight it looks less like a diagnosis than a prophecy.

According to Hegel's schema in the Lectures, the history of art is characterized by successive constellations of artistic form and content,

---

2   Arthur C. Danto, *The Philosophical Disenfranchisement of Art* (New York: Columbia University Press, 1986).

called symbolic, classical, and romantic. Art's highest purpose is to bring substance or spirit into sensuous appearance in such a way that the inner content has fully and without rest found expression in the outward form of an undifferentiated whole. This was achieved only in classical Greece because here art became the highest and fullest of the Greek's politico-religious essence, which Hegel refers to elsewhere as 'art-religion.' By contrast, both the pre-artistic symbolic phase (covering everything before and other than Greek art) and the later romantic phase, which begins with the rise of Christianity and lasts into Hegel's own present, are characterized by the discrepancy of form and content. Symbolic art suffers from the fact that form and content have not yet been fully separated but rather appear in an abstract unity exemplified by the enigmatic Egyptian pyramids. In post-classical romantic art, the content or substance—namely Christianity rather than Greek polytheism—no longer lends itself to outwardly visible representation. What is called the end of art marks the end of the third and final phase of art. Henceforth, art is for us a thing of the past because our spiritual essence has found other, more appropriate forms of expression, knowledge, and philosophy chiefly among them. In this regard, art's tombstone or grave is Hegel's own "Lectures on Aesthetics."

Countless critics have rebelled against the privilege Hegel accords to classical art, and just as many have also balked at the coincidence of (Hegelian) philosophy of art with the end of art as such. However, some, such as Odo Marquard, have argued conversely that Hegel actually relieves art from its philosophical duties.[3] Since its foundation in Baumgarten, the philosophical discipline of aesthetics had moved art to the center stage of philosophy. At the close of Idealism, Hegel offers a corrective to this persistent instrumentalization of art on the part of philosophy. With the end of art, Hegel sets art free, thus allowing it to assume functions other than representing philosophical truths. This still leaves Greek art as the unquestioned highpoint but because it is historically confined, no normative consequences issue from its privileged position.

The story of the end of art is told somewhat differently in Hegel's earlier *Phenomenology of Spirit*. At issue is the section in which Hegel describes the transition from Greek art-religion to revealed religion. In contrast to the *Lectures*, Hegel proposes in the *Phenomenology* a very different argument involving the succession of genres within Greek art and their dissolution. It is worth noting that Hegel did not identify the singular accomplishments of art in classical Greece as an end of

---

3 Odo Marquard, "Kant und die Wende zur Ästhetik," *Zeitschrift für philosophische Forschung* 16 (3), 363–74 (1962).

art but reserved it for his own time. By contrast, the end of art of the *Phenomenology* is, as it were, an exclusively Greek affair. According to Hegel, the emergence of the Homeric epics characterized the beginning of art in Greece. They were succeeded by tragedy (here figured as the highest form). They give rise to comedy, which now figures as the end of art, an end, however, that is not the demise of art but also its accomplishment. In the *Phenomenology* then, art ends as art in the art form of comedy. And this is so because comedy is the form in which art, as it were, ironically confesses that it has no substance of its own. This is why it is an ironic end. Irony is the end but, by the same token, the end is ironic because it is enacted by and as art, more specifically as comedy. The revelation of art's lack of substance, which according to the "Lectures" is philosophy's insight about art, is here generated by art itself and in a particular art form.

The ironic end of art in and as comedy in the *Phenomenology* can be linked to the posthumous *Lectures* by the latter's analysis of objective humor. Hegel had only disdain for the notion of Romantic irony as formulated by Friedrich Schlegel, because (unlike the objective irony of comedy as a form) irony in the sense of Schlegel was only about self-important subjectivity. As an alternative Hegel briefly mentions the notion of objective humor as a way for form and content to cohere even after the end of great art. Objective humor thus opens up possibilities for "serious" art after art's end. Among those who have drawn on Hegel's notion of objective humor for the purposes of developing a theory of genuinely modern art are the philosopher Dieter Henrich and the literary critic Wolfgang Preisendanz.[4] In different ways, they both illustrate how Hegelian aesthetics can be instructive for later periods not despite his verdict on the end of art but, rather, because of it.

The end of the artistic period according to Heinrich Heine

Hegel's fateful dictum from the *Lectures* has a curious analogy in the poet Heinrich Heine's almost simultaneous enunciation about the "end of the artistic period"[5] which he claims began with Goethe's arrival on the literary scene in the 1770s and ended with his death in 1832 (Hegel had already died a year earlier). Heine first voiced this opinion in a review of Wolfgang Menzel's literary history from 1828, once more in 1831, and again in 1833 in his book on "The Romantic School." Even

---

4 Dieter Henrich, *Fixpunkte. Abhandlungen und Essays zur Theorie der Kunst* (Frankfurt am Main: Suhrkamp Verlag, 2003). Wolfgang Preisendanz, *Humor als dichterische Einbildungskraft. Studien zur Erzählkunst des poetischen Realismus* (Munich: Wilhelm Fink Verlag, 1976).

5 Heinrich Heine, *The Romantic School and Other Essays*, ed. Jost Hermand and Robert C. Holub (New York: Continuum Publishing, 1985).

though Heine only refers to the previous sixty years and, also unlike Hegel, he harbored hopes for a new age with a new art, there are also some similarities. For example, Heine also believed that the upcoming interim would be dominated by subjectivism and humor. But critics tend to mobilize Heine as the one who proved that Hegel was mistaken with his idea of the end of art. Because Heine was the first to discover the literary possibilities of journalism, he is heralded as modern who succeeded in securing new modes of literariness after the end of the Romantic period. While this might be objectively true, this view fails to do justice to Heine's own ambivalence, regarding his own Romantic past and, above all, the towering figure of Goethe. Goethe's artworks may be lifeless like statues, but their "dead immortality" looms larger. Thus Goethe's works continue to exert an influence that artworks according to Hegel no longer have.

The anti-aesthetic affect (Nietzsche, Benjamin, Heidegger)

The Hegelian end of art could not be toppled by mere anti-Idealist rhetoric, yet it had to be challenged in order for modern art since Hegel to achieve (or retain) legitimacy as art. Equally pressing was an alternative philosophy of art capable of avoiding the trappings of idealism. Beginning in the nineteenth and increasingly in the twentieth century, deepening anti-Hegelianism inaugurated an anti-aesthetic tradition of theorizing art.

One of its most influential proponents, Friedrich Nietzsche, did not write a systematic aesthetics, yet his early writings are frequently deemed to be aestheticist. The notorious charge conveys the fact that in Nietzsche aesthetic attitude and artistic productivity are no longer and not even primarily confined to art. They rather designate a more general, even universal practice, rooted in our ability to produce metaphors, make stories, and delight in illusions. Defined in this way, aesthetic practice can be found in all areas of life. However, this exuberant notion of an aesthetic attitude did not keep Nietzsche from writing a book in which the death of art figures prominently. The book in question (which Nietzsche later claimed "smelled a little Hegelian") is the *Birth of Tragedy* (1872). In it the trained classical philologist Nietzsche offers a radically new and, by scholarly standards of the time, very idiosyncratic account of the emergence of Greek tragedy from the music of the Dithyramb as performed during the Dionysian festivals. The Greece presented in Nietzsche's is very different from Hegel's conception of Greek art-religion. Like Hölderlin before him, Nietzsche invented another Greece, opposed to the proverbial naiveté and serenity that held sway over Germany's cultural imagination between Winckelmann and Hegel. Nietzsche's Greeks had gained profound insights into the terror of all life and had to invent tragedy to be able to bear the terrible truth and continue living. What Hegel had conceived of as their "art-religion" was in Nietzsche's eyes a compensatory strategy. Still, Nietzsche seems not to have been able to give up the notion of an end of art, though its resemblance to Hegel is only superficial: the great art of tragedy, this unique synthesis of the opposed artistic drives of Dionysian immersion and Apollonian distance, begins to die in the comedies of Euripides. Threatened art eventually finds asylum in the Socratic dialogues. The new rationality that asserts itself in Plato's dialogues later gives rise to a scientific rationality Nietzsche also calls Socratic. Born in Athens it remained victorious into the present. While this seems to recall Hegel's claim that knowledge and philosophy have superseded sensuous art forms, Nietzsche's point is very different. For him, scientific rationality is not the other of art but only another mode in which the artistic drives realize themselves. The aesthetic attitude, the pleasure taken in play and metaphor, persists in the rational world, even if its representatives tend to believe themselves to be in the possession of truth. But because their truth is also only an aesthetic illusion, Nietzsche remains hopeful that at some point in the near future, the scientific age will pass over into an aesthetic age again. *The Birth of Tragedy* is written in the spirit of an imminent return of great art in a new age, which Nietzsche believed to be dawning in Wagner's music.

In his *The Origin of German Tragic Drama* (1927) Walter Benjamin contributes to the debates about the possibilities of tragedy in modernity sparked by Nietzsche. Benjamin turns to the then almost forgotten seventeenth-century tragedies by baroque German Protestant writers such as Lohenstein. Benjamin presents those works as an anti-aesthetic corrective to classicism, romanticism, and also to Nietzsche aestheticizations. He understands the bizarre mourning plays as inherently fragmentary artworks that by their fragmentariness object to an aesthetic tradition occupied with beautiful appearances and the work as a totality.

This tradition of anti-aesthetics is radicalized in the philosophy of Martin Heidegger, above all in his lectures on Nietzsche (1936–46, first published in 1962), the essay on the "Origin of the Artwork" (1935), and in the so-called "Contributions" (1938), often considered Heidegger's other main work after *Being and Time* (1927).[6] In the "Contributions" as well as in a number of other texts, beginning with lectures on the poet Friedrich Hölderlin in the early 1940s and later extending to reflections on the paintings of Cezanne and Klee, art becomes for Heidegger increasingly an alternative access to the world dominated by modern

---

6   Martin Heidegger, "The Origin of the Work of Art," in *Basic Writings*, ed. David Farrell Krell (New York: Harper & Row Publishers, 1977), 139–212.

technology. This return of art to the center stage of philosophizing and its endowment with a certain redemptive quality initially seems at odds with Heidegger's strong critique of the Western tradition of aesthetics as part of a metaphysical tradition in need of overcoming.

Against this background, Heidegger judges Nietzsche to be the last metaphysician, since the aesthetic logic of production—unmoored from aesthetics—reigns supremely in Nietzsche's notion of a will-to-power. Similarly, Hegel's aesthetics is explicitly called the last aesthetics but it is also judged to be the greatest. What Heidegger underscores in particular is the unquestioned validity of Hegel's verdict on the end of art. Precisely because aesthetics might be the medium in which art dies, Hegel's aesthetics reaches beyond the tradition by the very verdict on the end of art. In an addendum to his artwork-essay, Heidegger suggests that the decision whether great art still is still possible as an expression of truth cannot be separated from a decision on Western metaphysics as a whole. Since the so-called "turn," Heidegger insisted that there was no way to either overcome, outdo, or break with the metaphysical tradition because the very tradition already harbors the potential for its overcoming. This is especially true of the tradition of aesthetics, to which Heidegger attributes a self-destructive potential that allows the aesthetic discourse to pass beyond its limits. In Hegel, this potential is marked by the figure of the end of art.

Art, new media, and modern culture (Kracauer, Benjamin, Adorno)

Whenever new media emerge—photography in the nineteenth century, film, radio, television, and the internet—the rhetoric of ends tends to proliferate. In the twentieth century, the end of art can be observed in such contexts.

The sociologist and film theorist Siegfried Kracauer was also among the first to develop a theory of mass entertainment as a culture in its own right, different from but no less valuable than the once dominant bourgeois art. For Kracauer, the end of (bourgeois) art is a matter of fact rather than conviction. In a brief essay entitled "The Mass Ornament" dealing with the Tiller Girls and published in the *Frankfurter Zeitung* in 1927,[7] Kracauer notes that the geometrical patterns produced by the dancing girls no longer resemble any familiar forms either from geometry or from dance. Yet what begins to look like a lament about the new culture reproducing the soulless patterns of work on the assembly line takes a surprising turn towards the end. Kracauer emphatically

---

7   Siegfried Kracauer, "The Mass Ornament," in *The Weimar Republic Sourcebook*, ed. Anton Kaes, Martin Jay, and Edward Dimendberg (Berkeley: University of California Press, 1994).

supports the aesthetic enjoyment of those figures and forms because they bestow visible form on something that would otherwise remain invisible. As the Tiller Girls lend recognizable shape to the proletariat as a class they assume the same function that art-religion fulfilled for the essence of Greek life or as "great art" did for the bourgeoisie. While Kracauer believes in an end of art, he does not believe in the end of an aesthetic tradition that understood art as expression of a historical culture.

Kracauer stands at the beginning to a debate that has lasted into recent discussions about postmodernism and "closing the gap between high and low" (Leslie Fiedler). Another important contribution to this discussion stems once again from Walter Benjamin, whose essay "On the Artwork in the Age of Mechanical Reproduction" (1935) has long since become canonical. On the face of it, Benjamin seems to be championing film and its mass-reception over and against the old auratic artwork and its corresponding mode of contemplative reception. A closer look, however, reveals first of all a certain ambivalence regarding the decline of auratic art that comes to the fore in Benjamin's somewhat melancholic description of early portrait photography, into which the auratic cult value of art fled before its full liquidation in the street photographs by Atget. This ambivalence is not a matter of personal indecision but reflects the objective ambivalence of the historic-political situation in which Benjamin found himself. With the film industry not only in capitalist hands but abused by National Socialism for the purposes of propaganda, it was not clear whether the revolutionary potential of the new media would be given the chance to realize itself. In this regard, but for different reasons, Benjamin assumes an ambivalence familiar from Heidegger. Moreover, Benjamin also maintains that new media retroactively affect the old artistic forms. They effect a liquidation of the value of tradition of all previous culture. This is not a loss, or better, not only a loss, because it also suggests the redemption of the past; liberated from the authoritarian value of tradition, the objects of earlier culture are in a way born again. In later texts, Benjamin would indeed argue that any document of culture is also always a document of barbarism and that the past would be available only to a redeemed humanity.

This latter thought bears some resemblance to a tendency observable in the works of Theodor W. Adorno, who also believed that a fully reconciled humanity would have no more need for art, which is born from and remains bound to suffering (a motif familiar from Nietzsche). However, in Adorno, this is only one version of the end of art. The other is the annihilation of art by mass culture (which for Adorno, in contrast to Kracauer and Benjamin, is certainly not culture at all). Especially the chapter on the culture industry from the "Dialectic of Enlightenment" is an almost apocalyptical attack of Hollywood film and TV. Of course, Adorno knew full well that there had always been entertainment such as the circus, for example. But it had nothing to do with the industrialized film industry of Hollywood. Strictly opposed to mass culture are singular artworks that obey the ascetic logic of modernism, as with Beckett's plays, for example. However, in the end Adorno manages to find some truth in the lies of the culture industry. In its glaring light the problematic nature of high art is revealed. The culture industry's brutal reduction of style to self-sameness, for example, illuminates the usually hidden fact that any artistic style is the result of violence done to the material but also self-inflicted by the artist.

SEE ALSO: Truth

Twelve Allegory

J. D. Mininger

Allegory figures as a key concept in German aesthetics thanks to its revival and reconceptualization in the twentieth century. Despite the lasting influence and importance of the classical, medieval, and Renaissance forms of allegory, which typically involve a sustained metaphor in which a word, image, or character rather mechanically stands in for another, often abstract, idea, the rejuvenated interest in allegory in the twentieth century significantly resituated these traditional bearings. Motivated especially by Walter Benjamin's influential valorization of the term, several notable twentieth-century approaches to allegory eschewed its otherwise rigidly held conventional codes in favor of a reinterpretation of allegory as an operation that questions the assumed correspondence between meaning and object, sign and trope, designation and signification. The significance of allegory's "rebirth" in the twentieth century is not a matter of progress; rather, by effectively reinventing allegory, Benjamin and Paul de Man, among others, found a tool to address, if obliquely, some of the social and political tensions of their modern era, such as the aesthetic ideology(s) of fascism, or the commodification of art via the process that Adorno and Horkheimer termed the culture industry.

German aesthetic theorists and practitioners of the eighteenth and nineteenth centuries also addressed allegory; however, there was no ultimate unanimity as to its import or role in art and art's valuation. The twentieth-century reinterpretation of allegory proposed by Benjamin and de Man follows a historical narrative of allegory's supposed devaluation in the eighteenth and nineteenth centuries in favor of the symbol. In the eighteenth and nineteenth centuries, the traditional mode of allegory certainly had detractors. Rationalism frowned upon allegory as its proponents sought greater realism in art. Further, fed up with allegory's wooden, predictable, rationalist operation, Romantics aided "a shift in poetic discourse, which required the invention of symbolism as a stronger, more spiritual, and more vital form of expression."[1] Whatever their particular assessment of allegory, early Romantic writers such as August Wilhelm Schlegel, Friedrich Schlegel, Novalis, Schleiermacher, and Tieck, the philosophers Schelling and Solger, and Goethe too, all distinguished allegory in comparison to symbolism. For many Romantics, symbol rescued a sense of immediacy and proximity to the divine world that allegory failed to capture.

The example of Johann Joachim Winckelmann serves as an indication of the complexity of the eighteenth-century situation surrounding the shifting valuations of symbol and allegory. One of the pioneers of the discipline of art history and a figure largely responsible for the massive neoclassical revival in German thought, Winckelmann tended to conflate the two terms, at points using them interchangeably. In particular, his theory of painting emphasized the central role of allegory: as Frederick Beiser explains of Winckelmann's model, "since the aim of painting is to portray the insensible by sensible means, and since an allegory is essentially a sensible symbol for something insensible, the aim of painting should be allegory."[2] Thus, despite eventually succumbing to their positions as a highly charged oppositional pair, much of eighteenth-century aesthetics still noted the family resemblances of symbol and allegory. In *Truth and Method*, Hans-Georg Gadamer, whose book uses the history of the changing relationship between symbol and allegory as an example of the devaluation of rhetoric during the nineteenth century, notes some of these important shared characteristics:

> both [symbol and allegory] refer to something whose meaning does not consist in its external appearance or sound but in a significance that lies beyond it. Common to both is that, in both, one thing stands for another. This relation of meaning whereby the non-sensory is made apparent to the senses is found in the field of poetry and the plastic arts, as well as in that of the religious and sacramental.[3]

But while symbol and allegory share the potential to mean something other than what they may first appear to represent, their ways of completing this transfer of meaning proved too crucially divergent to

---

1 Jeremy Tambling, *Allegory* (London: Routledge, 2009), 62.
2 Frederick C. Beiser, *Diotima's Children: German Aesthetic Rationalism from Leibniz to Lessing* (Oxford: Oxford University Press, 2009), 189.
3 Hans-Georg Gadamer, *Truth and Method*, 2nd ed., revised, trans. Joel Weinsheimer and Donald G. Marshall (London: Continuum, 2004), 62–3.

the developing semantic trends of the eighteenth century, resulting in an emphasis on the terms' contrast.

Gadamer accounts for the promotion of symbol to the detriment of allegory as belonging part and parcel to the notion of genius cultivated in the age of Goethe: "the moment art freed itself from all dogmatic bonds and could be defined as the unconscious production of genius, allegory inevitably became aesthetically suspect."[4] According to this view of genius, the gap between experience and the expression of that experience can be transcended by the genius' poetic language, thereby promoting the notion that subjective experience can coincide directly with universal truth. Unlike allegory, a symbol, similarly to synecdoche, supposedly maintains an inherent connection between the sensible representation and the insensible meaning it represents. For this reason, writers such as Goethe privileged symbol as a natural sign capable of directly designating the spiritual world, without succumbing to what they deemed lesser aesthetic forms, such as allegory, which were too wooden, too sterile. Allegory involves an arbitrarily chosen sign, whereas symbol presupposes "the coincidence of the sensible and the nonsensible";[5] in other words, what allegory signifies by means of convention, the symbol suggests to be a natural link between sign and meaning. Allegory belongs to the sphere of *logos*—that is, to the truth of language and speech. At its etymological core allegory suggests the act of speaking figuratively, that is, of speaking otherwise than one seems to speak: literally, other speaking, or speaking to the other. An allegory offers the opportunity to speak, indicate, or represent one thing, and by it mean another thing—in effect signifying two things at once. But for Goethe and his long eighteenth-century contemporaries, and more profoundly for nearly all Romantic art and criticism of the nineteenth century, allegory's essentially contingent relation between sign and meaning meant that art remained fettered to rationalism, and the gap between individual experience and universal truth remained intact: no appeal to a "total, single, and universal meaning" was possible.[6] At the expense of allegory, symbol took pride of place in the eighteenth- and nineteenth-century German aesthetic tradition.

During the twentieth century the concept of allegory underwent significant reassessment as a critical concept. Two thinkers made especially prominent contributions to this renewal of allegory: Walter Benjamin and Paul de Man. Both privilege the concept of allegory

---

4   Ibid., 68.
5   Ibid., 64.
6   Paul de Man, "The Rhetoric of Temporality," in *Blindness and Insight: Essays in the Rhetoric of Contemporary Criticism*, 2nd ed., revised (Minneapolis: University of Minnesota Press, 1983), 188.

in the following ways: 1) allegory is a guiding optic for understanding that the category of the aesthetic is an essential part of any historical modernity whatsoever; and 2) the allegorical form is equally a fundamental feature of language that, by proposing an inescapable disjointedness between sign and meaning, places in question the very discourse of modernity understood as discourse (a signifying system), history (a narrative), or concept (a philosophical system).

Benjamin's major project during the 1930s, the *Arcades Project*, drew heavily on the concept of allegory as both a thematic basis—in this case, for theorizing the nineteenth-century culture of high capitalism—and a methodological guide for a philosophically responsible form of criticism. However, an earlier work, *The Origin of the German Tragic Drama* [*Ursprung des deutschen Trauerspiels*], "conceived 1916; written 1925,"[7] presents Benjamin's most sustained commentary on allegory. Like its successor project, the *Trauerspiel* book both addresses allegory as a key component of the content of the study and deploys allegory as a critical method.

As form and method, Benjamin justifies the allegorically informed structure of his book in the "Epistemo-Critical Prologue," where he denounces earlier aesthetic traditions' claims to systematically derived truths captured through symbolic representation. Because Benjamin understands human language as fundamentally allegorical, such symbolic representation threatens to mystify language use and maintain the illusion of human autonomy as a result. Benjamin advocates the idea of the constellation, which assists the allegorical method of drawing together fragments that, when read together, "mean" precisely in terms of the play of their relations. Hence, they are estranged and individuated, and yet necessarily entangled in a web of relations—a constellation—that expresses each fragment of the past through the perspective of the present. Benjamin's allegorical method refuses anything that smacks of an act of symbolic representation, in which a single, unified whole lays claim to a directly accessible truth.

The thematic materials on allegory in *The Origin of German Tragic Drama* pursue a renewal of the concept through a justification of the historical significance of the seventeenth-century baroque dramatic form called the *Trauerspiel*—in English, a play of mourning or lamentation. Through an analysis of the formal properties of the *Trauerspiel*, Benjamin separates *Trauerspiel* from classical tragedy by virtue of its allegorical techniques. By privileging allegory over symbol, Benjamin situates allegory alongside melancholy, which follows from the crisis of

---

7   Walter Benjamin, *The Origin of German Tragic Drama*, trans. John Osborne (London: Verso, 1998), 25.

meaning that allegory exposes in language, knowledge, and truth. This crisis unfolds as a plane of absolute contingency, the disenchanting powers of which prove destructive—hence the mournful attunement of what symbolic representation had conditioned us to expect, such as unquestioned modes of expression and their immediate relation to truth. Benjamin writes: "Any person, any object, any relationship can mean absolutely anything else. With this possibility a destructive, but just verdict is passed on the profane world: it is characterized as a world in which the detail is of no great importance."[8] The disenchantment of the world—or secularization, in which any transcendent anchor for truth claims is lost—uses allegorical form to express the contradictions that haunt it. On the one hand, allegory points to something other than itself, acting *as if* buoyed by a transcendent power, such as the example from the *Trauerspiel* form of the sovereign ruler stuck pathetically within the immanent world where only creaturely powers manifest themselves. In part, because the form of transcendence is impersonated, the "power which makes them appear no longer commensurable with profane things ... can, indeed, sanctify them."[9] On the other hand, allegory "ruins" thought, in the sense that it deforms contexts of meanings through its contingent historical foundations and the concomitant devaluation of individual things (signs) as expressions of truth unto themselves. This is the destructive side of the antinomy of allegory within the *Trauerspiel*. The ruin is the emblem of this side of allegory: "In the ruin history has physically merged into the setting."[10] Figures of transience activate allegorical meaning, such as with the emphasis on the corpse in the *Trauerspiel*—any sign that spatializes or figuralizes time takes on this allegorical power. Because allegory relies upon convention, the truth of transience appears (allegorically) with every allegorical expression.

The allegorical model that Benjamin finds in the *Trauerspiel* allegorizes modern experience itself, with its increasing structures of culture that serve to mediate the immanent world, devoid of transcendent anchors for truth claims. For this reason Benjamin extends his study of allegory to the culture of high capitalism and the works of Charles Baudelaire. One example Benjamin emphasizes in the unfinished *Arcades Project* is the commodity fetish as allegory, which he associates particularly with modern experience and culture, and which, he claims, had not fully developed in the seventeenth century, when allegory was in part still a "mere" artistic strategy.[11] The commodity fetish typifies

---

8   Ibid., 175.
9   Ibid., 175.
10 Ibid., 178.
11 Walter Benjamin, *The Arcades Project*, trans. Howard Eiland and Kevin

"the image of petrified unrest,"[12] in which the allegorical arrangement of contingency between sign and meaning allows a commodity to be given what appears to be a stable value (exchange-value), but at the great expense and devaluation of its immeasurable value, or value-in-itself (use-value). Images of "petrified unrest" allegorize eternal transience with the hope of challenging political, economic, and cultural mystifications. However, the important difference between allegory in the *Trauerspiel* book and allegory in the *Arcades Project* is the historical context: when modernity itself is allegorical—that is, disenchanted—such as in the nineteenth-century context of high capitalism, allegory's efficacy as a tool of social and political critique may be blunted.

Within the tradition of German aesthetics, Benjamin's inspiration and insight is nowhere more pronounced than in the work of Theodor W. Adorno. For example, Benjamin's theory of allegory from the *Trauerspiel* study animates both the form and content of Adorno's *Kierkegaard: Construction of the Aesthetic*, a slightly modified version of Adorno's *Habilitationsschrift* which establishes some of the fundamental themes and insights that persist throughout Adorno's prodigious body of work. Robert Hullot-Kentor argues in his foreword to the English translation of *Kierkegaard* that Benjamin's theory of allegory pulses at the very center of Adorno's thought: "The Hegelian dialectic, passed through Benjamin's idea of allegory, became in Adorno's work the form for the interpretation of all culture. No longer a dialectic of progress, the Hegelian dialectic, as the critique of any first, continually transforms meaning into the expression of transience."[13] For Adorno, Benjamin's theory of allegory helped develop the outward form of a way to say the unsayable: to point negatively to the always fleeting hope of culture beyond administered culture via the allegorical, which simultaneously represents and denies the truth it expresses.

This fundamental ambiguity at the heart of the allegorical operation also offered a model of critique in the work of Paul de Man. Like Benjamin, and certainly in part inspired by Benjamin's writings, de Man recuperates allegory from its (supposed) devaluation by Romantic writers and the critical reception of Romanticism. In "The Rhetoric of Temporality" de Man establishes his program to reclaim the importance of allegory. However, he does not merely denounce the Romantic use of symbol, which, whether willfully or ignorantly, brushes aside the rhetorical or figural dimension of language in its expression of

---

McLaughlin (Cambridge, MA: Harvard University Press, 1999), 347.
12　Ibid., 366.
13　Robert Hullot-Kentor, Foreword, "Critique of the Organic," in *Kierkegaard: Construction of the Aesthetic*, by Theodor W. Adorno, trans. Robert Hullot-Kentor (Minneapolis: University of Minnesota Press, 1989), xix–xx.

desire for a complete and unified subjectivity. Pairing allegory with a study of Romantic irony, de Man equally privileges Romantic poetics.

For de Man, allegory is not merely a tool of criticism and interpretation. Far from suggesting that allegory reduces texts to a hermeneutic dead-end in which rhetoric and figural language undermine the intended meaning, de Manian allegorical reading refuses to forget the necessarily representational and material nature of allegory. This involves a simultaneous two-fold procedure: unveiling a linguistic trope for what it is—namely, a figural use of language—and the deconstruction of that trope, understood as the explanation of how the trope (or any rhetorical dimension of language) places its own narration in question via the disjuncture between sign and meaning, or between the grammatical and rhetorical registers.[14] The lesson is: because of the irreducible figurality of language, language must always narrate. A sign must refer to somewhere or something else other than itself, even when the meaning appears self-evident. One of the most compelling examples of this in de Man's oeuvre comes in "Sign and Symbol in Hegel's *Aesthetics*," in which he discusses the position of "I," and the gap "between what the I is and what it says it is."[15]

In "The Rhetoric of Temporality" de Man applies these lessons to Romantic texts and the tension between symbol and allegory. In a passage that echoes Benjamin's crucial link between allegory and transience, de Man explains that "the prevalence of allegory always corresponds to the unveiling of an authentically temporal destiny. This unveiling takes place in a subject that has sought refuge against the impact of time in a natural world to which, in truth, it bears no resemblance."[16] Romantic art as well as its conventional critical reception falls prey to a danger inherent to symbolic presentation; yet in early Romantic literature de Man locates allegorical moments that unveil this danger: "allegory designates primarily a distance in relation to its own origin, and, renouncing the nostalgia and the desire to coincide, it establishes its language in the void of this temporal difference. In so doing it prevents the self from an illusory self-identification with the non-self, which is now fully, though painfully, recognized as a non-self."[17] The inherent danger that prompts de Man to favor allegory is both an act (self-mystification) and a desire (nostalgia): in short, aesthetic ideology.

---

14 See Paul de Man, *Allegories of Reading: Figural Language in Rousseau, Nietzsche, Rilke, and Proust* (New Haven, CT: Yale University Press, 1982).
15 Paul de Man, "Sign and Symbol in Hegel's *Aesthetics*," *Aesthetic Ideology*, ed. Andrzej Warminski (Minneapolis: University of Minnesota Press, 1996), 99.
16 de Man, "Rhetoric of Temporality," 206.
17 Ibid., 207.

Allegory and the problem of aesthetic ideology are bound up with one another as an urgent problem for contemporary philosophical aesthetics. In dialogue with de Man's texts, in "Romanticism's Paradoxical Articulation of Desire," Jochen Schulte-Sasse defines aesthetic ideology as:

> an ideology—or, more precisely, an institutionalized discursive practice—that seeks to suppress the structurality of structures in favor of an illusive experience of wholeness. To use Lacanian terminology, the aesthetic enables the subject to establish an imaginary relationship between self and text. Art serves here as a mirror in which the subject experiences itself as unified and as possessing an equally unified, privileged consciousness. Poetic language sustains this imaginary relationship because it allegedly transcends the rhetorical nature of language, which, in turn, is able to close the gap between experience and its representation.[18]

In Schulte-Sasse's reading, what most provocatively distinguishes allegory from symbol is its relationship to desire. Whereas a symbol expresses a longing for wholeness in a unified subjectivity, allegory suggests a subject position that accepts the subject's inherent fragmentation and lack. Similar in some respects to Manfred Frank's notion of infinite approximation in early German Romanticism,[19] Schulte-Sasse goes a step further than de Man's critical engagement with Romanticism, suggesting that "rather than arresting their thinking at the point of recognition that language is rhetorical, [the Romantics] may have accepted the pursuit of aesthetic ideology's ideal as necessary while simultaneously appreciating its 'impossibility.'"[20] Schulte-Sasse suggests that allegory can construct subject positions acknowledged as fictional: "an illusion that enables [the Romantic] to construct or 'synthesize' himself as unified, while always remaining aware of the fact that every construction is preliminary and incomplete."[21] In this way, by proceeding "as if," and supplemented by aesthetic reflection, the subject achieves the only "unity" possible.

The stakes of allegory are aesthetic ideology. Its structural effects include dangerous operations of identity politics such as nationalism,

---

18 Jochen Schulte-Sasse, "General Introduction: Romanticism's Paradoxical Articulation of Desire," *Theory as Practice: A Critical Anthology of Early German Romantic Writings*, ed. Jochen Schulte-Sasse et al. (Minneapolis: University of Minnesota Press, 1997), 2.
19 See Manfred Frank, *The Philosophical Foundations of Early Romanticism*, trans. Elizabeth Millán-Zaibert (Albany: State University of New York Press, 2008).
20 Schulte-Sasse, "Romanticism's Paradoxical Articulation of Desire," 7.
21 Ibid., 7.

fundamentalism, sexism, racism, and so on. Allegory's importance lies in confronting us with the matter of our desire. In this sense, an allegory does not hide its meaning, for a reader to decode or reveal. Rather, allegory exposes lack, fragmentation, transience—the condition of "hiddenessness" itself—as the absent center of signification that conditions desire. This implicates desire at the very heart of aesthetics. Whether, and in what ways, allegory continues to find appreciation in philosophical aesthetics therefore depends upon the historical, ethical, social, and, above all, political stakes of addressing the persistent desire—the problem of aesthetic ideology—that is always the "other" of allegory's signifying operation.

SEE ALSO: Irony; Value; Tragedy/*Trauerspiel*; Committed Art

Thirteen Value
A. Kiarina Kordela

In traditional approaches, aesthetic value is generally defined along the lines of the quality or merit of beauty possessed by a particular object or state of affairs—having largely to do with whether one experiences that object or state of affairs as pleasurable or unpleasurable. Yet, of all aesthetic concepts, value perhaps best foregrounds art's interlacing—or, more precisely, structural and conceptual homology—with the other fundamental constituents of human life and society: economy, ethics, and linguistics. Crucially, beyond aesthetic value, among others there are exchange values, moral values, and, as we know from Ferdinand de Saussure, linguistic values. For this reason, in distinction to those traditional definitions, this chapter repositions value, as it emerges in the philosophical aesthetics of secular capitalist modernity, within its homological network of aesthetics, economics, ethics, and linguistics/representation.

Aesthetic and economic values emerge in secular capitalist modernity in parallel with concomitant developments in ethics and modes of representation. There are four phases in this development: first, the movement of "ideal content," an incubator of modern value, lasting until Kant's intervention; second, the new paradigm of "abstractism" or "formalization," which erupts out of the Enlightenment; third, "structuralism," in which Romanticism advances the paradigm of formalization; and, fourth, "performative self-referentiality," a modern consequence of the third, formulated by, notably, Heidegger and Benjamin.

The ideal-content movement posits its task as defining good taste by means of concrete ideals. Pioneers of aesthetic theory in the second half of the eighteenth century prior to Kant (e.g. Baumgarten, Winckelmann, Lessing) unapologetically propose their personal tastes, including specific artworks, predominantly Greco-Roman (notoriously, Laocoön), as ideals for emulation regarding themes and technique.

"Ideal content" names this embryonic phase not because of its emphasis on topic rather than form (technique), but because there was no overarching sense that these values belonged to a larger paradigm or system. Content here may be understood in the structuralist sense of "content," as the filling that comes to occupy empty "sites" in a purely relational network.¹ This formal network (of values and valuation) not having yet been conceived, all there is for the ideal-content movement is exclusively content.

The ideal-content movement is exemplary of the "knowledge of order" that characterized "the *Classical episteme*" and aspired to maximum "taxinomia" and encyclopedization.² For instance, it demands, according to Winckelmann (1755), that "allegories," understood as "concrete ... figures by which general concepts ... [are] represented" according to fixed significations, be "classified" in a "compendium" so as "to instruct the artist in how to apply" them.³ Predating its distinction from symbol, allegory is here a remnant of the dominant conceptualization of representational value "since the Stoics," according to which the sign is grounded on "similitudes that link the marks [significant] to the things [signified]," so that this "link" is "organic."⁴ Secular representation gradually collapses these "similitudes," after which "things and words were to be separated" and signs would become arbitrary.⁵ Kant's severance of thing-in-itself and representation seals this process. As the first stage of the modern (i.e. secular capitalist), formation of a theory of value, the ideal-content movement still bases values and value judgments on the contiguity between sign and meaning, which relegates human expression, including art, to taxonomy—even as such pre-secular remnants begin to falter at that time.

The gradual shift from "organic" to "arbitrary" representational value corresponds to the economic shift from feudalism to "'mercantilism' [which] freed the value of money from ... [its] intrinsic value of metal," so that "money ... receives its value" arbitrarily, "from its

---

1 Gilles Deleuze, "How Do We Recognize Structuralism?" trans. Melissa McMahon and Charles J. Stivale, in *Desert Islands and Other Texts 1953–1974*, ed. David Lapoujade (Los Angeles: Semiotext(e), 2004), 174.
2 Michel Foucault, *The Order of Things: An Archaeology of the Human Sciences* (New York: Vintage, 1970), 71.
3 Johann Joachim Winckelmann, *Thoughts on the Imitation of the Painting and Sculpture of the Greeks*, trans. H. B. Nisbet, in *German Aesthetic and Literary Criticism: Winckelmann, Lessing, Hamann, Herder, Schiller, Goethe*, ed. H. B. Nisbet (Cambridge: Cambridge University Press, 1985), 52–3.
4 Foucault, *The Order of Things*, 42.
5 Ibid., 43.

form" or "pure function as sign."⁶ Exchange-value as a differential system of immaterial abstract values eventually finds its systematic formulation in Marx's *Capital, Volume 1* (1867), which states that there is "not an atom of matter" in "the objectivity of commodity as values," which is not "natural" but "purely social" or relational.⁷

Already in his first *Critique* (1781), Kant expresses this tendency toward abstract relational form by exhorting the abandonment of "the critique of taste," with its "merely empirical" "putative rules," in favor of a new "transcendental aesthetic" detached from "sensation" and based on *a priori* "pure intuition and ... mere form of appearances."⁸ His call entailed the degradation of technique as criterion of artistic value, since it pertains to the *a posteriori* empirical aspect of the artwork.⁹ But Kant's formalist move required the separation of aesthetic value from use-value—by analogy, anticipating Marx's separation of exchange-value from the "coarsely sensuous objectivity of ... physical objects" of utility.¹⁰ The modern concepts of aesthetic and economic value, as well as the distinct fields of aesthetics and political economy, emerge through this separation of aesthetic value from use-value, as is succinctly illustrated in the passage from David Hume to Adam Smith.

By mid-eighteenth century, the commodification of art begins to challenge the union of aesthetics and political economy within moral philosophy. "In order to maintain the reduction of beauty to utility," Hume's utilitarianism introduced the "tenuous distinction between ... immediate" and "deferred utility," the latter pertaining to artworks as "the pleasure of contemplating the beautiful objects of the rich man [rather] than ... the pleasure of possessing."¹¹ In *Theory of Moral Sentiments* [1759], Smith interiorized Hume's external distinction—that between artworks and other commodities—within every commodity, "between its being as means (its 'beauty') and its being as end (its 'use')," by arguing that "the desire for the object exceeds the gratification ... [of] its use," for otherwise "no economy would develop

---

6 Ibid., 175–7.
7 Karl Marx, *Capital: A Critique of Political Economy, Volume 1*, trans. Ben Fowkes (London: Penguin Books, 1990), 138–9.
8 Immanuel Kant, *Critique of Pure Reason*, trans. Paul Guyer and Allen W. Wood (New York: Cambridge University Press, 1998), 156–7; A21–2/B35–6, and note.
9 For example, see Johann Gottlieb Fichte, "On the Spirit and the Letter in Philosophy," trans. Elizabeth Rubenstein, in *German Aesthetic and Literary Criticism: Kant, Fichte, Schelling, Schopenhauer, Hegel*. ed. David Simpson (Cambridge: Cambridge University Press, 1984), 74–93.
10 Marx, *Capital*, 138.
11 John Guillory, *Cultural Capital: The Problem of Literary Canon Formation* (Chicago: The University of Chicago Press, 1993), 309–10.

beyond the ... production requisite for satisfying the minimal needs of human existence."[12] Thus, Smith establishes "aesthetic disposition as" the "invisible hand" or "motor of economic production," by finding "in the surplus 'beauty' of the commodity over its ...use the source of the social *surplus*": "wealth."[13] However, this conjunction of aesthetic and economic values could not last long because of the capitalist disequilibrium between production and consumption, which stubbornly belied moral philosophy's denial of the accumulation of surplus-value, and its postulate that "the exchange-value of the commodity ... express *both* the labor entailed in [its] production *and* the desire provoked in the consumer."[14] Faced with the incommensurability between economic cost of production and desire, classical economists "were forced to shift ... to ...production" and need, and to bracket "consumption" and desire "as irrelevant to the determination of price."[15] For example, in *The Wealth of Nations* (1776), Smith's invisible hand loses its aesthetic sensibilities to indulge in a utilitarianism grounded on benevolent self-interests: in aiming at "his own advantage ... and not that of society," "every individual" is "necessarily ... led by an invisible hand to promote" the "interest ... of the society," an "end which was no part of his intentions."[16] Thus, just as value in political economy refers to need and the double utilitarianism of use-value and self-interest, so aesthetic theory is born on the premises of the non-utilitarian character of art and the non-self-interestedness of aesthetic contemplation.

The abstraction from content—as both material thing (use-value) and (according to Kant, pathological) interest—accomplished by these premises of aesthetic theory marks the movement of formalization, the second stage of the development of value in secular capitalist modernity. Kant executed this abstraction of content on the three levels of reason, ethics, and aesthetics. His categorical imperative— "Act only according to that maxim by which you can ... will that it should become a universal law"[17]—and his definition of the beautiful in his third *Critique* (1790) as the object of an entirely disinterested satisfaction, both aim at evacuating ethical and aesthetic values of all content. Moreover, because aesthetic value involves subjective pleasure, and "from concepts there is no transition to ... pleasure or pain," aesthetic judgments, unlike those of reason and ethics, raise "a

---

12 Ibid., 311.
13 Ibid., 311–12.
14 Ibid., 313.
15 Ibid., 314.
16 Adam Smith, *The Wealth of Nations*, ed. Edwin Cannan (New York: The Modern Library, Random House, 2000), 482, 485.
17 See Immanuel Kant, *Foundations of the Metaphysics of Morals and "What Is Enlightenment?"* (Indianapolis: The Liberal Arts Press, 1959).

claim" not to objective but "to subjective universality." This means that aesthetic judgments have the character of an *"as if"*: "as if beauty were a characteristic of the object," and as if one had "reason for attributing a similar satisfaction to everyone."[18] Going beyond Locke's "secondary qualities" (subjectively distorted perception of matter), Kant points to perception as the result of an autonomous abstract relational network, independent from matter (both use-value and empirical body/subject)—whence his claim to "subjective *universality*."

By further linking aesthetics to the moral "Ideal," Kant eventually defines "beauty" as *"purposiveness* [*Zweckmäßigkeit*]," as opposed to *"purpose* [*Zweck*]," that is, as a teleology without *telos*, by analogy to reason's demand for the totality of experience (presented in Kant's first *Critique*).[19] Like the *Gesetzmäßigkeit* (conformity to law) of pure reason, *Zweckmäßigkeit* entails that a thing aims at its own *totality*, beyond any particular end or interest, and it is the attainment of the highest *Zweckmäßigkeit* (totality) that rouses the feeling of pleasure. But no human product, artistic or not, can comply with *Zweckmäßigkeit*, since its production is motivated by someone else's end-purpose of producing it. Eventually Kant concludes that only a thing that "bear(s) itself alternately as cause and as effect"—an *"organised* and *self-organising being"* that causes itself as its own *"natural purpose [Naturzweck]"* on the principle of "self-preservation"—can fulfill the requirement of *Zweckmäßigkeit*.[20] And this *"internal natural perfection"* of "organized beings" is "unthinkable," "inexplicable," and "not analogous to any ... faculty known to us ... not even ... [by] analogy to human art," for art presupposes "an artificer (a rational being) external to it."[21] "Nature," therefore, is for Kant a surface for projecting a causal model that "has ... nothing analogous to any causality we know."[22] Kant's favoritism of natural beauty as ideal beauty may have served subsequent philosophers, as Caygill, and Guillory after him, argue, to repress production and the "invisible hands [of] the wage-laborers."[23] But Kant's enlightened-bourgeois approach can easily *consciously* justify their oppression.[24] What Kant is indeed forced to repress—i.e. what is, in a sense, *unconscious* in Kant—is the true "aporia" behind the

---

18 See Immanuel Kant, *Kritik der Urteilskraft*. Werkausgabe, Band X, ed. Wilhelm Weinschedel (Frankfurt am Main: Suhrkamp, 2000), 56; §6.
19 Kant, *Kritik der Urteilskraft*, 90; Immanuel Kant, *The Critique of Judgment*, trans. J. H. Bernard (New York: Prometheus Books, 1974), 155; §17.
20 Kant, *Kritik der Urteilskraft*, 275, 278; Kant, *The Critique of Judgment*; 320, 322; §65.
21 Kant, *Kritik der Urteilskraft*, 278–80; §65.
22 Kant, *Kritik der Urteilskraft*, 279, §65.
23 Guillory, *Cultural Capital*, 312. See Howard Caygill, *Art of Judgement* (Oxford: Basil Blackwell, 1989), 38–102.
24 See Kant, *Kritik der Urteilskraft*, 352–8; §83.

"contradictory faculty" of a judgment that "can be deduced neither a priori nor empirically" but from a subjective, yet *a priori* "feeling of pleasure": the unknown causality of that which is *both its own cause and effect*.[25] For, in Kant's eyes, such causality amounts to either "hylozoism" or an external "soul" using "organised mater as [its] instrument"—in short, to the collapse of the Enlightenment. To be sure, the answer to this "aporia" had already been given in Spinoza's *Ethics* (1985 [1677]): "God is the immanent, not the transitive, cause of all things," an "immanent" cause being precisely a cause that is the effect of its own effects.[26] But the question remains, particularly at the peak of the Enlightenment: what is meant by "God"? Thus, this aporia was bequeathed to the Romantics.

If the Romantics see in Kant a failure to ground self-consciousness, it is because of his dualistic mirroring of subject and object, the transcendental "I" and "(the thing) which thinks." The Romantics understood that a third element is required in order for the subject to avoid narcissistically doubling itself in the object. As Gilles Deleuze explains it, to go beyond this narcissism there must be—beyond the distinction "real 'in truth'" and "imaginary double"—a "third order" or "symbolic element," "at once unreal, and … not imaginable," which breaks the mirroring between true and false, and "makes them communicate with each other, while … preventing the one [series] from imaginarily falling back on the other" in traditionally dialectical fashion.[27] This "symbolic … object=x," which "belongs to no series" but "is nevertheless present in both,"[28] is timidly indicated already in Kant's first *Critique*, as "the transcendental subject of thoughts=x," which is a "wholly empty representation (*Vorstellung*)" of "this I, or He, or It (the thing) which thinks."[29] But it is Schelling who really grasped its exact function.

In his *System des transzendentalen Idealismus*, Schelling intuits the object=x as a "third" by first noting that in the endless sequence of reflective acts—in which the subject becomes the object each time it becomes self-conscious of its own act of consciousness or intuition—"self-intuition could potentiate itself … to infinity," whereby "the series of products in nature [objects] would merely be increased, but consciousness would never arrive."[30] There must, therefore, be an

---

25 Guillory, *Cultural Capital*, 318; Caygill, *Art of Judgment*, 27.
26 Baruch [Benedict de] Spinoza, *The Collected Works of Spinoza*, Vol. 1, ed. and trans. Edwin Curley (Princeton, NJ: Princeton University Press, 1985), 428; part I, prop. 18.
27 Deleuze, "How Do We Recognize Structuralism?", 171–2, 185.
28 Ibid., 184–5.
29 Kant, *Critique of Pure Reason*, 414; A346/B404.
30 Friedrich Wilhelm Joseph von Schelling, *System of Transcendental Idealism*, trans. Albert Hofstadter, in *Philosophies of Art and Beauty: Selected Readings in Aesthetics*

"intuitive activity ... to the second power ... a purposive activity, which is, however, unconsciously purposive," that is, capable of intuiting all preceding intuitions, but *incapable of intuiting its own act of intuiting*—because, if it did, it would objectify it, the series of objectifications would commence again, and consciousness would never arrive.[31] This "ground ... can only lie outside the ego," as "another rational being" unconscious of its own reflective activity—an *unconscious consciousness that is no ego* but *a thing that thinks*, and which, without belonging to any of the series of objects and subjects constituted throughout the reflective acts, is present in both, for, without presupposing it, the two series would perpetually collapse in a bad infinity without consciousness.[32]

Thus, as Jochen Schulte-Sasse argues, far from committing "aesthetic ideology"—i.e. (imaginary) identity between subject and object—the Romanticist-structuralist movement "preempts the obfuscation of that desire" by revealing its cause: the fact that (the ground of) consciousness is a "necessary ... impossibility," or in Friedrich Schlegel's words, undoubtedly "a *fiction*. But an absolutely necessary one."[33] Hölderlin's premonition of an epistemology doomed to "become an empty infinity" concerns not Romanticism but (de Manian) "irony" itself—the eternal ironization/objectification of one's own reflective act.[34]

As necessary fiction—a transcendental function presupposed for the distinction between subject and object throughout the reflective series—unconscious consciousness (object=x) is the cause and effect of the series: the secular God, as Jacques Lacan's "true formula of atheism," "God is unconscious," indicates.[35] *Qua* immanent cause, object=x is both exception to and member of the series—not unlike capital in economic value. "By treating capital ... [or] money"—which classical economists considered an absolute exception to the other commodities—"as a commodity," Marx "identifies a paradox in which a class of the meta-level [capital] descends to the object level [commodity] ... to become a member of itself."[36] Both capital and (secular) consciousness are, therefore, self-referential.

---

from Plato to Heidegger, ed. Albert Hofstadter and Richard Kuhns (Chicago: University of Chicago Press, 1976), 376.

31 Ibid., 376.

32 Ibid., 376–7.

33 Jochen Schulte-Sasse, "General Introduction: Romanticism's Paradoxical Articulation of Desire," in *Theory as Practice: A Critical Anthology of Early German Romantic Writings*, ed. Jochen Schulte-Sasse et al. (Minneapolis: University of Minnesota Press, 1997), 21, 19.

34 Schulte-Sasse, "Romanticism's Paradoxical Articulation of Desire," 34.

35 Jacques Lacan, *The Four Fundamental Concepts of Psychoanalysis*, trans. Alan Sheridan, ed. Jacques-Alain Miller (New York: W. W. Norton, 1981), 59.

36 Kojin Karatani, *Architecture as Metaphor: Language, Number, Money*, ed. Michael

The logical consequence of the structuralist self-referentiality of cause and effect finds its expression in the last movement of the modern emergence of value, which postulates that any human product—intellectual, manual, and artistic—must have a self-referential relation to the rest of the world, as its immanent cause and effect. This relation is expressed in "performativity," as understood in speech-act theory as the function of language to perform the reality it describes, whereby reality is both the cause and effect of language, and vice versa. This performativity entails a radical indeterminability regarding both the direction between cause and effect and the purpose of whatever is performed. In this fourth movement of the modern emergence of value, the religious residue of the benevolence of Smith's "invisible hand" of the market is replaced by the radical indifference of our own unconscious (divine) "hand." Thus, fantasies of absolute control and of inhuman self-destruction become equally possible.

Undoubtedly, Nietzsche's re-evaluation of art in *The Birth of Tragedy* (1872) as a (Apollonian) defense against life's suffering relates to the anxiety underpinning the movement of performative self-referentiality; yet, the (Dionysian) "gospel of universal harmony," supposed to be compensated by art, was already a *fait accompli* and the very cause of modernist suffering.[37] The real defense is Nietzsche's own exhortation—to become (God or Übermensch)—for it gives the illusion that we are not yet it.

On the economic level, performative self-referentiality becomes manifest as financial capital. This is not real capital, but "nominal" or "signaling" or "productive" capital. The fact that it is required for its own production renders financial prognosis more uncertain than ever. The same uncertainty manifests itself in aesthetic theory, with Heidegger and Benjamin offering the first formulations of the dilemma facing the effect that knows that it is its own *arbitrary* cause.

Heidegger's grimace of the Greek middle voice, as in his *Der Ursprung des Kunstwerks* [*The Origin of the Work of Art*] (1936–7), in which "die Welt weltet [the world worlds]," expresses the fact that in "art"—i.e. the "setting-into-work of truth"—"world" or "truth is both the subject and the object of the setting," even as "subject and object are unsuitable names."[38] For at stake are not the agent and object of an

---

Speaks, trans. Sabu Kohso (Cambridge, MA: MIT Press, 1995), 69–70.
37 Friedrich Nietzsche, *The Birth of Tragedy and Other Writings*, ed. Raymond Geuss and Ronald Speirs, trans. Ronald Speirs (Cambridge: Cambridge University Press, 1999), 18.
38 Martin Heidegger, *The Origin of the Work of Art*, in *Aesthetics: A Comprehensive Anthology*, ed. Steven M. Cahn and Aaron Meskin (Oxford: Blackwell, 2008), 352, 357. Martin Heidegger, *Der Ursprung des Kunstwerks* (Stuttgart: Reclam, 1960), 41, 79–80.

action, but the cause and origin of truth or the world, the "primal" or "founding leap" (*Ursprung*) through which the world brings itself "into being out of the source of its nature."[39] Of course, if art is not "added to what is already there," and "we think of all this in reverse order," so that art "first gives to things their look and to men their outlook on themselves," then a slight inflection can introduce either fatalism—e.g., the "world is the ever-nonobjective to which we are subject"—or decisionism, whether revolutionary or authoritarian—e.g. Heidegger's call to take sides regarding the "either-or and its decision" between "art" as "origin" or "as a routine … phenomenon."[40]

Similarly, Benjamin argues in his "The Work of Art in the Age of Its Mechanical Reproducibility" (1936), because of the "thoroughgoing permeation of reality with mechanical equipment," technologically reproduced art "offers … an aspect of reality" that is structured according to "a new law" hitherto unnoticed, just as prior to the "Freudian theory" "a slip of the tongue passed … unnoticed."[41] Echoing Heidegger's rhetoric, we can say that, in expressing the unconscious laws of reality, art lets reality *be* reality. The undecidability of this performative self-referentiality between art and reality is reflected in Benjamin's essay in the "either-or" between a revolutionary art of "Communism" or an ideal tool for "Fascism," whose "imperialistic warfare" best realizes that "mass movements, including war, constitute a … human behavior which particularly favors mechanical equipment."[42]

Because performative self-referentiality regresses to such mirror-like reversals regarding the future, dialectics gained high currency in the Frankfurt School. Eventually, in Adorno's negative dialectic, as presented in his *Aesthetic Theory* (1970), "art is the social antithesis of society," and artworks "are after-images … of empirical life, inasmuch as they proffer to [it] what in the outside world is … denied them."[43] Like religion in Marx, "the moment of unreality … in art … is … an echo of the imperfections of real conditions, their constraints … and their potentialities"—just as "dreams" "of a better life … recall the negativity from which they were … extracted"—so that "what [artworks] say is literally true," presenting "the unresolved antagonisms of reality

---

39 Heidegger, *Origin*, 357. Heidegger, *Ursprung*, 80.
40 Heidegger, *Origin*, 352, 357. Heidegger, *Ursprung*, 40–1, 81.
41 Walter Benjamin, "The Work of Art in the Age of Mechanical Reproduction," in *Aesthetics: A Comprehensive Anthology*, ed. Steven M. Cahn and Aaron Meskin (Oxford: Blackwell, 2008), 335–6.
42 Ibid., 339, 343 n.31.
43 Theodor W. Adorno, *Aesthetic Theory*, ed. Gretel Adorno and Rolf Tiedemann, trans. C. Lenhardt (London: Routledge, 1984), 11, 6.

[as] immanent problems of artistic form."[44] Accordingly, the secular passion for contemplative "disinterestedness" vis-à-vis art indicates that "works of art ... evolve in a dialectic of interests and disinterestedness," and "underscores the ... posture of art's ... refusing to play the world game" which, since utilitarianism, is "brutal self-interest."[45]

If, however, Adorno turns to Kafka as an exemplary case of modernist literature, it is because by then art knows that the utilitarian myth is dead. In calling "forth ... responses of real anxiety" modernism "enabl[es] desire to survive in art," since any "psychic defense ... [has] more in common with desire than with ... Kantian disinterestedness."[46] Ever since, as postmodern art reconfirms, desire and interest are the true negative "after-image" of the capitalist mode of production. For, brainwashed by utilitarianism and individualism alike, we may imagine that we act according to our own interests and desires, but, as Hegel knew, we are actually pawns of the extant "Spirit of History," the accumulation of surplus-value. Still worse, according to performative self-referentiality, surplus-value is not a clear-cut external imposition on humanity, but a modulation, however distorted, of our own—mental, economic, and technological—unconscious.

SEE ALSO: Judgment; God is Dead; Truth

---

44 Ibid., 10, 17, 8.
45 Ibid., 17.
46 Ibid., 18.

Fourteen God is Dead
Silke-Maria Weineck

> Absolute beginnings make us speechless in the precise sense of the word.
> But this is what humans can bear the least.
>
> Hans Blumenberg

"God is dead" belongs to Nietzsche. To be sure, others—Hegel, Heine—have said so before him, but it was Nietzsche in whose voice the phrase gained its stark iconicity. Its ubiquity may well be unique—what other sentence from the history of philosophy has been scrawled on the giant billboards shadowing the highways of America?—but it remains, for that very reason as well as for more complicated ones, enigmatic. Its bearing on aesthetics has been mediated, via ethics and epistemology, and while it is one of those sentences that bear fruit in their most blatant misreadings, we should take some time to understand what it does *not* say.

The opposite of a good idea is a bad idea, to loosely paraphrase Niels Bohr,[1] but the opposite of a great idea will be another great idea. God was Bohr's prime example, for "there is a God" is just as great an idea as "there is no God." Both have been endlessly productive of different epistemologies, structures of experience, forms of human violence and of human creation, and in the end, after all the nuances had played out, such had been the choice before Nietzsche.

"God is dead," however, refuses this opposition; it is, so to speak, the opposite of either one. To atheism, God cannot have existed; to all the monotheisms that have mattered, including and particularly deism, he cannot die. This death, then, radically incompatible with occidental theism and atheism alike, marks more than a socio-historical process

---

1   Paul Dirac, "The Versatility of Niels Bohr," in S. Rozental, *Niels Bohr: His Life and Work as Seen by His Friends and Colleagues* (New York: John Wiley, 1967), 309.

of progressive, if fitful secularization, though it is often reduced to that. "Surely [Nietzsche] realized that it would be a category mistake to speak of the death of something which never existed," Eric von der Luft intones in exemplary misunderstanding, "thus, the distinction must be made between the death of God in itself and the death of God for us, or between God's own death and the death of our faith in God."[2] Well, no. This is precisely the distinction Nietzsche will *not* make, or rather the distinction that shatters under the hammer of his philosophy, though the shards, to be sure, continue to fly. It is high noon, and the ding-an-sich no longer casts its pale Königsbergian shadow.[3]

Before we can ponder the extent to which "God is dead" belongs to the "fundamental concepts of German aesthetics," then, we must consider whether it is a concept at all, or whether it rather troubles conceptuality at its core. Postulating the death of the immortal, it is in flagrant and gleeful violation of the principle of non-contradiction, "the premise of philosophy and the foundation of rational discourse,"[4] and to the extent that it changes what art is, it changes it in that liberating, fearful violation. Paradox is not merely a stylistic device here; it is program, a calculated assault on the center of Western philosophy. In the process, Nietzsche frees the image of the divine corpse from the heavy irony that weighed down Heinrich Heine's *On the History of Religion and Philosophy in Germany*, a text Nietzsche knew well, admired, and cannibalized freely for his own history. *Gay Science* 125—without a doubt the definitive text when it comes to Nietzsche's death of God—borrows the lantern, the stench, the cosmic imagery, even the trope of madness from Heine, but "Der tolle Mensch," usually though imprecisely translated "The Madman," barely has Kant, who was Heine's target, in its sights. It aims further back and deeper down.

In order to understand what is dying here, and perhaps also what is being born, we need to look more closely at the text that should not be reduced to that one flamboyant phrase. Its title may well be the right place to start, for "toll" does not mark generic madness: it is manic and aggressive, a synonym for "rabid" in its visceral, somatic sense; this man is mad like a mad dog is mad, hence dangerous. If there is a model for this mode of madness, though not its substance, it may be Ajax among the sheep, or Oedipus driving the pins of his wife's

---

2 Eric von der Luft, "Sources of Nietzsche's 'God is Dead!' and its Meaning for Heidegger," *Journal of the History of Ideas*, 45 (2) (April–June, 1984): 270.
3 Friedrich Nietzsche, *Sämtliche Werke: Kritische Studienausgabe* (= KSA), 15 vols, ed. Giorgio Colli and Mazzino Montinari (Berlin: de Gruyter, 1967–77). See *Götzendämmerung*: KSA 6:81.
4 Allan Bloom, *The Republic of Plato*, trans. Allan Bloom (New York: Basic Books, 1991), 457 n.25.

brooches into his eyes. This madman, in other words, is not simply a literary but a mythic figure, and as such acting at a particular but indeterminate and recurrent point in time. Hans Blumenberg, in his customary precision, notes that

> Nietzsche's affinity to myth emerges out of the fact that the norm of truth has become problematic for him. ... Nietzsche did not simply negate theology, he transformed it by giving god, instead of his attributes, *one* story the end of which is its punchline. He made use of the formal liberty of the mythologist and—this is the scandal of the paradox—transferred it to the Biblical god who, while he had entered *into* history [*Geschichte*], did not endure the form of stories [*Geschichten*].[5]

It is not in its fictional character—the category of fiction is much younger than that of myth—but in its formal freedom that myth precedes the "duty to truth" which anchors itself in the principle of non-contradiction.[6] Blumenberg is right to stress that the passage's formal—that is to say, aesthetic — qualities do far more than recuperate the possibilities of literature for purposes of philosophy—after all, Cartesian disavowals aside, philosophy had never lost touch with narrative and trope. Like many of Nietzsche's readers, however, Blumenberg tends to neglect the question of the speaker, who is not Nietzsche, the latter remaining much more of a philosopher of old than it may seem. Why is Nietzsche's messenger crazed? Why does he sound like one of those people who, pupils enlarged, buttonhole you in the park to tell you about their urgent insights into the nature of self, time, and other?

Here is the opening paragraph:

> Did you not hear of that crazed human being who lit a lantern during the bright morning hours, ran to the market place, and cried incessantly cried: 'I am searching for God! I am searching for God!' As many of those who did not believe in God were standing there together, he provoked great laughter. But did he get misplaced? said one. Did he get lost like a child? said another. Or is he hiding? Is he afraid of us? Has he boarded a ship? emigrated? —thus they yelled and laughed together.[7]

---

5 Hans Blumenberg, "Wirklichkeitsbegriff und Wirkungspotential des Mythos (1971)," *Aesthetische und Metaphorologische Schriften* (Frankfurt am Main: Suhrkamp, 2001), 352, my translation.
6 Ibid., 352.
7 Nietzsche, KSA, 3:480. All translations mine.

The man may be crazed, but it is the atheists who are stupid. Like many of Nietzsche's readers, they are convinced that it is a question of deliberate faith, that "not believing in God" will have erased God's existence while leaving their world otherwise intact. Atheism, however, is not the point here, the atheists are merely the uncomprehending bystanders of their own moment. After the madman's monologue, we hear no more of them than that they "stood silent and gazed upon him in estrangement [*befremdet*]."[8]

The atheists' estrangement, however, is above all an estrangement from themselves and their time, the time of the killing of God: "This monstrous event is still on its way and wandering—it has not yet reached the ears of humankind. Lightning and thunder take time, the light of the stars takes time, deeds take time even after they have been done in order to be seen and heard. This deed is still further from them than the furthest stars—and yet they committed it themselves."[9]

These sentences reveal that historical time, time of human deeds and human record, is merely one of Nietzsche's concerns, though he has often enough heaped contempt on all ahistorical philosophies. If nonetheless historical time can blend into cosmic time so easily here, it is precisely because the distinction between the two had been anchored theologically, and no longer holds. The death of God, then, is both a historical event—and as such, belongs to modernity and the last man—and something entirely different which throws light—though perhaps the invisible light of a lantern at noon—upon the nature of a reality that does not divide into in-itself and for-us. As such, it sweeps away a century of bad-faith materialism.

This distinction, however, had been so fundamental, so entirely crucial to human endeavor that the language of reason (which Nietzsche himself speaks even or particularly when he is most outrageous) cannot accommodate it. Nietzsche sends us a madman whose tones are distinctly religious in cadence, whose truth claims are grounded formally in the tradition of divine madness[10] because the death of God can only be articulated in the breach, as it were—for articulation itself, or the structure of representation, had still depended on the idea that signification could be anchored. This is true, narrowly, for all theological arguments that, from Aquinas to Descartes and beyond, had postulated the *adaequatio intellectus et rei*, a correspondence of mind and reality grounded in the divine. Kant's *Critique of Pure Reason* can justly be seen as finally dispensing with that tradition, at

---

8 Ibid., 3:480.
9 Ibid., 3:480.
10 Silke-Maria Weineck, *The Abyss Above. Philosophy and Poetic Madness in Plato, Hoelderlin and Nietzsche* (Albany: SUNY, 2002), 113ff.

least for the purposes of philosophy. It is also true, however, even if perhaps in less immediately obvious ways, for most modern thought that assumes it has freed itself from traditional metaphysical doctrine. Gotthold Ephraim Lessing's great dictum— "not all are free who mock their chains"— applies to all the bystanders who think it suffices not to believe in God to be free of him.

The immense threat and promise that hover over *Gay Science* 125 are articulated quite clearly in a chapter of the *Twilight of the Idols,* "How the True World Finally Became a Fable: History of an Error." True, here, it is not God but the idea of a "true world" generating the world of appearances that is at stake, but Heidegger, for once, is entirely correct in reading the death of metaphysics into Nietzsche's death of God (Heidegger, *passim*). In a tour de force, Nietzsche, not even pretending to do justice to his subjects, takes us through Plato ("the true world reachable for the wise"), Christianity ("unreachable for now, but promised ... 'to the sinner who repents'"), Kant ("unreachable, unprovable, unpromisable, but even as a thought a consolation, an obligation, an imperative"), positivism ("certainly unreached, and as unreached also unknown. hence neither consoling, redeeming, obligating"), and his own earlier work ("a useless, a superfluous idea, hence a refuted idea"). The turning point arrives at stage six: "We abolished the true world: which world remained? the apparent one perhaps? ... but no! along with the true world, we have abolished the apparent world as well." This is, we read, "the moment of the shortest shadow, the highest point of humanity," and the moment where Zarathustra enters.[11]

It is noon in the *Gay Science* as well, but it is either a different history, or, more plausibly, *Twilight* tells the history of what has remained a future. The end of the apparent world—i.e. the end of appearance as distinct from existence that underlies, *mutatis mutandis*, most models of representation—has not arrived, humanity has not reached its zenith, the meta-human (to avoid the hopelessly contaminated term Übermensch) is as far away as the furthest stars. This meta-human, whose modes of experience, cognition, and creation would be commensurate with the murder of God, simply cannot appear in the languages that are nothing but the sedimentation of the history of religious and metaphysical dualisms.

For now, then, God is not dead but rather undead, provided we hear in this term the uncanny simultaneity of contradictory meaning that so fascinated Freud when he wrote "Ueber den Gegensinn der Urworte" ("On the Antithetical Meaning of Primitive Words") in 1910. While most readers of *Gay Science* 125 focus on the crisis of morality and value

---

11 Nietzsche, KSA 6:81.

they see foreshadowed there, what dies with God is not the arbiter of good and evil but the postulate of this arbitration's ultimate singularity. As the history of the twentieth century has shown, substitutes for traded religious value systems are readily available, and nothing is sillier than to confuse the death of God with the rise of fascism, a system that, on Nietzsche's terms, was nothing if not rigidly and mendaciously metaphysical.

In general, God as transcendental signifier worked just as well, perhaps best, when it was empty, for beyond all determinate functions, God's work was to stop the buck, and in this regard, it is entirely irrelevant whether we call a structure's center by the name of God or by any other name—say, sexuality, science, politics, art, capital, or the human. In its rigorous paradoxical sense, the death of God remains unthinkable for all *logos*, as Derrida's classic essay on "Structure, Sign, and Play" elaborates, one of the most incisive engagements with Nietzsche's death of God.[12] Freud's solution—to acknowledge the end of negation but to relegate it to the unconscious so that we may continue to speak—may well have been the most brilliant strategy to date to both honor and forestall the event Nietzsche names, but in most regards, psychoanalysis, as well, remains blindly beholden to the undead god.

All of this is, in some regard, remarkably bad news for aesthetics to the extent that the term implies a notion of art as a privileged form of human activity, though this piece of news, too, will take its time to travel (it barely begins to arrive with Morris Weitz' essay "The Role of Theory in Aesthetics" which argued, in 1956, that aesthetics' "main contention that 'art' is amenable to real or any kind of true definition is false"[13]).

To be sure, in the 1870s, under the influence of Schopenhauer and Wagner, Nietzsche could still advocate art as the cure for metaphysics:

> The periphery of the circle of rational knowledge [*Wissenschaft*] consists of an infinity of points, and while it cannot yet be foreseen how that circle could ever be fully measured out, the noble and gifted human, before reaching the midpoint of his existence, will inevitably arrive at one of those liminal points where he will stare into that which cannot be illuminated. When here he sees, to his horror, how logic curls around itself at these borders and finally bites its own tail—then a new form of recognition breaks

---

12 Jacques Derrida, "Structure, Sign, and Play in the Discourse of the Human Sciences," in *Writing and Difference*, trans. Alan Bass (London: Routledge, 1978), 278–94.

13 Morris Weitz, "The Role of Theory in Aesthetics," *The Journal of Aesthetics and Art Criticism* 15 (1) (September 1956): 28.

through, *tragic recognition*, which, if it is to be endured, needs art as protection and curative.[14]

A decade later, when the *Gay Science* appears, however, Nietzsche has lost faith in the poets as well, though he will long remain associated with a stance he himself, in the postscript to *Birth*, had denounced as embarrassingly romantic.[15] Certainly, he continues to remain interested in the great restorative powers of un-truth, but his investments have shifted from the renewal of art to the reinvention of philosophy in a realm where the divide between mythos and logos will be yet another distinction to discard: "Why might not the world which concerns us be a fiction? And whoever then asks 'but does an author belong to the fiction?'—might he not be answered back with Why? Does not this 'belong' belong to the fiction?"[16]

If the death of God is bad news for aesthetics, it is, at least potentially, good news for art, even if it has lost, unbeknownst to most of its practitioners, the foundation to some of its more extravagant claims towards filling the vacuum which God's murder has created. Thematically, the death of God plays out in, say, the patricidal literature of German expressionism, or, far more ambivalently, in Kafka's work. It deeply informs the aesthetics of the Frankfurt School, particularly with regard to Adorno's articulation of negative dialectics (though Adorno keeps his distance from Nietzsche's stringent anti-dialectical screed), moves through French existentialism and echoes, though at times in strange distortions, through all emancipatory projects which ironically assume that Nietzsche's stark anti-foundationalism can anchor them theoretically.

While art has become just another manifestation of the will-to-power, ungrounded and ungrounding, Nietzsche's attack on the history of the West will prove fruitful formally as well. It would be quite silly to claim his proclamation as the defining force of developments that are surely overdetermined, but we may nonetheless think of a number of them in Nietzsche's terms. His praise of the surface, which is a direct corollary of his disdain for the metaphysics of profundity—"to stop courageously at the surface, the fold, the skin, to adore appearance, to believe in forms, tones, words"[17]—surely is at least deeply compatible with many of twentieth-century art's greatest formal experiments. More importantly, perhaps, the death of God marks the end of the ideal spectator—the human invention of God had also been the invention

---

14 Nietzsche, *Birth of Tragedy*, KSA 1:101.
15 Ibid., 1:21.
16 Nietzsche, *Beyond Good and Evil*, KSA 5:54.
17 Nietzsche, *Gay Science*, KSA 3:352.

of a god who invents humanity in turn and gazes upon its works. Art, then, can neither lay claim to essence—there is no more essence—nor can it address itself to the eternal—the immortal has died—and thus loses all unifying perspective twice over. All of this plays out in various, often wildly divergent ways, some of which are the subjects of essays to follow in this volume. But it is also worth noting that some of the most remarkable work will emerge out of opposition to Nietzsche's dictum. One must not agree with George Steiner's assertion that "remythologization in a time which has found secular agnosticism more or less unendurable may, in future, be seen as defining the spirit of the age"[18] to acknowledge that what Nietzsche contemptuously called "the *demand for certainty*, ... the *need* for faith"[19] produced not only some of the greatest atrocities of the twentieth century but some of its most astonishing achievements.

Not that this would have come as a surprise to Nietzsche, who, in Blumenberg's words, told "a story about this god of ongoing history."[20] Not only did his madman tell us that our history can always only be the history of the undead god; he himself enters the agora still in search of the very god he will declare dead.

SEE ALSO: End of Art; Value; Truth

---

18 George Steiner, *Real Presences* (Chicago: Chicago University Press 1989), 221.
19 Nietzsche, KSA 3:581-2.
20 Blumenberg, "Wirklichkeitsbegriff und Wirkungspotential des Mythos (1971)," 351.

Fifteen Tragedy / *Trauerspiel*
Ian Balfour

The idea and the tradition of tragedy cast a shadow over a good deal of the drama of the long twentieth century; yet it was all but impossible to write tragedies as such, or tragedies with a strong family resemblance to examples of the genre from any of its great periods and privileged locales: ancient Athens, Elizabethan and Jacobean England, or the golden ages of France and Spain with Racine and Calderón. Tragedy still had great critical and theoretical prestige in the twentieth century and remained a force for authors to reckon with even with the golden age of tragedy long since past. In the first part of the century Brecht distanced his work from especially the Aristotelian ethos and tradition, one that had established *Oedipus Tyrannos* as the model of a play that moved audiences and made perfect logical sense. On the several occasions when Brecht engaged tragedy most directly, in his rewritings of *Antigone*, *Coriolanus*, and Marlowe's *Edward II*, the originals are rendered far less tragic in their transformation. If the outlines of the plots remain largely the same, there is nonetheless a tendency to evacuate tragic pathos as well as to de-heroicize the heroes. One reads in *The Life of Galileo*: "Unhappy is the land that needs heroes."[1] Indeed, the focus on individual heroes was one of Shakespeare's (historical) shortcomings that had to be overcome, in Brecht's view outlined in "The Little Organon." Like Heiner Müller after him, Brecht would revise ancient and early modern tragedies to speak in such a way as to confront and affront his own time with the material of epochs no longer "actual," not least to force the present to understand itself as precariously historical. Not so much *plumpes Denken* (crude thinking) as *plumpes Schreiben*, crude writing.

In the second half of the century, Heiner Müller's relation to tragedy

---

1   Bertolt Brecht, *The Life of Galileo*, trans. John Willet (New York and London: Penguin, 2008), 95.

is at once extreme for the pervasiveness of tragedy traversing his work and yet not atypical of what becomes of tragedy when it is re-fashioned in a post-tragic world, far from either the metaphysical gloominess of a Schopenhauerian worldview or the remarkably upbeat tragedies (often with a "happy" or serene ending) of Goethe and Schiller. Müller repeatedly ransacked the corpus of canonical tragedies to translate, adapt, dissect, distill, and mutilate: from *Medea* to *Oedipus* to *Philoctetes* to any number of Shakespearean tragedies (*Macbeth, Titus Andronicus*). Müller's relation to tragedy shares the insouciance of Brecht: there is not the slightest reverence for masterpieces—he is close to Artaud in this—whose canonicity precedes them. Yet Müller takes tragedy far more seriously than Brecht, at least as an antagonist. He has, in his own terms, an "obsession" with Hamlet/*Hamlet* from his first encounter as a teenager onward.[2] His passion for the play included not only translating it but, in perhaps his most remarkable achievement, writing *Hamletmaschine*, a *reductio* almost *ad absurdum* of motifs and characters from the play, stitched together in disparate monologues with far-flung quotations from Mao to Marx to Hölderlin, with characters speaking not the lofty or ornate phrases typical of tragedy but the nitty-gritty idioms of everyday life. Müller's gesture was nothing if not Oedipal: he sought to "destroy" Hamlet/*Hamlet*.[3] If Müller thought tragedy was possible at all, it was in the mode of "proletarian" tragedy: the resistance to the older tragic forms was in part political. Müller transformed both the high canon of tragedy and Brecht's too moralizing fables in a post-tragic vein by stretching the limits of sense to their breaking points: resistance was in the first instance resistance to meaning. His plays, some of which might be called "screwball tragedies," reassemble motifs from tragedies without having them make tragic sense. When he reaches back to Sophocles he filters it partly through Hölderlin (as Brecht did), retaining bits of the poet's translation that defy, in their literality, German syntax and sense. Oedipus is no longer the paradigm he was, as Müller opines: "... in the century of Orestes and Electra that is upon us, Oedipus will seem a comedy."[4] That is perhaps because, for all their horrors, the plays bearing Oedipus' name issue not in his death but in survival a kind of surpassing knowledge beyond the mere senses (perhaps one reason for the philosopher Aristotle promoting it as the paradigm of the genre). All's well that ends well. Müller's encounters with tragedy stage historical interventions by reinventing earlier ones.

---

2   Heiner Müller, *Germania*, trans. Bernard and Caroline Schütze (New York: Semiotexte, 1990), 55.
3   Ibid., 55.
4   Heiner Müller, *A Heiner Müller Reader*, ed. and trans. Carl Weber (Baltimore, MD: Johns Hopkins University Press, 2001), 51.

He followed Carl Schmitt's *Hamlet oder Hecuba* essay in conceiving of tragedy as entailing "the intrusion of history into the play" (*"Einbruch der Zeit in das Spiel"*). If time was out of joint in *Hamlet* it was doubly so in *Hamletmaschine* and as in a good many other of Müller's radical translations.

If tragedy's afterlife was ambiguous in actual drama and theater, its life in theory and criticism was far more robust. Tragedy had never been simply one genre among others for philosophy, nor for "theory" broadly understood: it is the kind of literature that has most solicited philosophical attention from Plato's early fascination, given the writing and then burning of his tragedies, to Aristotle's promotion of it as the exemplary literary genre, to Hegel's folding in of tragic plots into the very substance of philosophical analyses of social dynamics. German philosophy, above all, took to the genre like no other, it being the key literary mode to think about and even *with* for Schelling, Schopenhauer, and others—a tradition whose specificity has been sketched in magisterial fashion by Peter Szondi.[5] Tragedy thrived too as a premiere object of philological attention, a discipline that flourished in Germany as nowhere else. If one were to look for philologically informed, sensible accounts of tragedy in the late nineteenth and early twentieth centuries, one might turn first to figures such as Ulrich von Wilamowitz-Moellendorff and Karl Reinhardt respectively.[6] Yet the two texts that seem most resonant and suggestive in the period, both poised midway between philosophy and philology, are Nietzsche's *The Birth of Tragedy from the Spirit of Music* (1872), a work that influenced even cultural production and thinking far beyond academia, and Walter Benjamin's *The Origin of German Tragic Drama* (1928), an extreme study of literary extremities.

When Nietzsche, a young professor of classical studies, turned to tragedy as the subject for his first book, he was hardly content to perform the protocols of the still emerging discipline of philology. *The Birth of Tragedy* could scarcely have been more provocative to the reigning classical philology, given its strict canons of evidence and its studiously distanced relation to its objects of study. Nietzsche was clearly bent on unsettling his scholarly readers, questioning the very project of *Wissenschaft* (organized knowledge, not just 'science') as well as his more popular audience (bourgeois, imagined to be complacent) not least with the repeated claim that the world could be "justified only

---

5   Peter Szondi, *Essay on the Tragic*, trans. Paul Fleming (Stanford, CA: Stanford University Press, 2002).
6   Ulrich von Wilamowitz-Moellendorff, *Einleitung in die griechische Tragödie* (Berlin: Weidmann, 1907). Karl Reinhardt, *Tradition und Geist. Gesammelte Essays zur Dichtung* (Göttingen: Vandenhoeck & Ruprecht, 1960).

as an aesthetic phenomenon,"[7] a slogan encapsulating his attempt to strip culture of its purported morality and to strip the discourse of morality, mainly of the Christian sort, of its pretensions. In retrospect, even Nietzsche would call it an "impossible" book[8] but without recanting its principal claims.

Nietzsche engages tragedy as something of existential import: its stakes are high and so are those in thinking about it. The ancient past, especially the Greek, and especially its art, as in Marx, is not over and done with. The examples of Schiller and Goethe, who did much to "revive" and rework Greek (or, more precisely, Athenian) tragedy, were still fresh in the minds of many German playgoers and readers. Moreover, Athenian tragedy was undergoing, according to Nietzsche, a belated reinvention, in the music dramas of Richard Wagner, whom Nietzsche had met as a budding classicist of twenty-four.

The Birth of Tragedy does not take the form of close or slow reading Nietzsche would elsewhere invoke as the great virtue of classical philology or that he would practice in his lectures and seminars on *The Libation-Bearers* around this time. It is a wide-ranging speculative work of cultural critique concerned to elucidate the grand driving forces behind tragedy, its skeletal structural features (chorus, satyr, actor, spectator, prologue, etc.), and its reception by the paradigmatic spectator, almost always with an eye to resonances to modern German and European culture in his own time. Nietzsche casts tragedy as the product of two powerful forces: the Apollonian is predicated on individuation, intelligibility, and the very principle of form; the Dionysian is a matter of primal, ecstatic, anarchic energy that annihilates the self or leaves it far behind. The energy of Nietzsche's text is drawn especially to the Dionsyian, to the ecstatic surpassing of the individual in touch with the primal will, even if a good many formulations stress the co-presence and intertwining of the Apollonian and Dionysian in tragedy, especially in those that take the form of theses, e.g. "Apollo could not live without Dionysus"[9] or "... we grasp, intuitively, the reciprocal necessity of these two things."[10] This balance varies, however, in practice and over time. If the Dionysian is at the origin of tragedy, it is, far more present in Aeschylus and Sophocles than in Euripides, despite Euripides being popularly known as author of *The Bacchae*, his last surviving play and arguably the most overtly Dionysian tragedy. Nietzsche argues for the presence of Dionysus in all

---

7   Friedrich Nietzsche, *The Birth of Tragedy and other Writings* (Cambridge: Cambridge University Press, 1999), 8.
8   Ibid., 5.
9   Ibid., 27.
10 Ibid., 26.

tragedies: Oedipus and Prometheus are versions of this originary god. The paradox is that when tragedy represents Dionysus most directly, in *The Bacchae*, the genre is betrayed, perhaps because Dionysus appears explicitly and in the mode of knowledge not wisdom. What Nietzsche diagnoses in Euripides as a bad tendency toward non-Dionysian knowledge is not based on thematic predilections of the last of the trio of great tragedians but something registered in sheer formal terms, especially in the prologue, which spells out the essentials in advance, and in the *deus ex machina* endings (not confined only to Euripides). Despite the title of the book announcing its being about the *birth* of tragedy, Nietzsche is equally worked up about its development and its endpoint in ancient Greek culture: the decline and fall of the genre in the hands of Euripides and his philosophical fellow traveler Socrates, for having made tragedy a too theoretical affair, too much a matter of knowledge—for which the debilitating motto is "Know Thyself." Euripidean tragedy also fatally took its distance from the chorus that was originally at its core as well as from a sense and performance of totality, the chorus being a version of and figure for a collectivity, a public not speaking in the mode of a subjective "I." (In an excursus on the lyric, inextricably bound up originally, with music, Nietzsche notes how there the "I" is only apparently subjective and contends that to be a subjective artist is not to be an artist at all.) The addition of one after another actor, even if wearing a mask with a fixed "expression," only propels the genre more precipitously toward individuation and the (Apollonian) dissolution of the genre that, from different vantage points, had seemed to be developing. Taken together these changes result in not only the death but in the "suicide" of tragedy.[11] It should be clear by now that Nietzsche is concerned to *judge* this and that tragedy, as well as this and that tragedian far more explicitly than is the norm in academic criticism, hardly resting content to be descriptive or to put things in dispassionate historical perspective.

Nietzsche's text often has the appearance of a history: birth, genesis, first this, then that, et cetera. The denouement is also a *telos*. At any number of points it sounds as if the debacle that is Euripidean drama, linked so closely to the philosophical Socrates, comes well after Sophocles and yet the lifetimes of Sophocles (c. 496–404 BCE) and Euripides (c. 480–406 BCE) overlap a great deal. Even though Sophocles began writing tragedies before Euripides, it is somewhat misleading to think of Euripides as decisively coming *after* Sophocles and thus as the "end" of tragedy. Yet this makes for a better story, or at least a story, even if Euripides' last play is the final nail in the coffin.

It is a complicated story, not least because of the complexity, indeed

---

11 Ibid., 54.

instability of the prime categories as unfolded in this exuberant text. *The Birth of Tragedy* starts out by seeming to want to track the interplay between the polar(ized) drives of the Apollonian and Dionysian. In general Nietzsche characterizes and even critiques the Apollonian as a mode of representation (over against the non-mimetic Dionysian) but the prized folk song is said to be a "musical mirror of the world"[12] and the even more highly valued chorus in proto-tragedy is glossed as "the self-mirroring of Dionysiac man."[13] That is to say, the Dionysian is characterized in terms usually associated with the Apollonian. Similarly, whereas the Apollonian often comes across as an affair of surfaces, to the extent that it is a structure of illusion, necessarily conceals a depth, a category that first seems linked to the Dionysian, except that the "deep" Dionysian tends to collapse distinctions of subject–object, inside and outside, and thus is more surface than depth.

This vertigo of even the most fundamental categories of *The Birth of Tragedy* extends to and has consequences for the very execution of the text. One would presume that the text wants to tell the truth about tragedy and many of its statements are in that mode but the text is at the same (or in alternating fashion) time a dithyrambic performance of a pronounced "I," hardly disguising its subjective, non-universal position based on something other than knowledge. The text attempts to perform what it in part states as a thesis, namely the irrelevance of the categories of subjective and objective when it comes to the aesthetic, the only domain in which the world can be justified. In its very writing, then, *The Birth of Tragedy out of the Spirit of Music* marks itself as a performance in keeping with the origins of tragedy and aligned with the music dramas of his older contemporary Richard Wagner, whose sublime, non-mimetic works operate at or beyond the limits of representation. (Nietzsche would later change his tune about Wagner, considering his operas the antithesis of ancient Greek culture.)

Benjamin welcomes a crucial aspect of Nietzsche's position in *The Birth of Tragedy*: its historicism in recognizing that tragedy is hardly a genre for all times and places, nor a recurrent, fundamental expression of the human condition. Indeed, tragedy had a finite beginning, middle, and end in ancient Greece, with some resurgences in later antiquity and modernity (Seneca, Shakespeare, Wagner). This Benjamin finds congenial in combating a loose humanism fixated on a universal that simply does not exist. On the other hand, Benjamin considers much of what was good in Nietzsche's first book vitiated by his wallowing in an "abyss of aestheticism,"[14] closing off an opening to the world that could

---

12 Ibid., 33.
13 Ibid., 42.
14 Walter Benjamin, *The Origin of German Tragic Drama*. trans. John Osborne

have been consistent with the *geschichts-philosophisch* (historico-philosophical) approach Benjamin advocates. It is partly in a Nietzschean spirit that Benjamin shows, and more in keeping with Rosenzweig than Schopenhauer, how little the baroque *Trauerspiele* have in common with Greek tragedies. If the word *Trauerspiel* starts out as a homegrown German term for "tragedy," in Benjamin's analysis it soon gains, or aspires to gain, a certain autonomy, naming a quite distinct literary phenomenon. What Benjamin calls, after the convention of the German dramatists themselves, *Trauerspiel* by no means applies to only this national-linguistic formation but rather constitutes a pervasive mode of baroque culture in Western Europe. Indeed, Benjamin considers Calderón and Shakespeare the great masters of the *Trauerspiel*, with *Hamlet* and its melancholic hero as paradigmatic of the genre. When Benjamin refers to Shakespeare's "tragedies"[15] he does so just like that, in scare quotes because the best term to characterize the genre is *Trauerspiel* not tragedy, a term that would mask the differences between the two modes. Shakespeare's publishers should have had a title-page saying *Hamlet*, a *Trauerspiel* in five acts (that the title pages of the quartos read *The Tragicall Historie* and not "Tragedy" is partly in keeping with Benjamin's point).

One mistakes the texture of the baroque *Trauerspiel*, according to Benjamin, if one construes it as an outgrowth of Renaissance tragedy (and more distantly of Greek antiquity). The baroque *Trauerspiel*, so marked by the Counter-Reformation and the post-Reformation more generally (and thus by a kind of resurrection of Christianity after the embrace of classical antiquity), in many respects vaulted back over the Renaissance to connect with medieval, Christian culture, as legible in the affinity between the passion plays and martyr dramas of the earlier period with the "mourning-play" (the literal sense of *Trauer-spiel*) of the later. The example of Shakespeare's *Richard III*, for example, points to the way the baroque *Trauerspiel* harks back to a medieval and Christian heritage (Richard as Satan, as Vice). The modern *Trauerspiel* has little of ancient tragedy's logic of sacrifice, not least because, in the bleak vision shared by the baroque dramatists, all of fallen nature is guilty from the start. The character of the "tragic hero" is also markedly different: the *Trauerspiel*, Benjamin contends, "knows neither heroes nor selves, but only constellations."[16]

Perhaps the most salient difference between ancient tragedy and modern *Trauerspiel* lies in the respective relations to and presentations of history. Tragedy, according to Benjamin, is based on

---

(London: Verso, 1977), 103.
15 Ibid., 228.
16 Ibid., 141.

materials of historical legend, indeed, of the order of myth, whereas *Trauerspiele* are far more given over to history. Historical life is, in so few words, "the content, the true object" of the *Trauerspiel*.[17] From some vantage points, it is an encompassing, even all-encompassing form: it engages cosmology (via more or less learned astrological discourse), the state, and kingdom (via the drama of sovereignty), and in it history is absorbed into and presented as "natural history."[18] The history on display in the *Trauerspiele*, which do *not* directly address German history or legend, tends to be circumscribed to the machinations of a few key figures such as the sovereign, the latter being the "representative of history. He holds the course of history in his hand like a scepter."[19] Yet Benjamin can also say, perhaps hyperbolically: "Baroque drama knows no other historical activity than the corrupt energy of schemers."[20] This sort of activity is concentrated in the "intriguer," though a sovereign such as Shakespeare's Richard III, given the plotting involved in usurpation and irregular succession widespread in Shakespeare, can embody both. These plots unfold in a world in which, Benjamin maintains, the "Baroque writer felt bound in every particular to the ideal of an absolutist constitution, as was upheld by the Church of both confessions." In such a politico-juridico setting, the state of exception theorized famously by Carl Schmitt (whom Benjamin cites and with whom he corresponded) takes on a special weight: the sovereign comes into his own, as it were, in the state of emergency, an extreme situation which lays bare the stakes and lines of power, the effective sovereignty of the sovereign.

The *Trauerspiel* tends not to take the shape of the well-written, dialectical plot of ancient Greek tragedy but rather something processional, loosely on the model of the sequences of the *trionofi*, whose logic is sometimes not much more compelling than that of one thing after another, indeed the piling up of one thing after another in a "rubbish heap,"[21] in the ongoing "catastrophe"[22] that is world history. This sequential performance of history, in the hands of these dramatists, becomes strangely repetitive, fixed, and static: "When, as is the case in the Trauerspiel, *history* becomes part of the setting, it does so as *script*."[23] The plays emphasize and draw attention to their writing or

---

17 Ibid., 62.
18 Ibid., 40, 120, inter alia.
19 Ibid., 65.
20 Ibid., 88.
21 Ibid., 139.
22 Ibid., 66.
23 Ibid., 177.

script through the violence of their gestures at every level of language: plot, word (archaisms, neologisms), and even letter (with the stark capitalization of nouns making everything potentially allegorical). The effect and force is summarized by Benjamin thus: "The language of the baroque is constantly convulsed by rebellion on the part of the elements which make it up."[24] Benjamin posits a homology between the order of language and history: "the desire for a vigorous style of language, which would make it seem equal to the violence of world-events."[25]

The texture of the *Trauerspiel* is also distinct from ancient tragedy to the extent that is pervaded by frameworks of allegory, which much of the baroque embraces as a privileged and almost as a default mode of presentation. Allegory, in Benjamin's influential account, is the mode of violent, arbitrary discourse best suited to the tendency of the *Trauerspiel* to mourning and death, subtended in performance by the stage prop and the material corpse, all of which serve as prods to contemplation in the hero (e.g. Hamlet) and occasion to something of the same in the onlooker/critic who needs to "pause for breath"[26] for critique to be possible, in the fulfillment of the work that Benjamin calls, strikingly, "mortification."[27] The rest is history.

SEE ALSO: Beauty; End of Art; Allegory; Nothingness

---

24 Ibid., 207.
25 Ibid., 55.
26 Ibid, 44.
27 Ibid., 182.

Sixteen Saying/Showing

Fabian Goppelsröder

Over the last decades the growing importance of perception and picture theory in German aesthetic discourses has brought new fame and importance to the concept of "Zeigen" (showing). Relegated to the eye and the senses, "showing" previously played a rather inconspicuous role in the Western philosophical tradition. Just a series of footnotes to Plato, as Alfred North Whitehead would have it, philosophy apparently valued the reflective functions of reason more than the sensual abilities of the body. Its concern was the eternal, immaterial realm of thought, not the historical, material world of things. Its domain was precise concepts, not vague sensuous impressions. The physiological perception apparatus was dominated by a rhetoric of the inner eye, able to see the ideal form behind its imperfect material appearance; vision turned into "theoria," the Greek word for beholding the eternal divine, and from there developed into the modern notion of theory. Even Alexander Gottlieb Baumgarten's 1750 *Aesthetica* did not really change this trend. His attempt to draw attention to the senses as a kind of lower cognitive faculty, allowing for genuine and, in its own way, perfect knowledge was quickly absorbed by a discourse on aesthetic judgment instead of aesthetic cognition. Similarly, the *Gefühlsästhetik* (aesthetics of emotion) of *Sturm und Drang* was replaced by classical formal aesthetics and Hegel's "sensual appearance of the idea," which privileged content over material expression.

Thus, "showing" remained no more than a subordinate of reason. "Showing" could illustrate abstract data; it was able to turn complex thought into something palpable and thus popular; but popularity also meant a loss of accuracy. Like Plato, who called a picture an imperfect copy of the idea, "showing" in general fell prey to philosophy's logocentrism, its apotheosis of reason.

The technological and sociological change over the last hundred years, however, has led to a revaluation of the visual.[1] The philosophical debate about showing belongs intimately to these developments. Toward the end of the nineteenth century the mass printing press first made graphs, drawings, and sketches a natural, ubiquitous part of popular culture. Catchy images complemented and even outdid the written word. In order to keep the print runs high, not only the message itself, but also equally if not more importantly its appearance had to pique people's curiosity. Photography and new ways of technical reproduction further pushed this trend. Since the 1950s new media such as television have proliferated images into the ordinary person's living room. Today they permeate virtually all areas of human culture. They move smoothly back and forth between private and public, and transgress national borders and natural barriers. Digitalization has made it easy to take pictures and to circulate them. Almost instantaneously they can make their way from one end of the world to the other. What previously took days, weeks, or months is now a matter of fractions of seconds.

More specifically, pictures have also gained new importance within the sciences. The computational possibilities allow for numerical descriptions of the world, boosting the complexity of the traditional mechanistic model. Complex networks no longer simply represent, but instead rebuild reality on the basis of non-linear mathematics. This attempt to approximate reality not as one line of history but with all its inherent uncertainties ends in a flood of data, which the human brain is no longer able to process, at least all at once; a mediation between humans and computer is needed. Climate research, medicine, and biology need imaging techniques to produce visual interfaces that allow the researcher to access and to interpret his or her data. Network models, computer tomography, or scanning probe microscopy are just some of the most notable examples. While breaking up phenomena into binary code seems to be the last step to fully detaching the epistemic process from the senses, it actually ends up being the contrary: digitalization has inundated the sciences with pictures.[2]

All this undoubtedly strengthens the cultural importance of the visual—and at the same time makes the otherwise supposedly

---

1   See: Hans Belting, ed., *Bildfragen: Die Bildwissenschaften im Aufbruch* (Munich: Fink, 2007); Horst Bredekamp, "Bildwissenschaft," in *Metzler Lexikon Kunstwissenschaft* (Stuttgart: Metzler, 2003); Gottfried Boehm, "Bildsinn und Sinnesorgane," in *Neue Hefte für Philosophie* 18/19 (1980): 118–32; Boehm, ed., *Was ist ein Bild?* (Munich: Fink, 1995); Boehm, *Wie Bilder Sinn Erzeugen. Die Macht des Zeigens* (Berlin University Press, 2007).

2   See Fabian Goppelsröder and Nora Molkenthin, "Mathematik/Geometrie", in *Bild. Ein interdisziplinäres Handbuch*, ed. Stephan Günzel and Dieter Mersch (Stuttgart/Weimar: J. B. Metzler, 2014).

self-evident nature of a "picture" more precarious.³ The painted canvas in a wooden frame is no longer the standard. The traditional format seems to almost dissolve between film, computer screen, or digital snapshots, or between performances, tableaux vivants, or media installations. Moreover, even the ontological status of a "picture" is changing. Similarity with the picture object as defining criterion for what counts as picture has become problematic. If the picture is no longer a direct projection from the original but a (re-)construction based on binary code, the principal arbitrariness and pragmatic (cultural) relativity of the choice of colors, format, size, or shape are undeniable. Instead of being a representation of something absent, visual interfaces have become the gateway through which we access reality and as such are constitutive of our understanding of the world.

The intrusive omnipresence of the image in digital culture eventually also demands a philosophical re-evaluation of the visual. This is the context within which the recent debate has to be seen. It emerged as a critique of the academic discipline that seems to naturally claim expertise concerning the picture: art history. Taking "the painting" as just another object of historical study, however, fails to perceive the complexity of the actual quest for the nature of the "picture" as such. Yet also neither the proliferation of formats nor its peculiar role as some kind of Heideggerian "existential" category that harnesses the organization patterns of a human's world captures "picture" any longer. Following thinkers like Aby Warburg or Max Imdahl, scholars such as Horst Bredekamp, Gottfried Boehm, and Hans Belting have thus claimed a new form of *Bildwissenschaften*, or picture sciences, to replace the art historical approach, in order to cover the broad cultural and epistemic relevance of the picture. Belting's 1983 book *Das Ende der Kunstgeschichte?* poses as a question what he claims some ten years later as a fact: namely, the end of art history. Beyond this criticism of a specific academic discipline, however, the picture sciences from the beginning have been a decidedly interdisciplinary movement. Philosophy, literary criticism, and cultural studies, but also non-humanist disciplines such as the neuro- and computer-sciences, physics, and mathematics, are on board, an approach that almost naturally shows a tendency to transgress the narrow borders of national academies. And yet, despite links to similar research around the globe—for example, the discussion between Gottfried Boehm and W. J. T Mitchell in Chicago as documented in Elkins' *What is an image?*—the debate has gained a particular intensity and importance in Europe. Institutionally it has led to a whole series of research clusters and scholarly networks pushing the agenda of *Bildwissenschaften* inside and outside the established

---

3 For example, see Boehm, *Was ist ein Bild?*

university infrastructure. The *eikones* institute in Basel or the Berlin graduate schools, and their studies in "Schriftbildlichkeit" ("Notational Iconicity") and "Sichtbarkeit und Sichtbarmachung. Hybride Formen des Bildwissens" ("Visuality and Visualization. Hybrid Forms of Pictorial Knowledge") are recent examples.

The geographical centers of interest in the topic seem to be linked to movements and trends in continental philosophy in the twentieth century. The traditional disdain for the body was at least called into question by a new thinking that was skeptical of the undisputed rule of the intellect. Anthropological and sociological research has brought the cultural relativity of human judgment to the fore. Instead of pure reason socially trained, sensuous perception conditions the intellectual evaluation of the world. In a different way, existentialism's rejection of the opposition of subject and object in favor of humans' condition as always already thrown into the world forces a new valuation of the body. Phenomenology too, particularly in Maurice Merleau-Ponty's French variation, decries the insufficiency of an exclusively rational worldview.

Martin Heidegger is an important source and inspiration for both of these philosophical strands. In his own playfully etymological appropriation of the Western philosophical tradition, Heidegger emphasizes the distinction between the "apophansis" (saying) and the verb "apophainestai" (showing or manifesting itself). In his reflection on the phenomenological method—§7 of *Sein und Zeit*—he defines phenomenology as "apophainestai ta phainomena" and translates this as "to let what shows itself be seen from itself, just as it shows itself from itself." Thus Heidegger philosophically draws on the particularity of the German concept of *Zeigen*, the many facets of which the English term "showing" only partially translates. It can mean to present or to point at something; and it can also mean to demonstrate or perform and thus to show oneself and through showing oneself accentuate something else. But there is also the completely self-referential allusion of *sich Zeigen*, which translates best as "to manifest itself." Heidegger takes this dimension of *sich Zeigen* as the experience of something coming toward us, something that remains unrecognized as long as we stay within a technical, referential relation to the world. What manifests itself cannot be shown and cannot be said. It makes the specific richness of the experience of otherness. In this sense Heidegger's phenomenological reflection informs the thought of ethicists like Emmanuel Levinas, but also of thinkers like Bernhard Waldenfels, who conceptualizes our experience of *das Fremde* (the foreign) as the self-manifestation of what the human intellect cannot categorize or control.

Thus the complexity of the German term *Zeigen* makes it a good fit for grasping the anthropological and epistemic importance of the visual field. Conceptually *Zeigen* sponsors the attempt to modify the traditional epistemological paradigm. Cognition is no longer thought to be immaterial and mind-based, but a genuinely sensual process.[4]

The title of Gottfried Boehm's 2007 book *Wie Bilder Sinn erzeugen: Die Macht des Zeigens* (*How Pictures Make Sense: the Power of Showing*) succinctly points to the stakes of the debate. Not only language, but also pictures engender meaning—they "make sense." There is a genuine visual layer in human understanding, a layer irreducible to *logos*. This peculiar power cannot be understood by referring to the artifact itself. It is something that pictures do, an effect of their dynamic presence.[5]

The philosophical roots of the concept of showing lead back to a philosopher whose impact on our understanding of the visual is yet to be developed: Ludwig Wittgenstein. Known often as merely a philosopher of language, the unconventionality of his succinct wording and creative, even playful phrasing has made him a favored reference within the so-called pictorial sciences. But despite the many quotes and allusions, the real potential Wittgenstein's thinking holds for the concerns of the pictorial discourses has hardly been tapped.[6]

In his *Tractatus Logico-Philosophicus* Wittgenstein introduces the distinction between "Sagen und Zeigen," saying (sometimes also translated as telling) and showing. Though readers' typical impressions seem to be that Wittgenstein privileges "saying," he in fact does not renew the claim of language's superiority over the senses. His distinction anchors itself elsewhere: the core of Wittgenstein's language philosophy is made of a picture theory. Wittgenstein's anthropological presupposition is his understanding of a human as a picture producing being. In 2.1 of the *Tractatus* Wittgenstein claims: "We picture facts to ourselves."[7] The notion of representation supporting this basic claim, however, is everything but ordinary. It constitutes a crucial part of the peculiar understanding of language that buoys the entirety of the *Tractatus*. Here, picturing is not based on similarities, but on structural

---

4   See Fabian Goppelsröder and Martin Beck, *Präsentifizieren. Zeigen zwischen Körper, Bild und Sprache* (Berlin/Zürich: diaphanes, 2014); Dieter Mersch, *Was sich zeigt. Materialität, Präsenz, Ereignis* (Munich: Fink, 2002); Dieter Mersch, *Epistemologien des Ästhetischen* (Berlin/Zürich: diaphanes, 2015).
5   See Emmanuel Alloa, *Das durchscheinende Bild. Konturen einer medialen Phänomenologie* (Berlin-Zürich: diaphanes, 2011). As a position contesting the idea of the pictures themselves being active agents and yet emphasizing the importance of showing as part of man's practice of communication, see Lambert Wiesing, *Sehen lassen—Die Praxis des Zeigens* (Berlin: Suhrkamp, 2013).
6   See Fabian Goppelsröder, *Zwischen Sagen und Zeigen. Wittgensteins Weg von der literarischen zur dichtenden Philosophie* (Bielefeld: transcript, 2007).
7   Ludwig Wittgenstein, *Tractatus Logico-Philosophicus* (London: Routledge, 2001), 9.

identity: the picture, or image, does not resemble the pictured; it shares the same logical structure.

One of the critical results of this foundational claim is that, although the *Tractatus* may appear to be merely a treatise about the sentence, it turns out to be a manifesto for a new philosophy. Wittgenstein writes:

> 1. The world is all that is the case. 1.1 The world is the totality of facts, not of things … 1.13 The facts in logical space are the world … 2. What is the case—a fact—is the existence of states of affairs. 2.01 A state of affairs (a state of things) is a combination of objects (things).[8]

The dogmatic-apodictic style of these first lines makes unmistakably clear that there is more at stake than just the discussion of a logical or semantic problem. Veiled in exact numbering and an attitude of neutral objectivity, the *Tractatus* begins with a redefinition of the world: not physical existence, but, instead, logical form is decisive. The world is no accumulation of independent things, and is not built of atoms. Its basic unit is the fact, the "state of affairs," that which is the case. Its basic unit is thus a constellation, a configuration of things.[9] This configuration, however, has (and is) a logical structure. The states of things, which are the world, are "facts in logical space."

Point 2.1 should be understood within this context: "We picture facts to ourselves." The picture is a picture because "its elements are related to one another in a determinate way."[10] It becomes what it is because the configuration of its parts is identical to the configuration of the pictured fact. Thus, "pictorial form is the possibility that things are related to one another in the same way like the elements of the picture."[11] Only if such structural identity applies is it possible to speak of a picture at all: "What any picture, of whatever form, must have in common with reality, in order to depict it—correctly or incorrectly—in any way at all, is logical form, i.e. the form of reality."[12] However, this means that the picture as just a configuration in logical space has the same ontological value as what it depicts. Or, as Wittgenstein phrases it: "A picture is a fact."

Wittgenstein's concept of a picture is thus symmetrical and reflexive. In traditional, normative picture theories it is assumed that, for instance, a map actually pictures the landscape it purports to reflect and control.

---

8   Ibid., 5.
9   Ibid., 8, point 2.0272.
10 Ibid., 8, point 2.14.
11 Ibid., 10, point 2.151.
12 Ibid., 11, point 2.18.

Based on structural identity, as in Wittgenstein, the picturing relation could also be the other way around. The consequences are crucial. If points 3 and 4 determine thought as picture and, in turn, this picture as a meaningful sentence, halfway through the *Tractatus* a structural identity of world, picture, thought, and sentence is established. The difference between picture and language—that is, the gap between mind and world—has collapsed.

This also affects the distinction between saying and showing. Point 4.1212 of the *Tractatus* states: "What can be shown cannot be said."[13] But if showing is what pictures do and the meaningful sentence is defined as a picture of facts, how can saying and showing be particularly distinct? In fact, the seemingly simple distinction gains unexpected complexity, and showing becomes the central concept of the *Tractatus*.

The meaningful sentence says something because it pictures a fact and, thus, "propositions show what they say."[14] Logical sentences, however, do not describe a configuration within logical space but rather perform its limits (such as in a contradiction or tautology). They do not picture a fact but manifest the condition of meaningful sentences. They are senseless but transcendental.[15]

A third kind of showing becomes important toward the end of the *Tractatus*. It is neither meaningful nor senseless: "There are, indeed, things that cannot be put into words. They make themselves manifest. They are what is mystical."[16] Here Wittgenstein claims a dimension of experience beyond the factual world—the experience of something that eludes and manifests itself. It does not show a recognizable pattern, a logical configuration, but indicates the moment of insight into the world's facticity, into its "that." It is not a focused view, but an undirected gaze. Wittgenstein calls it, "feeling the world as a limited whole."[17] Thus the tractarian concept of showing implies not only a revaluation of the senses for philosophical epistemology; equally, it altogether refuses the traditional hierarchy between intellectual and sensuous capacities.

The symmetrical and reflexive correlation between picture and the pictured leads to a pragmatic understanding of the image. It does not primarily depend on the intrinsic qualities of the artifact, but becomes what it is in relation to the vantage point of the person who, through it, relates to the world. Within Wittgenstein's later philosophy of language game(s), this aspect of context-sensitivity will gain even

---

13 Ibid., 31.
14 Ibid., 41, point 4.461.
15 Ibid., 78, point 6.13.
16 Ibid., 89, point 6.522.
17 Ibid., 88, point 6.45.

greater importance. But, already in the *Tractatus*, Wittgenstein poses the overcoming of the ontological hierarchy between picture and the pictured. That way also the distinction between saying and showing does not deepen the gap between abstract conceptuality and concrete perception, but has to be understood as a distinction inherent to visuality itself. Parallel to Roland Barthes' notions of "studium" and "punctum," one could speak with Wittgenstein of the saying- and the showing-itself dimension of a picture. If the former is the unambiguously identifiable structure of the canvas, the latter is the irritation, the *je ne sais quoi* of aesthetic experience that will never be put into words or succumb to the rules of logic.

Artists such as Joseph Kosuth and Bruce Naumann, Robert Rauschenberg, or Jochen Gerz were influenced by this philosophy. The play between transparency and opacity, between saying and showing in their artwork, reflects an examination of Wittgenstein's thought. Art critics like Michael Fried base their valuation of photography as an important modern art form at least in part on the ideas and observations found in Wittgenstein's writings. These reflections on the different modes of language equally touch the poetic core of writers such as Peter Handke and Ingeborg Bachmann.

All this makes Wittgenstein's *Zeigen* not just an interesting concept within a specific philosophy. In fact, it is capable of covering the crucial consequences inherent to visual thinking. Wittgenstein himself was a visual thinker. The more than 1,300 sketches and graphics in his posthumous estate are an unambiguous sign—but this is hardly the point. The point in visual thinking is not to shorten abstract thought through diagrams and illustrations, but the assumption that thinking generally works other than traditionally suggested. Instead of transforming sensuous impressions into abstract data that can then be processed as such, visual thinking stands for the idea of sensuously concrete thinking. It is directed against the successful but artificial reduction of complexity through rational disambiguation. From his earliest work Wittgenstein's thinking was directed against such a reduction. Not in order to play off Wittgenstein against the discourse of *Bildwissenschaften*, but so as to support both in their full philosophical relevance, Wittgenstein's showing must be further investigated to ascertain whether and how far it is actually able to bridge the still existing gap between advocates of the respective so-called linguistic and iconic turns, or simply the static between philosophies of language and art theory.

In 1980 Gottfried Boehm demanded a revision of the traditional understanding of the picture.[18] The focus on the picture as merely a

---

18 Boehm, "Bildsinn und Sinnesorgane," 120.

copy of reality neglects the other, genuinely aesthetic dimension of *deixis*, the "showing-itself." This "showing-itself" Boehm describes as a particular form of knowledge that cannot be retranslated into the linear linguistic structure. Depending on logical means of identification language is unable to cope with the picture's flowing complexity.[19] Boehm contrasts iconic dynamic density with the static distinction of language and thus highlights a difference that, as previously shown, had become secondary in Wittgenstein's thinking. But if it is the picture as copy that prefigures an inauthentic aesthetic insight, that stops "the flow of sensible experience ... in the firm outline of the *Eidos* or Concept,"[20] then the medial differentiation cannot be definite.

The ongoing debate about *Zeigen* as an aesthetic and epistemological concept should have as its goal to finally end the traditional fight between body and intellect, between *aisthesis* and reason. The epistemic value of the picture, the "visual *logos*," must become the paradigm for a new analysis of humans' organization and understanding of their world.[21] Dieter Mersch calls this "visual *logos*" a non-non-classical logic. It is neither the same nor the opposite of classical logic. It is something new: knowledge that remains sensuous, that includes the shades and nuances otherwise suspended by the law of the excluded middle (*tertium non datur*).[22] The ambiguity of sensuous impressions that traditional philosophy has often attempted to erase may now turn productive.

---

19 Boehm, *Wie Bilder Sinn Erzeugen. Die Macht des Zeigens*, 206.
20 Boehm, "Bildsinn und Sinnesorgane," 118, my translation.
21 See Dieter Mersch and Martina Heßler, eds, *Logik des Bildlichen. Zur Kritik der ikonischen Vernunft* (Bielefeld: transcript, 2010).
22 See Mersch, *Epistemologien des Ästhetischen*.

Seventeen Nothingness
Kenneth Haynes

Alongside the traditional philosophical and religious understandings of nothingness, such as logical negation, ontological absence, personal annihilation, or apophatic theology, the nineteenth century developed two more: the nihilism that was feared to be intrinsic to reason in its modern form and an influential misunderstanding of Buddhism as the embrace of nothingness. These new versions of nothingness are marked by the distinctive use of a new vocabulary, in particular the terms "nihilism" and "nirvana," and they can be given at least rough dates.

In an open letter to Fichte in 1799, Jacobi accuses him (and by implication Kant) of "nihilism," investing the term with all the animus previously conveyed by charges such as "atheism" and "Spinozism" and using it to create a powerful image of Enlightenment philosophy as all-destroying, a depiction that would culminate in Hegel's depiction of the Enlightenment as terror. Jacobi was not the first to accuse critical philosophy of harboring "nihilism" within it,[1] but he popularized it in the controversy with Fichte and helped establish it as a major obstacle which subsequent philosophers would have to overcome. It radicalized old anxieties about the destructive power of criticism and thereby motivated a new function for art, that of the *Bildung* of a citizenry. However, nihilism, with its apparent threat not only to philosophy but to all Western institutions, outlasted the solutions attempted by idealism. It would become a recurrent theme throughout Nietzsche's work and later was the object of Heidegger's protracted scrutiny of both Nietzsche and modernity, and in both thinkers it lay near the center of their aesthetics.

The term "nirvana" appears in Kant's lectures on geography, briefly but richly in Schopenhauer's *World as Will and Representation*

---

1 Frederick C. Beiser, *German Idealism: The Struggle against Subjectivism, 1781–1801* (Cambridge, MA: Harvard University Press, 2002), 643.

(1818), and in Hegel's lectures on philosophy and on the philosophy of religion throughout the 1820s. Hegel's misapprehension that the religion of the Orient equates God and nothingness was certainly not new: in eighteenth-century Europe, the Buddha had frequently been depicted as a secret atheist who deceptively preached exoteric superstitions (his alleged death-bed confession was often recounted), and a number of writers, including Bayle and Diderot, imagined that "oriental religion" was another name for Spinozism.[2] In addition, however, Hegel eventually assimilates it within his own philosophical system and interprets it as a philosophical problem, so that it ceases to be a destructive nothingness that stands in a simple opposition to being. In *The Science of Logic* (1812–16, rev. 1832), he writes that pure being and pure nothing are the same, insofar as they are both indeterminate, and that in the dialectical process of unity (that is, in becoming) the path to the absolute is cleared. Although in *The Science of Logic* Hegel identifies "Buddhist Nirvana" with un-dialectical unconsciousness and annihilation, in the 1827 lectures he finds the religion philosophically richer in its grasp of God as nothing, if still insufficiently dialectical.[3] Schelling offers the main alternative to Hegel's formulation of being and nothing. In *Ages of the World* (written c. 1815), in the lectures posthumously published as *The Philosophy of Mythology* (1856), and elsewhere he revives the ancient metaphysical, and with Böhme theosophical, distinction between two kinds of nothingness, *ouk einai* and *mê einai*: nothing at all and a potentially productive non-being that is also the ground of being.[4] That nothingness can be potentially productive is developed within idealist aesthetics as evidence for the freedom of the art work and as a hint to what may lie antecedent to the subject–object division.

The new problematic of nothingness—foregrounding the radical destructiveness of the will to reason on the one hand and the potentially productive non-being on the other—is most fully developed for aesthetics in a philosophical tradition running from Schopenhauer through Nietzsche to Heidegger. The three read eclectically and sometimes deeply in Asian religion and philosophy, finding there a theory or practice of nothingness that seemed to offer an alternative to

---

2   Urs App, *The Birth of Orientalism* (Philadelphia: University of Pennsylvania Press, 2010).
3   Roger-Pol Droit, *The Cult of Nothingness: The Philosophers and the Buddha*, trans. David Streight and Pamela Vohnson (Chapel Hill: University of North Carolina Press, 2003).
4   On Hegel, see Urs App, "The Tibet of the Philosophers: Kant, Hegel, and Schopenhauer," in Monica Esposito, ed., *Images of Tibet in the 19th and 20th centuries*, Vol. 1 (Paris: EFEO, 2008), 5–60. On Schelling, see Jean W. Sedlar, *India in the Mind of Germany* (Washington, DC: University Press of America, 1982).

Western metaphysics; they were each concerned with the threat posed by the nihilism that seemed to lurk behind assertions of the will (and sometimes within the suspension of will); and they each believed, at least in some moments, that the philosophical investigation of nothingness or will-lessness, especially as experienced or revealed in certain kinds of aesthetic experience, could properly illuminate possibilities for salvation.

Schopenhauer first published *The World as Will and Representation* in 1818. He aimed to correct Kant's account of the thing-in-itself, replacing it with a description of the metaphysics of will, to which we have access both through our representation of phenomena and through our inner experience of ourselves as willing. Unfortunately, the will, the world itself, is an evil: first, since willing as such stems from suffering and since no satisfaction of the will can compensate for the suffering and silence the will; second, because in suffering we will ("disinterestedly") the suffering of others; and third because in pangs of conscience we cannot evade the knowledge, notwithstanding its corruption by the will, that tormentor and tormented are the same and that our individuation is a delusion hiding our nothingness from us.[5]

The solution is to abolish the will. The "complete self-effacement and denial of the will" is the only thing that "stills and silences for ever the craving of the will;" it "alone gives that contentment that cannot again be disturbed."[6] To deny the will is to abolish the world, a goal which Schopenhauer carefully sets out in the work: the volume culminates in a final chapter on the nothingness that is arrived at when the will has been denied through saintly ascetic practice (a state that is transiently anticipated in the aesthetic experience). Once we recognize "incurable suffering and endless misery as essential to the phenomenon of the will, to the world," and then once we see "the world melt away with the abolished will and retain before us only empty nothingness," we can replace the will with knowledge. We hesitate to do this because we fear nothingness "as children fear darkness," but this is a mistake, and Schopenhauer exhorts us in the last words of his book:

> We must not even evade it, as the Indians do, by myths and meaningless words, such as *reabsorption* [*Resorption*] in *Brahman*, or the *Nirvana* of the Buddhists. On the contrary, we freely acknowledge that what remains after the complete abolition of the will is, for all who are still full of the will, assuredly nothing. But also conversely, to those in whom the will has turned and

---

5 Arthur Schopenhauer, *The World as Will and Representation*, 2 vols, trans. E. F. J. Paynes (New York: Dover Press, 1969), I:363–7.
6 Ibid., 362.

denied itself, this very real world of ours with all its suns and galaxies, is—nothing.⁷

In his conclusion, Schopenhauer contrasts several responses to nothingness: the frightened aversion of the willful to what appears to them only as "empty nothingness,"⁸ the evasions of Hindus and Buddhists on the topic, and the experience of "ecstasy, rapture, illumination, union with God, and so on"⁹ available to those who have completely denied the will and to whom, in consequence, it is the world of the willful, not its negation, that is truly nothing. This last state, however, moves beyond the remit of philosophy, as it moves beyond knowledge and communicability, and so it cannot form part of his investigation, which must limit itself to relative nothingness and can express itself only negatively as the denial of the will.¹⁰

"Nihilism," the misery of the Western experience of will, is implicitly present in Schopenhauer's account of nothingness, and the "Nirvana" of ascetic Hindus and Buddhists is explicit there.¹¹ In 1844 the second volume of *The World as Will and Representation* appears, consisting of four supplements to the four chapters of the first volume. In it he concedes preeminence to Buddhism and takes pleasure in finding his doctrine "in such close agreement with a religion that the majority of men on earth hold as their own." At the same time, he insists on the independence of philosophy from religion, and on the specific independence of his thought in 1818 from Buddhism, when "there were to be found in Europe only a very few accounts of Buddhism, and these extremely incomplete and inadequate."¹² Yet he does not change the wording of his conclusion from 1818, which refers to the Hindu term "brahman" and the Buddhist "nirvana" indifferently as "myths and meaningless words" which evade nothingness (the distinction between Hinduism and Buddhism was not always drawn by Westerners at that time or before). However, toward the end of his life he adds a comment in his working copy of the volume, finding the "nothingness" with which it concludes to be the same as the prajñā pāramitā of the Buddhists, "the 'beyond all knowledge,' in other words, the point where subject and object no longer exist." The comment first appears in print (as a footnote keyed to the last word of the text) in the fourth,

---

7   Ibid., 411–12.
8   Ibid., 409.
9   Ibid., 410.
10 See Julian Young, *Schopenhauer* (Abindgon: Routledge, 2005).
11 On the latter, see especially Droit, *The Cult of Nothingness*, 91–103, and Urs App, *Schopenhauer's Compass* (Rorschach: UniversityMedia, 2014).
12 Schopenhauer, *The World as Will*, 169.

posthumous edition of 1873. The result, for most subsequent readers, has been a strangely incoherent conclusion, in which two evidently irreconcilable descriptions of Buddhism are juxtaposed, one taking it to be delusion and the other a way to attain a subject-less and object-less knowledge beyond the will.[13] It is clear, nonetheless, that he is aspiring in his philosophy to the latter.

This goal—salvation in which the will is denied, and subject and object no longer exist—is anticipated in aesthetic experience. Art delivers us, blissfully but momentarily, from the "fierce pressure of the will"; aesthetic pleasure in the beautiful raises us "for the moment above all willing," rids us of ourselves.[14] In aesthetic experience, we no longer perceive an object in the ordinary way with reference to the will, by considering "the where, the when, the why, and the whither in things, but simply and solely the *what*." This results not only in raising ourselves to the "*pure*, will-less, painless, timeless *subject of knowledge.*" At the same time that we as subjects are transformed, so too is the object of aesthetic experience, which becomes the "*Idea* of its species." In the idea, subject and object, knower and known, can no longer be distinguished; the subject exists only as mirror of the object.[15]

In addition to negating distinct subject- and object-identities and canceling the will-driven *principium individuationis*, the experience of nothingness in art takes on occasion more intensive forms. In tragedy, the highest art apart from music (which, uniquely among the arts, copies the will itself and is independent of the phenomenal world), we experience not only the beautiful but also the sublime, "in fact, the highest degree of this feeling."[16] In the sublime, the peculiar double nature of consciousness is highlighted most distinctively. In the dynamically sublime (Schopenhauer adopts Kant's terms), the subject feels himself at once "a vanishing nothing in the face of stupendous forces" and "the eternal, serene subject of knowing"; in the mathematically sublime, we "feel ourselves reduced to nothing," but "against such a ghost of our own nothingness" we have the immediate consciousness that what is so reducing us exists "only in our representation, only as modifications of the eternal subject of pure knowing."[17] Negation is experienced differently in the beautiful and the sublime, but both

---

13 App, however, interprets Schopenhauer's reference to the "meaningless words" of the Indians in a positive sense. See Urs App, "The Tibet of the Philosophers: Kant, Hegel, and Schopenhauer," 57.
14 Schopenhauer, *The World as Will*, 390.
15 Ibid., 178–80.
16 Schopenhauer, *The World as Will*, II:169.
17 Schopenhauer, *The World as Will*, I: 205–6.

provide a glimpse into the more enduring salvation achieved through ascetic practices or philosophical knowledge.

Nietzsche's distinction of the Apolline and Dionysian impulses in art innovates upon Schopenhauer's several contrasts between will and representation, music and the other arts, and the beautiful and sublime. He expounds the contrasting types in his first major work, *The Birth of Tragedy* (1872; rev. 1886). Apolline art provides the illusion by which "great and sublime forms" delight us in their individuality; it gratifies our sense of beauty and permits us to "comprehend in thought the core of life contained within them."[18] It tears us out of the "orgiastic self-destruction" of the Dionysian, although the latter is the "true idea of the world."[19] At its greatest, that is, in Greek tragedy, it does not merely distance tragic spectators from the Dionysian; rather, it overcomes them "by that certain foreknowledge of a supreme delight reached by a path through destruction and negation, so that the spectator believes he is hearing the innermost abyss of things speaking audibly to him."[20] In this way, Greek tragedy temporarily synthesizes Apolline illusion and Dionysian music, enabling the spectators not only to share the "utter delight in semblance" but also, simultaneously, to negate this pleasure by finding "a yet higher satisfaction in the destruction of the visible world of semblance."[21] The Greeks devised, for a short time, an art form that not only recognized tragic reality but also enabled them to bear it triumphantly. The synthesis was not stable, and it died, by suicide, with Euripides, through whom Socratic rationalism defeated Dionysian myth.

Nietzsche's analysis is not oriented toward understanding antiquity but in using it to face the crisis of the present. Socrates' "determination to destroy myth" led directly to the "abstract man" of the present, formed by an "abstract education, abstract morality, abstract law, the abstract state"; to the culture of the present, "which has no secure and sacred place of origin," and which is "condemned to exhaust every possibility" as it ransacks the past and other cultures for legitimation; and to "dissatisfied modern culture," with its "feverish and uncanny agitation."[22] In the absence of the Greek tragic synthesis, two historical trajectories are available. One moves in the direction of "Indian Buddhism," characterized by its longing for nothingness borne

---

18 Friedrich Nietzsche, *The Birth of Tragedy and Other Writings*, ed. Raymond Geuss and Ronald Speirs, trans. Ronald Speirs (Cambridge: Cambridge University Press, 1999), 102.
19 Ibid., 103.
20 Ibid., 100.
21 Ibid., 112.
22 Ibid., 108–9.

(if at all) by rare ecstatic states and philosophical attempts to overcome the "indescribable apathy" in the intervals between those states; the other is the extreme worldliness of Roman *imperium*, grand, terrifying, coarse, and enduring.[23] Attic tragedy gave an alternative to these destinies, but it was short-lived; nonetheless, Nietzsche believed in 1872, the solution it once offered could be recreated through Wagner's music of the future.

The Apolline impulse, as delighted illusion, is in tension with truth, and as triumphant deification of everything that exists, whether "good or evil,"[24] it conflicts with moral judgment. The Dionysian, as embracing ugliness and disharmony, challenges aesthetic delight,[25] and in its "longing to deny the will as the Buddhist does" it risks negating life.[26] Finally, the Socratic lust for knowledge and happiness[27] keeps the Apolline and the Dionysian from joining in a mutually-remedying union and so leads to the nihilism of the present. Nietzsche's position changes drastically by the time of *Human, All-Too-Human* (1878–80) in which, having outgrown metaphysics, our needs are better met by science than by art; and it changes again with subsequent works. The relationship among life, art, and truth is scrutinized anew in the major works, where with great subtlety Nietzsche examines the hidden springs of nihilism, decadence, and pessimism in our acts of valuation and knowledge. His diagnoses are diverse, and his term "nihilism" protean, encompassing among other phenomena pessimism, Platonism, Christianity, Romanticism, and Schopenhauer's philosophy, as well as Indian thought and Buddhism.[28] His prescriptions are correspondingly diverse: at different moments, art is to save or protect us from nihilism by satisfying a loving superficiality, or by exemplifying self-fatedness, or by exciting or overexciting the desire for life. One of his most succinct formulations came in 1888, "We have *art* so that we do not die of *truth*": truth is the negation of life, but art is the negation of truth, or at least insulation or a prophylactic against it.

Retrospectively, Nietzsche was turned into the philosopher of nihilism, especially with *The Will to Power* (1901, rev. 1906), a posthumous selection and ordering from his notebooks in which the problem is foregrounded (it begins, "Nihilism is at the door: where

---

23 Ibid., 99.
24 Ibid., 22.
25 Ibid., 113.
26 Ibid., 40.
27 Ibid., 86.
28 On the latter, see: Mervyn Sprung, "Nietzsche's trans-European eye," in Graham Parkes, ed., *Nietzsche and Asian Thought* (Chicago: University of Chicago Press, 1991), 76–90; and Robert G. Morrison, *Nietzsche and Buddhism: A Study in Nihilism and Ironic Affinities* (Oxford: Oxford University Press, 1997).

does this uncanniest of guests come from?"). With the First World War, nihilism was seen as the defining problem of modernity. It was studied as such early on by Max Scheler and then, with the crises leading to the Second World War, by Karl Jaspers, Karl Löwith, and others. The most extended meditation is by Martin Heidegger, who lectured and wrote intensively on Nietzsche and nihilism from the 1930s until just after the war; prior to this, Heidegger had studied nihilism in relation to modernity in the *Introduction to Metaphysics* (1935). He presented the first systematic elaboration of the problem of nothingness in his inaugural lecture at Freiburg, "What is Metaphysics?" (1929), which introduces the claim, made notorious by Carnap, that "The nothing itself nihilates" (the neologism "nichtet" has also been translated as "noths" and "nothings"). Here, as in a few other cases, Heidegger uses strange and apparently tautological syntax in order to bypass traditional misunderstandings: "nothing" is not to be understood as an entity, or as negation, or as annihilation. It is not the nothing which must appear empty to scientific questioning; rather, it enables a fundamental questioning of metaphysics. By the 1930s, Heidegger had identified the forgetting of such questions as the modern condition of nihilism.

After *Being and Time* (1927), the character of Heidegger's writing increasingly deviated from that of conventional philosophical discourse, in both style and formulation. The energetic use of neologism, etymologizing, word-play, poetic quotation, and strained syntax was to create distance from the propositions of Western metaphysics, which he came to understand as the history of an ever-increasing forgetfulness of being, culminating in the nihilism of the present. He sought out alternatives to this nihilism, above all through his vision of archaic Greece, uniquely free from the domination of metaphysics. He also paid close attention to Daoism and Zen Buddhism—his dialogue with several Japanese thinkers began in the 1920s, he read Zhuangzi in Buber's edition in 1930, and in 1946 he collaborated on an aborted translation of Laozi—and found there an analogous alternative to Western metaphysics, where the sameness of being and nothing could be affirmed.[29]

Being and nothing belong together as the simultaneous disclosing and concealing which Heidegger understands as the nature of truth. Truth, moreover, "can happen as art, or even must so happen."[30] In

---

29 The extent of Heidegger's indebtedness to Asia is discussed in Reinhard May, *Heidegger's Hidden Sources: East Asian Influences on His Work*, trans. Graham Parkes (London: Routledge, 1996); and Lin Ma, *Heidegger on East–West Dialogue: Anticipating the Event* (London: Routledge, 2008).
30 Heidegger, Martin. *Off the Beaten Track*, ed. and trans. Julian Young and Kenneth

"The Origin of the Work of Art," he calls the two aspects of truth "world" and "earth." The art work sets up a world where "world" is not a "collection of the things ... that are present at hand," nor the "imaginary framework" of our representation of the things. It is not an object that we can create, or which we confront as an object. Rather, "*world worlds*";[31] it is "the self-opening openness of the broad paths of simple and essential decisions in the destiny of a historical people."[32] But there is another aspect to truth. In the art work the world sets itself back into earth and allows earth to come forth into the open.[33] Earth is essentially self-secluding and escapes attempts at controlling, structuring, or willing it; it "shows itself only when it remains undisclosed and unexplained."[34] ("Earth," in this usage, is close to the productive sense of nothingness.) In setting forth the earth, in letting the earth be an earth, the art work allows the world to appear as consecrated, divine. The two essential characteristics of setting up a world and setting forth the earth belong together in the being of the art work.[35] In this way art is the happening of truth.

In the essay, Heidegger develops Nietzsche's distinction between Apolline and Dionysian into a contrast between disclosed, articulate, and grasped form and an unwilled, nonconceptual yet authoritative area beyond intelligibility.[36] Although he will change his vocabulary in later essays (replacing "earth" with a number of other terms), and although he will alter major features of his own account—eschewing, in particular, the role of primordial strife in the happening of truth; conceding that the art work does not necessarily set up a world as binding historical community; and developing the will-lesssness of *Gelassenheit*[37]—the double essence of truth as disclosure and concealment remains fundamental to his thinking.

Aesthetic theory in Schopenhauer, Nietzsche, and Heidegger shares a number of features: an insistence that the art work is not to be finally understood from within an autonomous aesthetic domain but instead has a salvific relation to life; a strong orientalizing tendency whereby the state of will-lessness, potentially to be experienced in art, is understood to characterize the Asian world in contrast to the Western experience of power; and a meditation on nothingness, conducted

---

Haynes (Cambridge: Cambridge University Press, 2002), 33.
31 Ibid., 23.
32 Ibid., 26.
33 Ibid., 24.
34 Ibid., 25.
35 Ibid., 26.
36 Julian Young, *Heidegger's Philosophy of Art* (Cambridge: Cambridge University Press, 2001), 40.
37 See Young, *Heidegger's Philosophy of Art*.

especially through contrasting pairs (will and representation, Apolline and Dionysian, world and earth) that are exemplary within, or even constitutive of, the work of art.

SEE ALSO: God is Dead; Truth

Eighteen Messianism
Peter Fenves

Wilhelm Traugott Krug, who assumed Kant's chair in philosophy after marrying the former fiancée of Heinrich von Kleist, places the following definition in his *Allgemeines Handwörterbuch der philosophischen Wissenschaften*:

> Messianism is an idea that stems from Judaism and was transferred to Christianity. *Messiah* (*moshiach*, from *moshah*, 'he has anointed') and *Christ* (*christos*, from *chrein*, 'anoint') originally meant the same thing: the anointed one, hence the king. The Christians believed that they found in their Christ what the Jews expected in their messiah—a savior from all kinds of evil, with no precise differences among physical, moral, and political evil. Both Jews and Christians embellished their idea of a redeemer with aid of the imagination.[1]

Krug's dismissive remarks on messianism are remarkable only because they appear in a "universal lexicon of the philosophical sciences." Earlier German philosophers often discussed topics such as the Jewish concept of the messiah and the notion of Jesus as savior but only rarely mentioned messianism, understood as a mode of theory and practice oriented toward a redemptive moment in which history or even time itself comes to an end. Krug probably included messianism in his lexicon so that he could describe the phenomenon of "philosophical messianism," which occurs whenever the disciples of a philosopher— he explicitly refers to Saint-Simonism and implicitly to G. W. F. Hegel and Friedrich Schelling, whom he elsewhere attacks—are convinced that their master "teaches the purest truth and thereby secures the

---

[1] Wilhelm Traugott Krug, *Allgemeines Handwörterbuch der philosophischen Wissenschaften*, 5 vols (Leipzig: Brockhaus, 1838), 5:29.

salvation of humanity."[2] As a loose disciple of Kant, who famously asserted that Enlightenment consists in the "exit from self-imposed tutelage,"[3] Krug warns his readers of the danger that philosophical messianism poses to the scientific status of the discipline.

It is ironic that the first positive use of the term *messianism* in the German philosophical tradition can be found in the work of Hermann Cohen, founder of the Marburg school of neo-Kantianism, who grounds his system of philosophy in "the fact of science."[4] An influential figure in German Judaism from the 1880s until his death in 1918, Cohen first discusses messianism in a small treatise written in defense of the Jewish citizens of Marburg: "The thought that 'God loves the foreigner' connects the thought with which Judaism begins, that of election, with the thought with which the vocation of Judaism concludes, that of the messianic unity of humanity."[5] As the repeated use of the word *thought* suggests, Cohen's messianism is a function of his idealism, which represents thinking as the sole source of knowledge and the only adjudicator of action. The "messianic unity of mankind" cannot be located in space or time but is, instead, the ever-receding goal of world history, an ethical *telos* that corresponds to the "infinite task" of the empirical sciences. Unlike most major terms in Western philosophy, which derive from Greek or Latin, *messianism* comes from Hebrew and attests, in Cohen's view, to the ethical idealism that propels the development of the Jewish religion. In *Ethik des reinen Willens* and then again in various writings on religion and politics, including his pamphlets in support of Germany during the First World War, Cohen discusses the essential characteristic of messianism, which Greek and Roman ethics, for their part, consistently neglect: care for the poor. The "messianic unity of humanity" thus expresses itself as progress toward the ideal condition of universal socialism. Furthermore, as Cohen claims in the conclusion to his posthumously published *Religion der Vernunft aus der Quelle des Judentums*, "the unity of human consciousness is expressed by the peace of the soul," and because the messiah relieves the soul of its divisiveness, he is called "the prince of peace."[6] The transcendental unity of consciousness and the final unification of humanity are correlated ideas, both of which contain the promise of eternal peace.

---

2   Ibid., 5:29.
3   Immanuel Kant, *Gesammelte Schriften*, hrsg. Königlich-Preußische [später, Deutsche] Akademie der Wissenschaften zu Berlin, 27 vols to date (Berlin: Reimer; later, de Gruyter, 1900–), 8:35.
4   Hermann Cohen, *Ethik des reinen Willens* (Berlin: Cassirer, 1904), 9.
5   Hermann Cohen, *Die Nächstenliebe im Talmud* (Marburg: Elwert, 1888), 8.
6   Hermann Cohen, *Religion der Vernunft aus den Quellen des Judentums* (Leipzig: Fock, 1919), 447.

Cohen's promotion of messianism thus combines his devotion to Judaism with his loyalty to Kant, whose critical project culminates in the 1795 treatise entitled *Zum ewigen Frieden*,[7] often translated "Perpetual Peace" but more accurately rendered by "Toward Eternal Peace." Kant may have sensed that *Zum ewigen Frieden* veers in the direction of a certain messianism, for he wrote a series of contemporaneous polemics against millenarian and mystagogic tendencies, including "Das Ende aller Dinge"[8] and "Von einem neuerdings erhobenen vornehmen Ton in der Philosophie."[9] Nevertheless, Kant could not suppress the tantalizing suggestion that his *Critiques* contain something like a messianic promise, and some of his boldest readers in the late 1790s saw him as "the Moses of our nation."[10] Although he never reached the Promised Land, he shows the way to the Germans. For Hölderlin and his friends, including Hegel and Schelling, the most promising of the *Critiques* is doubtless the last, namely the *Kritik der Urteilskraft*, which brings together the analysis of beauty and sublimity with an inquiry into the legitimacy of teleological judgment. Schelling concludes his treatise of 1800, *System des transzendentalen Idealismus*, by presenting the work of art as the revelation of the mystery of the world. Whereas the subject necessarily distinguishes between itself and its object, the work of art unconsciously unifies subjectivity and nature, thus concluding "the history of self-consciousness."[11] Schelling's system cannot be called an aesthetic messianism, however, for it ultimately adopts a cyclical view of history, such that the final revelation of art becomes the starting point of another era, whereupon the "odyssey of spirit"[12] begins anew. Similar patterns can be found in many of his contemporaries, including Hölderlin, Kleist, and the founders of early German romanticism (Friedrich Schelling and Friedrich Hardenberg), all of whom combine messianic motifs with cyclical theories of history. Hegel, for his part, does not conclude his own system of philosophy with the revelatory character of art but, on the contrary, claims that the completion of his system, in conjunction with the establishment of the modern bourgeois state, marks the conclusion of the world-historical process and demonstrates, in turn, that works of art can no longer satisfy "the highest need of spirit."[13]

---

7 Kant, *Gesammelte Schriften*, 8:343–60.
8 Ibid., 8:327–39.
9 Ibid., 389–406.
10 Friedrich Hölderlin, *Sämtliche Werke*, ed. Friedrich Beißner, 6 vols (Stuttgart: Kohlhammer, 1943–85), 6:304.
11 Friedrich Schelling, *Ausgewählte Schriften*, ed. Manfred Frank, 7 vols (Frankfurt am Main: Suhrkamp, 1985), 1:702.
12 Ibid., 1:696.
13 Georg Wilhelm Friedrich Hegel, *Werke.*, ed. Eva Moldenhauer und Karl Markus

Cohen develops his version of philosophical messianism in explicit opposition to theories of history akin to Hegel's. Although Cohen is also a strong proponent of the modern state, he does not locate the end of history with its emergence, much less with the publication of his philosophical system; rather, history comes to its end only when the world is entirely free of injustice. Cohen thus draws on one version of the Jewish messianic tradition, according to which the arrival of messiah is the culmination of a process that has been prepared from the first day of creation. According to an alternate version of the same tradition, the messiah can arrive at any moment. Not only is this arrival not the culmination of an historical process; it interrupts every such process, thus bringing history to an end. The end (*eschaton* in Greek) has nothing to do with a putative goal (*telos* in Greek). Struck by the devastation of the First World War, which discredited idealistic theories of historical progress, a number of sophisticated students of Kantian critique and German idealism aligned themselves with the alternate strain of the Jewish messianic tradition. By insisting on an insuperable distinction between eschatology and teleology, they developed programs of critical thought that escape a range of disjunctive formulations. Messianic critique dispels dogmas of rationalism and positivism but does not therefore dispose of reason and replace it with vitalist or voluntarist irrationalism. While rejecting the claim of historical progress, the program likewise denounces its ideological inversion, which glorifies a mythical past and justifies reactionary politics. And even as messianic critique disregards any version of Marxism that claims insight into the scientific laws of historical development, it finds common ground with proponents of the Marxist tradition who see in revolutionary situations the possibility for a counter-history—or something other than history as it has hitherto been understood.

Whereas Kant's *Kritik der Urteilskraft* brings together aesthetics and teleology, messianic critique keeps the two apart. As Kant emphasizes and Schelling reiterates, the creation of artworks is distinguished from the production of utensils because only the former transcend the goals that guide their creation. By conceiving of this transcendence in terms of the genius, who "gives the rule to art" by virtue of a "natural endowment,"[14] the *Kritik der Urteilskraft* binds its discussion of the artwork with its subsequent inquiry into "natural purposes." Kant's conception of genius not only fostered the emergence of both German romanticism and German idealism; it also played a central role in Cohen's aesthetics. Perhaps nothing is more characteristic of the critical mode of messianism that emerged in the early years of the

---

Michel, 20 vols (Frankfurt am Main: Suhrkamp, 1971), 13:42.
14 Kant, *Gesammelte Schriften*, 5:307.

twentieth century than its elimination of "genius" from the field of aesthetic discourse and its tentative replacement by terms associated with redemption. Instead being primarily defined in relation to its "genial" origin, the work of art is seen as the cipher of a future that is as far removed from the sphere of established culture as it is from that of organic nature. And the task of the critic consists in discovering the lineaments of this "eternal" future and in thus releasing its messianic potential.

Among the earliest and most prolific proponents of critical messianism is Ernst Bloch, beginning with his 1918 manifesto *Geist der Utopie*. Declaring that "everything in us is already somehow prepared in Kant,"[15] Bloch freely draws on the *Critiques* for much of his Expressionist-styled study, and he specifically adopts Kantian terminology in its dramatically entitled conclusion, "Karl Marx, Death, and the Apocalypse": "the soul, the messiah, the apocalypse are the *a priori* of all politics and culture."[16] Bloch's *a priori* corresponds to the tripartite moment of relation in Kant's table of categories: the soul is the substance of politics and culture; in the event of the apocalypse, as both revelation and destruction, there is political-cultural community; and the messiah is the nexus of "psychic" interaction. In the absence of messianic hope, which facilitates relations among souls, regardless of their social roles, there can be no community. Such is the case, for Bloch, not only with mechanistic systems like Newton's but also with vitalist worldviews like Bergson's. *Geist der Utopie* begins with a description of an outmoded utensil, specifically an old jug, which can be seen as a symbol of the authentic work of art once it is viewed from the perspective of messianic hope: not only does the jug bear the traces of its fragile history on its surface; its depth is formed by an emptiness that silently calls for fulfillment.

Around the time Bloch published *Gesit der Utopie* Franz Rosenzweig arrived at the intuition underlying his 1921 treatise *Der Stern der Erlösung*. Just as Judaism is symbolized by an eternal star, so Christianity can be seen as its world-historical radiance. The category of redemption, emphasized by the title of Rosenzweig's *magnum opus*, acquires its full range of significance only in the context of two other, equally primordial categories: creation and revelation. All three categories are relational modes in which one of the three elements of being—God, the world, the human being—is bound with another element: the world is created by God, who reveals himself to human beings, who are called upon to redeem the world. By presenting redemption as a human–world

---

15 Ernst Bloch, *Geist der Utopie. Faksimile der Ausgabe von 1918* (Frankfurt am Main: Suhrkamp, 1985), 271.
16 Ibid., 433.

relation, Rosenzweig shows how messianism can acquire a dangerous dynamism. When redemption is divorced from revelation, on the one hand, and the created world is seen as mere matter, on the other, messianism assumes the form of expansionist nationalism, which invests certain peoples with the mission of redeeming humanity at large. This disastrous form of secularization can be averted only if messianism is kept apart from all world-historical processes. And this is what Judaism does: "the eternal life of the eternal people must always remain foreign and irksome to world history."[17] In contrast to Christianity, which gains historical concretion by filling in the time between the Incarnation and the Second Coming, the Jewish people abide by an unchanging calendar that doubtless repeats itself year by year but does so only in the liturgical context of reliving creation and revelation, thus breaking with the cosmic cycles that Rosenzweig associates with the "pagan" proto-world. The Christian counterpart to the Jewish calendar is not so much its own liturgy as its arts—but not the "fine arts" of secular culture, understood along Kantian lines as the objects of disinterested pleasure or along Hegelian lines as objective formations of world-historical spirit. Christianity establishes a counterpart to the Jewish liturgy in the craftwork of cathedral architecture, church music, and popular performance (*Volksspiel*): "Only when works emerge from the magic circle of their ideal space and enter into an actual space, only then will they be fully actual and stop being merely art."[18]

Instead of following Cohen and locating the systematic place of messianism within the sphere of ethics and politics, Rosenzweig lays it into the foundation of his epistemology. According to the "messianic theory of knowledge"[19] with which *Der Stern der Erlösung* concludes, truth does not consist in the correspondence between thought and reality or in the identity of subject and object but, rather, in the event of *Bewährung*. In legal contexts this term signifies "probation" or "suspended sentence," but the verb, *bewähren*, strongly associated with the word "true" (*wahr*), means "to prove its worth" or "to verify by means of severe testing." In a summary description of his epistemology, Rosenzweig emphasizes that the "verification" of truths beyond those of the mathematical sciences not only does not converge onto a single, highest Truth; for human beings, there are always only higher truths,

---

17 Franz Rosenzweig, *Der Stern der Erlösung* (Frankfurt am Main: Suhrkamp, 1988), 371.
18 Ibid., 394.
19 Franz Rosenzweig, *Der Mensch und sein Welt. Gesammelte Schriften III. Zweistromland: Kleinere Schriften zu Glauben und Denken*, ed. Reinhold und Annemarie Meyer (Dordrecht: Nijhoff, 1984), 159.

one of which is accessible in the form of Jewish messianic hope, the other by way of Christian faith:

> From the most unimportant truths of the type '2 × 2 = 4,' to which people easily agree, ... the way leads through truths for which human beings are willing to pay, to those they can verify [*bewähren*] in no other other way than through the sacrifice of their lives, and finally to those truths that can be verified only by risking the life of all generations. This messianic theory of knowledge, which ranks truths according to the price of their verification and the bond that they institute, cannot lead beyond two irreconcilable expectations of the messiah: the expectation of the one to come and the expectation of the returning one.[20]

The most influential and arguably the most consequential version of critical messianism can be found in the work of Walter Benjamin. From his earliest essays—including ones published before *Geist der Utopie* and *Der Stern der Erlösung*—to his very last writings, Benjamin sketches concepts of history that reject theories of progress without fostering fantasies of regression or promoting doctrines of cyclical return. The opening remarks to his 1915 essay "Das Leben der Studenten" are paradigmatic in this regard:

> There is a conception of history that, confident in the infinitude of time, distinguishes only the tempo ... with which human beings and epochs advance along the path of progress. This accords with the incoherence, lack precision, and laxity of demand such a conception imposes on the present. The following meditation, by contrast, concerns a particular state [*Zustand*] in which history rests concentrated as a focal-combustive point [*Brennpunkt*], which it has been in the images of thinkers from time immemorial. The elements of the final state [*Endzustand*] do not appear as formless progressive tendencies but are deeply embedded into every present moment as the most endangered, scandalous, and ridiculed creations and thoughts. The historical task consists in purely forming this immanent state of perfection, making it visible and dominant in the present. This state cannot be circumscribed with pragmatic descriptions of details ... but can be grasped only in its metaphysical structure, like the messianic kingdom or the French-revolutionary idea.[21]

---

20 Ibid., 159.
21 Walter Benjamin, *Gesammelte Schriften*, ed. Rolf Tiedemann and Hermann Schweppenhäuser, 7 vols (Frankfurt am Main: Suhrkamp, 1972–91), 2:75.

The "historical task" does not therefore consist in working toward a goal prescribed by either reason or a particular tradition; rather, the task is already solved in those "creations and thoughts"—in other words, artworks and speculative adventures—where history is already completed in the form of images that are at once concentrated ("focal") and explosive ("combustive"). The task of the critic thus lies in identifying and describing these focal-combustive images of history at its end.

It may be an exaggeration to say that all of Benjamin's subsequent writings follow the program of research thus articulated in 1915; but he remains loyal to its underlying impulse. Instead of seeing history as either a teleological process or a senseless series of accretions, the thinker *cum* critic looks for literary, philosophical, and cultural artifacts that may appear retrograde or recalcitrant but harbor a certain order of redemptive elements. One of Benjamin's major works of criticism is therefore an analysis of the German baroque *Trauerspiel* (mourning play), which is generally seen as deficient in comparison to its Western European counterparts; another is a massive study of the world associated with the outdated arcades of Paris. When, by contrast, he analyzes a consummate work of art—as is the case with his study of Goethe's novel *Wahlverwandtschaften*—he represents critique as the destruction of beautiful appearance and the concomitant disclosure of an unfinished "torso," which gestures toward a state of perfection transcending the sphere of art.

Just as Rosenzweig finds a systematic place for messianism in epistemology rather than ethics, so Benjamin rejects political versions of messianism, and in a short text of uncertain date he claims that the primary accomplishment of Bloch's *Geist der Utopie*[22] lies in its refutation of political messianism. Instead of seeking to install an earthly replica of the heavenly kingdom, the profanation of an already "profane" politics has no other goal than the attainment of happiness, which is saved, as it were, from "profane" purposes because it is forever fleeting. To the extent that legal, social, and cultural formations are meant to persist, they run counter to the eternal transience of happiness. The proper "method" of politics consists in the nullification of these happiness-destroying formations and should be called "nihilism"[23]—not "messianism"—for this reason.

SEE ALSO: End of Art; Truth

---

22 Benjamin, *Gesammelte Schriften*, 2:203.
23 Ibid., 2:204.

Nineteen Mediation/Medium

James A. Steintrager and Rey Chow

In *The Genealogy of Morals* (1887), Nietzsche asserts that the appropriate methodological color for his topic is not blue but gray: no speculation, lofty notions, and gazing at the sky; rather, eyes cast downward at "that which has been documented, the really-establishable, actually-happened-that-way, in brief, the whole long, difficult to decipher hieroglyphic text of the moral past of humanity [das Urkundliche, das Wirklich-Feststellbare, das Wirklich-Dagewesene, kurze die ganze lange, schwer zu entziffernde Hieroglyphenschrift der menschlichen Moral-Vergangenheit]."[1] In one of the earliest attacks on the history of ideas, Nietzsche insists that we attend to language, or what would eventually come to be called "discourse," embedded in a material support. As the argument unfolds, he elucidates that other types of support for ideas are not neutral: from the body, including the digestive system, to the will-to-power—which Nietzsche would develop as a properly material system of differences—which colors our access to truth with perspective. *The Genealogy of Morals* describes the workings of two conceptions of medium. First, there is medium as something that serves as the carrier of form, information, signification, or meaning: the voice, print, or strings of binaries stored on a hard drive. Second, there is medium as something that stands *between* us and, broadly put, the world—including others and ourselves.[2] Here "medium" entails a barrier to immediate experience or access. Although these two conceptions are not mutually exclusive—and often blur—we will maintain the distinction provisionally to help lay out a genealogy of medium and mediation in the German tradition.

---

1 Friedrich Nietzsche, *Jenseits von Gut und Böse/Zur Genealogie der Moral* (Berlin: Walter de Gruyter [Deutscher Taschenbuch Verlag], 1999), 254, our translation.
2 Georg Christoph Tholen, "Medium, Medien," in *Grundbegriffe der Medientheorie*, ed. Alexander Roestler and Bernd Stiegler (Stuttgart: Uni-Taschenbücher, 2005), 150–72.

Medium as In-Between

Kant is the dominant figure in the lineage of medium as an ineluctable between, and in the *Critique of Pure Reason* (1781) the adjectives *mittelbar* and *unmittelbar* ("mediate" and "immediate") appear with a frequency that confirms their conceptual importance. Kant's celebrated Copernican turn put off limits "things-in-themselves," or *noumena*, and focused instead on how we experience and, more radically, construct *phenomena*. This approach is carried over in the *Critique of Judgment* (1790), where neither beauty nor sublimity are objective attributes but rather occasions of the free play of reason and imagination (beauty) and the overwhelming of imagination in a way that leads to respectful recognition of our freedom from natural determination (sublimity). Kant's project was not to reduce everything to mediacy, however, but rather to discover what could count as immediate and what not. Thus, in the transcendental aesthetic in the *Critique of Pure Reason*, we initially approach phenomena through intuitions that Kant characterizes as immediate: "In whatever way and through whatever means a cognition may relate to objects, that through which it relates immediately to them, and at which all thought as a means is directed as an end, is intuition [Auf welche Art und durch welche Mittel sich auch immer eine Erkenntnis auf Gegenstände beziehen mag, so ist doch diejenige, wodurch sie sich auf dieselbe unmittelbar bezieht, und worauf alles Denken als Mittel abzweckt, die Anschauung]."[3] The fundamental intuitions are time and space, and the immediacy that remains embedded in any cognitive relation to objects—the thinking of objects through the understanding, that is, the conceptual synthesis of the manifold of experience—comes not from the objects themselves but is embedded in our primary, constitutional sensibility. This sensibility gives us not the matter of experience, which would be *a posteriori*, but its form, which is *a priori*.

We must also recognize Herder's contribution to the genealogy of mediation: he helped shift from the ideal of language as transparent representation to an understanding of language as a formative power in its own right. Whereas, for example, Frederick II of Prussia would subscribe to the Enlightenment ideal that German might be remodeled along the lines of French for greater clarity—that its very role as a medium might be effaced and the particularities of different languages ideally tuned to the representation of universals—Herder insisted that language is the medium of thought: an interposition that shapes us as much as it shapes things. Further, particular languages express

---

[3] Immanuel Kant, *Critique of Pure Reason*, trans. and ed. Paul Guyer and Allen W. Wood (Cambridge: Cambridge University Press, 1998), 155; German: Immanuel Kant, *Kritik der reinen Vernunft*, Vol. 1 (Frankfurt am Main: Suhrkamp, 1997), 69.

national and what would eventually be called cultural differences. This shift in what language is and does motivated the development of both anthropology and hermeneutics, with writers such as Wilhelm von Humboldt, Schleiermacher, Dilthey, and Gadamer focusing on language as a fundamental constituent of human differences and as the tool to cross such divides.

At heart, Hegel's epistemological project was the wedding of the Kantian concern with the mediate and immediate to Herder's historical turn. In *The Phenomenology of the Spirit* (1807), Hegel uses the term *Medium* frequently—often qualified as "abstract general Medium [*abstrakte allgemeine Medium*]"—to signify something along the lines of matter that has yet to receive determination. Hegel provides several glosses on *Medium* in this sense, which indicates the semantic problem of specifying the unspecifiable and inevitably particularizing the abstract: "thinghood [Dingheit]" (recalling Kant); "pure essence [reine Wesen]"; or the "here and now" as a "simple togetherness of a plurality [das Hier und Itzt … als ein einfaches Zusammen von vielen]."[4] In Hegel's terminology and epistemology, therefore, it is not so much *Medium* that is in-between, but various mediations that simultaneously provide us with whatever access to truth we may attain and preclude immediate access to "thinghood" or "pure essence." His choice of the term "negation" to characterize the mediation of the *Medium* captures nicely how positive gains of knowledge are achieved privatively. Hegel gives these mediations a dialectical movement and epochal trajectory. For example, the consciousness of the master is mediated by the recognition of the bondsman and, later, the Stoic consciousness appropriates objects to consciousness through labor on the world. Art, moreover, is taken as a stage of mediate consciousness that will be overcome with the advent of absolute knowledge, when the work of mediation will sublate itself into immediacy.

Hegel's idealism—his insistence on the primacy of ideas as determinants of consciousness and motors of historical change—would be inverted in the writings of Young Hegelians such as Ludwig Feuerbach and in Marx, who would emphasize the material determination or at least conditioning of the ideational. The very notion of ideology as developed in Marxist theory treats ideas as mediate: far from presenting reality or morality as such, they bear within them in occluded form the mark of the forces of production and of the concrete, social relations of production. Ideology includes the cultural sphere, so that literature and art become expressions of—and covers for—class conflict. Schopenhauer in *The World as Will and Representation*

---

4   Georg Wilhelm Friedrich Hegel, *Phänomenologie des Geistes*, Werke 3 (Frankfurt am Main: Suhrkamp, 1970), 94, our translation.

(1818) would also posit the necessity of mediation and the dream of its overcoming, and provides a different perspective on the Kantian inheritance. Schopenhauer treats the world of representations—of ideas and appearances—as one aspect of reality, and a thoroughly mediated one. Thus bodily mediation is the prerequisite for knowledge ("Erkennen ... ist durchaus vermittelt durch ein Leib"), but the body itself can be known mediately as an idea—and thus as "an object among others"—or immediately as will.[5] Similarly, knowledge is treated as the "medium of motives [Medium der Motive]" and as such influences the "appearance" of the will in actions.[6] Music, the least obviously representational of the arts, Schopenhauer championed as the most immediately expressive of the will: not a "copy of ideas [Abbild der Ideen]" but a "copy of the will itself [Abbild des Willens selbst]."[7] This bifurcation is present in the early Nietzsche as well, where Dionysian art puts forward the dream of unmediated access—at the cost of dissolution—and Apollonian art brings order and individuation through mediation. The compromise solution at the time of *The Birth of Tragedy* (1872) was Wagner's operatic melding of the two tendencies, although Nietzsche later not only repudiated Wagner but also attempted a thorough rejection of any notion of immediate access. The universal assertion that *all* observation is perspectival—that is, particular—can be seen as paradoxical. A similar paradox lies at the heart of the psychoanalytic project with the positing of "primary processes" to which our only access is mediated. We get to the unconscious only through the language of dreams, slips, and jokes—and we never really get to the bottom of the unconscious, which remains a kernel of psychic reality that recedes behind every attempt to finally crack it open.

Phenomenology, which we can trace back to Kant's initial move, continued to grapple with mediation—and with ever more reflexive maneuvering. Husserl's *epoché* or philosophical bracketing of anything outside of perceptual experience was fundamentally an attempt to suspend the question of mediation. In *Speech and Phenomena*, Derrida memorably exposed Husserl's privileging of the inner voice, and elsewhere critiqued attempts to make language the vehicle of presence by pointing out that signification is a system based not on positive values but rather on differences and so inevitably entails absence and lack. One of Derrida's chief targets—and influences—was Heidegger, who gathered up the strands of phenomenology, hermeneutics, and historicism, and turned them to a questioning of Being as opposed to sundry

---

5 Arthur Schopenhauer, *Die Welt als Wille und Vorstellung*, 2 vols, in *Sämtliche Werke* (Wiesbaden: F.U. Brodhaus, 1966), 1:118.
6 Ibid., 1:350.
7 Ibid., 1:04.

beings. As Heidegger puts his case in his "Letter on 'Humanism,'" thinking must start from the so-called *ek-sistence* [Ek-sistenz] of human beings: our position within "the openness of being, into the open region that first clears the 'between' within which a 'relation' of subject to object can 'be.'"[8] Within this line of questioning, language took on an increasingly crucial role. Memorably calling language the "house of Being [das Haus des Seins]," for Heidegger language becomes the means of approaching being, in a simultaneous and paradoxical movement of occlusion and revelation.[9] True thinking *through* language is exemplified in pre-Socratic fragments and the poetry of Hölderlin, for example, and contrasts with technology as a mediating frame (*Ge-stell*) that holds being at bay as objects and as instruments.[10]

It would seem that the interrogation of mediation *qua* in-between accompanied by inevitably paradoxical attempts to secure immediacy is one way to define the German philosophical project from Kant through the nineteenth century and beyond. Kant thus proposed intuitions to serve as the immediate, transparent grounding of universal and therefore necessarily mediating concepts in relation to particularities. Hegel projected an end to mediation with the advent of the absolute idea and concomitant self-certainty and self-transparency. Similarly, for Marx alienation—which can be understood as the mediation of one's true self by class divisions—will end with the historical end to the capitalist relations of production. The consistency and duration of this project of bringing mediation as an in-between to an epochal close can be grasped in Herbert Marcuse's attempt in *Eros and Civilization* (1955) to conjoin Marxism with Freud's later thought. In *Beyond the Pleasure Principle* (1920) and *Civilization and Its Discontents* (1930), Freud had followed Schopenhauer and (early) Nietzsche along the path of self-annihilation as the only end to mediation by hypothesizing the "death drive" as the ultimate psychic, biological, and indeed cosmic principle—a principle from which we can infer that life itself is nothing but death temporarily suspended or mediated. Freud considered civilization in general as a force of repression of not just *Eros* but also of *Thanatos*. Modernity further forces these drives into the unconscious, although they re-emerge in sublimated form, as well as in the form of symptoms such as a generalized neurosis and the increasing risk of release in aggressive form. Marcuse held out the hope that resolving the contradictions of capitalism could unfetter *Eros* without the taint of the death drive. Social and psychic mediacy would end at the same

---

8   Martin Heidegger, *Pathmarks*, ed. William McNeill (Cambridge: Cambridge University Press, 1998), 266.
9   Ibid., 239.
10 See ibid., 259.

time. The humanist and seemingly utopian dream, however, had long since given rise to a concomitant reflection on the impossibility of immediacy and the omnipresence of epistemological latency—that is, knowledge ungraspable by reflection—that the "in-between" entails. For good reason Marx, Nietzsche, and Freud have been grouped under the rubric of the "masters of suspicion." Moreover, critique, which describes the mode of inquiry proper to making the latent manifest, almost inevitably shades off into paradox. In fact, we might restate the so-called liar's paradox as the fundamental mediation paradox: all statements about mediation are themselves mediated and therefore suspect, including this one. Or, as Friedrich Kittler, in a formulation that shifts the focus of ideology from economics narrowly construed to technology, paradoxically explained his own project: "Understanding media—despite McLuhan's title—remains an impossibility precisely because the dominant information technologies of the day control all understanding and its illusions."[11]

Medium as material carrier

In spite of its paradoxicalness, Kittler's statement directs us away from the conundrums of circularity and toward a seemingly much more grounded sense of medium or what have been called "materialities" of communication in response to the perceived immaterialism of certain trends in French poststructuralist thought (most dramatically Baudrillard's notion of the death of reality[12]). Whereas Kant demonstrated little interest in a more materialist sense of medium, and Herder broached the matter only occasionally, Lessing in his *Laocoön or On the Limits of Painting and Poetry* had already made a major statement in German on the topic in 1776. In Lessing's argument, the "representations [Nachahmungen]" of painting, along with other visual arts, uses—or ought to use—different "means [Mittel]" or "symbols [Zeichnen]" than poetry. For the former, "figures and colors in space [Figuren und Farben in dem Raume]" are required; for the latter "articulated sounds in time [artikulierte Töne in der Zeit]."[13] Lessing was most interested in how media constrained the representation and communication of suffering. Whereas Virgil, using the time-bound medium of epic poetry, could depict the Greek priest expressing his

---

11 Friedrich Kittler, *Discourse Networks 1800/1900*, trans. Michael Metteer with Chris Cullens (Stanford, CA: Stanford University Press, 1990), xl.
12 See K. Ludwig Pfeiffer, "The Materiality of Communication," in *Materialities of Communication*, ed. Hans Ulrich Gumbrecht and K. Ludwig Pfeiffer, trans. William Whobre (Stanford, CA: Stanford University Press, 1994), 1–12.
13 Gotthold Ephraim Lessing, *Laokoon*, in *Werke*, Vol. 3 (Munich: Carl Hanser Verlag, 1982), 103.

torment—the moment passes, the scream is not truly heard—and thereby effect sympathy in his hearer, the sculptor of the Laocoön group could not fix the priest's mouth in a scream without producing effects that would be grotesque and alienating, that is, antithetical to sympathy. Conversely and inhumanly, gladiators must dissociate their inner suffering from the plane of expression: wounds may appear as natural signs of pain, but the decorous warrior must negate them by expiring gracefully.

Although Marx focused on materiality, this was largely limited to the forces and relations of production, and ideology itself tended toward conceptualization as the immaterial counterpart and skewed reflection of this base. We can see this in Marxists such as Lukács, who focused on the novel, a class-bound genre, or in Brecht, who came at the restraints of drama as medium in a way that largely inverted Lessing: hoping to shake his audience into a consciousness of their own alienation under the current relations of production (the so-called *Verfremdungseffekt*). In psychoanalysis, Freud would give new communication technologies such as the telegraph and telephone a prominent place in *Civilization and Its Discontents* as examples of how human ingenuity promises to ensure contentment by, for example, overcoming distance, but tends to undermine itself simultaneously. Yet Freud thought that the ultimate reason for civilization's discontents lay in the death drive, which means that these discontents are irreducible to any technological factor.

Walter Benjamin would resist such reduction to natural forces and emphasize rather the constitutive powers of history. Different from Hegel or Marx, moreover, Benjamin extended historical analysis to the new media of his day—from photographs to film, phonographs, and radio—as materialities in their own right. Thus, in "The Work of Art in the Age of Its Technological Reproducibility," Benjamin writes that it is not just the forms of collective human existence that change over time but that the "way in which human perception is organized—the medium in which it occurs—is conditioned not only by nature but by history [Die Art und Weise, in der die menschliche Sinneswahrnehmung sich organisiert—das Medium, in dem sie erfolgt—is nicht nur natürlich sondern auch geschichtlich bedingt]."[14] Although this statement has become a *locus classicus* in media studies,[15]

---

14 Walter Benjamin, *The Work of Art in the Age of Its Technological Reproducibility and Other Writings on Media*, ed. Michael W. Jennings, Brigid Doherty, and Thomas Y. Levin (Cambridge, MA: Harvard University Press, 2008), 23. German: Walter Benjamin, *Gesammelte Schriften*, Vol. 1, part 2, ed. Rolf Tiedemann and Hermann Schweppenhäuser (Frankfurt am Main. Suhrkamp Verlag, 1974), 478.
15 See Tholen, "Medium, Medien," 163.

Medium was not actually a term to which Benjamin had frequent recourse. Here it implies all those factors that shape perception by supporting and framing it, including the body and historical-cum-social forces. He did, however, show consistent interest in what we would call technological mediation. Among other mediating factors, for instance, an oil painting is materially different from a technologically reproducible art object such as a film. The former in its singularity is tied to the outmoded sacred and lends its aura to, for example, patrons, be they aristocratic or bourgeois. The latter strips away aura through the very fact of reproducibility. It thereby also provides the grounds for muted optimism concerning film's technical capacity to break apart and analyze social experience and the medium's potential as a revolutionary tool for turning the masses into self-conscious critics of their situation, or so Benjamin believed at the time.

The advent and aftermath of the Second World War produced a darker vision of mass mediation in Frankfurt School thinkers such as Adorno and Horkheimer, who could only see the purported culture of jazz records and Hollywood movies as so much entertainment opiate for the hopelessly alienated masses. Approaching the matter with more attention to historical detail, Jürgen Habermas in his *Structural Transformation of the Public Sphere* would consider "coffee houses, salons, and Tischgesellschaften" as spaces where the discussion of art and politics could take place outside of aristocratic and courtly institutions.[16] Free conversation was then translated into nascent print media such as journals and newspapers, and the novel further helped build the sense of autonomous individuality and interiority essential to the public sphere. Habermas wavered on whether the "medium of a critical public" that emerged in the eighteenth century was an illusion or a brief historical reality soon transformed by the very forces that gave rise to it into a "medium of advertising."[17] Either way, the ideal of rational communication that first emerged in Habermas's work in media studies and historical sociology became his quest and some would say will-o'-the-wisp.

A major counter-voice to Habermas in Germany was the sociologist Niklas Luhmann. Luhmann turned sociology from the empiricist dream of analyzable "action systems" to the various paradoxes of communication and second-order observation. For Luhmann, the observation of "reality" is never immediate; rather, it is a distinction between system and environment drawn within the system itself,

---

16 Jürgen Habermas, *The Structural Transformation of the Public Sphere: An Inquiry into a Category of Bourgeois Society*, trans. Thomas Burger (Cambridge, MA: MIT Press, 1989), 51.
17 Ibid., 84, 189.

for which the environment as such is strictly speaking inaccessible; it must be constructed. With this, the Copernican turn that Kant realized for epistemology is extended in willfully reflexive and knowingly paradoxical form to society. In *Social Systems*, Luhmann specifies three different types of *media*: "language"; "media of dissemination" such as writing, print, and broadcasting; and "symbolically generalized communication media."[18] The last, taken up from the American sociologist Talcott Parsons, indicates distinctions such as "truth, love, property/money, power/law ... religious belief, art, and, today, standardized 'basic values'" that serve to differentiate social subsystems.[19] These three media types "mutually enable one another, limit one another, and burden one another with consequent problems."[20] For example, language extends communication beyond perception through the use of signs but, because of this very extension—by which almost "any random event can appear and be processed *as information*"[21]—topics, codes, and eventually symbolical generalizations emerge to limit and guide communication. Philosophy appears when the medium of writing, which separates information from its enunciation, sunders the apparent unity of these aspects of communication in oral culture and compensates by insisting on self-standing truth claims—an insistence that can always be read with skepticism. Print speeds up this process: "Only writing and printing suggest communicative processes that react, not to the unity of, but to the difference between utterance and information: for example, processes for controlling truth, for articulating suspicion, with the accompanying psychoanalytic and/or ideological universalization of suspicion."[22]

Luhmann followed the arguments of seminal writers on medium such as Eric Havelock and Walter Ong—a reminder that what we have called the German tradition is highly porous. Similarly, Friedrich Kittler, the most prominent of post-war German media theorists, conjoined the work of French post-structuralists such as Derrida, Lacan, and Foucault to the McLuhanite insistence that it is not content or information that makes the difference historically but the way or means by which it is delivered. Crucially, borrowing from Foucault the notion of the historical *a priori*—that there are contingent, historical factors underlying any claims to knowledge—Kittler turned discourse analysis and genealogy toward the priority and determinant force of

---

18 Niklas Luhmann, *Social Systems*, trans. John Bednarz, Jr., with Dirk Baecker (Stanford, CA: Stanford University Press, 1995), 160–1.
19 Ibid., 161.
20 Ibid., 160.
21 Ibid., 160.
22 Ibid., 162.

media as materialities. Freud had likened the structure of the mind to the "mystic writing pad," on which the traces of the stylus that mark the wax remain (the unconscious), even when the plastic sheet (repression) is lifted and so erases what appeared on the surface (conscious). Similarly, Kittler's notion of the "alphabetization" of the child by the mother's voice makes the mind—an outcome of the ears and eyes working in concert—a medium that bears the marks of this process. Thus, the printed word—after the mother's voice has been internalized by the alphabetized child—serves as a medium in a playful sense: it channels the "spirit" of the author.[23] Reminiscent of Benjamin, for Kittler it is the material form of print as historical *a priori* coupled with pedagogical and institutional practices that put into place hermeneutics as the attempt to recapture and evoke this spiritual presence in the act of interpretation. Yet what we might call the ruse of print is revealed as such when it enters into competition with the new media of gramophones, typewriters, and film that break apart the sensorium and assert their own materialities and concomitant forms of experience and social organization.[24]

Kittler's major historical studies put the workings of formerly new media into relief in part by drawing comparisons with the new regime of digitization. He and other theorists such as Georg Christoph Tholen have since increasingly moved media studies in the direction of computing, hardware, and binary coding as the most important "in-betweens" of our time.[25] Meanwhile, as exemplified by Siegfried Zielinski's *Deep Time of the Media: Toward an Archeology of Seeing and Hearing by Technical Means*, historians have extended the story of past media in their diversity and often seeming eccentricity when viewed from the perspective of the present. Other media have also been added to the list. In *Rules for the Human Zoo* Peter Sloterdijk has taken up culture and genes as media—much to the chagrin of Habermas, for whom the topic alone recalled fascism. Revisiting Heidegger's critical assessment of humanism—and inadvertently recalling Lessing—Sloterdijk has proposed that we must face up to the ancient Roman media struggle of "books" (the codification of humanism) against the "amphitheater" (inhuman spectacle as agent of political control) as it is currently playing out in our post-print, mass-mediated, and increasingly globalized world.[26] If mediation doggedly appeared and reappeared as irresolvable paradox, medium as materiality now risks

---

23 See Kittler, *Discourse Networks*, 25–69.
24 See Friedrich Kittler, *Gramophone, Film, Typewriter*, trans. Geoffry Winthrop-Young and Michael Wutz (Stanford, CA: Stanford University Press, 1999).
25 See Tholen, "Medium, Medien," 5–7, 14–16.
26 Peter Sloterdijk, "Rules for the Human Zoo: A Response to the *Letter on*

ubiquity to the point of vacuity. One might even say that the pressing question has become not so much what a medium is, but what is not one?

SEE ALSO: Film; Montage/Collage

Humanism," trans. Mary Varney Rorty, *Environment and Planning D: Society and Space* 27 (2009): 16.

Twenty Truth

Kai Hammermeister

Plato postulated an inseparable connection between the beautiful, the true, and the good. This triad, however, would only truly merge in the realm of ideas. In the material world, the junction was fragile and tainted by matter's inherent drift toward chaos. What we call fine art today was excluded from the triad altogether precisely because it was that sphere in the material world in which truth was most corrupted. Yet art's epistemological degeneration was dangerously hidden under a veil of pleasure. Thus was initiated a long philosophical separation of art from beauty and from truth.

In the eighteenth century, the term "art," long understood to include all skill-based production, was narrowed down to refer mostly to the fine arts. Simultaneously, the aesthetic rationalism of Leibniz, Wolff, Baumgarten, Gottsched, Mendelssohn, and Winckelmann extended the triad of beauty, truth, and goodness as facets of perfection to include objects of fine art. For them, perfection consisted in harmony defined as unity in variety. Such perfection is based on rules that can be extracted by the philosopher from existing works of art and set up as guiding principles for the production of new artworks. Following these eternal rules provides the artist with a guarantee that his creation will be beautiful, truthful, and ethically inspiring.

Kant in his 1790 *Critique of Judgment* put an end to such rationalist aesthetic optimism. This third Critique was meant to reconcile the previous two that were in serious danger of collapsing from the strain that the divergent forces of nature and freedom, phenomenon and noumenon, had imposed on the system. Judgment was introduced as the splint that was meant to hold together sensuality and cognition as much as sensuality and morality. The judgment of taste takes for its object beauty, both natural and man-made. But beauty cannot be defined by recourse to rules of perfection; rather, it announces itself as a sense of pleasure in the observer. An aesthetic judgment is therefore not cognitive or logical, but it is based on the pleasure derived from the free play of the faculties involved in this judgment. Thus Kant had severed the connection between the beautiful and the true, despite the fact that for him aesthetic judgments still tend to seek validation in a collective affirmation that prevents them from being merely subjective.

German romanticism and idealism are responses to Kant's system that appeared magnificent in its aspirations, yet plagued by inconsistencies. Ten years after the publication of the third Critique, the most brilliant and influential attempt at its refutation was published by the young F. W. J. Schelling in his *System of Transcendental Idealism*. For the very brief period of just a couple of years, Schelling elevated art to the privileged embodiment of truth that surpasses both theology and philosophy in its epistemological potency. Whereas subject and object remain separate by necessity in every linguistic utterance, art can unify the two and thus grant access to the absolute. While art is useless for all practical purposes, its truth claim replaces that of philosophy, respectively science. As an embodiment of the absolute, art consequently only exists as one unified field of beauty; individual works of art are just so many manifestations of it that ultimately all repeat the same message, namely that the absolute is present in art's beauty.

Schelling soon retracted this elevation of art over conceptual thought, and in his *Philosophy of Art* he insisted again on the necessity of philosophy to interpret the achievements of art. Hegel too, whose thought would go on to dominate the nineteenth century, insisted on philosophy's superior aptitude to handle truth claims compared to those of art. Art's springtime as ideal vehicle of truth lasted but a few romantic years. For the next century, philosophy and science reasserted themselves as the rightful venues to pursue epistemological investigations. Only with Nietzsche's arrival on the philosophical scene would another attack in the name of art be ridden against philosophy's claim to truth. In his early book publication *The Birth of Tragedy* he suggests that life cannot be comprehended rationally, but that art provides the means for its elucidation. In the course of his writing life, Nietzsche came to redefine the notions of truth and beauty both of which were considered to be manifestations of power. Truth was given a pragmatist spin, reconceived as a tool for the self-affirmation of the speaker, and beauty was regarded as an increase in power. Art as just one manifestation of the beautiful was conceptualized as a stimulus to power, i.e. expansion and self-glorification above and beyond mere survival. Heidegger takes his cue from these reconceptualizations, but broadens and refines them considerably.

Heidegger

From 1936 to 1940 Heidegger lectured on Nietzsche, in the subsequent six years he elaborated on these lectures in a series of essays. These writings were published in the two volumes *Nietzsche I/II*.[1]

Heidegger argues that for Nietzsche art is the highest expression of the will-to-power, and as such it becomes the exemplary counter-movement against nihilism. However, just like Nietzsche's "reversal of all values" is a counter-movement against nihilism *within* nihilism, Nietzsche's conception of art and aesthetics remains tied to the metaphysical history of Western thought. Nihilism does not end with Nietzsche, nor anywhere in the twentieth century, but will continue for hundreds of years to come. Yet nihilism is necessity and fate, and therefore the precondition for the possibility of a return of the Gods.

In the context of his discussion of Nietzsche's *will-to-power* as manifested in art Heidegger advances six theses about philosophical aesthetics which are sadly neglected in the discussion of Heidegger's theory of art, because it focuses mostly on the essay *The Origin of the Work of Art* that was published at the same time. It becomes clear from these theses, though, that for Heidegger art and its philosophical reflection are fundamentally at odds. Aesthetic theory is a phenomenon of decadence and late cultures. Art requires no assistance from the thinkers. In summary, the theses are as follows:

1. In ancient Greece, the truly great art exists and thrives in the absence of all philosophical reflection on it.
2. Aesthetic theory comes into existence in Greece when the period of great art is over.
3. Great art reveals being in its entirety. In the modern age, art loses its essence, namely the representation of the absolute. The aesthetic attitude toward art that turns it into a being among others destroys art's genuine capacity.
4. The triumph of aesthetic theory marks the end of great art. Hegel's aesthetics make this end explicit.
5. Within nihilism, art cannot rescue itself. Nietzsche's hopes for Wagner's *Gesamtkunstwerk* are false. While the *Gesamtkunstwerk* is a serious attempt to revoke art's loss of its essence, the dominance of the musical element in it reduces it to an art of mere sensual stimulation. The advocated return of the absolute in art turns out to be a dissolution into nothingness.
6. Aesthetic theory in Nietzsche's hands turns into applied physiology. The basic aesthetic state is that of intoxication, i.e. increase of power, fullness (openness to everything), and mutual penetration of all active and passive faculties. Aesthetic intoxication moves

---

1 See Martin Heidegger, *Nietzsche I/II*, 2 vols (Frankfurt am Main: Klostermann, 1996).

beyond both subjective and objective theories of art. It lets the subject transcend itself, but the beauty of the artwork that gave rise to this state also places the object on a trajectory toward a recipient.

Heidegger concludes that both beauty and truth keep Being open, beauty in a sensual, and truth in a cognitive manner. But since beauty transcends mere sensuality, ultimately an essential affinity between the two exists.

In his 1935 lecture *The Origin of the Work of Art* Heidegger connects back to Schelling's elevation of art to the singular disclosing event of truth. While he emphatically agrees with the romantic notion of art as a privileged access to truth (without ever crediting Schelling), he abstains from postulating its exclusiveness. Other human acts may disclose truth just as effectively.

In the lecture, Heidegger discusses a painting by Vincent van Gogh in which a pair of farmer's boots is depicted (they belonged to the painter). From the image of the worn shoes we learn about the land and the hardship and joy of farming. No insights would have been gained from looking at a pair of work boots directly, mostly because muddy shoes are not meant to be contemplated in the first place. Boots are *Zeug*, tools, the nature of which is unobtrusiveness. The connection to the soil emerges only from the shoe's image in and as a work of art. Art has a decidedly epistemological function by disclosing to us what we do not perceive directly. Thus he arrives at his famous definition of the artwork as *"das Sich-ins-Werk-Setzen der Wahrheit des Seienden,"* the emergence of the truth of being in the work.[2]

Heidegger accuses philosophical aesthetics of being unable to comprehend this fundamental epistemological difference between the work of art and other objects, thereby reducing art to *Bestand*, objects to be manipulated at will. Thought must oppose aesthetics and recover art's basic function of disclosing the truth of being as an event. Art decidedly does not express the self of the artist who is entirely irrelevant. Nor does the truth of art consist in a mimetic representation of reality. Works rest in themselves rather than signifying something else which would require a pointing away from themselves. Yet in this restfulness the world can be present. In the openness of the artwork the world itself is opened up. "The work erects a world. The work holds the openness of the world open."[3]

Being presents itself to man in language. Such primal disclosure needs to occur before any artwork can come into existence. Naturally, poetry therefore takes pride of place among the arts: not because it is

---

2   Martin Heidegger, *Der Ursprung des Kunstwerks* (Stuttgart: Reclam, 1997), 30.
3   Ibid., 41.

closest to the conceptual truth of philosophy, as Hegel had argued; rather, in poetry being achieves its utmost openness. It is not the poet who speaks in order to express his self; rather, a historical people speaks through him. Furthermore, such openness cannot be grasped conceptually. Every work of art contains a moment of resistance against subsumption under a philosophical concept, in fact against all comprehension. Heidegger calls the moment of withdrawal and refusal "earth." In artworks, earth is that which both resists cognition and which simultaneously announces its perpetual resistance so that it cannot be forgotten or ignored. No artwork gives pleasure only; each one dispenses its share of frustration as well. Yet such frustration is not only unavoidable, but beneficial. While other objects might give us the illusion of total control in our handling of them, artworks are precisely those objects that announce the limits of our cognition and our dominance. "The earth lets every attempt to intrude upon it crash against it. It turns every calculating intrusion into destruction."[4] It is art in which the object can find shelter in an age of calculation and exploitation.

To be sure, the truth of art must not be misunderstood as openness. Art's truth is exactly the struggle between openness and concealedness, between the disclosing of world and the hiddenness of earth. Truth is a relation to being that accepts its moments of darkness. Art brings such darkness into light as darkness.

While Heidegger grants truth claims to philosophy, art, and also certain political acts like the founding of a state, he explicitly excludes science. Science merely operates in the realm of correctness (*Richtigkeit*) that in turn depends on a previous disclosure by truth. In this sense, art much like thought is indispensable for the establishment of a historical space in which concrete acts of research can be carried out. In other words, science never establishes its own paradigms, but operates within those that have been laid out by artworks or philosophical disclosures. In this sense, Heidegger can even argue that "art is history in the essential sense that it founds history."[5]

Gadamer

Gadamer expands Heidegger's "hermeneutics of facticity" into a general philosophical hermeneutics. Moving much beyond traditional hermeneutics as a method to guarantee an accurate comprehension of texts, Gadamer reconceptualizes understanding as a fundamental human way to relate to the world and oneself. In this model, aesthetics too becomes an aspect of hermeneutics, albeit a privileged one. Traditional

---

4   Ibid., 43.
5   Ibid., 80.

aesthetic theories post Kant, however, so Gadamer argues in *Wahrheit und Methode*, have failed to properly respond to the truth claim of art. Yet this particular truth claim of art must not be confused with scientific truth. Just like Heidegger, Gadamer distinguishes between truth and the operative model of the natural sciences. He argues that Kant had discredited all notions of cognition that did not conform to the model worked out by the natural sciences. Yet when the humanities attempt to conform to this mode of operating, they lose the specificity of their objects and approach them with methodological tools that ultimately destroy the unique truth of these objects.

Kant had largely limited the analysis of art to the subjective response to it as "disinterested pleasure." For Gadamer, this does violence to the artwork by cutting it off from its seat in life, its social, historical, or religious world. Hermeneutics is called to reintegrate the work of art into the fullness of its origin. In the work, its world is always understood as well.

The truth claim of art, though, emerges from its genuine ontological status in the world. Gadamer reverses the Platonic claim that art is an ontologically flawed object because it is that type of object in the world furthest removed from the realm of ideas. For Gadamer, artworks somehow increase the ontological density of normal objects and thus contain their essence. Ultimately, artworks can claim an ontologically superior status. Cognition of the world becomes much easier via a detour through art which ultimately proves to be a short cut.

Heidegger had hesitated to elevate art above philosophy. Gadamer takes this step with conviction. "We do not read philosophical texts like a poem that knows everything. We rather read a philosophical text as one that will also not know, but whose author has inquired and thought for longer."[6]

Three of the most important contributions to twentieth-century philosophical aesthetics in Germany, namely those of Heidegger, Gadamer, and Adorno, all insisted on the truth claim of art. Their notion of truth, though, was a clear departure from the Aristotelian correspondence theory of truth. Therefore, none of them was tied to an imitative notion of the relation of artwork and world. Since all of them regarded the natural sciences more as tools of exploitation than as guardians of truth, art became almost by necessity the privileged locus of truth. To a greater or lesser degree, though, it still depended on philosophy's assistance in order to reveal the truth it contained. At the same time, the history of philosophical aesthetics was largely

---

6 Hans-Georg Gadamer, *Wahrheit und Methode*, 6th ed. (Tübingen: Mohr und Siebeck, 1990), 170.

rejected as collaborative in the efforts to measure art by the standards of natural science.

Heidegger's reconstruction of the romantic notion of aesthetic truth found echoes in such diverse thinkers as Richard Rorty, Manfred Frank, and Giorgio Agamben to name just a few.

SEE ALSO: Judgment; Beauty; Value

Twenty-one Uncanny
Thomas Pepper

Ever since Freud's 1919 essay, "das Unheimliche,"[1] translated as "[T]he Uncanny," this word-thing has become ever more urgent, not only in psychoanalysis, but in aesthetic thought and beyond. But despite its having become a commonplace, its definition is a comfort resisted by both word and thing. Reasons for this resistance cut to the kernel of the matter.

"The uncanny" is Freud's term for a subject's experience of the familiar when, having been repressed into the unconscious because of the discomfort it induces for the subject, it returns to consciousness as defamiliarized or estranged, along with anxiety (conscious or not). The discomfort of this anxiety is the echo of the unpleasantness at the root of the original repression.

Yet despite naming an experience, "the uncanny" very often slides into being attributed to an object of experience. This slippage—from an experience to an object of that experience—recalls the crucial difference between the ancient and early modern sublime, where sublimity is the name for a quality of an object, and the sublime after Kant's *Critique of the Faculty of Judgment*, where sublimity is the name for the destabilization of the subject's faculties by an object. This analogy is borne out by the negative affective coloring, both in Kant's epochal reworking of the sublime in his third *Critique* and in what Freud calls the uncanny.

For pinpoint accuracy on the sublime in literary language and Freud's words in *un-*, here is Empson, from the Table of Contents of *Seven Types of Ambiguity*: "CHAPTER VII(:) The seventh type is that of full contradiction, marking a division in the author's mind. Freud invoked."[2]

---

1 Sigmund Freud, "The 'Uncanny,'" in *Writings on Art and Literature* (Stanford, CA: Stanford University Press, 1997), 193–233.
2 William Empson, *Seven Types of Ambiguity* (New York: New Directions, 1947 [1930]), ix.

In keeping with Kant's and Freud's very different purposes, one of the major specific differences between the experience Kant calls sublime and the one Freud calls uncanny is Freud's offering the more powerful account of causal reasoning for the negative feeling tone. While the critical Kant calls beautiful what fosters harmonization of the subject's faculties and sublime the experience of their dissonance and its unpleasantness, Freud, long before 1919, had already explained negative affective coloration as the cause of the subject's repression of it into the unconscious in the first place. For the critical Kant makes it clear that it is only the beautiful that is the realm of aesthetic experience as such. This is the power of Kant's gesture of taking the sublime from being the quality of an object and making it into a name of something accompanying the subject's experience of that object. That, in the first part of Kant's third *Critique*, the "Analytic of the Sublime" follows upon his "Analytic of the Beautiful," does not constitute a philosophical argument that both of these sections pertain to the aesthetic as such. The error of thinking this is precisely to miss the radicality of Kant's taking the Greek *aisthesis*, a word for perception in general, and making of it a modern name for what we now call aesthetic experience, experience of the beautiful. For the ancients "aesthetic experience" would have been the tautological usage of a non-reflective person, who did not speak properly or philosophically. For Kant "aesthetic experience" is no tautology: there is plenty of experience that is not accompanied by the predicate beauty. The demarcation of the "Analytic of the Sublime" from the "Analytic of the Beautiful" is an attempt at a conceptual firewall between the two sections and the respective realms of experience discussed in them. On one side is the beautiful, which is the concern of aesthetics; on the other is the sublime, which is not the realm of aesthetics, properly speaking. Thus it is at this firewall that the conceptual space of an art that is not aesthetic (or pleasurable for the beholder) opens up, whether the philosopher (Kant or anyone else) realizes it or not. One who does not understand this division as a part of the internal necessity of Kant's argument thinks wishfully of an idealized, harmonized Kantian System. But this is not the thinking of Kant himself, who, in the radicality of his redefinitions, logically defines the sublime as outside the realm of the aesthetic.

The example to be used here in order to set up a tableau vivant of Freud's uncanny is the last footnote of Freud's essay. It follows a long paragraph in the essay's third and final section (less than five pages in Freud's *Gesammelte Schriften*, where the essay occupies forty pages before the end of both the section and essay). This is the only note in this last section, the last note. (In contrast, the first section of the text has a note of more than a full page, while the second contains a few notes, but nothing the size of that earlier monster.)

The sentence upon which this last note follows reads: "Therefore what is at issue here is purely an occasion of reality testing, that is to say of material reality." The note reads as follows:

> Since the uncanny effect of a "double" is also of this kind, it is interesting to experience what the effect [*Wirkung*] is on the occasion that it is the image, not deliberately summoned and unexpected, of one's own person, that appears to us. E. Mach reports two such observations in *The Analysis of Sensations*, 1900, page 3. The first time he was more than a little terrified as he recognized that the face seen was his own, the other time an unfavorable judgment occurred to him regarding an apparent stranger who got on to his [*sic*] bus: "what a broken-down schoolmaster is the one getting aboard."—I can tell a similar adventure: On that occasion I sat alone in the compartment of the sleeper-car, when a considerable jolt in the motion of the train swung back the door of the adjoining washing cabinet, and an older man, wearing a traveler's cap and a nightshirt, came into my compartment [*bei mir*]. I assumed that, upon leaving the W.C. that was between two compartments, he had erred in direction and incorrectly had entered my compartment, jumped up in order to enlighten him, but soon recognized [myself to have been] confused, [and] that the intruder was my own image, conceived by the mirror in the joining door [*Verbindungstür*]. Furthermore I know that this appearance had deeply displeased me. Thus, instead of being terrified, both of us—Mach as I—had simply not identified [*nicht agnosziert*] him [*den Doppelgänger*]. But as to whether the accompanying displeasure was rather not in fact a remainder of some archaic reaction, which perceives the Doppelgänger to be unheimlich [...]?[3]

The conjuring of the great Mach, before what in German is called a "thought dash," only after which Freud's "I" appears, uses the former to serve as guarantor of the probity of Freud's own tale. This sequence, which politely accords the first place to the account of the distinguished other, also casts the light of Mach's name upon Freud himself. Mach is thus used as Freud's good double or model figure. This wishful thought, accomplished thus by sequence, is intensified in a fact of simultaneity: in 1919 any reader of Freud's essay will know that the founder of psychoanalysis himself had also published his own signal work, *The Interpretation of Dreams*, in 1900.

---

3   Sigmund Freud, *Gesammelte Werke*, 18 Bde. u. Nachtragsbd (Frankfurt am Main: Fischer, 1999 [1941–68]), 12:229–68, translation modified.

This simultaneity is pointed at, without being said, in the note itself. Indeed, in the logic of the unconscious, it does not hurt the "argument" (also called the conceit, a word that comes from the same root as concept) that Mach's name is one small *t* short of *Macht*, power. Freud's citing Mach invokes Mach's authority as source of an influx of power for himself, Freud. Furthermore, Freud's own name ends in *d*, the voiced version of the missing *t* in the power of Mach's own name.

Thus Freud is also the donor of Mach's own power and influence: and, if anything, the missing palatal of Mach's own name, where Freud's own has a voiced one, castrates Mach in Freud's refusal to give, hand over, or share his own, while also waving it, as a triumphal nursery-school child would. He, Freud, has it; Mach does not. Such is the ambivalence, along with doubling, that is a major mark of Freud's uncanny. His own greatness here not only rides on the coattails, or nightshirt, of Mach's "own bus," but the role model suffers dearly for the now dubious privilege. It is the uncanny logic of the double that explains (via some help on the part of Freud's disciple, Otto Rank[4]) why both men's doubles are placed in lower positions than their observers. Freudian reasoning explains the derogation of these split-off, bad doubles, as well as Mach's own "unfavorable judgment" of what he himself derisively calls a "fallen schoolmaster" (*"ein herabgekommener Schulmeister"*), who is certainly no famous professor, as were Mach and Freud.

According to one thread, the logic of the uncanny apparently splits off the bad doubles, themselves mere appearances of the two great men; according to another thread, Mach and Freud are twinned in the sign of their shared wondrous destiny. Freud's note displays the revered, empiricist, anti-metaphysical Mach, and Freud too, on powered mechanical vehicles, moving from 1900 into the twentieth century and beyond. And given the discussion to which the note is adjoined, the stakes of riding with Mach are as high as can be. For it is Freud's greatest ambition to ground his science in the "material reality" Mach and he both held to be the causal ground of everything.

This illustration via Freud's note thus enacts his own compulsively repeated wish to lodge himself incontrovertibly at and as the acme of science. It stages this wish in an uncanny encounter with one who is himself now a ghost. Mach had died in 1916. To close off this reading of Freud's note, it is necessary to revisit its last two sentences: "Thus, instead of being terrified, both of us—Mach as I—had simply not identified [*nicht agnosziert*] him [*den Doppelgänger*]. But as to whether the accompanying displeasure was rather not in fact a remainder of some

---

4 See Otto Rank, *The Double: a Psychoanalytical Study* (London: Karnac, 1989 [1925]).

archaic reaction, which perceives the *Doppelgänger* to be *unheimlich* [...]?" Here the uncanny comes home. After all the (ambivalent) prizing and praising, Freud has to break off the thread of his fantastical identification. The translation, with its incomplete final sentence, followed by a question mark, demonstrates this. But this literal act of breaking off is itself necessitated by the weirdness of the negated verb, "nicht agnosziert," at the end of the penultimate sentence. Like Empson's heading of his own seventh chapter, in which the critic describes the highest development of what he means by ambiguity, Freud writes what is correctly rendered in the already given translation.

The German verb *agnoszieren* itself is strange. Clearly based on the Latinization of a Greek word for non-recognition (as in the diagnostic term *agnosia*), the German verb means the opposite. "Agnoszieren" means "to acknowledge" or "to recognize" something or someone with a decidedly positive valence, as in the case of recognizing someone by bestowing an honor. This is oxymoronic in relation to the sense of the root in the ancient, "dead" languages. But "agnoszieren" is also the technical word for identifying a corpse. *Agnoszieren* and its preceding *nicht* are so tense here as to cause the ungrammatical break in the last sentence, as well as to retroactively give right to the preceding text of Freud's note as being charged with extreme ambivalence. Freud read both Ancient Greek and Latin. Furthermore, he wrote enough papers to fill a book of essays, only recently printed as a single volume, on the subject of *aphasia*, a genus of illnesses that contains a subordinate subgenus called *agnosia*. He cannot not know what this word means in Greek or Latin—neither as one who had studied them, nor as a German-speaking neurologist of his time, let alone as the author of the papers for which he was acknowledged, *agnosziert* in his own time (even if these were left out by the editors of his *Gesammelte Schriften* as well as by those of *The Standard Edition of the Complete Psychological Works of Sigmund Freud*, overlapping but not identical editorial and textual sets).

"Mach as I—[we had] simply not recognized him": this is written by one who has seen many corpses as part of his training, who has been trained in Classical Greek and Latin, and who has become a *professor*. Having come in as an "I" here on the coattails of Mach, himself dead at the time of Freud's writing, and in thus acknowledging and praising himself in his fantasy of identification with the former, as well as in the simultaneous supplemental mutilation of him (name and works are all that remain of Mach in 1919), Freud has little choice but to break off, lest he be in the position of identifying or recognizing his own corpse. Of course, in 1920, he will become even more famous by publishing *Beyond the Pleasure Principle*, with its renowned-in-being-disputed thesis that death is the aim of life; with its proclamation of a *death drive* evinced in the repetitions that had formerly belonged to life and its pleasure principle alone; in its announcing of the *compulsion to repeat* as this death drive's very calling card; and in the repeating of the idea that each finite biological existence is the way in which the eternal germ plasm of the species reproduces itself.

Psychoanalysis works out and recognizes the logic of the preceding unfolding of this note, of this strangely folded space where something simultaneously is both x and not-x, in the flickering in-and-out of the peripheral vision of the everyday unfamiliarity of the familiar. Indeed, "the Unfamiliar" is another uncanny-translation. "Heimlich," the adjective alone, without the negation, is hardly used as much in contemporary German as its formal negation: the ambivalence of this apparently non-negative word is strong enough that, with its connotations of secrecy, among others, it can also mean *unheimlich*.

In Freud's note the *unheimlich* is thus enacted, just as the themes immediately above are all present in "The Uncanny," even if history since has chalked all of these up to the next year and its own major book from Freud's pen. This enactment of being-in-vacillation, in ambivalence, of things lapsing into their opposite, of x-and-not-x, is one of the central axes of Freud's nervous-*unheimlich* system of the psyche. As a leitmotiv it runs from *The Interpretation of Dreams* (1899/1900),[5] through Freud's eponymous review of Karl Abel's "Über den Gegensinn der Urworte"[6] ("The Antithetical Meaning of Primal Words"), permeates "On Narcissism: An Introduction,"[7] pushes through "Die Verneinung,"[8] to "Constructions in Analysis"[9] and "The Splitting of the Ego in the Processes of Defense."[10]

It is by right that Freud is anxious about the uncanny. For the philosophers have trouble with psychoanalytic logic and its anaesthetizing of Aristotle's law of non-contradiction. The psychologists of more recent but not necessarily more advanced times have had to invent "cognitive dissonance" to try to say the same thing, without mentioning Freud. It is a shock for big science to learn that, in the aforementioned major work of 1920, it was he who first gave a robust account, in his discussion of traumatically induced repetition, of what is today called Post-Traumatic Stress Disorder. Socrates and Plato already knew about mania, narcissism, and ambivalence, and the troublesome intercourse between beings and their copies or images. This is not to say that

---

5   Sigmund Freud, *Gesammelte Werke*, vols 2–3.
6   Ibid., Vol. 8.
7   Idid., Vol. 10.
8   Ibid., Vol. 14.
9   Ibid., Vol. 16.
10 Ibid., Vol. 17, containing posthumous works.

purported founders of Western philosophy liked these transporting deportations or derangements of the full wakefulness of reason. Plato's banishment of mimetic art is the punishment for mimesis's leading to the vicious regress of "how much like, how much unlike?" Lacan, too, points in this direction when he responds to a young philosopher, who asks him "what the ontological status of the unconscious is" with his famous "the ontological status of the unconscious is that it is pre-ontological."[11] The unconscious has other characteristics of things not cordoned off by strictly philosophical accounts of being—of eggs, larvae, pupae—stages before the Imago arrives: it knows no time nor negation (these emerge with repression, and belong to the fortified border of the preconscious, not to the unconscious).

Too often the omnibus, the literal meaning of which is "for all," has been forgotten as the site of the radicalized uncanniness/*Unheimlickeit* of what was once called experience. Experience there still is, no matter how fragile, despite loud and reactive proclamations of its end. Uncannily enough, this is what remains too real for comfort.

SEE ALSO: Sublime; Shudder

---

11 See Jacques Lacan, *The Seminar of Jacques Lacan. Book XI. The Four Fundamental Concepts of Psychoanalysis*, trans. Alan Sheridan (New York: W. W. Norton 1981), 37.

Twenty-two Mood/Attunement
Darío González

In order to properly assess the constellation of meanings attached to the German word *Stimmung* in modern aesthetics, it seems necessary to pay attention to both the genesis and the grammar of the concept. Without forgetting its morphological proximity to *Stimme* (voice), *Bestimmung* (determination), and other related terms, *Stimmung* is used in a variety of contexts whose common denominator is the allusion to a certain fusion of the "objective" and the "subjective" dimensions of aesthetic experience. Even when the English word *mood* aptly describes both the inner character of a feeling and, by extension, the external conditions for its recognition or the possibility of its projection, the German concept refers in some cases to a sort of prior "accord" or "attunement" between the observer and the observed situation. The use of expressions taken from the sphere of music in the explanation of the English term reflects the alluded connection between *Stimme* and *Stimmung*. But even here it would be difficult to decide whether the "attunement" at issue is the accord of the mind to the world, or the mind's capacity to comprehend the play of the different "voices" or "tones" that constitute the world. This is what the Austrian philologist Leo Spitzer has in mind when, in the investigation of the origins of the concept, he describes the development of the motif of "world harmony" in classical and Christian thought. From a historical point of view, the revival of Neoplatonism in the Italian Renaissance should be mentioned as the most important link between that tradition and modern aesthetics. *Stimmung,* in this sense, is first of all the "musicalization" of the soul, its mystical attunement to the beautiful order of the universe expressed, in turn, by the idea of the "music of the stars." But the German word was also capable of covering other uses of the concept of "harmony." Spitzer shows that the expression *"Concent der Stimmung"* appears, for instance, in a 1547 translation of Vitruvius, that is, in the domain of the so-called *"Massästhetik,"* the aesthetics of measurement and proportions. The general applicability of the concept to different empirical fields seems to indicate that the use of the word *Stimmung* was related to the practice of synesthesia:

> It is thanks to this practice that the musical term could be freely used, not only in the other arts, but also in the realm of the human psyche. Consequently, we will find in Renaissance poetry many passages in which the poet (conceived of as a musician) is represented as 'attuning his instrument' to accord with the song he is to sing.[1]

Although the continuity between this conception of poetical activity and the modern use of the notion cannot be denied, it is important to take into account, following D. E. Wellbery, the historical "turning point" through which some aspects of the traditional idea of harmony pass from a "speculative-symbolic theology" into a "reflective aesthetic theory."[2] After quoting Goethe's characterization of the artist as the one able to "see everywhere the sacred vibrations and quiet tones through which Nature unites all objects," Wellbery observes that this unity is "not the organic purposiveness" of Nature, but the fact that "the artistic view unfolds the given objects as a game of echoing tonal variations and, thus, it perceives the different objects in an encompassing unity that transmits a surplus of meaning."[3] It is not difficult to recognize in these remarks an allusion to a particular motif in Kant's theory of judgment, namely the distinction between the "objective purposiveness" of teleological judgments (concerning things as *natural ends*) and the "subjective purposiveness" of aesthetic judgments of reflection (concerning "indeterminately purposive *natural forms*").[4] In the second case, the only basis determining the judgment is "the harmonious play of the two cognitive faculties [...], the imagination and the understanding."[5] Deprived from the cosmological background of the traditional concept of harmony, the very notion of the "free play" between faculties marks the transition towards what has been called a "reflective aesthetic theory." In fact, Wellbery suggests that the incorporation of *Stimmung* into the vocabulary of aesthetics goes

---

1 Leo Spitzer, *Classical and Christian Ideas of World Harmony. Prolegomena to an Interpretation of the Word "Stimmung"* (Baltimore, MD: Johns Hopkins, 1963), 134.
2 David E Wellbery, *Stimmung*, in Karlheinz Barck et al., *Historisches Wörterbuch Ästhetischer Grundbegriffe*, ed. 5:703–33 (Stuttgart & Weimar: Metzler, 2003), 706.
3 Ibid., 705.
4 Immanuel Kant, *Kritik der Urteilskraft* (Hamburg: Meiner, 2006), 531–2.
5 Ibid., 520.

back to Kant's use of it—albeit mainly as a "metaphor"— in the *Critique of Judgment*.[6] The possibility of a representation's "attunement (*Zusammenstimmung*)," not to the object through a determined concept, but to the "conditions of universality" required by understanding, can from now on be conceived of as the criterion for the aesthetic use of the faculty of judgment.[7] Previous to the feeling of pleasure attached to representations, those conditions of universality constitute the ground of communicability of our judgments of taste. As to the sphere of "feeling" as such, some scholars have insisted on the fact that the author of the *Critique of Judgment* does not neglect its significance. According to Walter Biemel, for instance, Kant attributes to feelings and moods "a function of disclosure" that before him "had been granted only to logical cognition", "implicitly" giving them "a veritative import that only in our days, with Heidegger and Scheler, has found its appropriate justification."[8]

It is Schiller, however, who in his reassessment of Kant's theory of beauty interprets the "free play" of the faculties as the removal of the opposition between sense experience and reason, as much as between feeling and thought, in a specifically "aesthetic disposition of the mind [ästhetische Stimmung des Gemüths]."[9] Leading the sensuous man to "form" and the spiritual man to "the world of sense," beauty allows the human mind to traverse an "intermediary disposition in which sensibility and reason are *at the same time* active, and thus they mutually destroy their determinant (*bestimmende*) power." The mediating function of aesthetic disposition corresponds to the role assigned to the "play drive" as unifying factor between the "form drive" and the "material drive." In so far as the mind "is neither physically nor morally constrained and yet is in both ways active," this "free disposition" is obtained when we "step backwards" from determination to "a state of pure determinability [einen Zustand der bloßen Bestimmbarkeit]."[10] It would be possible to invoke the same arguments in order to explain why the "aesthetic state," in spite of its indeterminate character, is also the "state of the highest reality" and "the most productive in relation to knowledge and morality."[11] An important corollary of this view within Schiller's idealistic theory of the arts is

---

6   Wellbery, *Stimmung*, 707–9.
7   Kant, *Kritik der Urteilskraft*, 69.
8   Walter Biemel, *Die Bedeutung von Kants Begründung der Ästhetik für die Philosophie der Kunst* (Köln: Kölner Universitäts-Verlag, 1959), 145.
9   Friedrich Schiller, Über die ästhetische Erziehung des Menschen in einer Reihe von *Briefen. Werke*, Vol. 12 (Stuttgart & Tübingen: Gottaschen Buchhandlung, 1838), 90.
10 Ibid., 85.
11 Ibid., 90–1.

that "the excellence of a work of art" is understood as proportional to "the universality of the disposition" it produces beyond the diversity of material forces operating in the specific media. Thus, "the different arts come to resemble each other more and more in the action which *they exercise on the mind.*"[12]

The abandon of the question concerning the universal communicability of aesthetic judgments—which had been the frame of Kant's theory of beauty—becomes even clearer in the tradition of German Idealism after Fichte. In the context of romantic aesthetics, subjectivity is not just the site of the formal conditions for the appreciation of beauty but, rather, the inner power whose "movements" or "vibrations" are to be conveyed by the artist. As one might expect, the field in which this conception finds its utmost application is the theory of lyric poetry. According to Hegel's *Lessons on Aesthetics*, "since in lyric it is the *subject* who expresses himself, [...] subjectivity as such is the proper content of the poem, so what matters is only the soul of sensation and not what the respective object is."[13] An interesting point here is that, rather than referring to the continuity of "an objective action," the lyric poem can concentrate on "the most fleeting mood of the moment [die flüchtigste Stimmung des Augenblicks]."[14] Parallel to the Hegelian account of the significance of moods in poetry, however, is the description of that phenomenon in the *Philosophy of Subjective Spirit*. The context for the characterization of *Stimmung* in Hegel's philosophical anthropology is the investigation of the "relation of the outer sensations with the interiority of the sentient subject."[15] Illustrated by our ability to indicate certain moods through colors, sounds—among which the human voice occupies a particular place—odors, flavors, etc., that relation is previous both to self-awareness and to the awareness of an alien object. Conceptually distinguished from the more encompassing term "feeling", "sensation [Empfindung]" involves sensitivity or sentimentality [Empfindsamkeit], and, as such, it emphasizes "the side of passivity or of finding [die Seite der Passivität, des Findens], i.e. the immediacy of the determinateness in feeling [der Unmittelbarkeit der Bestimmtheit im Fühlen], whereas feeling rather refers to the selfhood involved in it."[16] With important variations, the ambiguity of the notion of *Stimmung*—as content of the poetic experience and as a form of

---

12 Ibid., 93.
13 Georg Wilhelm Friedrich Hegel, *Vorlesungen über die Ästhetik. Dritter Band. Jubiläumsausgabe*, Vol. 14 (Stuttgart: Frommann, 1964), 424.
14 Ibid.
15 Georg Wilhelm Friedrich Hegel, *System der Philosophie. Dritter Teil. Die Philosophie des Geistes. Jubiläumsausgabe*, Vol. 10 (Stuttgart: Frommann, 1958), 134.
16 Ibid., 148.

sensation prior to the distinction between the self and the world—is preserved in Kierkegaard's reception of Hegel's philosophy. On the one hand, the description of the "aesthetic" sphere of life in Kierkegaard's *Either/Or* implies the critique of a personality that only "exists in the mood [Stemning]." Unable to attain the stability required by ethics, the aesthetic personality "dissolves" in a series of ephemeral moods marked by the tension between melancholy and frivolity. On the other hand, in *The Concept of Anxiety,* Kierkegaard attempts to identify "the mood that properly corresponds" to the notion of "sin," suggesting that the right mood—"earnestness"—only can be found in the individual's ethical and religious address to another individual.[17] More important for the later history of the concept, nevertheless, is the fact that *anxiety* is indicated in that work as the existential mood corresponding to the "real possibility" of sin. The manifestation of anxiety in the stage of "dreaming spirit"—that is, before "the difference between myself and my other is posited"—is characterized in terms taken over from Hegel's *Philosophy of Subjective Spirit,* albeit through the exposition of those topics by Karl Rosenkranz in his *Psychology or Science of Subjective Spirit*. It is precisely in that stage that the mood of anxiety is said to have "an intimated nothing" as its object.[18]

The crisis of the metaphysics of German idealism resulted in the transformation of the role performed by the notion of *Stimmung*. From Hegel to Nietzsche, the process of dissolution of the traditional disciplines devoted to the study of the human soul made it possible to redefine that notion on the basis of historical, sociological, and rhetorical investigations. Towards the end of the nineteenth century, at least two positions are to be mentioned. The first one is represented by Hugo von Hoffmannsthal in the 1896 essay "Poetry and Life." Hoffmannsthal's return to the idea of the "ephemeral state of the soul [...] that we call mood" is accompanied by a clear acknowledgment of the role of language as the concrete materiality of the poem. The entire problem consisting in the lyric construction of the relation between the inner and the outer world takes a new orientation as soon as subjectivity itself has lost its metaphysical density. The second case is that of the Austrian art historian Alois Riegl. In his 1899 article entitled "Mood as the Subject Matter of Modern Art," Riegl develops the assumption that our longing for *redemption through harmony*—a harmony we cannot find in nature—is the fundamental drive of artistic activity. In the same way as the mere presence of primitive fetishes, the classical ideal of bodily beauty, and the Christian expression of spiritual perfection were

---

17 Søren Kierkegaard, *Begrebet Angest. Skrifter,* Vol. 4 (Copenhagen: Gad, 1994), 322–3.
18 Ibid., 347.

responses to that demand, "our" time finds in the scientific worldview the possibility of a redeeming harmony, in so far as it allows us to take hold, beyond the particularity of conflicting phenomena, to a complete range of those phenomena *seen from a distance*. A similar preoccupation can be detected in Georg Simmel's *Philosophy of Landscape*, published in 1913: we are only aware of "seeing a landscape" when our consciousness attains a unitary whole that transcends the mechanical composition of the elements. As in earlier phases of the German aesthetic tradition, *Stimmung* seems to designate a non-reducible meaning that can become perceptible under the condition of a unifying vision. What seems to constitute a new turning point in the interpretation of the phenomenon, however, is the increasing awareness of the necessity of that kind of vision in the modern world.

Taking into account the complexity of its historical and systematic presuppositions, Martin Heidegger's philosophical re-evaluation of the notion of *Stimmung* deserves particular consideration. The essential characteristic of Heidegger's approach in the 1927 treatise *Being and Time* is the reference of the "ontic" phenomenon of "mood [Stimmung]" or "Being-attuned [Gestimmtsein]" to an ontological structure, i.e. to a specific feature of our Being-in-the-world.[19] That ontological structure is indicated through the term *Befindlichkeit*, rendered in English as "state-of-mind" or "attunement," and further explained by one of its translators as "the state in which one may be found." Following a path of investigation sketched in his 1924 lecture course on "The Basic Concepts of Aristotelian Philosophy," Heidegger suggests in *Being and Time* that the earliest systematic interpretation of πάθη [affects] takes place in Aristotle's *Rhetoric:* before being described within the framework of a "psychology" in terms of feelings and emotions, "moods" are that in which and out of which the orator speaks.[20] From an ontological point of view, what is at issue here is the *function of disclosure* of the state-of-mind, its role in shaping the "reliance on the world out of which we can encounter something that matters to us."[21] Thus, the mood "comes neither from 'outside' nor from 'inside'"; on the contrary, it "has in every case already disclosed the Being-in-the-world as a whole, and makes it possible first and foremost to direct oneself towards something."[22] Strictly speaking, our "encounter" with entities is not just a "sensing [Empfinden]" or "staring at" something; if entities can be "touched [gerührt]" and "have a meaning for ... [Sinn haben für]" something, it is only because "the 'senses' [die 'Sinne']"

---

19 Martin Heidegger, *Sein und Zeit* (Tübingen: Niemeyer, 1993), 134–40.
20 Ibid., 139.
21 Ibid., 137–8.
22 Ibid., 136–7.

belong ontologically to a Being-in-the-world that shows itself in the state-of-mind.[23] These remarks are consistent with Heidegger's account of "state-of-mind" as co-original with "understanding" within the structure of the "disclosedness" of our Being-in-the-world.[24] In a similar fashion, the emphasis on the function of disclosure attached by the later Heidegger to the poetic word, particularly in his lectures and seminars on Hölderlin, is based on the idea that the "fundamental mood [Grundstimmung]" of poetry "de-termines [be-stimmt]" the ground [Grund] on which language institutes a historical world.

Heidegger's view on the "disclosive" character of moods in *Being and Time* is influenced by Kierkegaard's conception of anxiety, although the merely "psychological" scope of that conception is now referred back to its ontological condition of possibility. The importance of the "fundamental state-of-mind of anxiety" among the diversity of our moods can be comprehended against the background of Heidegger's distinction between, on the one hand, our relation to the "entities" we encounter "within the world" and, on the other hand, our "Being-in-the-world as such." Different from the mood of "fear" regarding a determinate entity, anxiety seems to be confronted with "nothing," but in such a way that this "nothing" is "grounded in the most primordial 'something'—in the *world*." In so far as our "Being-in-the-world itself is that in the face of which anxiety is anxious," anxiety implies the experience of our own being-*thrown* into existence, in a world we never fully master.[25] The *fundamental* character of the mood of anxiety consists in the fact that this mood brings us face to face with "the uncanniness [die Unheimlichkeit]" of our "everyday" and "familiar" Being-in-the-world, our "not-being-at-home [Nicht-zuhause-sein]."[26] This fundamental disclosure, however, is at the same time the revelation of the possibility of an "authentic" existence.[27]

Interestingly, the idea of a suspension of our everyday attitude on the basis of certain "fundamental moods" is developed by another author of the time. According to Fritz Kaufmann in his 1929 essay "The Meaning of Artistic Attunement," artworks are particularly able to suggest the feeling of a whole of being, making visible the relation of life and world. Compared to this view, Heidegger is doubtlessly more inclined to emphasize the ambiguous and disruptive character of the event of disclosure. Close to the "uncanny" revelation of anxiety described in *Being and Time*, the experience of *nostalgia* (*Heimweh*)

---

23 Ibid., 137.
24 Ibid., 160.
25 Ibid., 187.
26 Ibid., 342, 189.
27 Ibid., 343.

is mentioned as one of the "fundamental moods" of philosophy in the 1929–30 lecture course *The Basic Concepts of Metaphysics: World, Finitude, Solitude*.[28] Another remarkable feature of that lecture course is the extensive section devoted to the "fundamental mood" of *boredom* (*Langeweile*), a phenomenon that Heidegger would characterize later, in *Contributions to Philosophy*, as the hidden destination of modernity.

SEE ALSO: Judgment; Beauty; Feeling; Truth

---

28 Martin Heidegger, *Die Grundbegriffe der Metaphysik. Welt—Endlichkeit—Einsamkeit* (Frankfurt am Main: Klostermann, 2004), 7.

Twenty-three Film

Johannes von Moltke

In his "Thoughts on an Aesthetics of the Cinema," first published in 1913, Georg Lukács writes: "something new and beautiful has come to be and yet instead of taking it as it is, one attempts to strip it of its true meaning and confine it to old, inappropriate categories."[1] Criticizing the treatment of cinema either in purely pedagogical terms as a medium for instruction, or in economic terms as competition for the theater, Lukács was an early advocate for an aesthetic approach to the new medium.

But even for those, long in the minority, who implicitly agreed that film amounted to a new art form,[2] the question of how to formulate an "aesthetics of the cinema" remained a vexed one. The birth of film at the end of the nineteenth century posed a challenge to the history and philosophy of aesthetics; the task of theory was initially to work out the encounter between the new medium and existing aesthetic categories. Here, three lines of inquiry offered themselves: first, theorists could take the new medium as an occasion for applying existing aesthetic criteria and insights to new material, resulting in the medium's *integration* into an established system that otherwise remained fundamentally unaltered. Such a view would appear to have fueled Béla Balázs' early call to assign film "a chapter in ... the great aesthetic systems" of the time,[3] and it formed the explicit object of Rudolf Arnheim's influential account in *Film as Art*—a book designed to "demonstrate that the art of film did not fall from the sky but operates according to the same

---

1 Georg Lukács, "Thoughts on an Aesthetics of the Cinema," *Polygraph* 13 (2001): 13–18.
2 See Anton Kaes, ed., *Kino-Debatte: Zum Verhältnis von Literatur und Film 1909–1929* (Tübingen: Niemeyer, 1984).
3 Béla Balázs, *Early Film Theory: Visible Man and The Spirit of Film*, ed. Erica Carter, trans. Rodney Livingstone (New York: Berghahn, 2010), 3.

age-old laws and principles as do all the other arts."[4] Second, the addition of film as the "seventh art" could occasion a new branch of aesthetic inquiry—"film theory"—that treated the medium *sui generis*, but still left intact the established aesthetic categories inasmuch as the other arts are concerned; this would amount to an *expansion* of aesthetics and aesthetic categories to cover new phenomena. Lukács' "Thoughts" steer in this direction, drawing on received notions of the beautiful in both nature and art to formulate a theory of cinema's fantastic naturalism; and three years after Lukács, Hugo Münsterberg would devote an entire book to the psychology and aesthetics of *The Photoplay*, having set out to "study the right of the photoplay, hitherto ignored by esthetics, to be classed as an art in itself ...."[5] But we also find later film theorists of this persuasion—among them Siegfried Kracauer, whose classic treatise *Theory of Film* develops a new set of aesthetic criteria drawn from the history of photography to argue that "if film is an art at all, it should certainly not be confused with the established arts."[6]

Both of these approaches fall short from a third perspective, according to which the new medium challenged the very foundations of aesthetic theory, much like quantum physics unsettled long-held Newtonian beliefs. "To a quantum physicist," writes a leading quantum physicist (borrowing his metaphor from the movies), "classical physics is a black-and-white image of a Technicolor world. Our classical categories fail to capture that world in all its richness."[7] The discovery of quantum behavior, he notes, "forces us to rethink how we look at the universe and accept a new and unfamiliar picture of our world."[8] To a film theorist of this third persuasion, classical aesthetics similarly offers a still image of a moving object, its categories inadequate to understanding the new and unfamiliar world of art after the advent of the motion picture. This version of the encounter between philosophical aesthetics and the new medium would amount to nothing short of a paradigm change, or a *revolution* of aesthetics—a view famously taken by Walter Benjamin in his essay on "The Work of Art in the Age of its Mechanical Reproducibility." Here, Benjamin advanced the thesis, among others, that the quintessentially modern medium of cinema had revolutionized the very foundations of the aesthetic, requiring the

---

4   Rudolf Arnheim, *Film as Art* (Berkeley: University of California Press, 1957), 16.
5   Hugo Münsterberg, *Münsterberg on Film. The Photoplay: A Psychological Study and Other Writings*, ed. Alan Langdale (New York: Routledge, 2001), 39.
6   Siegfried Kracauer, *Theory of Film: The Redemption of Physical Reality* (Princeton, NJ: Princeton University Press, 1997), 40.
7   Vlatko Vedral, "Living in a Quantum World," *Scientific American* 304 (6) (June 2011): 38.
8   Ibid.

introduction of new concepts into the theory of art (concepts which, Benjamin claimed, would be "useful for the formulation of revolutionary demands in the politics of art").[9] Henceforth, Benjamin argued, it was futile to ask simply whether film could be considered art and to neglect the far more fundamental question of "whether the invention of photography [and consequently of cinema]—had not transformed the entire character of art."[10]

To be sure, Benjamin could point to numerous aspects of the medium that apparently burst asunder traditionally held notions of aesthetic philosophy: cinema, he claimed, countered contemplation with distraction, it did away with the notion of the beautiful (*schöner Schein*). In place of the individual bourgeois subject, it enthroned the masses as the subject of aesthetic reception, and its technological basis appeared to undermine some of the basic assumptions about representation, aesthetic imagination, and originality—or what Benjamin famously, if somewhat cryptically, defined as "aura." As his friend Theodor W. Adorno would also argue (though he remained far less enthusiastic than Benjamin concerning the implications of this argument), the mechanical recording device that made film possible drew into question the vaunted "autonomy" of the art work.

The notion that cinema ushered in a paradigm shift in the philosophy of aesthetics has an undeniable radical appeal that may account, in part, for the currency of Benjamin's thinking in film studies; but the watershed that divides pre-cinema aesthetics from a modern(ist) theory of art is also a rhetorical construction that hides significant underlying continuities. For it can hardly be claimed—*pace* Benjamin—that the advent of cinema did away with the categories of philosophical aesthetics, or that the latter lost all relevance in the face of exponential media change during the twentieth century. Especially during the early years of theorizing about film—in the texts now collectively viewed as "classical film theory"—we can trace the persistence of aesthetic categories derived from German idealism and romanticism; even though the cinema may have strained their conceptual boundaries, these remained the categories in which a generation of film critics and theorists, all of them steeped in the traditions of German aesthetics, made sense of the new medium. Looking back, David Rodowick rightly finds it "curious that early in the twentieth century film would

---

9   Walter Benjamin, "The Work of Art in the Age of Its Technological Reproducibility," Second version, *The Work of Art in the Age of Its Technological Reproducibility and Other Writings on Media*, ed. Michael Jennings, Brigid Doherty, and Thomas Y. Levin (Cambridge, MA: Harvard University Press, 2008), 20.
10 Ibid., 28.

become associated with theory, rather than with aesthetics or the philosophy of art."[11]

Hardly a theoretical account of cinema during the first half of the twentieth century, for example, can do without a comparison between theater and film, as if one could only make sense of the new by comparing it with the known. From Lukács's "Thoughts on an Aesthetics of the Cinema" and Hugo Münsterberg's *Photoplay* (1916) through Arnheim's *Film as Art* (1931) and Kracauer's *Theory of Film* (1960), critics measured the artistic merits of the cinema against established aesthetics of the stage. The goal, in each case, was to defend the cinema against the claim that it was nothing but a reproduction, "canned theater" at best (and mere *Schund* [schlock; trash] at worst), and to demonstrate the specific capabilities and promises, as well as limitations, of cinema as an art form. The debt to classical aesthetics was similar in all these cases, but became explicit in an essay penned by Rudolf Arnheim in 1938, and included in the heavily revised English edition of *Film as Art* in 1957: under the title "A New Laocoön: Artistic Composites and the Talking Film," Arnheim took up the comparison between film and theater to argue the specificity of silent film (and draw into question the legitimacy of sound film as a "composite" medium). But Lessing looms large in other accounts as well, all the way down to Siegfried Kracauer who would still invoke his comparative treatment of poetry and painting to argue that "the achievements within a particular medium are all the more satisfying aesthetically if they build from the specific properties of the medium."[12] Although the pervasive "medium-specificity arguments" of classical film theory meanwhile have been roundly critiqued by Noël Carroll, they testify to the endurance of classical aesthetics in theorizations of the new medium.

But even more than Lessing, it is Kant who continues to loom large in the texts of classical film theory—nowhere more so, perhaps, than in the early contribution by Hugo Münsterberg,[13] a German-born psychologist who was invited by William James to teach at Harvard, where he spent the better part of his career. Influenced by the neo-Kantian school and especially his close friend Heinrich Rickert, Münsterberg's writings and activities ranged broadly across the nascent discipline of psychology and philosophy; at the end of his life, he discovered a passion for the cinema and promptly wrote a short book on the subject that counts as

---

11   David N Rodowick, "An Elegy for Theory," *October* 22 (Fall 2007): 92.
12   Siegfried Kracauer, *Theory of Film: The Redemption of Physical Reality* (Princeton, NJ: Princeton University Press, 1997), 12.
13   See Hugo Münsterberg, *Münsterberg on Film. The Photoplay: A Psychological Study and Other Writings*, ed. Alan Langdale (New York: Routledge, 2001).

one of the first sustained theoretical contributions. Fascinated by what he considered to be parallels between the technological and aesthetic potential of cinema on the one hand, and the functioning of the mind on the other, Münsterberg undertook a transcendental investigation of the new medium. Not only does the "photoplay" (as the recently established feature-length narrative cinema was called at the time) offer particularly successful examples of artistic play, or what Kant famously defined as purposiveness without a purpose. In addition, one might sum up the Kantian premises of Münsterberg's argument by suggesting that he mines cinema for the conditions of possibility of aesthetic judgments.[14] As he insists throughout *The Photoplay*, cinema shapes and molds the outer world to correspond to the inner, subjective movement of the mind. For Münsterberg, this is a double process, in which the aesthetic object is first "isolated" from its external, instrumental connections and then sublimated into a purposive unity that can become the object of aesthetic judgment.

Münsterberg explicitly builds the culminating aesthetic argument of his treatise on a psychological foundation. As an experimental psychologist, Münsterberg is particularly interested in the fact that cinema can generate the impression of movement and depth from a series of still, two-dimensional representations; in a chapter devoted to the problem of depth and movement, he relates this crucial technological aspect of the medium to experiments in visual psychology to conclude that the depth and motion we see are "created by [our] own mind[s]" and that we consequently "invest the impressions" we receive in the cinema with *a priori* categories located in the subject rather than in the object. Having thus established the profoundly idealist character of the new medium, Münsterberg then proceeds to unfold a series of aesthetic categories that are not only operative in the cinema, but for which the technical and narrative devices of cinema would appear to offer ideal representations: in the close-up, Münsterberg argues, we find an analogon for the faculty of attention; the cut from one space of action to another both enacts and represents—or, as Münsterberg writes, "objectifies"—an act of imagination; the flashback both draws upon and instantiates the faculty of memory. Like Lukács before him, Münsterberg celebrates all these devices for their new possibilities— and he celebrates them for their apparent independence from the laws of space, time, and causality. It is in this (idealist) sense that Münsterberg considers the cinema an art form: bound far closer to the workings of the mind than to the exigencies of everyday reality, and yet held together by the narrative "unity" of the "photoplays" that

---

14 See Donald Laurence Fredericksen, *The Aesthetic of Isolation in Film Theory: Hugo Münsterberg* (New York: Arno Press, 1977).

Münsterberg considered the medium's fullest realization (as opposed to the many non-fictional uses to which it could be put), the cinema was perhaps the ultimate art form, serving no ulterior purpose and yet intensely bound up with the faculties of judgment, the laws of perception and cognition.

Though Münsterberg ties these arguments into a highly normative aesthetic toward the end of his book, his emphasis on the cognitive and perceptive dimensions of the new medium has remained influential over the intervening century, up to and including recent cognitivist accounts of film narrative and cinematic perception by David Bordwell and Noël Carroll, among others. In this tradition, Rudolf Arnheim's important *Film as Art*, originally published in 1931 and translated into English (in a significantly altered version) in 1957, serves as an important relay. Münsterberg himself already cites psychological experiments by Max Wertheimer, under whom Arnheim would acquire his foundational training in Gestalt psychology; although the latter was apparently unaware of Münsterberg's work at the time he wrote *Film as Art*, his approach shares a number of premises, and even some conclusions, with *The Photoplay*: Arnheim, too, approaches film from the point of view of perception in order to argue its aesthetic value; and although he strategically emphasizes the medium's productive limitations rather than its novel possibilities, he similarly concludes that these limitations put enough daylight between cinema and reality to allow us to speak of the former as an art form. Against those who claim that the cinema is bound to reproduce what is already before the camera, thereby offering no aesthetic surplus-value in its own right, Arnheim points out the form-giving powers inherent in the cinema's technical reduction of the world to framed, two-dimensional, gray scale images: "by the absence of colors, of three-dimensional depth, by being sharply limited by the margins on the screen, and so forth," Arnheim argues, "film is most satisfactorily denuded of its realism."[15] Taking a position paradigmatic for what would later be labeled "formalist" film theory, Arnheim assumes—much like Münsterberg did a quarter century before him—that "art begins where mechanical reproduction leaves off, where the conditions of representation serve in some way to mould the object."[16] The implicit premise remains, of course, the Kantian claim that the aesthetic world exists at a remove from reality, that its own sense of purposiveness will not and should not be confused with a world in which actions have practical consequences.

As in Kant, however, the corresponding forms of perception and

---

15 Arnheim, *Film as Art*, 26.
16 Ibid., 55.

judgment on the side of the spectator are not linked exclusively to the form-giving powers of aesthetics and to artistic beauty, but obtain also in the face of natural phenomena, whether in terms of the sublime or of what Kant calls *das Naturschöne*, the beauty of nature. Here, too, theorists considered the cinema ideally positioned to enable heightened forms of aesthetic perception, but the focus shifted from cinema's unique formal capabilities to its technologically inscribed mimetic powers. Where "formalist" critics such as Münsterberg and Arnheim had emphasized the distance between the film image and the "pro-filmic" world that it ostensibly represents, an equally influential thinker such as Béla Balázs would point out the new medium's power to reveal the "physiognomy" of things as they already existed. The face in cinema, isolated and enlarged by the device of the close-up, exemplified this notion, much like the close-up had objectified the mental act of "attention" for Münsterberg. But for Balázs, the concept of physiognomy extended well beyond the legibility of the face to the realm of objects and the natural world. In this sense, it approximated the notion of the *Naturschöne*, though the exalted language of Balázs' contributions as a film critic and author of two of the most influential books of classical film theory[17] pointed more in the direction of the appropriations and revisions of Kant's aesthetics by the Romantics than to the *Critique of Judgment*. This is particularly evident in the recurrent trope of immediacy in Balázs' writings, the sense that the truly popular medium of film helps retrieve a lost visual language that circumvents the mediations of verbal language and fuses subject and object, spectator and image, in a quasi-spiritual union.

Although Balázs was arguably closer to the contemporary "impressionists" among French film-makers and theorists of the young medium than to later "realists" such as Siegfried Kracauer, the latter would reference Balázs' work throughout his career, up to and including his *Theory of Film*, hardly a work that could be mistaken for an heir to romantic aesthetics. And yet, Kracauer shared with Balázs what Malcolm Turvey has usefully termed the "revelationist" outlook of many classical theories, i.e. the argument that film—whether conceived as a mimetic medium or celebrated for its anti-mimetic powers of form—could not only record but also reveal aspects of physical reality that were hidden or otherwise inaccessible to human vision. In order to argue this case, Kracauer developed a sustained account of film as an extension of photography; both media, he stipulated, were defined by their inherent "affinities" toward the unstaged, the fortuitous, the indeterminate, endlessness, and, in the case of film, the "flow of life." According to Kracauer's phenomenological argument, the

---

17 See Balázs, *Early Film Theory*.

specific "explorative powers"[18] of photographic media lay not in the construction of a separate, aesthetic universe but in re-connecting the spectator, at the level of experience, with the concrete reality of the material world. In this sense, Kracauer, too, remained invested in a "physiognomic" reading of the world, a tradition that extended from Balázs backwards through the Romantics, to the works of Goethe, and—as Aitken has argued—to Kant's notion of the *Naturschöne*.[19]

Alongside André Bazin, who was developing astonishingly similar arguments in France, Kracauer is generally considered a "realist" film theorist, in contradistinction to the "formalists" from Münsterberg through Eisenstein to Arnheim. In recent years, it has become clear, however, that this distinction between formalism and realism has perhaps obscured some equally, if not more important underlying concepts that unite the apparently divergent approaches of classical film theorists. Turvey's recovery of the "revelationist tradition" provides one starting point from which to reconsider these overlaps, as does Aitken's account of "intuitionist" approaches. Building on such relatively recent interventions, which themselves reflect a return to aesthetic concerns after several decades of theorizing driven by linguistic, psychoanalytic, and sociological paradigms, we may now want to "zoom out" even further, opening the lens widely enough to encompass some of the concepts and theoretical premises that continue to lurk behind revelationist or intuitionist, let alone formalist or realist paradigms. Given the philosophical training of most classical film theorists, these concepts and premises will inevitably still have their roots in aesthetic philosophy, no matter how much the advent of the new medium might have contributed to uprooting those traditions. Idealist and romantic conceptions of art and the aesthetic, of the faculties of imagination and perception, remain operative in classical film theory as much as does the debate about medium-specificity. And at a more fundamental level, virtually all film theorizing takes place under the assumption, operative from Baumgarten through Adorno, that the aesthetic describes what is known through the senses, as opposed to through concepts: as a medium that is, in Christian Metz's tentative phrase, "more perceptual" than other media, the cinema has provided a particularly fertile ground for exploring aesthetic knowledge in this sense.

SEE ALSO: Medium/Mediation; Montage/Collage

---

18 Kracauer, *Theory of Film*, 22.
19 Ian Aitken, *European Film Theory and Cinema: A Critical Introduction* (Edinburgh: Edinburgh University Press, 2001), 172.

Twenty-four Montage/Collage
Patrizia McBride

A key term in the reconceptualization of art in the twentieth century, montage involves strategies of citation, juxtaposition, and combination that cut across diverse media and genres, including literature, drama, painting, sculpture, photography, film, radio, and the plethora of media born of the digital revolution. The term denotes an intertextual or intermedial exchange that hinges on readily identifiable operations of quotation and appropriation. Its emphasis on the moment of construction and the "found" quality of the incorporated materials sets it off from the conceptually proximate category of pastiche. While it is true that practices involving quotation, the recycling of found materials, and intermedial boundary-crossing well predate the twentieth century, montage art reflects a specific cultural constellation at the century's onset that was shaped by the development of technologies of mechanical reproduction and the rise of the modern mass media, the advent of a consumer culture, the demise of a normative aesthetics, and the blurring of the nineteenth-century divide between high art and popular forms. Accordingly, montage art relates to new ways of seeing and experiencing shaped by life in the metropolis, the world of machines and assembly-line production, and the leisure culture of a mass society.

Originally tied to the domains of industrial production and the military, in German the term "montage" migrated to the realm of art in the 1920s to become the overarching category encompassing "cut-and-paste" practices in diverse media and genres ranging from verbal and visual collage to photomontage, film editing, and sculptural assemblage. While it is true that after the mid-1920s the use of the term was bolstered by reception of the film theory of influential Soviet directors (Eisenstein, Kuleshov, Pudovkin, Vertov) who saw in editing a key principle of film poetics, the word "montage" is by no means a simple extension of a principle of film to non-filmic media. An understanding of montage as an activist practice that blurs the boundaries of media and genres was operative as early as 1920 within Dadaism, as witnessed by George Grosz's designation of John Heartfield as artist-laborer or "Monteur" (literally: mechanic or assembly-fitter). Indeed, within Dadaist and Constructivist circles the term montage was chosen over the French "collage" because of its ties to the world of modern technology and industrial labor, as well as its emphasis on the constructed nature of the artwork and its dependence on found materials and ready-made parts. The montage practices of Dadaism and Constructivism continued and often radicalized the inquiry into the boundaries of verbal and visual expression that had driven the experiments of French Cubism and Italian Futurism. In the visual arts this gave way to a rejection of illusionistic compositions and an exploration of non-naturalistic, often non-figurative arrangements bound to interrogate the semiotics of visual communication and its interplay with verbal codes (see the collages and photomontages of Hannah Höch, Raoul Hausmann, Kurt Schwitters, John Heartfield, László Moholy-Nagy, and Marianne Brandt as well as the graphic work of pioneers of the new typography like El Lissitzky and Jan Tschichold). In the realm of literature the works of Richard Huelsenbeck, Raoul Hausmann, and Kurt Schwitters defied established narrative and lyric conventions to explore the materiality of language and its operation as a medium of communication, often by foregrounding the sonoric qualities and visual appearance of the linguistic inserts. For the new medium of film, debates hinged on the privileged position of editing in film aesthetics and poetics, a viewpoint championed by Soviet film-makers and incisively developed by Walter Benjamin, yet also challenged by influential critics like Rudolf Arnheim (*Film as Art*, 1932).[1]

In the 1920s montage emerged as an umbrella term for describing influential attempts at reviving traditional artistic genres, often under the rubric of a modernist aesthetics of shock and defamiliarization that fed off the cacophonous and disjointed quality of modern life. In Bertolt Brecht's project for an epic theater, which drew on the stage innovations of Erwin Piscator while moving beyond them, the montage principle resulted in the contrapunctual deployment of disparate devices (discontinuous plot, non-naturalistic acting, the use of posters, film clips, and projections on stage) that prevent narrative and ideological closure and shatter aesthetic illusion. The ultimate aim is to foil the spectators' identification with characters on stage in order to foster active engagement in the unfolding performance. In the domain of the novel, Walter Benjamin singled out Alfred Döblin's

---

1   See Rudolf Arnheim, *Film as Art* (Berkeley: University of California Press, 1957).

montage novel, *Berlin Alexanderplatz* (1930), as the epitome of a new epos suited for the presentation of collective experience in massified modern societies. Benjamin especially praised the narrative's montage of unsublimated inserts culled from the socio-economic underworld of the metropolis, which in his view helped shatter the artificial closure of the bourgeois *Bildungsroman*. Critics also cited the work's proximity to the montage technique of James Joyce's *Ulysses* (1922) and John Dos Passos' *Manhattan Transfer* (1925). In the poetry of Gottfried Benn the unsettling montage of phrases and images drawn from the debased reality of trench warfare and metropolitan life served to express the hallucinatory intensity of an ecstatic experience that sheds the shackles of subjectivity to return to the biological roots of undifferentiated life.

Art historian Franz Roh was among the first to illustrate the effects of modernist montage by pointing to the confrontation it stages between the realism of inserted fragments and the abstraction (or anti-naturalism) of the overall composition (*Post-Expressionism*, 1925). Indeed, the defamiliarizing potential of montage operates at two levels. In the first place, the direct incorporation of found objects, be they images, things, or linguistic material, destroys the bounded contours of the artwork, since the collaged fragments unremittingly point back to the extra-artistic contexts from which they were culled. Second, the anti-illusionistic reshuffling of elements from everyday experience produces unfamiliar and startling juxtapositions. The ambiguity and open-endedness of this procedure prevent hermeneutic closure and stable readings and engage the recipient actively in the moment of reception. As noted by Viktor Žmegač,[2] montage displays two primary features to this phenomenon. One is metapoetic and hinges on the ways in which the montage artifact self-reflexively calls attention to the moment of construction. The second rests on the cognitive reframing that results from the moment of defamiliarization.

The productivity and conceptual reach of montage can be measured by the influence it exerted on the aesthetic and philosophical reflection of prominent modernist thinkers in the decades spanning the 1930s to the 1970s, especially, though not exclusively, within the Frankfurt School. The term traverses Walter Benjamin's oeuvre as a multi-dimensional category that names phenomena ranging from Brecht's epic theater as the model for a dramatic form whose discontinuous structure helps uncover the contradictions of capitalism ("Author as Producer," 1934) to the principle of a new epos that overcomes the strictures of the bourgeois novel ("The Crisis of the Novel," 1930) and a mode of historical inquiry that dispenses with historicism's causality in order

---

2 Viktor Žmegač, "Montage/Collage," in *Moderne Literatur in Grundbegriffen*, ed. Dieter Borchmeyer and Viktor Žmegač (Tübingen: Niemeyer, 1994).

to juxtapose shards of past and present experience in constellations that are bound to unleash imponderable moments of insight (*Arcades project*, 1927–40). More importantly, perhaps, Benjamin identified filmic montage as a crucial point of interface between modern technologies of mechanical reproduction and a human sensory apparatus trained on the rhythms of alienated labor and sensory overstimulation of metropolitan life. Notably, this premise allowed him to argue that montage in film assaults and productively innervates the human sensorium, engendering a scattered mode of reception that inoculates individuals against the contemplative pull of fascism's aesthetic spectacles and lays the foundation for an emancipated collective (*The Work of Art in the Age of its Technological Reproducibility*, 1936–9).

In *Heritage of Our Times* (1935) Ernst Bloch recognized in montage the signature of a collapsing bourgeois culture whose fragments had become available for the empty play of disaggregation and recombination characteristic of the New Objectivity (and itself symptomatic of the exploitative irrationality of capitalism). In the mediated use of montage Bloch also glimpsed the possibility of constructing not-yet existing, emancipatory contexts by releasing the material traces of utopian future embedded within the decaying present. Theodor W. Adorno saw in montage a procedure that shatters the false semblance of totality summoned by what he termed the culture industry. In assembling heterogeneous materials within pointedly constructed compositions, montage defies the hermeneutic operations that allow for endowing experience with sense and leads to works that prevent the misuse of art as a tool of reconciliation with a reality fraught with the contradictions of capitalism. As he pointedly concluded, "in terms of this microstructure all modern art may be called montage."[3]

Adorno's reflections form a bridge between the debates on montage that unfolded prior to the Second World War and the interest that developed in the post-war period. In the pop and conceptual art of the 1960s and 1970s montage often signaled an emphatic orientation towards everyday contexts and the ensuing desire to bridge the divide between high art and popular culture. At the same time, the appropriation of montage in explicit reference to the activism of the pre-war avant-garde often helped to ground the social and political engagement of contemporary art. In the concrete poetry of the 1950s and 1960s, montage procedures drove operations of quotation that foregrounded the materiality of language as a visual and sonoric medium and reflexively explored the mechanisms of signification (Helmut Heißenbüttel,

---

3   Theodor W. Adorno, *Aesthetic Theory*, ed. Gretel Adorno and Rolf Tiedemann, trans. Robert Hullot-Kentnor (Minneapolis: University of Minnesota Press, 1997), 15.

Ernst Jandl, H. C. Artmann). Since the mid-1950s, montage practices have run the gamut of experimental and countercultural art in a broad variety of media, ranging from Wolf Vostell's décollages and the happenings and mix-media events of Fluxus, the punctual music of Karl-Heinz Stockhausen, Sigmar Polke's ironic appropriation of pop art in his collages and assemblages, the enigmatic photographic *Atlas* of Gerhard Richter, and Valie Export's intermedial montages of videos, electronically-simulated images, and live performers. These diverse interventions share a now playful, now polemical relation to mass culture and a high degree of self-reflexivity in the way they interrogate prevalent concepts of representation, authorship, spectatorship, and the processes of mediation made possible by old and new technologies.

If in the first half of the twentieth century montage art conjured positive associations with the experimental and countercultural, in the aftermath of the Second World War the ubiquitous proliferation of montage practices in advertisement and commercial art, their inclusion in the revised canon of modern art (as instigated by influential exhibitions of leading art museums such as MoMA's 1961 "Art of Assemblage"), as well as their continuous morphing in the relentless cycle of technological advances that shape mass culture (the spread of television, the introduction of photo-silk-screen methods, the propagation of electronic synthesizers in music, and the more general proliferation of electronic media since the 1980s) prompted critics to undertake more discriminating evaluations of its potential as a tool of artistic dissent. In his *Theory of the Avant-Garde* (1974)[4] Peter Bürger emblematically asked how the return, in the aftermath of the Second World War, of the appropriation strategies developed by the interwar avant-garde should be assessed in the face of what he considered the gimmicky and exploitative pop art of the 1960s. While Bürger polemically (and unconvincingly) dismissed much activist art of the post-war period as ultimately self-promoting and ideologically disingenuous, his reflections pointed to a real quandary that hounds montage and appropriation art. This lies in the fundamental ambiguity of the gesture of citation that is proper to montage, which is bound to pay homage at the same time as it critiques. In recognizing that strategies of citation and iteration tend to oscillate ambivalently between denunciation and affirmation, more recent criticism has treated the moment of appropriation as a tactical step that does not inherently possess subversive value, and whose ideological appraisal requires a broad contextualization within relevant sociocultural frameworks.

In the wake of the linguistic turn and the momentous reception of

---

4   Peter Bürger, *Theory of the Avant-Garde*, trans. Michael Shaw (Minneapolis: University of Minnesota Press, 1984).

Walter Benjamin's works in the 1960s and 1970s, some critics called for applying the lesson of montage to the domain of philosophical writing, all the while noting that montage art had increasingly seeped into mainstream artistic circuits. As Gregory Ulmer argued in "The Object of Post-Criticism" (1983),[5] the appropriation of montage for philosophy and criticism involved a "paraliterary" mode of writing that bypassed conceptual abstraction and mimetic representation by enlisting the allegorical and physiognomic modalities of montage (as exemplified for Ulmer by Jacques Derrida's *Glas*). Since the 1990s, montage practices have been the object of historically and geographically localized investigations that tend to focus on media-specific aspects and generally lack the normative premises that drove theoretical discourse on montage through the 1970s. Inquiries informed by visual studies and the cultural analysis of space and place have also broadened the focus beyond the semiotic and hermeneutic frameworks of previous investigations. For instance, in his study of the cultural function of photography Bernd Stiegler[6] pleads for treating montage as a historically inflected practice in order to uncouple the concept from the linguistic and textual bias of poststructuralism. Analyses of the non-linear, recursive, and interactive poetics of digital media also occasionally enlist a heuristic concept of montage, for instance to describe the complex spatio-temporal configuration of hypertext (Manovich[7]) or the specific operations of appropriation made possible by the electronic media in pop music (Diederichsen[8]).

SEE ALSO: Medium/Mediation; Film; Shudder

---

5 Gregory Ulmer, "The Object of Post-Criticism," in *The Anti-Aesthetic. Essays on Postmodern Culture*, ed. Hal Foster (Port Townsend, WA: Bay, 1983).
6 Berndt Stiegler, *Montagen des Realen. Photographie als Reflexionsmedium und Kulturtechnik* (Paderborn: Fink, 2009).
7 Lev Manovich, *The Language of New Media* (Cambridge, MA: MIT Press, 2001).
8 Diederich Diederichsen, "Montage, Sampling, Morphing," http://www.medienkunstnetz.de/themen/bild-ton-relationen/montage_sampling_morphing/ (accessed June 22, 2011).

Twenty-five Normality

Jürgen Link

Translated by Mirko M. Hall

The following text deals with the role of a fundamental, yet often overlooked category for the culture of modernity: that of normality or of the normal. This chapter addresses its main features and provides a few exemplary illustrations, mainly from the German-speaking world.

Normality is something different from normativity

An etymological confusion partially explains why most theories of modernity, as well as cultural studies, have overlooked normality: one is too busy with normativity (with the norm, the normative, the breach of norms, etc.) and overlooks its fundamental difference to normality. In fact, both categories go back etymologically to the Latin "norma" (right angle, metaphor for rule), but later developed as two different discursive complexes since around 1800. Normativity designates ethical and legal complexes—i.e. social rules of behavior (imperative norms) through which offenses (breaches of norms) are sanctioned. Without normativity, human society is inconceivable. On the other hand, with regard to normality, we are dealing with a modern European and North American emergence since the eighteenth-century that represents a historical particularity.[1] The historical prerequisite for the emergence of the normal was the formation of data-processing societies. These societies make themselves statistically transparent, both comprehensively and regularly, in order to be able to regulate their mass dynamics. This allows the normal to be quantitatively calculated as the middle zone of a mass distribution or as including a certain distance from the average (from the "middle"). The first historical

---

1 For historical and systematic information, see Jürgen Link, *Versuch über den Normalismus. Wie Normalität produziert wird*, 4th ed. (Göttingen: Vandenhoeck & Ruprecht, 2009).

instances included body size (normality between giants and dwarves), life expectancy, and economic growth. Later, complex phenomena such as sexuality and "intelligence" were normalistically determined.

"Normalism" is the name for the entirety of procedures and institutions through which normalities (and their opposite—abnormalities) are produced and reproduced in modern cultures. The borders of the normal range in the "middle"—i.e. the borders to abnormality—are important here. These borders are called the borders of normality. They create a new, highly important form of cultural borders through which, for example, inclusion and exclusion are regulated. What distinguishes these borders of normality (in contrast to normative norms) is their instability: distribution curves of masses are mathematically constant, that is, continuous; they do not have any intrinsic discontinuities (like those between ethical or legal guilt and innocence). As the phenomenon of addiction clearly shows, one can easily glide over the borders of normality. This gliding of normality into abnormality can be called "denormalization." It corresponds to a fundamental fear of modernity—the "fear of denormalization," i.e. the fear of losing normality and becoming abnormal.

Normalities (in the limited sense of normalism) are (in contrast to normativities) not ahistorical—i.e. they are neither biologically constituted nor identical with an ahistorical everydayness. The nature of their historicity lies in the fact that normalties fulfill the important function of insuring modern cultures against the risks of the (symbolically) "exponential" growth of modernity. The dynamic growth (of people, capital, and knowledge) in modernity must be normalized as a logistic curve (an elongated s-shaped curve) in order to prevent its "explosion." Such a normalization is typically achieved through processes of inclusion or redistribution within a mass distribution. Examples are the inclusion of homosexuality into a normal spectrum or the redistribution of the standard of living through the social welfare state in order to reach a bell-shaped distribution with a broader "middle."

Historical dynamics: Protonormalism and flexible normalism

The fact that the borders of normality (as opposed to normative norms) are on a statistical continuum, and always moveable, accounts for the historical dynamic of normalism. The two opposing poles of this dynamic are recognizable as ideal types and imply a chronological component:

1) Protonormalism, which dominated from 1800 to around 1945. It is characterized by a narrow spectrum of normality and corresponds

to expanded zones of abnormality as well as the massive, frightening borders of normality (typically as the walls of prison and psychiatric wards, and later concentration camps). The rigidity of these borders of normality is reinforced through their close pairing with normative (ethical and legal) rules. The protonormalistic fight against a wide spectrum of sexual abnormalities ("perversities") is exemplary here. This protonormalistic method of regulation corresponds—on the side of subjectivity—to an "authoritarian" [Adorno], "disciplined" [Foucault], and "other directed" [Riesman] character. In other words, protonormalism produces mainly abnormalities (and only indirectly though deterrence and a bad conscience). It is mainly concerned with exclusion. Or, to riff on an analogy of Foucault, protonormalism means: "make abnormality and allow normality."

2) Flexible normalism, which achieved cultural hegemony after the Second World War in "rich" Western countries. In contrast to protonormalism, it uses the statistical continuum to expand the middle spectrum of normality as far as possible. It not only pushes outward the borders of normality, but also renders them porous through wider transitional zones. The zones of abnormality, thereby, become smaller. This occurred through the inclusion of possibly much earlier abnormalities (e.g. the inclusion of mostly earlier sexual "perversities"). This flexible method of regulation involves a similarly flexible subject of "self-management" and "self-normalization," who "adjusts" its very own borders of normality through the procedure of testing. The middle spectrum of normality is internally (i.e. "pluralistically") differentiated through such inclusions and individualizations. One could, therefore, say that flexible normalism produces mainly normalities and is primarily concerned with inclusion. Stated differently, "make normality and allow abnormality."

The flexible border of normality implies two consequences that have wide-ranging consequences for contemporary ("postmodern") culture. First, the border of normality becomes attractive in an ambivalent way. It promises *fun and thrill* and increased intensities—as in drug use and doping. At the same time, addiction lurks (as the impossibility of returning to normality). Second, the question arises as to where the flexible spectrum of normality ends. It is a question of the absolute borders of normality. In the field of sex, for example, this concerns rape (as sadomasochistic sex becomes normalized) and pedophilia (as homosexuality becomes normalized).

Protonormalism and flexible normalism are ideal types. In historical reality, there are and were various mixtures between them, which constantly cause conflicts. These conflicts are about hegemony. Protonormalism always remains an alternative and could even theoretically regain its hegemony. How does this normalistic typology, outlined here, behave vis-à-vis Foucault's category of a "normalizing society?"[2] And how does this category behave vis-à-vis his typology of "law" and "norm?"[3] ("Law" refers, here, to the above field of "normativity.") Is Foucault's "norm," therefore, identical with "normality?" The role of data-processing and statistics is in no way overlooked by him. It is just not considered to be fundamental. "Normalization" (*normalisation*) does not mean a statistically supported *floating* in the spectrum of normality, but rather "standardization" in the sense of an industrial norm. Foucault's "normalizing society" is, thus, nearly synonymous with a "disciplinary society." His society of the "norm" as well as his epoch of "bio-power" could be largely identified with protonormalism.

As already suggested, a main function of normalism for modern cultures exists in its combination of objective (mass distribution) and subjective normality. This corresponds to the development of objective (typically sociological) and subjective (typically psychological) sciences and technologies that are statistically supported (such as growth-bound and social welfare states, and the therapy culture of personal growth). Discourses and other cultural formats play a key role in this connection. Important statistical data and trends must be publicly disseminated so that individuals of modern mass societies can orientate themselves to statistical "landscapes" and eventually normalize their behavior. This occurs through normalistic mass media and (artistic) narratives, both in a broad and narrow sense.

Normalism and culture: Normalistic narratives and the "(not) normal trip"

For all the literary arts, the emergence of normalism was an epochal break in several respects:

- A new type of protagonist arose: the "average man" as a statistically grounded man of the masses—and its opposite, the abnormal man.
- A new collective symbolism of the "life journey" arose, typically in technical vehicles (railroad, car, motorcycle) and within modern mass transit.
- A new type of narrative arose: the normalistic case study, which first developed in medicine and psychiatry, especially around "abnormal" individuals.
- A new type of "realistic" story arose: the epic of denormalization.

---

2 Michel Foucault, *Discipline and Punish: The Birth of the Prison*, trans. Alan Sheridan (New York: Vintage Books, 1977).
3 Michel Foucault, *The History of Sexuality*, Vol. 1: *The Will to Knowledge*, trans. Robert Hurley (New York: Vintage Books, 1978).

- New forms of perspective arose: first-person narrations of "normal" or "abnormal" protagonists with the related speech forms of jargon and slang.

The combination of these new processes, which originated in normalism, generated the fascination type of the "(not) normal trip." As an ideal type, this is the combination of trips in technical vehicles and the story of a great denormalization. The trip begins in normality and, then, gradually or suddenly "*de-viates*" into abnormality. As an ideal type this trip is the (auto)biography. The protagonists are normal people and the dominant problems are normalistic complexes: sexuality and its "deviations," crime, psychopathology, addiction, insanity, and suicide. On the level of the symbolic vehicle, the accident (or the crash) symbolically corresponds to denormalization. The accident symbolizes, above all, coincidence and contingence as the typically normalistic form of narrative linkages. As a result, a form of narration develops that is a-teleological and non-entelechial.

This fascination type is nearly ideally realized in Louis-Ferdinand Céline's novel *Journey to the End of the Night* (1932). The hero is a doctor, who is involved with various abnormalities, and whose life is always—and seemingly by chance—connected with that of a criminal. The journey of denormalization goes through many countries, including the United States and those in Africa, and ends with murder in a car in Parisian traffic. The first-person narration of the protagonist is in the tone of a "*cool*" cynical slang. Céline was an important model for Jack Kerouac's *On the Road* (1957), which, in turn, inspired the genre of road stories and road movies. The close symbiosis between high and low culture is revealed here, which is typical for all normalistic narratives. In combination with crime, psychopathology, and other abnormalities, the individual motives of (not) normal trips—like wild trips in cars and motorcycles with chases, dead-end streets, lost ways, and accidents—are typical components of popular, "trivial" mass culture. In this regard, film has long had a greater effect than literature. Henri-Georges Clouzot's 1953 French film *The Wages of Fear* (starring Yves Montand) is exemplary here. It involves a trip over adventurous paths which is constantly threatened by a deadly explosion and the psychology of four not-normal protagonists.

Naturalism

The first explicitly normalistic epochal style developed with naturalism—and after normality/abnormality, as a definition and concept, had already played an increasing role in Realism. Wilhelm Bölsche programmatically proclaimed normality as the principle and goal of art, indeed of culture: "Its tendency is in the direction of the normal, the natural, the consciously lawful. Poetry has nurtured so far, with few ... exceptions, all sorts of abnormal love. In the future, it must try to paint for the reader the normal as the goal of striving, as in the eminent sense of the ideal."[4] This "German" naturalism was to form a "positive" alternative to the "French" naturalism of Émile Zola, which Bölsche repudiated through his fascination with the "abnormal." He did not understand that normality is inseparable from abnormality (its opposite). Likewise, he failed to see that any restriction of the normal would necessarily be ridiculous and boring, because it would remove the fear of denormalization as a source of specific normalistic *thrills*.

The fascination with Zola's cycle of *The Rougon-Macquarts* (1871–93) relates to the epic's narration of a large, frequently tragic denormalization across four generations. The individual novel *The Human Beast* (1890) once again established the ideal type of a (not) normal trip. The protagonist is a train engineer, who is closely connected with the technical vehicle and its trips in the normal transportation network. As a psychopathological case, he is simultaneously an extremely abnormal person with a disposition toward compulsive sex crimes. This disposition appears as inherited in Zola. This inheritance theory, which results in increasing "degeneracy" (which is today superseded through modern, up-to-date genetics) creates a scheme for the escalating denormalization of two families. It is not this scheme that has created one of the classic myths of modernity, but rather it is the intensive use of all normalistic narratives, including popular, "trivial" ones like crime thrillers.

Luckily, even German Naturalism of note does not follow Bölsche's program, but rather one of fascination through denormalization. Gerhart Hauptmann's drama *Before Sunrise* (1889) is exemplary here. Its protagonist, a sociologist, who is oriented toward the theory of degeneracy, nearly quotes Bölsche: "I am thoroughly satisfied with the normal stimuli that touch my nervous system." However, he does not overcome—in tragic irony—the battle with abnormality (alcoholism). In the end, he provokes the suicide of his beloved.

Antinormalistic polemics in the age of the aesthetic avant-gardes

Around 1900, the problematic of normality and abnormality as a fundamental element of modern culture was generally recognized and discussed (psychologically in Freud and sociologically in Durkheim). Normalization was explicitly elevated to a program for individuals and for society. It developed a psychological "therapy culture" around the

---

4   Wilhelm Bölsche, *Die naturwissenschaftlichen Grundlagen der Poesie. Prolegomena einer realistischen Ästhetik* (Tübingen: Niemeyer, 1976), 46.

project of sexual normalization for an increasingly wider audience. The aesthetic avant-gardes and their periphery strongly fought against and rejected this tendency. For Surrealism, on the contrary, the "abnormal" was the condition to be achieved and the so-called door to a utopia of aesthetic intensities. Robert Musil's novel *The Man without Qualities* (1930–43, postum 1952) details the process of denormalization in the space of one year (1913/14) leading up to the First World War. Several of the protagonists are explicitly abnormal (the sex murderer Moosbrugger, the art lover Clarisse, and the different members of protofascist all-male associations [Männerbündler]). A "line of flight" (Deleuze/Guattari) to a utopian "other condition" is sought in these abnormalities and denormalization just like in Surrealism, although with a completely different stylistic tone. This search remains—like in the novel—unfinished and problematic.

The antinormalistic polemic in the early twentieth century was naturally directed against protonormalism as the exemplary case of Karl Kraus shows. Its highpoint was the attack against Maximilian Harden in the Eulenburg Scandal (which exposed the homosexual network around Kaiser Wilhelm II). Through grotesque humor, Kraus destroyed the definition of sexual normality as such: all the inhabitants of "Bettenhausen" were revealed to be (through psychoanalysis) "unconsciously homosexual." A few of them, nevertheless, still secretly "procreated": "The fulfillment of this obligation of citizens was now made impossible, because it was now merely regarded as an alibi. Each one was ashamed to be normal, because he feared that his normal behavior would create the suspicion of a homosexual disposition. Whoever lived, was considered to be homosexual, but if he shot himself, the proof was right there."[5]

Flexible normalism and postmodernity

Normalism was also overlooked in the many partially contradictory attempts to capture the essence of "postmodernity" or "postmodern culture." If one can consider Leslie Fiedler's programmatic essay "Cross the Border—Close the Gap" (1972)[6]—with its proclamation of abolishing the borders between high and low culture or literature—as one of the foundational manifestos of postmodernity, then, therein, lies an implicit reference to normalism. First of all, the chapter is about the normative border between low and high culture: it deals with aesthetic norms, canons, and standards. At the same time, there

---

5 See Karl Kraus, *Die Fackel* (The Torch), 12 Bde. Zweitausendeins (Frankfurt am Main, 1977), #259–260, 11.7.1908, 22ff.
6 Leslie Fiedler, "Cross the Border—Close the Gap," *Collected Essays*, 2 vols (New York: Stein, 1971), 2:461-85.

is a statistical and, thus, normalistic aspect hidden within it. The "modern" (or "modernistic") conception of the border between high and low literature regarded the facts of mass character and popularity as evidence of "triviality" and "banality"—i.e. of aesthetic and cultural insufficiency. Normalistically formulated, this means that mass culture, popular culture, and mainstream culture (i.e. normal culture) fall into exclusion based on aesthetic norms. According to Fiedler, this exclusion should be replaced in the future by inclusion. The claim of the avant-gardists for extreme originality and a radical breach of norms as the condition of aesthetic quality means—in normalistic speech—nothing less than the demand for "abnormality" and the exclusion of normality. This exclusion should have been abolished according to Fiedler.

Ten years after Fiedler, Hans Magnus Enzensberger's essay "In Defense of Normality" (Enzensberger 1982) appeared in Germany. Together with his book "Average and Illusion," this text can also be considered a manifesto of postmodernity. Prior to this, Enzensberger had previously emerged as a main representative of the modern aesthetics of the avant-garde. Here, polemical attacks against normality were appropriate. For example, in the "Ballad of Taylor" in *Mausoleum*: "Always healthy and normal: shapelessly he dozes while sitting, sleeplessly on shapeless mountains of pillows. A social machine. Impotent his life long."[7] This shows, here, the necessity of distinguishing between protonormalism and flexible normalism. Of course, Enzensberger did not renounce his critique of protonormalism—what he newly defended was flexible normalism.

If postmodern literature can be generally identified through the inclusion of mass cultural narratives, then flexible-normalistic narratives form an important part of this. They are the (auto)biographical narratives of an ambivalent—and usually simulated—game with the borders of normality and of denormalization. In the German-speaking world, Rainald Goetz and Sibylle Berg serve as exemplary illustrations. Goetz's trilogy *Fortress* (1993), with its central book *1989*, consists of a colorful media collage that simulates the result of a seemingly contingent *zapping*. Of course, its secret theme is reunification and the so-called "normalization" of German history. The corresponding fragmented discourses and narratives are seemingly coincidently mixed with sports and entertainment: "taping it all"—as it is typically called in English. In the entire "media salad," which is seemingly and completely contingent, certain signifiers appear—as if by chance—with increasing insistence. The signifier "normal" itself appears more than others. This conspicuousness results in an alienation effect. We suddenly

---

7   Hans Magnus Enzensberger, *Mausoleum* (Suhrkamp: Frankfurt am Main, 1975), 100.

become attentive to the fact that our entire postmodern culture is based on a discursive complex that we "normally" overlook—even as it fundamentally determines our culture. This includes the truly "stunning" re-ascent of Germany to a world power (i.e. Germany's "normalization" that also includes a denormalization).

Sibylle Berg's novels also simulate the uninterrupted *flow* of a normalistic, mass-medial *fun and thrill* tape. "Trivial" narratives (mostly sexual "relationships") and the deep structure of computer games dominate here. The novel *A Couple of People Look for Happiness and Laugh Themselves to Death* (1997) functions like a simulated computer game. Ten normal men and women are sent out separately on a (not) normal trip, which is linked thematically to the typical denormalization in flexible normalism: drugs, alcohol, promiscuity, sexual deviances, and intentional unemployment. All the trips are escapes from normality and follow the ambivalent attraction of the flexible borders of normality. All the trips end in deadly accidents, addiction, or suicide—the tone is cynically cool. Flexible normalism appears as a *vicious circle*. Normality is boring and that is why normal people want to escape it. They fail, however, in their ambivalence to these borders of normality. There is no easy way out of the circle. "The really smart ones have realized that boredom is the normal condition of people who do not work hard." A consequence of this insight is that a couple can simply watch TV instead of looking for supernormal sex.

In the context of normalism, the "postmodern condition" (Lyotard) can be understood as a renunciation of a fundamental critique of flexible normalism. It is not merely a rejection of Marxism or other master narratives or utopias, but also a rejection of all transnormalistic alternatives like those exemplified in Enzensberger's development. The result is a specifically "cynical" and "*cool*" tone, especially when it is exaggerated through the macabre in Goetz and Berg. It unfolds a critical power and brings about in various places (particularly with Berg) a neo-existentialist accusation: Would it not be absurd if—instead of all the alternatives and concrete utopias—normalism should be the last word of Western cultural history?

SEE ALSO: Ugly

Twenty-six Ugly
Richard Leppert

The concept of the beautiful assumes one for the ugly; the significance of each term emerges from perceptions of the other. As the antithesis to beauty, the ugly maintains a significant presence in aesthetic assessments. A Google search of hits (3 April 2011) for the two terms, whatever the sloppiness of the results, is instructive:

	Ugly	Beautiful
Art (web)	48,500,000	521,000,000
Music (web)	62,700,000	50,000,000
People (web)	350,000	61,600,000
People (images)	24,600,000	330,000,000
People (images)	"really ugly" 25,200,000	"really beautiful" 257,000,000

Among these search categories, only ugly music outnumbers its beautiful counterpart. On average, ugly produces roughly 14 percent as many hits as those for beauty.

As an aesthetic category, the ugly (or ugliness) associates itself with imbalance, chaos, disruption, dissonance, and noise, just as beauty conventionally encodes the opposites to these terms. A great deal of cultural, and for that matter moral, negatives were attached to the concept of ugly, which Nina Athanassoglou-Kallmyer has nicely characterized as the "all-purpose repository for everything that did not quite fit … [the] elevated norm" constituting beauty. "Beauty was one. Ugliness had many faces,"[1] and these faces were deformed. The case for music in this regard is instructive.

---

1 Nina Athanassoglou-Kallmyer, "Ugliness," in *Critical Terms for Art History*, Robert S. Nelson and Richard Shiff, ed. 2nd ed. (Chicago: University of Chicago Press, 2003), 281–95.

Eduard Hanslick, in his influential *Vom Musikalisch-Schönen* (1854), suggested that "The logic [i.e., order] in music, which produces in us a feeling of satisfaction, rests on certain elementary laws of nature which govern both the human organism and the phenomena of sound."[2] Hanslick thus posits a kind of universal *natural* order encompassing the macrocosm. "All musical elements are in some occult manner connected with each other by certain natural affinities, and since rhythm, melody, and harmony are under their invisible sway, the music created by man must conform to them—any combinations conflicting with them bearing the impress of caprice and ugliness."[3] For Hanslick, to state the matter succinctly: Order = Form = Beauty. Hanslick is insistent: "The form (the musical structure) is the real substance (subject) of music—in fact, is the music itself."[4] (Hanslick's famous antipathy toward Wagnerian music drama located itself in what he heard as the music's "formlessness exalted into a principle."[5]) Hanslick might as well be channeling the Platonic metaphor of music of the spheres; the form and order of art, as an Ideal, constitutes a utopian conception of the world put right. Anything less by definition is ugly.

Adorno remarked that for traditional aesthetics "the ugly is that element that opposes the [art]work's ruling law of form," adding that "the impression of ugliness stems from the principle of violence and destruction."[6] Hanslick, coming at the end of a line stretching back to Plato and Aristotle, locates beauty in purposeful order, from which pleasure derives. The deformed, like the unformed, was philosophically, and maybe even socially and culturally, intolerable, though Aristotle duly acknowledged that the ugly could be beautifully represented, a position that held sway for centuries thereafter. In this regard, Lessing, articulating the Greek's seriousness of purpose in defense of beauty (which presumes formal coherence), noted that "the law of the Thebans commanded idealization in art and threatened digression toward ugliness with punishment."[7]

During the Renaissance the terms ugly and grotesque were synonymous, and both terms were commonly used as descriptors not

---

2   Eduard Hanslick, *The Beautiful in Music* (7th ed., 1891), ed. Morris Weitz, trans. Gustav Cohen (Indianapolis: Bobbs-Merrill, 1957), 51.
3   Ibid., 51.
4   Ibid., 92.
5   Ibid., 6.
6   Theodor W Adorno, *Aesthetic Theory*, ed. Gretel Adorno and Rolf Tiedemann, trans. Robert Hullot-Kentor (Minneapolis: University of Minnesota Press, 1997), 46.
7   Gotthold Ephraim Lessing, *Laocoön: An Essay on the Limits of Painting and Poetry*, trans. Edward Allen McCormick (Baltimore, MD: Johns Hopkins University Press, 1984), 13.

only for deformed objects but also and more importantly for people, those for whom today the term Other is often applied: the poor and downtrodden, ethnic and racial minorities, and the like: in short, the lower social orders, and the colonized. The eighteenth-century English term for those *not* Others was the Quality; accordingly, the Others in essence were the Non-Quality. In the end, the metaphors associated with beauty and ugliness boiled down to the linguistic imagery of economics: *worth*, broadly defined and broadly applied.

All this notwithstandiung, the long dominance of form as the foundation for assessing beauty or ugliness was challenged in the course of the eighteenth century and thereafter, in part on the unfolding principle that aesthetic value could not adequately be decided on formal grounds alone.

The importance of beauty, it must be noted, locates its long philosophical history not only in perceived paradigms of Truth and the Ideal but also in the presumed actuality of so much in and about life that was not beautiful and hence ugly. Ugly, we might say, was the default standard; beauty was the exception, even if ugliness was the less talked about prior to the advent of modernity, by which time the insistence of the ugly to have its philosophical day in court could no longer be denied, the reasons for which have rather less to do with isolated advancements in philosophical discourse and far more with the changing nature of political economy, social thought, and the attendant and general upheavals of lived history. Put simply, social-political revolutions impact thought, including thought about art (thus Modernism, what Stuart Hall has aptly termed "modernity experienced as trouble").

Clement Greenberg, never at a loss to stake out a position and, like Adorno, to make effective use of hyperbole when the occasion seemed to merit, uttered the oft-cited defense against the common denigration of modern art, by which he meant so-named abstract visual representation: "All profoundly original art looks ugly at first." Well, hardly; nonetheless what his overstatement encompasses reflected profound aesthetic upheaval that was well underway well before the mid-twentieth century. In a lecture in 1954, "Abstract and Representational," published later that year in *Art Digest*, he alluded to the prevalence of the stakes of the new art. Although he did not evoke the specter of ugliness, its shadow is distinctly visible in the symptoms he identifies in the diagnoses of art's alleged decline: "Our present abstract art is considered therefore a symptom of the cultural—and even moral—decay of our time," a position against which Greenberg argued.

For Adorno, whose concern with aesthetics centered on the relation between the philosophical concept of beauty, on the one hand, and its realization in art works, on the other, the significance of the ugly attained particular urgency in the late-modern world. To Adorno, the presence of ugliness *in* art was wholly necessary; its presence at once defined and mediated what any concept of beauty must acknowledge in order to claim truth. Aesthetic truth-content (*Wahrheitsgehalt*) for Adorno implied a social truth immanent to the form of art—itself dependent upon the mutuality shared with content, the one always a part (indeed, the sum and substance) of the other. In modern art, for Adorno, "powerlessly the law of form capitulates to ugliness,"[8] and ultimately to good purpose: "By absorbing the ugly, the concept of beauty has been transformed in itself, without, however, aesthetics being able to dispense with it. In the absorption of the ugly, beauty is strong enough to expand itself by its own opposite."[9]

The dynamism of ugliness—as with the dynamism of the concept of the beautiful—"mocks" what Adorno calls the "definitional fixation" of aesthetic norms. Put differently, ugliness in art represents the return of the repressed and suppressed: otherness and the Other. For Adorno, most important of all, ugliness acquires oneness with suffering (a condition of being Other) for which social emancipation, broadly understood, is the antidote. Art at its best may provide a semblance (only that) of what emancipation would be or look like.

Schlegel pointed out that "there has not even been a significant effort to establish a *theory of ugliness*," and this despite the fact that "beauty and ugliness are inseparable correlates."[10] In his briefly stated attempt to close the theoretical gap, requiring just a couple of pages, he takes up the beauty–ugly dyad in the fraught condition of the sublime. Sublime pleasure, he suggests, provides "a complete pleasure." *Sublime ugliness* (Schlegel italicizes this side of the binary but not its opposite) "is *despair*, essentially an absolute, unmitigated pain."[11] On this score, the line of thought from the German early Romantics to Adorno, though hardly straight, was for all intents and purposes well drawn.

Kant has very little to say about ugliness, allowing it no place in art, unless, per Aristotle, it is (however paradoxically) beautifully represented *and* so long as it does not produce disgust:

> Beautiful art displays its excellence precisely by describing beautifully things that in nature would be ugly or displeasing. The furies, diseases, devastations of war, and the like, can, as harmful things, be very beautifully described, indeed even represented in painting; only one kind of ugliness cannot be represented in

---

8 Adorno, *Aesthetic Theory*, 46.
9 Ibid., 273.
10 Friedrich Schlegel, *On the Study of Greek Poetry*, ed. and trans. Stuart Barnett (Albany, NY: State University of New York Press, 2001), 68.
11 Ibid., 69.

a way adequate to nature without destroying all aesthetic satisfaction, hence beauty in art, namely, that which arouses loathing.[12]

Hegel goes further to recognize that ugliness lurks in the shadow of the aesthetic; beauty and ugliness sometimes collide in the same object or entity, which he describes as a transgression, one "that cannot remain as such but must be superseded," the solution to which itself invokes in Hegel the language of violence: "collision as such requires a solution which follows on the battle of opposites"; such situations, he says, "rest on transgressions and give rise to circumstances which cannot subsist but necessitate a transforming remedy,"[13]

> But the beauty of the Ideal lies precisely in the Ideal's undisturbed unity, tranquility, and perfection in itself. Collision disturbs this harmony, and sets the Ideal, inherently a unity, in dissonance and opposition. Therefore, by the representation of such transgression, the Ideal is itself transgressed, and the task of art can lie here only, on the one hand, in preventing free beauty from perishing in this difference, and, on the other hand, in just presenting this disunion and its conflict, whereby out of it, through resolution of the conflict, harmony appears as a result, and in this way alone becomes conspicuous in its complete essentiality.[14]

For Hegel, the scenario outlined may successfully achieve the desired results in, for example, poetry, far less so (if at all) painting and (especially not) sculpture on account of what he sees as their being "fixed and permanent": ugliness which in poetry can be superseded, in the visual arts is not fleeting but frozen, locked. It cannot be ablated. In these arts, Hegel concludes, "It would be a blunder to cling to the ugly when the ugly cannot be resolved." By contrast, dramatic poetry "lets an ugly thing appear just for a moment and then vanish again."[15] In sum, Hegel regards ugliness, in the words of Athanassoglou-Kallmyer, as "an aesthetic ill, a symptom of cultural deficiency."[16]

Lessing, like Hegel after him, readily acknowledged the place of ugliness in poetry and for similar reasons, just as he was troubled by its presence in the plastic arts, though he hedged his bet: "May painting

---

12 Immanuel Kant, *Critique of the Power Judgment*, ed. Paul Guyer, trans. Paul Guyer and Eric Matthews (Cambridge: Cambridge University Press, 2000), 190.
13 Georg Wilhelm Friedrich Hegel, *Aesthetics: Lectures on Fine Art*, trans. T. M. Knox, 2 vols (Oxford: Clarendon Press, 1975), I: 204-5.
14 Ibid., 205.
15 Ibid.
16 Athanassoglou-Kallmyer, "Ugliness," 288.

make use of ugly forms to attain the ridiculous and the terrible? I will not venture with an unequivocal 'no'"—not least in the face of emerging theories of the sublime and the attendant concern less with form per se (*pace* Hanslick) and more with (aesthetic) experience: less, that is, a matter of form and more one of affects—though he almost immediately points out that the situation for poetry is different. In poetry, Lessing suggests, "ugliness of form loses its repulsive effect almost entirely by the change from coexistence to the consecutive"; that is, ugliness in poetry is transformed[17]: "The poet's use of ugliness becomes possible for the very reason that in his description it is reduced to a less offensive manifestation of physical imperfection and ceases, as it were, to be ugly in its effect."[18]

Schlegel, Hegel's contemporary, acknowledged the degree to which the ugly inhabited the terrain of beauty in a comment about the state of modern poetry:

> Almost everywhere you will find just about every other principle silently presupposed or implicitly put forth as the highest goal and fundamental law of art, as the ultimate measure for the worth of their works. Every principle, that is, except that of *beauty*. This is to such an extent not the governing principle of modern poetry that many of its most splendid works are openly representations of the *ugly*. One must finally, if reluctantly, admit that there does indeed exist a representation of confusion in all its plenitude, of despair characterized by boundless vigor, that demands an equal if not greater creative power and artistic wisdom than is required for the representation of abundance and vigor in complete harmony.[19]

For Schlegel, Shakespeare provided the perfect example: "None of his dramas are beautiful *in their entirety*; beauty never determines the arrangement of the whole. As in nature, even the particular beautiful elements are only rarely free of *ugly adjuncts*; they are only the *means* to another purpose. They serve the characteristic or philosophical interest." And then, the better to make his point, Schlegel gets down and dirty: "Nothing is so revolting, bitter, outrageous, disgusting, uninspired, and hideous, that [Shakespeare] would not depict it as soon as he sees a purpose to it. He often *flays* his subjects, and digs as if with an anatomical knife in the revolting decay of moral corpses."[20]

---

17 Lessing, *Laocoön*, 128.
18 Ibid., 121.
19 Schlegel, *On the Study of Greek Poetry*, 18.
20 Ibid., 34.

Simply put, Schlegel acknowledges the ugly as an aesthetic necessity, an insight that constitutes a predicate for modernism.

Romanticism pushed German aesthetic theory towards a greater openness to the inclusion of the ugly within the terrain of the beautiful. The actuality of social ugliness as well as the closely related and abiding presence of ugliness in nineteenth-century art (and beyond) argued for reconsideration evident in the writings of Hegel's students, Kuno Fischer, Arnold Runge, Friedrich Theodor Vischer, Christian Hermann Weisse, and, in particular, Johann Karl Friedrich Rosenkranz (*Aesthetik des Hässlichen*, 1853), for whom the ugly deserved its own monograph, a long one at that, within which unfolds a catalogue and taxonomy of a wide range of what can constitute the ugly in art and well beyond art, to include as well what he terms *Naturhässliche* and *Geisthässliche*. For Rosenkranz, the ugly is the *negation* of the beautiful. As regards questions of formal lack, he devotes sections to what he terms the amorphous, the asymmetrical, and the disharmonious. He also devotes more than one hundred pages to a category he names the Repulsive, incorporating the plump (*das Plumpe*), the dead and the empty, the horrible, the degenerate, the disgusting, and the evil, with subcategories for the criminal, the ghostly, the diabolical, and sub-subcategories for the demonic, the witchlike [Hexenhafte], and the satanic. The possibilities for ugliness are patiently catalogued and explained; indeed he requires an additional hundred pages to work through the possibilities that fall under the trivial, the weak, and the lowly. Rosenkranz readily acknowledges that the ugly possesses the agency of its own autonomy which, when encompassed within the beautiful, must be sublated (the ugly cannot be ignored). Contrasted with the beautiful, the ugly results not only from want of formal order or balance, but also from the lack of truth, and absence of "self-determination and freedom."[21] Put differently, the ugly presents an ethical challenge for art, and this is no accident in the new modernity for which art is assigned the task as replacement for the hope once engendered by religion.

For Adorno, the ambiguousness of the ugly (Rosenkrantz's categorization is impressively large and diverse) is a necessary result of the fact that aesthetics marks as ugly anything and everything that art conventionally condemns. Echoing Rosenkrantz, Adorno points out that the concept of art *depends* upon that of the ugly. Here Adorno goes a large step further to suggest that ugliness, the antithesis to beauty, maintains a presence that, as he puts it, "gnaws away correctively

---

21 Karl Rosenkranz, *Aesthetik des Hässlichen* (Stuttgart-Bad Cannstatt: Friedrich Frommann, 1968). Kai Hammermeister, *The German Aesthetic Tradition* (Cambridge: Cambridge University Press, 2002), 107.

on the affirmativeness of spiritualizing art,"[22] reminiscent of what he elsewhere claims for the presence of kitsch which "lurks in art, awaiting ever recurring opportunities to spring forth."[23]

Adorno pushes inclusion somewhat farther down the road than his German Idealist forebears by insisting that "art must take up the cause of what is proscribed as ugly,"[24] not in order to integrate or mediate or even to sublate ugliness within the beauty of the artwork, but instead to enable art to remark truth, though to do so comes with considerable risk. He insists that "art must denounce the world that creates and reproduces the ugly in its own image, even if in this too the possibility persists that sympathy with the degraded will reverse into concurrence with degradation."[25] In other words, within the artwork the ugly must be given its due; as a stand-in for what *is* (dystopian actuality), any claim by art for what *might be* (utopia) must acknowledge what stands in the way. Art overcomes this potential aporia (or surrender) through its formal processes—form again—that engage head-on form's proclivities for affirmation that too easily attach to an understanding of form as a kind of problem solving: "Appeals for more humane art ... regularly dilute the quality and weaken the law of form."[26] Ultimately, artworks lay claim to being beautiful in the degree to which they oppose what "simply exists'";[27] they do so *in form*. For Adorno the relation between the ugly and the beautiful is defined by history, just as the forms and formal processes through which the relation is engaged in art are themselves always already historical. Adorno takes form as seriously as the ancients; the stakes are high: "Form is the law of the transfiguration of the existing, counter to which it represents freedom... Form converges with critique."[28] In modern art, "it is for the sake of the beautiful that there is no longer beauty."[29] The beautiful in the end, whatever the ugliness of its truth, posits a semblance (definitely not the reality) of utopia: "By their very existence artworks postulate the existence of what does not exist and thereby come into conflict with the latter's actual non-existence... . [which is to say that] only what does not fit into this world is true."[30]

SEE ALSO: Beauty; Normality; Shudder; Committed Art

---

22 Adorno, *Aesthetic Theory*, 47.
23 Ibid., 239.
24 Ibid., 48.
25 Ibid., 48–9.
26 Ibid., 50.
27 Ibid., 51.
28 Ibid., 143–4.
29 Ibid., 53.
30 Ibid., 59.

Twenty-seven Shudder
Karyn Ball

In his unfinished, posthumously published *Aesthetic Theory* (1970), Theodor W. Adorno introduces the *shudder* (*Erschütterung*) to describe the impact of a modernist artwork that is "visceral" to the extent that it capsizes the modern subject's reified egocentrism. Adorno's understanding of reification presupposes Friedrich Nietzsche's diagnosis of "bad conscience" as the "civilizing" inversion of aggressive and creative instincts (the "will-to-power"). What Nietzsche calls the "internalization of man," Adorno re-names "second nature" to designate social adaptations that compel individuals to replicate the forces of their own domination by hardening themselves against affect, difference, and even their own survival instincts in the interests of self-sovereignty. Capitalism's hierarchical instrumentalization of collective needs according to their exchange values promotes efficient personal relations at the expense of compassionate responses to anxious vulnerability. Second-natured subjects scorn this anxiety as an archaic residue of a primeval age when nature prevailed. Adorno prizes artworks that humiliate this scorn by evoking a *déjà vu* of primal terror before an unruly nature that technological progress has all but neutralized. The syntax of Adorno's shudder conjoins the Kantian sublime with the Freudian uncanny: it registers the unsettling force of artworks that salvage a sensory memory of threatened survival and thereby derail self-rationalization.

Adorno's shudder aesthetics contributes a dialectical approach to the critique of *aesthetic ideology*, which Jochen Schulte-Sasse defines as an endeavor "to suppress the structurality of structures in favor of an illusive experience of wholeness."[1] Schulte-Sasse borrows Lacanian

---

1 Jochen Schulte-Sasse, "General Introduction: Romanticism's Paradoxical Articulation of Desire," in *Theory as Practice: A Critical Anthology of Early German Romantic Writings* (Minneapolis: University of Minnesota Press, 1995), 2.

terminology to foreground the imaginary impetus of this longing for wholeness that invests art with the power to resolve the subject–object split by orchestrating a harmonious fusion between the ideal and the real, the universal and the particular. This fantasy of fusion mirrors the fragmented subject's desire to "[possess] an equally unified, privileged consciousness."[2]

According to Schulte-Sasse, German idealists reproached Immanuel Kant for failing "to ground his theory of knowledge in an adequate notion of self-consciousness."[3] In the first *Critique*, the *Ich* of *apperception* is ultimately empty—it comprises nothing more than a *feeling* [*Empfindung*], the "sensual experience of self as self" as Schulte-Sasse translates it[4] that limns every cognitive act.[5] What has come to be known as the "philosophy of identity" emerged through various endeavors to correct Kant by laying out the aesthetic conditions for a unified self-consciousness and an impossibly endoscopic self-transparency that would halt an infinite proliferation of reflective acts.[6]

Where the philosophy of identity leaves off and the Jena Romantics begin is precisely in the latter's recognition that an artwork quintessentially bears out the paradoxical consequences of upholding an ideal of unified self-consciousness that cannot be fulfilled. Friedrich Schlegel and Novalis are remarkable in Schulte-Sasse's view for adhering to "a notion of subjectivity that accepts the impossibility of overcoming its inherent fissures and rifts *while simultaneously accepting the ideal of a unified self as an ethical imperative.*"[7] The Jena Romantics teach Adorno to disdain an aesthetics of reconciliation that misrecognizes a "concept of a harmonious, closed, and complete work of art" as a union between the universal and the particular and as a mirror of a coherent self.[8]

Schulte-Sasse's outline of aesthetic ideology offers a coda for parsing Adorno's *Aesthetic Theory* as a continuation of the critique of the philosophy of identity and metaphysical *méconnaissance* as such. Adorno's shudder concept works through the German-Idealist anxiety about Kant's "failure" to establish a unity of apperception as well as his Romantic reappraisal that formalizes the ramifications of a split subject. The artwork's form is social, as Adorno insists, because it recodes a naively mimetic desire to *perform* wholeness and self-mastery, or the "pure I" to recall Idealist terms, *for others*. At the same time, the

---

2 Ibid., 2.
3 Ibid., 10.
4 Ibid., 15.
5 Ibid., 13.
6 Ibid., 14.
7 Ibid., 25.
8 Ibid., 25.

German-Romantic investment in irony, stylistic fragmentation, and play inflects Adorno's affinity with the dissonant gestures of radical modernism.

Adorno's anti-identitarian ethos leads him to reject Hegel's definition of art "as the effort to do away with foreignness."[9] Despite this rejection, Adorno faces up to the implications of Hegel's prognosis that "our present in its universal condition is not favourable to art." The third paragraph of the *Aesthetic Theory*[10] already alludes to Hegel's ominous pronouncement from the *Introductory Lectures* that "art is and remains for us, on the side of its highest destiny ['höchsten Bestimmung'], a thing of the past." The problem, Hegel explains, is not limited to "the universal habit of having an opinion and passing judgment about art" that "infects" artworks with abstraction. The threat to art also mounts from "the whole spiritual culture [*geistige Bildung*] of the age" which corrodes an artist's ability to bring about through education or reflection that "peculiar solitude" that falls under the rubric of aesthetic autonomy.[11]

Adorno's scrupulous attention to the social conditions of autonomy propels his reconsideration of Hegel's conflation between "the objectivity of the artwork and the truth of spirit"[12] by transvaluing the latter's criticism of F. W. J. Schelling to the effect that "only qua *Schein* can the aesthetic image speak truth."[13] "If the spirit of artworks flashes up in their sensual appearance," Adorno writes, "it does so only as their negation."[14] Hence, the ineffable "spirit" that illuminates artworks as "things among things"[15] is inseparable from their impact as *Schein*: the artwork points beyond the form with which it is inextricably bound up.

In the "Society" chapter of the *Aesthetic Theory*, Adorno elaborates on art's double character: its status as a "fait social" (a social phenomenon) and its "autonomy." The dialectic sustaining this two-fold status emerges with the historical development of the bourgeois consciousness of freedom, which shores up art's claim that it rebuffs a puritanical and technocratic insistence on use-value. The idea of autonomy gains

---

9   Theodor W. Adorno, *Aesthetic Theory*, trans. Robert Hullot-Kentor (Minneapolis: University of Minnesota Press, 1997), 80.
10 Ibid., 3.
11 G. W. F. Hegel, "The Range of Aesthetic Defined, and Some Objections against the Philosophy of Art Refuted," in *Introductory Lectures on Aesthetics*, ed. Michael Inwood, trans. Bernard Bosanquet (New York: Penguin Books, 1993), 12.
12 Adorno, *Aesthetic Theory*, 89.
13 Espen Hammer, "The Touch of Art: Adorno and the Sublime," *Sats: Nordic Journal of Philosophy* 1 (2) (2000): 100–1.
14 Adorno, *Aesthetic Theory*, 89.
15 Ibid., 86.

credence through the artist's experience of his or her own work as an act of freedom from an "administered society" that mandates emotional and corporeal subjugation wherever goods and services are produced, exchanged, or consumed. The artwork *appears* to objectify this sense of freedom by thwarting an instrumental prioritization of use-value, yet this same operation of resisting utilitarian dictates also affirms their inescapability by negation. If, for Adorno, "every successfully realized correction" confirms the latent presence of "a collective subject yet to be realized" who watches over the artist, then the artwork bears the unconscious imprint of internalized surveillance as a social universal.[16] Artistic correction folds an imaginary *We* into an external interlocutor; for this reason, artworks can never be entirely non-conciliatory[17] because "something in their law of form implies [collective appeal]."[18] This is why the charge of false consciousness hangs over works that disavow their status as social and material products. In a "universally, socially mediated world," Adorno insists, "nothing stands external" to the "primordial guilt" that saturates the fundamental antagonism between physical and spiritual labor. He nevertheless predicates art's "social truth" on its "fetish character," which generates a particular work's "nexus of guilt" as the negated condition of its utopic aspirations.[19]

The impact of radically modernist artworks that seem to "renounce communication" is "aporetic" according to Adorno in a social totality that "swallow[s] whole whatever occurs."[20] By enunciating its own apparent "uselessness" as a source of consolation and transcendence, modernist hermeticism desultorily repels art's aesthetic-ideological function as a vehicle of *Sinnstiftung*, that is to say, as an affirmation of a non-alienated social identification. This hermeticism promises a "plenipotentiary of things that are no longer distorted by exchange, profit, and the false needs of a degraded humanity,"[21] yet because the artwork ineluctably fails to make good on this promise, it permits an iridescent determinacy for the "nonexisting as if it did exist." In representing both "what does not allow itself to be managed and what total management suppresses,"[22] modernism is inversely utopian: it beckons beyond the confines of an instrumental economy that barely tolerates it and toward a transformed order in which the division between an

---

16 Ibid., 231.
17 Ibid., 237.
18 Ibid., 238.
19 Ibid., 227.
20 Ibid., 237.
21 Ibid., 227.
22 Ibid., 234.

occulted physical labor and a parasitic spiritual labor will have ceased to exist along with the guilt that this opposition spawns.[23]

Adorno's *Aesthetic Theory* addresses the question of how the artwork comes to miss its "genuine truth and life" in modernity — not only its meaning, then, but its illusion of *necessity*.[24] In posing this question in Hegel's shadow as it were, Adorno recapitulates a thematics of "romantic anti-capitalism" that traverses the writings of Friedrich Nietzsche, Oswald Spengler, Ernst Jünger, Martin Heidegger, Gyorgy Lukács, and Walter Benjamin, among others. Though Lukács identified "romantic anti-capitalism" with "a reactionary current, tending toward the Right and fascism,"[25] more broadly applied, his formulation also spotlights a range of melancholic motifs in the criticism of capitalist-bourgeois society. This melancholic criticism bemoans the disappearance of a pre-capitalist idyll distinguished by faith-based communal values, non-alienated labor, and a spiritual vitality manifest in morally uplifting art forms. While Adorno did not stoop to chauvinistic rants about the dissipation of "German" or "European" *Geist*, his writings nevertheless participate in an ongoing lament about the decline of *Kultur* and *Gemeinschaft* in the age of *Zivilisation* and *Gesellschaft* that deepens with industrialization.

On the reactionary anti-liberal side of "romantic anti-capitalism," Jünger's shudder aesthetics discover an antidote to spiritual decline in the shocking immediacy of the extreme situation. Jünger's shudder wrests a visceral wisdom from a confrontation with imminent death, when survival is unequivocally at stake. Overwhelming life-and-death confrontations trigger *archaic regression*, a reversion to primal intensity that shreds the numbing filters of secular reason. Carl Schmitt's decisionism and Martin Heidegger's impassive resoluteness in the face of one's "own-most death" infamously channel Jünger's longing for a mystical clarity forged, ever so suddenly and intuitively, in the fires of extremity.

On the Marxist-sociological end of the romantic-anti-capitalist continuum, Walter Benjamin speculates about the memory and experience fracturing impact of the modern subject's heightened exposure to shock in everyday life. Benjamin's reactions to modernization evoke an irrationalist anthropology that posits unconscious regression as a condition for re-catalyzing senses torpidly habituated to modern life's battering pace. To specify the various effects of mass industrialization, Benjamin's "On Some Motifs in Baudelaire"

---

23 Ibid., 233.
24 Hegel, "The Range of Aesthetic Defined," 13.
25 Robert Sayre, and Michael Löwy, "Figures of Romantic Anti-Capitalism," *New German Critique* 32 (1984): 481.

cites Freud's biologistic allegory from *Beyond the Pleasure Principle* where he conjures the image of a "fragment of living substance" that accrues a hardened outer layer in response to a barrage of stimuli. Freud subsequently frames an analogy between this "baked through" cortex and the protective-selective operations of the perceptual-conscious system.[26] Benjamin borrows this analogy to represent sensory numbness as a defense mechanism against a crowded urban existence: the displacement of *Erfahrung* (long-range experience that integrates the present with the past) by *Erlebnis* (isolated present-tense experience) transpires the more this "deadened" cortical layer seeps inward to protect monadic consciousness from successive assaults on self-absorption. This petrifying individuation corrodes a fundamental human-animal responsiveness and, with it, the instinctual basis for survival itself.

Benjamin assembles his modernist poetics from Baudelaire's reckoning with the disintegration of the artwork's aura in his time. In its recourse to the trope of defamiliarization, the paradoxical character of this poetics aligns it with Adorno's shudder aesthetics: both call for an unexpectedly *demobilized* comportment, which re-attunes defense-fossilized senses to the sensual intimations of things. For an animist Benjamin reading between Baudelaire, Proust, and Freud, an object's startling power to "look back" punctures a habit-worn perceptual selectivity that wards off unmanageable stimuli.

Adorno revisits aura when he represents the shudder as a response to the artwork's mimesis of natural beauty in a noumenal mode—what Espen Hammer describes as a silent and ineffable "expression of an ungraspable otherness, or that which lies beyond the negative totality of subjective reason's intentions and projections."[27] This semblance stirs up the sensation of a missed encounter with "the mythical power of uncontrollable fate,"[28] a *déjà vu* reverberation of nature's disavowed danger, its transcendent non-identity, its terror, strangeness, and sublimity "at one remove."[29] Adorno's aesthetics also echoes Benjamin's primitivist enchantment with the poetic potential of an

---

26 Walter Benjamin, "On Some Motifs in Baudelaire," in *Walter Benjamin: Selected Writings Volume 4: 1938–1940*, ed. Michael W. Jennings (Cambridge, MA: Harvard University Press, 2003), 316–18. Sigmund Freud, *The Standard Edition of the Complete Psychological Works of Sigmund Freud. Volume XVIII: Beyond the Pleasure Principle, Group Psychology, and Other Works*, ed. James Strachey in collaboration with Anna Freud (London: Vintage, 2001), 27.
27 Hammer, "The Touch of Art," 100.
28 Ibid., 101.
29 J. M. Bernstein, *The Fate of Art: Aesthetic Alienation from Kant to Derrida and Adorno* (University Park, PA: The Pennsylvania State University Press, 1992), 220.

unconscious regression from perceptual defensiveness that endows art with the ability to move under patient contemplation. As "afterimages of prehistorical shudders in an age of reification,"[30] artworks surpass the "world of things by what is thinglike about them"[31] and thus rekindle a momentary sense of primal antagonism against self-individuating rationality.

J. M. Bernstein links this definition of shudder aesthetics to the account of "originary repression" from the *Dialectic of Enlightenment*. In this context, Horkheimer and Adorno narrate the sacrifice of instinctual "first nature" into socially-adaptive "second nature," a term that translates Rousseau's social contractual self into Nietzsche's figuration of "bad conscience" as a discipline deformed will-to-power. This deformation transpires as reason's subjugation of "external nature" enforces "the inhibition and domination of drives and desires," a mastery of "inner nature" that exacerbates the compulsion to identity. From Adorno's perspective, this compulsion is pursued as external nature is deadened at the expense of inner nature, or what Bernstein characterizes as a "sacrifice of self for its own sake."[32]

As an epitaph to the spirit in the era of ubiquitous reification, the artwork's intrusive "foreignness" as a thing is antagonistic to this anomic self.[33] Spectators "shudder" when they "forget themselves and disappear in the work" and, thus, *involuntarily* "lose their footing" with the shocking "irruption of objectivity into subjective consciousness."[34] Like Jünger, Adorno portrays the shudder as a trauma to sensory capacities calcified by socio-economic tunnel vision. In stark contrast to Jünger, however, Adorno divests the solace of a sharpened self-sovereignty arising from the ashes of its sense-dulled inauthenticity. Instead, the shudder dislodges the *Ich* by resuscitating the dread of weakness and finitude it disdains.

The shudder obtains a *memorial* valence insofar as it registers the nerve-crackling anxiety of an era that preceded the domination of inner and outer nature and the formation of a unitary subject ideal through repressive socialization.[35] Dialectically speaking, form "objectifies" an artist's struggle to master the nature of his or her materials, and this process of objectification unconsciously writes a history in which reason's ruthless advancement of technology, socio-economic stratification, and cultural commodification liquidates the

---

30 Adorno, *Aesthetic Theory*, 79.
31 Ibid., 80.
32 Bernstein, *The Fate of Art*, 219.
33 Adorno, *Aesthetic Theory*, 84.
34 Ibid., 244–5.
35 Bernstein, *The Fate of Art*, 220. Hammer, "The Touch of Art," 101.

"sensuous particularity" of negated suffering.³⁶ The object's disconcerting primacy and otherness as a thing pierces the normative subject's "self-aggrandizing narcissism."³⁷ This primacy is therefore crucial on an ethical level according to Bernstein since it stimulates a reified subject into remembering a repressed "ontic substratum,"³⁸ a mortal depth of exposure that cannot be directly cognized or expiated.

Adorno's most explicit comments on the shudder in the "Society" chapter of the *Aesthetic Theory* delineate it in part through reference to the "power of the subject" as the "precondition" of Kant's aesthetic of the sublime.³⁹ In Kant's construction of the sublime, as Gene Ray recounts it, the "power of reason and its moral law" presses "the great evil of natural catastrophe" into service as "a foil for human dignity."⁴⁰ The subject temporarily loses a sense of grounding in fumbling to produce an intuition, a comprehensive image of the magnitude of "rude nature" (the mathematical sublime) or nature's violent power (the dynamic sublime). Yet while imagination is painfully humiliated "before the power or size of nature," Ray observes, the faculty of reason triumphs as "[t]error and shame give way to a proud and enjoyable self-contemplation," thereby reinstalling a sovereign subject. Even though it begins with a negation of mastery in the intimate domain of intuition, in the end, Kant's emplotment of the sublime serves to elevate "humanity above mere sensible nature, however mighty or boundless it may be."⁴¹

The re-entrenched reason that finalizes the sublime is, as Kant himself admits, the culturally specific luxury of a bourgeois subject who safely contemplates disaster or chaos from a distance.⁴² Actual terror neutralizes the self-affirming pleasures this distance facilitates. In contrast, Adorno's "modernist sublime" relishes the eclipse of mastery in Kant's plot while dispatching its identitarian compensation. The shudder transpires as "the I is seized by the unmetaphorical, semblance-shattering consciousness: that it itself is not ultimate, but semblance."⁴³ From the subject's standpoint, this seizure "transforms art into what it is in-itself, the historical voice of repressed nature [den geschichtlichen Sprecher unterdrückter Natur], ultimately critical of

---

36 Adorno, *Aesthetic Theory*, 92.
37 Bernstein, *The Fate of Art*, 222.
38 Adorno, *Aesthetic Theory*, 258.
39 Ibid., 245.
40 Gene Ray, "Reading the Lisbon Earthquake: Adorno, Lyotard, and the Contemporary Sublime," *The Yale Journal of Criticism* 17 (1) (2004): 11.
41 Ibid., 9.
42 Ibid., 7.
43 Adorno, *Aesthetic Theory*, 245.

the principle of the I, that internal agent of repression."[44] Kant's empty I of apperception seemingly resurfaces here as an element of "the objective truth of art," which the shudder refracts.[45]

In its potential to reawaken a pre-rational first nature, the syntax of Adorno's shudder seems to be as beholden to the Freudian uncanny as it is to the Kantian sublime. In his 1919 essay on "The Uncanny," Freud traces a connotative convergence between *heimlich,* meaning homelike or familiar, and its apparent opposite, the *unheimlich,* or unfamiliar. His analysis of E. T. A. Hoffmann's "The Sand-Man" culminates in an explanation for this convergence: the uncanny registers the return of the repressed (the familiar) in an unfamiliar domain. Throughout his writings, Freud aligns the repressed with leftovers from our phylogenetic heritage—"infantile" or "primitive" beliefs in the omnipotence of thoughts, or generally speaking, "the over-accentuation of psychical reality in relation to material reality."[46] Normally buried in the adult's unconscious, these puerile beliefs become "uncanny" when they unexpectedly recoup their claims on the rational adult consciousness that has long since repudiated them. The psychic grammar of Adorno's shudder translates the uncanny into the unsettling effect of a pre-rational "first nature" erupting within the "unhomelike" space of reified "second nature."

"What would art be as the writing of history," Adorno asks, "if it shook off the memory of accumulated suffering?"[47] A work of art indirectly records this memory in remaining "strictly for-itself" while "nonetheless [submitting] to integration as one harmless domain among others."[48] Artworks succeed for Adorno when they reveal themselves "as the wounds of society and the social ferment of their autonomous form." Through the eloquence of their dirempted resistance, "the untruth of the social situation comes to light. It is actually this against which the rage at art reacts."[49]

SEE ALSO: Sublime; Uncanny; Film; Montage/Collage

---

44 Ibid., 246.
45 Ibid., 246.
46 Sigmund Freud, "The 'Uncanny'" (1919), in *The Standard Edition of the Complete Psychological Works of Sigmund Freud. Volume XVII: An Infantile Neurosis and Other Works.* ed. James Strachey in collaboration with Anna Freud (London: Vintage, 2001), 244.
47 Adorno, *Aesthetic Theory,* 261.
48 Ibid., 237.
49 Ibid., 237.

Twenty-eight Committed Art

Andrew Lyndon Knighton

If there is a single figure in twentieth-century aesthetic theory whose thought crystallizes debates about the relationship of art to politics, it is Theodor W. Adorno, for whom the problems of committed art demanded attention not only in a number of essays directly addressing the topic, but also more broadly throughout his aesthetic theory. It is difficult, however—given his penchant for a relentlessly dialectical thought that almost magically consumes itself—to pin him to a single, perfectly consistent position on the question. As each standpoint is absorbed and transcended, only tentative conclusions and provisional solutions seem to be left behind. The richness of this thinking nevertheless becomes evident when it is crystallized into a series of intellectual confrontations—with Walter Benjamin, Bertolt Brecht, Gyorgy Lukács, and Jean-Paul Sartre—that, in conjunction with his own theory of art's historical truth-content, make clearer the contours of his ideas and their relation to the vicissitudes of his time. Such an account might help to reveal the oversimplification that has laid open Adorno and his Frankfurt School colleagues to charges of resignation or evasion; it certainly makes incontrovertible the claim that the concept of "commitment" is unthinkable without him.

In Adorno's general estimation, artworks that surrender themselves to mere sloganeering are not only doomed to political irrelevance but risk invalidating themselves as art. Brandishing a so-called "message," in the earnest fashion of "propagandist plays against syphilis, duels, abortion laws or borstals," such works become indistinct from the purposive activity of practical, everyday life.[1] Yet, as he makes clear, such overtly tendentious works hardly exhaust the varieties of committed art; as with many of Adorno's subtle conceptualizations,

---

1 Theodor W. Adorno et al., *Aesthetics and Politics* (London and New York: Verso, 1977), 180.

one can come away with the impression that the exact location of "committed art" tends to shift in the time that it takes to comment upon it. The very historical dynamism of the twentieth century, and especially the coalescence and intensification of a seemingly totalizing culture industry, surely necessitated an ongoing process of definition. Indeed, as Peter Bürger has observed, the very notion of committed art is all but inconceivable prior to the insurrection by the twentieth-century avant-garde against the institution of art—which institution had the effect of containing and neutralizing radical aesthetic content.[2] Something of the novelty of this historical situation is captured by the exploratory way in which Adorno, in his now-canonical exchanges with Walter Benjamin in the 1920s and 1930s, tinkered with theories of the political potentials of both aesthetic modernism and mass culture.

Benjamin had compellingly argued in his essay on the reproducibility of artworks that superstructural and technological transformations such as those embodied in the cinema would augment the political potentials of creative expression—by relieving art of its "aura," ushering in more collective and populist forms of production, and linking intellectual and manual labor. Adorno, detecting in these ideas the lurking radical influence of Brecht, rejected Benjamin's argument on multiple fronts. Most critically, Adorno charged that the liquidation of aura achieved by fitting the artwork to the mass cultural horizon of economic exchange had the consequence of hypostatizing the work's marketable fragments: the hook, the gimmick, the star, the isolated motif. The consumer of a work disseminated under conditions of distracted overstimulation could hardly be expected to attain a sense of the aesthetic whole, and thus has impeded the supple dialectic between subject and object—in other words, the very tension that made aesthetic experience meaningful. One could not, Adorno argued, assume the existence of a proletariat equipped with either the spontaneous intellect or the critical remove to combat mere identification with the work. Later, in his *Minima Moralia*, the stakes of this argument were signaled rather more bluntly in an aphorism directly speaking to both the difficulty of solidarity and the experience of film spectatorship: "every visit to the cinema leaves me, against all my vigilance, stupider and worse."[3]

Also crucial to his rebuttal of Benjamin was Adorno's insistence that technicization was not the exclusive prerogative of modern nonauratic art forms, but that such innovation was inherent to the formal

---

2 Peter Bürger, *Theory of the Avant-Garde*, trans. Michael Shaw (Minneapolis: University of Minnesota Press, 1984), 90.
3 Theodor W. Adorno, *Minima Moralia*, trans. E. F. N. Jephcott (London and New York: Verso, 1974), 25.

logics of the most advanced modern art. This celebration of the formal possibilities of the modern autonomous artwork put him at odds with Gyorgy Lukács, whose later writings, adhering to Soviet thinking about the proper political tendency and perspective of revolutionary art, expressed unambiguous hostility to modernism. The latter Lukács derided as mere "formalism," an exhibition of individual idiosyncrasy and meaningless stylization that lacked a commitment to the politically valuable task of exhibiting reality as an object of knowledge. In his 1958 essay on Lukács, "Reconciliation under Duress," Adorno draws a lamenting contrast between the younger, more vital, Lukács and his ossified Soviet counterpart; the latter, he asserts, "willfully misinterprets" the formal elements of the modern work as merely "arbitrary," and fails to recognize that the purported failure of authors like Joyce and Beckett to lionize official praxis is an objective product of a society in which the corollary to actual subjective impotence is the inability to realistically represent reality. In Adorno's words, "the monadological condition persists universally, despite all assurances to the contrary," and this is the basic truth conveyed by such modernists.[4]

Lukács's championing of the realist novel might be numbered among those misleading "assurances to the contrary." Conceived by Lukács as an organic totality, the novel was to testify to the empirical knowability of reality, and hence to serve as a kind of guarantee that one can move from knowledge of that reality to action within it. Adorno responds by accusing Lukács of capitulating to a "cult of immediacy" driven by the "dubious faith in the face value of things,"[5] and notes that the realist novel, like any other artwork, has to be understood not as a mere reflection of reality but as a stylized production contrived through formal techniques no less subjective than those deployed by modernism. Far from producing an empirical knowledge of reality, such representations instead ideologically produce only reality effects. The organic coherence that they thereby acquire is deceptive, formally promoting—for all the critical or progressive tendencies their content might harbor—the semblance of a reconciled world. "Art does not provide knowledge of reality by reflecting it photographically or 'from a particular perspective,'" Adorno concludes, insisting that its autonomous status instead enables it to contrarily reveal that which is "veiled by the empirical form assumed by reality."[6]

This critique of Lukács' empiricism and faith in immediacy is echoed in the essay "Commitment," which responds to Jean-Paul Sartre's suggestion, in *What is Literature?*, that the artist must strive for

---

4 Adorno et al., *Aesthetics and Politics*, 153, 166.
5 Ibid., 162, 161.
6 Ibid., 162.

relevance and engagement with political reality. Noting a bit wryly that objections to the hermetic or autonomous artwork mirror each other on both wings of the political continuum—both right and left imploring that "art should say something"—Adorno commences a riff on Sartre's seemingly self-evident claim that "the writer deals with significations." True as far as it goes, the claim nevertheless betrays Sartre's assumption that conceptual meaning is both transparent and readily transmissible, as well as his failure to account for the formal mediation performed by the artwork. For one cannot guarantee, Adorno rejoins, that meanings may be unproblematically "transferred from art to reality";[7] to deploy a linguistic sign in a literary text means not only that the residues of everyday speech remain attached to the sign, but also that any meaning, no matter how mundane or spontaneous, undergoes a transformation when subjected to the specific formal context of the art-work: "Even an ordinary 'was,' in a report of something that was not, acquires a new formal quality from the fact that it was not so."[8] The work of art cannot be reduced to its external, extra-artistic meanings without underestimating the power of the objective material to dialectically transform those meanings.

Sartre thus prunes from art its quintessential quality—the formal demands of the artistic material—while compensating for it with a hypertrophied account of subjective intent. The specifically artistic context for such individual intentions and transportable meanings is forgotten, with the result that in Sartre "commitment ceases to be distinct from any other form of human action or attitude" and the specifically artistic context of such political expression is neglected. This mistake, Adorno argues, is reinforced by Sartre's thematic embrace of the abstract principle of "choice," which overestimates the agency of the individual in the face of an objective world that is not merely individual but "inherently collective."[9] Tellingly, the critique of Sartre's notion of political engagement—ostensibly Adorno's object in this important essay—gives way to an extended attack on Brecht, who reproduces Sartre's naiveté about the formal rigors of the artwork, and intensifies it, in Adorno's opinion, by further revealing the political ineffectiveness of a politicized aesthetic. Adorno's assault on Brecht is both harsh and occasionally quite personal—perhaps in its sometimes cartoonish extremity inadvertently reflecting Adorno's awareness of his adversary's intelligence and seductiveness—but certain of his tendentious works are singled out on exceptional occasions for praise, and he is explicitly lauded as more sophisticated than Sartre. Similarly,

---

7   Ibid., 182.
8   Ibid., 178.
9   Ibid., 181.

in his conclusion to the *Aesthetics and Politics* collection, Jameson credits Brecht with a particularly nuanced understanding of the epistemological logics of political art, one that transcends the ossified positivist certainties of Lukács. Adorno affirms this contrast in characterizing Brecht's work as akin to "practical, well-nigh manual activity" and as promising a means of "annulling the separation between physical and mental activity and the fundamental division of labor (not least that between worker and intellectual) that resulted from it."[10] As such, the Brechtian theater functioned as something like an orchestrated experiment with truth.

Despite the fact that the formal innovations of such an experimental theater were designed to transcend the simple repackaging of empiricist messages, Adorno argues that Brecht's approach nonetheless overvalorizes subjective artistic agency, and furthermore, driven by "the exigencies of agitation," necessarily oversimplifies and hence misrepresents the political realities it attempts to confront. The "theatricality of total plain-spokenness"[11] belies these works' claim to truth, Brecht's "didactic style [being] intolerant of the ambiguity in which thought originates."[12] Adorno's diagnosis is that, troubled by the persistence of doubt about the verity of its doctrine and the effectiveness of its means, Brecht's politicized art requires ever more strident declarations of the rightness of the subject, a stridency which redoubles its latent falsehoods by adding to them that of the ability of the subject to master his world by eliminating real ambiguity. Adorno concretized this later in his 1965 lecture series on negative dialectics, offhandedly referring to the political "organizer" committed to agitation: "the more you suspect that this is not true practice, the more doggedly and passionately you become attached to such activities."[13]

Adorno's impatience with the likes of Sartre, Brecht, and Lukács registers a consistent critique of their neglect of the artwork's specific formal complexity, and their reliance on notions of immediacy, spontaneity, and the empirical self-evidence of conceptual knowledge. Their conception of the artwork as a mere instrument of the sovereign political artist reduces the work to nothing more than a code to be deciphered; "the work dies as soon as philologists have pumped

---

10 Ibid., 204.
11 Ibid., 184, 188.
12 Theodor W. Adorno, *Aesthetic Theory*, ed. Gretel Adorno and Rolf Tiedemann, trans. Robert Hullot-Kentor (Minneapolis: University of Minnesota Press, 1997), 242.
13 Detlev Claussen, *Theodor W. Adorno: One Last Genius*, trans. Rodney Livingstone (Cambridge, MA and London: The Belknap Press of Harvard University Press, 2008), 337.

out of it what the artist pumped in, a tautological game."[14] The idea of meaning merely being "pumped in" and "pumped out" of the artwork is revisited elsewhere in the *Aesthetic Theory* and beyond: Adorno repeatedly cautions that a message cannot "be squeezed out" of Shakespeare or Beckett;[15] in "Commitment" he credits Sartre's popularity to his facility not just with "solid plot" but with readily "extractable" ideas.[16] This stable of imagery—pumping, squeezing, extraction, and the like—perhaps conjures a grotesquely purposeful erotic grappling, or, better, the processes of an industrial manufactory. In either case, Adorno classes its manipulation of the artwork as an indignity. But such versions of committed art furthermore represent to Adorno a philosophical shortcoming, in that they fail to account for the mediation by which no subjective message can remain untransformed by the dialectical encounter with the objective material of the work. "Art in its most emphatic sense lacks the concept even when it employs concepts, and adapts its façade to comprehension," he claims. "No concept that enters an artwork remains what it is,"[17] and what the artist thinks he puts in never emerges in a perfectly legible form. Art's "enigmaticalness," he concludes, makes problematic the very category of understanding.[18]

Rejecting these politicized aesthetics as limited by the elusiveness of conceptual meaning and the impoverishment of the thinking subject, Adorno's aesthetic theory nonetheless regards the artwork as thoroughly social, historical, and political. The work's very existence rejects society in favor of constructing its own order. This relentlessly negative gesture of critique manifests a longing—itself political—for an alternative order to that which is proffered by bourgeois society, but it lacks the leverage to succeed in liberating the work entirely from that society. "Whereas art opposes society, it is nevertheless unable to take up a position beyond it; it achieves opposition only through identification with that against which it remonstrates."[19] This contradiction is formally inscribed in the work. Simultaneously gesturing toward utopia and necessarily renouncing it as actually impossible, the work may only ideologically resolve itself. Such irresolution and contradiction is crystallized in its form, therein embodying the truth of an unresolved and mystified social order.

At once aligned with and resistant to bourgeois reality, the artwork's

---

14 Adorno, *Aesthetic Theory*, 129.
15 Ibid., 128.
16 Adorno et al., *Aesthetics and Politics*, 182.
17 Adorno, *Aesthetic Theory*, 132.
18 Ibid., 121.
19 Ibid., 133.

ambivalent social character is microcosmically reproduced in aesthetic experience itself. Shierry Weber Nicholsen has persuasively suggested that Adorno's understanding of such experience depends on a kind of oscillation between the mimetic and the enigmatic. For while art demands the assimilation of the self to the other and the surrender to an affinity with it, so too does it necessitate otherness and distance. The two—the identificatory impulse and its rational, philosophical corrective—are dialectically co-dependent and ceaseless in the demands they place on the subject. Thus does the enigmaticalness of the artwork deny not only mere identification but also summary resolution into a pat and total form of knowledge. An artwork worthy of its name does not, according to Adorno, "unfold to contemplation and thought without any remainder,"[20] but rather persists in egging cognition on to complement aesthetic experience with philosophy. As Kai Hammermeister observes, "while interpretation of art is mandatory, its result is never sufficient";[21] in that dynamic there inheres the infinite renewal of aesthetic yearning—simultaneously a lack to be suffered and glorious abundance of possibility.

That the versions of a political aesthetic championed by Brecht, Lukács, and Sartre variously neglect this ambivalence explains to Adorno their relatively easy assimilation into the very institutions responsible for sustaining an unjust order. According to Adorno, Sartre's faith in the unmediated relation between art and reality has, whatever his intent, left him "acceptable to the culture industry,"[22] just as Jameson retrospectively notes Brecht's own absorption in "the burgeoning Brecht-Industrie";[23] of Lukács, Adorno can only sarcastically note his co-opted status as the Soviets' "officially licensed dialectician."[24] Claussen's recent recounting of Adorno's uneasy relationship with the 1960s student movements shows how his objections to those activist endeavors similarly pivoted on their faith in the rightness and transparency of their thought, which to him was a mere positivity easily enough incorporated, a "conformist fad disguised as left-wing radicalism."[25]

Yet any attempt to characterize Adorno's position on social practice should meet his own dialectical standard, and resist the univalent conceptual conclusion that he rejected outright committed art and the

---

20 Ibid., 121.
21 Kai Hammermeister, *The German Aesthetic Tradition* (Cambridge: Cambridge University Press, 2002), 206.
22 Adorno et al., *Aesthetics and Politics*, 182.
23 Ibid., 208.
24 Ibid., 152.
25 Claussen, *Theodor W. Adorno*, 326.

praxis to which it sought to contribute. The great political hibernator and emblem of intellectual resignation himself inhabited a complicated position, torn between sympathetic identification and critical restraint. This much is indicated in a passage from a late draft preface to *Dialectic of Enlightenment*, penned by Adorno in 1969, and containing the following illuminating reflection:

> Young people at least have set out to resist the transition to the totally administered world. ...The protest movement in all the countries of the world, in both blocs as well as the Third World, testifies to the fact that wholesale integration does not necessarily proceed smoothly. If this book assists the cause of resistance to achieve a consciousness that illuminates and that prevents people from submitting to blind practice out of despair and from succumbing to collective narcissism, that would give it a genuine function.[26]

He thereby registers, in one rich stroke, his affinity with, and his rational suspicion of, praxis. The difficulty of accounting for both positions at once is the truth of Adorno's enigmatic position on commitment; such an accounting is a burden analogous to that borne by any thinker wishing to understand the relationship of art to practice. "The truth-content of artworks is the objective solution of the enigma posed by each and every one. By demanding its solution, the enigma points to its truth-content. It can only be achieved by philosophical reflection." Such reflection, rendered impossible by the simple judgments and subjective assuredness of most committed art, would acknowledge the deeply political nature of all artworks, while refusing to explain their complexities away. "This alone"—the obligation of philosophical reflection to respect the unique historical force of the work of art—"this alone is the justification of aesthetics."[27]

SEE ALSO: Ethics; Allegory; Ugly

---

26 Adorno, in Claussen, *Theodor W. Adorno*, 338.
27 Adorno, *Aesthetic Theory*, 127–8.

Bibliography

Adorno, Theodor W. (1970). *Aesthetic Theory*. Edited by Gretel Adorno and Rolf Tiedemann. Translated by Robert Hullot-Kentnor. Minneapolis: University of Minnesota Press, 1997.
Adorno, Theodor W. *Aesthetic Theory*. Edited by Gretel Adorno and Rolf Tiedemann. Translated by C. Lenhardt. London: Routledge, 1984.
Aitken, Ian. *European Film Theory and Cinema: A Critical Introduction*. Edinburgh: Edinburgh University Press, 2001.
Alloa, Emmanuel. *Das durchscheinende Bild. Konturen einer medialen Phänomenologie*. Berlin/Zürich: diaphanes, 2011.
App, Urs. "The Tibet of the Philosophers: Kant, Hegel, and Schopenhauer." In *Images of Tibet in the 19th and 20th Centuries*, Vol. 1. Edited by Monica Esposito. 5–60. Paris: EFEO, 2008.
App, Urs. *The Birth of Orientalism*. Philadelphia: University of Pennsylvania Press, 2010.
App, Urs. *The Cult of Emptiness: The Western Discovery of Buddhist Thought and the Invention of Oriental Philosophy*. Rorschach: UniversityMedia, 2012.
App, Urs. *Schopenhauer's Compass*. Rorschach: UniversityMedia, 2014.
Arendt, Hannah. *Lectures on Kant's Political Philosophy*. Edited by Ronald Beiner. Chicago: University of Chicago Press, 1982.
Aristotle's Poetics. A Translation and Commentary for Students of Literature. Edited by O. B. Hardison, Jr. Translated by Leon Golden. Englewood Cliffs, NJ: Prentice-Hall Inc., 1968.
Arnheim, Rudolf. *Film as Art*. Berkeley: University of California Press, 1957.
Athanassoglou-Kallmyer, Nina. "Ugliness." In *Critical Terms for Art History*, 2nd ed. Edited by Robert S. Nelson and Richard Shiff. 281–95. Chicago: University of Chicago Press, 2003.
Auerbach, Erich. *Mimesis. The Representation of Reality in Western Literature*. Translated by Willard R. Trask. Princeton, NJ: Princeton University Press, 1991.
Babbitt, Irving. *Rousseau and Romanticism*. Boston and New York: Houghton-Mifflin, 1919.
Balázs, Béla. *Early Film Theory: Visible Man and The Spirit of Film*. Edited by Erica Carter. Translated by Rodney Livingstone. New York: Berghahn, 2010.
Baumgarten, Alexander Gottlieb. *Reflections on Poetry*. Translated by Karl Aschenbrenner and William B. Holther. Berkeley: University of California Press, 1954.
Baumgarten, Alexander Gottlieb. *Theoretische Ästhetik. Die grundlegenden Abschnitte*

aus der 'Aesthetica' (1750/58). Translated and edited by Hans Rudolf Schweizer. Hamburg: Felix Meiner, 1983.

Baumgarten, Alexander Gottlieb. *Aesthetica*. Frankfurt an der Oder: Johann Christian Kleyb, 1750, and *Aesthetica pars altera* (1758); modern edition with facing German translation by Dagmar Mirbach, 2 vols. Hamburg: Felix Meiner Verlag, 2007.

Beiser, Frederick C. *German Idealism: The Struggle against Subjectivism, 1781–1801*. Cambridge, MA: Harvard University Press, 2002.

Beiser, Frederick C. *Diotima's Children: German Aesthetic Rationalism from Leibniz to Lessing*. Oxford: Oxford University Press, 2009.

Belting, Hans, ed. *Bildfragen: Die Bildwissenschaften im Aufbruch*. Munich: Fink, 2007.

Benjamin, Walter. *Gesammelte Schriften*. Edited by Rolf Tiedemann and Hermann Schweppenhäuser. 7 vols. Frankfurt am Main: Suhrkamp, 1972–91.

Benjamin, Walter. *The Origin of German Tragic Drama*. Translated by John Osborne. London: Verso, 1998.

Benjamin, Walter. *The Arcades Project*. Edited by Rolf Tiedemann. Translated by Howard Eiland and Kevin McLaughlin. Cambridge, MA: Harvard University Press, 1999.

Benjamin, Walter. "On Some Motifs in Baudelaire." In *Walter Benjamin: Selected Writings Volume 4: 1938–1940*. Edited by Michael W. Jennings. Translated by Harry Zohn. 313–55 Cambridge, MA: Harvard University Press, 2003.

Benjamin, Walter. *The Work of Art in the Age of Its Technological Reproducibility and Other Writings on Media*. Edited by Michael W. Jennings, Brigid Doherty, and Thomas Y. Levin. Cambridge, MA: Harvard University Press, 2008.

Bernstein, J. M. *The Fate of Art: Aesthetic Alienation from Kant to Derrida and Adorno*. University Park: Pennsylvania State University Press, 1992.

Biemel, Walter. *Die Bedeutung von Kants Begründung der Ästhetik für die Philosophie der Kunst*. Köln: Kölner Universitäts-Verlag, 1959.

Bloch, Ernst. *Geist der Utopie. Faksimile der Ausgabe von 1918*. Frankfurt am Main: Suhrkamp, 1985.

Bloom, Allan. *The Republic of Plato*. Translated, with notes, an interpretive essay, and a new Introduction. New York: Basic Books, 1991.

Blumenberg, Hans. "Wirklichkeitsbegriff und Wirkungspotential des Mythos (1971)." In *Aesthetische und Metaphorologische Schriften*. Edited with an afterword by Anselm Haverkamp. 327–405. Frankfurt am Main: Suhrkamp, 2001.

Boehm, Gottfried. "Bildsinn und Sinnesorgane." *Neue Hefte für Philosophie* 18/19 (1980): 118–32.

Boehm, Gottfried, ed. *Was ist ein Bild?* Munich: Fink, 1995.

Boehm, Gottfried. *Wie Bilder Sinn Erzeugen. Die Macht des Zeigens*. Berlin: Berlin University Press, 2007.

Bohrer, Karl Heinz. "Am Ende des Erhabenen: Niedergang und Renaissance einer Kategorie." *Merkur* 43 (1989): 736–50.

Bölsche, Wilhelm. *Die naturwissenschaftlichen Grundlagen der Poesie. Prolegomena einer realistischen Ästhetik*. Tübingen: Niemeyer, 1976.

Bonds, Mark Evan. *Music as Thought: Listening to the Symphony in the Age of Beethoven*. Princeton, NJ: Princeton University Press, 2006.

Brecht, Bertolt. *The Life of Galileo*. Translated by John Willet. New York and London: Penguin, 2008.

Bredekamp, Horst. "Bildwissenschaft." In *Metzler Lexikon Kunstwissenschaft: Ideen, Methoden, Begriffe*. Ed. Ulrich Pfisterer. 56–8. Stuttgart: Metzler, 2003.

Burke, Kenneth. *Language as Symbolic Action: Essays on Life, Literature, and Method.* Berkeley: University of California Press, 1966.
Byron, Lord. *Don Juan by Lord Byron.* Edited by Leslie A. Marchand. Boston: Houghton Mifflin, 1958.
Canguilhem, Georges. *On the Normal and the Pathological.* Edited by Robert S. Cohen. Translated by Carolyn R. Fawcett. Boston: Reidel, 1978.
Caygill, Howard. *Art of Judgement.* Oxford: Blackwell, 1989.
Chua, Daniel K. L. *Absolute Music and the Construction of Meaning.* New York: Cambridge University Press, 1999.
Cohen, Hermann. *Die Nächstenliebe im Talmud.* Marburg: Elwert, 1888.
Cohen, Hermann. *Ethik des reinen Willens.* Berlin: Cassirer, 1904.
Cohen, Hermann. *Religion der Vernunft aus den Quellen des Judentums.* Leipzig: Fock, 1919.
Cole, Andrew. *The Birth of Theory.* Chicago: University of Chicago Press, 2014.
Coleridge, Samuel Taylor. *Biographia Literaria,* 2 vols. Edited by James Engell and W. Jackson Bate. Princeton, NJ: Princeton University Press, 1983.
Costelloe, Timothy M. "Aesthetics and the Faculty of Taste." In *Oxford Handbook of British Philosophy in the Eighteenth Century.* Edited by James A. Harris. 430–49. Oxford: Oxford University Press, 2014.
Dahlhaus, Carl. *The Idea of Absolute Music.* Translated by Roger Lustig. Chicago: University of Chicago Press, 1989.
Danto, Arthur C. *The Philosophical Disenfranchisement of Art.* New York: Columbia University Press, 1986.
Deleuze, Gilles. "How Do We Recognize Structuralism?" In *Desert Islands and Other Texts 1953–1974.* Edited by David Lapoujade. Translated by Melissa McMahon and Charles J. Stivale. 170–92. Los Angeles: Semiotext(e), 2004.
Dennis, John. *The Critical Works.* Edited by Edward Niles Hooker. Vol. 2. Baltimore, MD: Johns Hopkins University Press, 1943.
Derrida, Jacques. "Structure, Sign, and Play in the Discourse of the Human Sciences." In *Writing and Difference.* Translated by Alan Bass. 278–94. London: Routledge, 1978.
Diederichsen, Diederich. "Montage, Sampling, Morphing" http://www.medienkunstnetz.de/themen/bild-ton-elationen/montage_sampling_morphing/ (accessed June 22, 2011).
Dirac, Paul. "The Versatility of Niels Bohr." In *Niels Bohr: His Life and Work as Seen by His Friends and Colleagues.* Edited by S. Rozental. 306–9. New York: John Wiley, 1967.
Droit, Roger-Pol. *The Cult of Nothingness: The Philosophers and the Buddha.* Translated by David Streight and Pamela Vohnson. Chapel Hill. University of North Carolina Press, 2003.
Eggebrecht, Hans Heinrich. *Die Musik und das Schöne.* Munich and Zürich: Piper, 1997.
Empson, William. *Seven Types of Ambiguity.* New York: New Directions, 1947 [1930].
Enzensberger, Hans Magnus. *Mausoleum.* Frankfurt am Main: Suhrkamp, 1975.
Enzensberger, Hans Magnus. *Politische Brosamen*: Frankfurt am Main: Suhrkamp, 1982.
Enzensberger, Hans Magnus. *Mittelmaß und Wahn. Gesammelte Zerstreuungen.* Frankfurt am Main: Suhrkamp, 1988.
Faas, Ekbert. *The Genealogy of Aesthetics.* Cambridge: Cambridge University Press, 2002.

Fichte, J. G. *Science of Knowledge, with the First and Second Introductions.* Translated and edited by Peter Heath and John Lachs. Cambridge: Cambridge University Press, 1982.

Fichte, J. G. "On the Spirit and the Letter in Philosophy." In *German Aesthetic and Literary Criticism: Kant, Fichte, Schelling, Schopenhauer, Hegel.* Edited by David Simpson. Translated by Elizabeth Rubenstein. 74–93. Cambridge: Cambridge University Press, 1984.

Forkel, Johann Nicolaus. *Allgemeine Geschichte der Musik.* 2 vols. Leipzig: Schwickertschen, 1788–1801.

Foucault, Michel. *The Order of Things: An Archaeology of the Human Sciences.* New York: Vintage, 1970.

Foucault, Michel. *Discipline and Punish: The Birth of the Prison.* Translated by Alan Sheridan. New York: Vintage Books, 1977.

Foucault, Michel. *The History of Sexuality,* Vol. 1: *The Will to Knowledge.* Translated by Robert Hurley. New York: Vintage Books, 1978.

Frank, Manfred, *The Philosophical Foundations of Early Romanticism.* Translated by Elizabeth Millán-Zaibert. Albany: State University of New York Press, 2008.

Fredericksen, Donald Laurence. *The Aesthetic of Isolation in Film Theory: Hugo Münsterberg.* New York: Arno Press, 1977.

Freud, Sigmund. "The 'Uncanny.'" In *Writings on Art and Literature.* 193–233. Stanford, CA: Stanford University Press, 1997.

Freud, Sigmund. *Gesammelte Werke.* 18 Bände und Nachtragsband. Frankfurt am Main: Fischer, 1999 [1941–1968].

Freud, Sigmund. *The Standard Edition of the Complete Psychological Works of Sigmund Freud.* Translated from the German under the General Editorship of James Strachey. In collaboration with Anna Freud. Assisted by Alix Strachey and Alan Tyson, 24 vols. London: Vintage, 2001.

Gadamer, Hans-Georg. *Wahrheit und Methode.* 6th ed. Tübingen: Mohr und Siebeck, 1990.

Gadamer, Hans-Georg. *Truth and Method,* 2nd ed., revised. Translated by Joel Weinsheimer and Donald G. Marshall. London: Continuum, 2004.

Gebauer, Gunter and Christoph Wulf. *Mimesis: Culture, Art, Society.* Berkeley: University of California Press, 1995.

Goethe, Johann Wolfgang von. *Goethe's Faust.* Edited by R-M. S. Heffner, Helmut Rehder, and W. F. Twaddell. Boston: Heath, 1954.

Goethe, Johann Wolfgang von. *Essays on Art and Literature.* Edited by John Gearey. Goethe's Collected Works, Vol. 3. Princeton, NJ: Princeton University Press, 1994.

Goethe, Johann Wolfgang von. *Die Leiden des jungen Werther.* Edited by Katharina Mommsen and Richard A. Koc. Frankfurt am. Main: Insel Verlag, 2001.

Goethe, Johann Wolfgang von. *The Sufferings of Young Werther.* Translated by Stanley Corngold. New York: W. W. Norton, 2011.

Goppelsröder, Fabian. *Zwischen Sagen und Zeigen. Wittgensteins Weg von der literarischen zur dichtenden Philosophie.* Bielefeld: transcript, 2007.

Goppelsröder, Fabian and Martin Beck. *Präsentifizieren. Zeigen zwischen Körper, Bild und Sprache.* Berlin and Zürich: diaphanes, 2014.

Goppelsröder, Fabian and Nora Molkenthin. "Mathematik/Geometrie." In *Bild. Ein interdisziplinäres Handbuch.* Edited by S. Günzel and D. Mersch. 408–13. Stuttgart: J. B. Metzler, 2014.

Gottsched, Johann Christoph. "Critical Poetics." In *Eighteenth Century German Criticism*. Translated by Timothy J. Chamberlain. German Library Vol. 11, 3–5. New York: Continuum, 1992.

Gramit, David. *Cultivating Music: The Aspirations, Interests, and Limits of German Musical Culture, 1770–1848*. Berkeley: University of California Press, 2002.

Guillory, John. *Cultural Capital: The Problem of Literary Canon Formation*. Chicago: University of Chicago Press, 1993.

Guyer, Paul. *A History of Modern Aesthetics*. 3 vols. Cambridge: Cambridge University Press, 2014.

Habermas, Jürgen. *The Structural Transformation of the Public Sphere: An Inquiry into a Category of Bourgeois Society*. Translated by Thomas Burger. Cambridge, MA: MIT Press, 1989.

Hall, Mirko M. "Friedrich Schlegel's Romanticization of Music." *Eighteenth-Century Studies* 42 (2009): 413–29.

Halliwell, Stephen. *The Aesthetics of Mimesis. Ancient Texts and Modern Problems*. Princeton, NJ: Princeton University Press, 2002.

Hammer, Espen. "The Touch of Art: Adorno and the Sublime." *Sats: Nordic Journal of Philosophy* 1 (2) (2000): 92–105.

Hammermeister, Kai. *The German Aesthetic Tradition*. Cambridge: Cambridge University Press, 2002.

Hanslick, Eduard. *The Beautiful in Music* (7th ed. 1891). Edited by Morris Weitz. Translated by Gustav Cohen. Indianapolis: Bobbs-Merrill, 1957.

Hegel, Georg Wilhelm Friedrich. *System der Philosophie. Dritter Teil. Die Philosophie des Geistes. Jubiläumsausgabe*, Vol. 10. Stuttgart: Frommann, 1958.

Hegel, Georg Wilhelm Friedrich. *Vorlesungen über die Ästhetik. Dritter Band. Jubiläumsausgabe*, Vol. 14. Stuttgart: Frommann, 1964.

Hegel, Georg Wilhelm Friedrich. *Hegel's Philosophy of Right*. Translated by T. M. Knox. London: Oxford University Press, 1967.

Hegel, Georg Wilhelm Friedrich. *Werke*. Edited by Eva Moldenhauer and Karl Markus Michel. 20 vols. Frankfurt am Main: Suhrkamp, 1971.

Hegel, Georg Wilhelm Friedrich. *Phenomenology of Spirit*. Translated by A. V. Miller. Oxford: Oxford University Press, 1977.

Hegel, Georg Wilhelm Friedrich. "The Range of Aesthetic Defined, and Some Objections against the Philosophy of Art Refuted." In *Introductory Lectures on Aesthetics*. Edited by Michael Inwood. Translated by Bernard Bosanquet. 3–16. New York: Penguin Books, 1993.

Hegel, Georg Wilhelm Friedrich. "Earliest Program for a System of German Idealism." In *Theory As Practice: A Critical Anthology of Early German Romantic Writings*. Edited by Jochen Schulte-Sasse. 72–3. Minneapolis: University of Minnesota Press, 1997.

Hegel, Georg Wilhelm Friedrich. *Aesthetics: Lectures on Fine Art*. Edited and translated by T. M. Knox. Oxford: Oxford University Press, 1998.

Heidegger, Martin. "Nietzsches Wort: 'Gott ist tot'." In *Holzwege*. 193–247. Frankfurt am Main: Vittorio Klostermann, 1950.

Heidegger, Martin. *Der Ursprung des Kunstwerks*. Intro. Hans Georg Gadamer. Stuttgart: Reclam, 1960.

Heidegger, Martin. "The Origin of the Work of Art." In *Basic Writings*. Edited by David Farrell Krell. 139–212. New York: Harper & Row Publishers, 1977.

Heidegger, Martin. *Sein und Zeit*. Tübingen: Niemeyer, 1993.

Heidegger, Martin. *Nietzsche I/II*. 2 vols. Frankfurt/Main: Klostermann, 1996.

Heidegger, Martin. *Pathmarks*. Edited by William McNeill. Cambridge: Cambridge University Press, 1998.
Heidegger, Martin. *Off the Beaten Track*. Edited and translated by Julian Young and Kenneth Haynes. Cambridge: Cambridge University Press, 2002.
Heidegger, Martin. *Die Grundbegriffe der Metaphysik. Welt–Endlichkeit–Einsamkeit*. Frankfurt am Main: Klostermann, 2004.
Heine, Heinrich. *The Romantic School and Other Essays*. Edited by Jost Hermand and Robert C. Holub. New York: Continuum Publishing, 1985.
Heine, Heinrich. *Zur Geschichte der Religion und Philosophie in Deutschland*. Ditzingen: Reclam, 1997.
Henrich, Dieter. *Aesthetic Judgment and the Moral Image of the World: Studies in Kant*. Stanford, CA: Stanford University Press, 1992.
Henrich, Dieter. *Fixpunkte. Abhandlungen und Essays zur Theorie der Kunst*. Frankfurt am Main: Suhrkamp, 2003.
Herder, Johann Gottfried. *Schriften zu Literatur und Philosophie 1792–1800*. Edited by Hans Dietrich Irmscher. Frankfurt am Main: Deutscher Klassiker Verlag, 1998.
Hoeckner, Berthold. *Programming the Absolute: Nineteenth-Century German Music and the Hermeneutics of the Moment*. Princeton, NJ: Princeton University Press, 2002.
Hoffmann, E. T. A. *Sämtliche Werke*. Edited by Hartmut Steinecke and Wulf Segebrecht. 6 vols. Frankfurt am Main: Deutscher Klassiker, 2003.
Hoffmann, E. T. A. *E.T.A. Hoffmann's Musical Writings: Kreisleriana, The Poet and the Composer, Music Criticism*. Edited by David Charlton. Cambridge: Cambridge University Press, 2004.
Hölderlin, Friedrich. *Sämtliche Werke*. Editied by Friedich Beißner. 6 vols. Stuttgart: Kohlhammer, 1943–85.
Hölderlin, Friedrich. "Judgment and Being." In *Essays and Letters on Theory*. Edited and translated by Thomas Pfau. 37–9. Albany: State University of New York Press, 1988.
Hullot-Kentor, Robert. "Critique of the Organic." In Theodor W. Adorno, *Kierkegaard: Construction of the Aesthetic*. Translated by Robert Hullot-Kentor. x–xxiii. Minneapolis: University of Minnesota Press, 1989.
Hume, David. "Of the Standard of Taste." In *Essays, Moral, Political, and Literary*. Edited by Eugene F. Miller, rev. ed. 226–49. Indianapolis: Liberty Fund, 1987.
Hutcheson, Francis. *An Inquiry into the Original of Our Ideas of Beauty and Virtue in Two Treatises*. Edited by Wolfgang Leidhold. Indianapolis: Liberty Fund, 2004.
Kaes, Anton, ed. *Kino-Debatte: Zum Verhältnis von Literatur und Film 1909–1929*. Tübingen: Niemeyer, 1984.
Kant, Immanuel. *Gesammelte Schriften*, hrsg. Königlich-Preußische [später, Deutsche] Akademie der Wissenschaften zu Berlin. 27 vols to date. Berlin: Reimer; later, de Gruyter, 1900–.
Kant, Immanuel. *Foundations of the Metaphysics of Morals and "What Is Enlightenment?"* Indianapolis: The Liberal Arts Press, 1959.
Kant, Immanuel. *Kant's Critique of Judgement*. Translated by James Creed Meredith. Oxford: Clarendon, 1964.
Kant, Immanuel. *The Critique of Judgment*. Translated by J. H. Bernard. New York: Prometheus Books, 1974.
Kant, Immanuel. *Critique of Judgment*. Translated by Werner S. Pluhar. Indianapolis: Hackett Publishing Co., 1987.

Kant, Immanuel. *Anthropology from a Pragmatic Point of View*. Translated by Victor Lyle Dowdel. Carbondale: Southern Illinois University Press, 1996.
Kant, Immanuel. *Critique of Pure Reason*. Translated by Werner S. Pluhar. Indinapolis: Hackett Publishing Co., 1996.
Kant, Immanuel. *Critique of Pure Reason*. Translated by Paul Guyer and Allen W. Wood. New York: Cambridge University Press, 1998.
Kant, Immanuel. *Critique of the Power of Judgment*. Edited and translated by Paul Guyer and Eric Matthews. Cambridge: Cambridge University Press, 2000.
Kant, Immanuel. *Kritik der Urteilskraft*. Werkausgabe, Band X. Edited by Wilhelm Weinschedel. Frankfurt am Main: Suhrkamp, 2000.
Kant, Immanuel. *Kritik der Urteilskraft*. Hamburg: Meiner, 2006.
Kant, Immanuel. "Remarks in the *Observations on the Feeling of the Beautiful and Sublime*." In *Observations on the Feeling of the Beautiful and Sublime, and Other Writings*. Translated by Thomas Hilgers, Uygar Abaci, Michael Nance, and Paul Guyer. 65–204. Cambridge: Cambridge University Press, 2011.
Karatani, Kojin. *Architecture as Metaphor: Language, Number, Money*. Edited by Michael Speaks. Translated by Sabu Kohso. Cambridge, MA: MIT Press, 1995.
Kern, Andrea. *Schöne Lust: Eine Theorie der ästhetischen Erfahrung nach Kant*. Frankfurt am Main: Suhrkamp Verlag, 2000.
Kierkegaard, Søren. *Begrebet Angest. Skrifter*, Vol. 4. Copenhagen: Gad, 1994.
Kittler, Friedrich. *Discourse Networks 1800/1900*. Translated by Michael Metteer with Chris Cullens. Stanford, CA: Stanford University Press, 1990.
Kittler, Friedrich. *Gramophone, Film, Typewriter*. Translated by Geoffrey Winthrop-Youn and Michael Wutz. Stanford, CA: Stanford University Press. 1999.
Kompridis, Nikolas, ed. *The Aesthetic Turn in Political Thought*. New York: Bloomsbury, 2014.
Kracauer, Siegfried. "The Mass Ornament." In *The Weimar Republic Sourcebook*. Edited by Anton Kaes, Martin Jay, and Edward Dimendberg. 404–7. Berkeley: University of California Press, 1994.
Kracauer, Siegfried. *Theory of Film: The Redemption of Physical Reality*. Princeton, NJ: Princeton University Press, 1997.
Krug, Wilhelm Traugott. *Allgemeines Handwörterbuch der philosophischen Wissenschaften*. 5 vols. Leipzig: Brockhaus, 1838.
Kuspit, Donald. *The End of Art*. Cambridge: Cambridge University Press, 2004.
Lacan, Jacques. *The Seminar of Jacques Lacan. Book XI. The Four Fundamental Concepts of Psychoanalysis*. Translated by Alan Sheridan. Edited by Jacques-Alain Miller. New York: W. W. Norton, 1981.
Lactantius, *The Divine Institutes*. Translated by Mary Francis McDonald, Vol. 49 of *The Fathers of the Church*. Washington, DC: Catholic University of America Press, 1964.
Lessing, Gotthold Ephraim. *Laokoon*. In *Werke*, Vol. 3. Edited by Herbert G. Göpfert. 9–188. Munich: Carl Hanser Verlag, 1982.
Lessing, Gotthold Ephraim. *Laocoön: An Essay on the Limits of Painting and Poetry*. Translated by Edward Allen McCormick. Baltimore, MD: Johns Hopkins University Press, 1984.
Lessing, Otto Eduard. "Irving Babbitt's *Rousseau and Romanticism*." *Journal of English and Germanic Philology* 18 (1919): 628–35.
Link, Jürgen. "Normal/Normalität/Normalismus." In *Ästhetische Grundbegriffe*. Edited by Karlheinz Barck et al., Vol. 4. 538–62. Stuttgart: Metzler, 2002.

Link, Jürgen. "Normalization" (four essays). Translated by Mirko Hall. *Cultural Critique* 57 (2004): 14–90.
Link, Jürgen. *Versuch über den Normalismus. Wie Normalität produziert wird*, 4th ed. Göttingen: Vandenhoeck & Ruprecht, 2009.
Locke, John. *An Essay Concerning Human Understanding*. Edited by R. S. Woolhouse. London: Penguin Books, 1997.
Longinus. *On Sublimity*. Translated by D. A. Russell. Oxford: Oxford University Press, 1965.
Luhmann, Niklas. *Social Systems*. Translated by John Bednarz, Jr. with Dirk Baecker. Stanford, CA: Stanford University Press, 1995.
Lukács, Gyorgy. "Thoughts on an Aesthetics of the Cinema." *Polygraph* 13 (2001): 13–18.
Ma, Lin. *Heidegger on East–West Dialogue: Anticipating the Event*. London: Routledge, 2008.
Man, Paul de. *Allegories of Reading: Figural Language in Rousseau, Nietzsche, Rilke and Proust*. New Haven, CT: Yale University Press, 1982.
Man, Paul de. "The Rhetoric of Temporality." *Blindness and Insight: Essays in the Rhetoric of Contemporary Criticism*, 2nd ed. rev. 187–228. Minneapolis: University of Minnesota Press, 1983.
Man, Paul de. "The Concept of Irony." In *Aesthetic Ideology*. Edited by Andrzej Warminski. 163–84. Minneapolis: University of Minnesota Press, 1996.
Man, Paul de. "Sign and Symbol in Hegel's *Aesthetics*." *Aesthetic Ideology*. Edited with Introduction by Andrzej Warminski. 91–104. Minneapolis: University of Minnesota Press, 1996.
Manovich, Lev. *The Language of New Media*. Cambridge, MA: MIT Press, 2001.
Marquard, Odo. "Kant und die Wende zur Ästhetik." *Zeitschrift für philosophische Forschung* 16 (3) (1962).
Marx, Karl. *Capital: A Critique of Political Economy, Volume 1*. Translated by Ben Fowkes. London: Penguin Books, 1990.
May, Reinhard. *Heidegger's Hidden Sources: East Asian Influences on his Work*. Translated by Graham Parkes. London: Routledge, 1996.
Mendelssohn, Moses. *Philosophische Schriften*, 2nd ed. Berlin: Voss, 1771.
Mendelssohn, Moses. *Philosophical Writings*. Edited and translated by Daniel O. Dahlstrom. Cambridge: Cambridge University Press, 1997.
Mersch, Dieter, ed. *Was sich zeigt. Materialität, Präsenz, Ereignis*. München: Fink, 2002.
Mersch, Dieter, ed. *Bild. Ein interdisziplinäres Handbuch*. Stuttgart and Weimar: J. B. Metzler, 2014.
Mersch, Dieter, ed. *Epistemologien des Ästhetischen*. Berlin/Zürich: diaphanes, 2015.
Mersch, Dieter and Martina Heßler, eds. *Logik des Bildlichen. Zur Kritik der ikonischen Vernunft*. Bielefeld: transcript, 2010.
Mirandola, Gianfrancesco Pico della. *Liber de imaginatione/On the Imagination*. Latin text with English translation by Harry Caplan. New Haven, CT: Yale University Press, 1930.
Moritz, Karl Philipp. "From: 'On the Artistic Imitation of the Beautiful'." In *Classic and Romantic German Aesthetics*. Edited by J. M. Bernstein. 131–44. New York: Cambridge University Press, 2003.
Morrison, Robert G. *Nietzsche and Buddhism: A Study in Nihilism and Ironic Affinities*. Oxford: Oxford University Press, 1997.
Muecke, D. C. *The Compass of Irony*. London: Methuen, 1969.

Müller, Heiner. *Germania*. Translated by Bernard and Caroline Schütze. New York: Semiotexte, 1990.
Müller, Heiner. *A Heiner Müller Reader*. Edited and translated by Carl Weber. Baltimore, MD: Johns Hopkins University Press, 2001.
Münsterberg, Hugo. *Münsterberg on Film. The Photoplay: A Psychological Study and Other Writings*. Edited by Alan Langdale. New York: Routledge, 2001.
Nazar, Hina. *Enlightened Sentiments: Judgment and Autonomy in the Age of Sensibility*. New York: Fordham University Press, 2012.
Nietzsche, Friedrich (1872). *Sämtliche Werke: Kritische Studienausgabe*. 15 vols. Edited by Giorgio Colli and Mazzino Montinari. Berlin: de Gruyter, 1967–77.
Nietzsche, Friedrich (1872). *The Birth of Tragedy out of the Spirit of Music*. Edited by Raymond Geuss and Ronald Speirs. Translated by Ronald Speirs. Cambridge: Cambridge University Press, 1999.
Nietzsche, Friedrich (1872). *Jenseits von Gut und Böse/Zur Genealogie der Moral*. Berlin: Walter de Gruyter [Deutscher Taschenbuch Verlag], 1999.
Novalis. "Last Fragments." In *Philosophical Writings*. Edited by Margaret Mahony Stoljar. 153–66. New York: State University of New York Press, 1997.
Pederson, Sanna. "Defining the Term 'Absolute Music' Historically." *Music & Letters* 90 (2) (2009): 240–62.
Pfeiffer, K. Ludwig. "The Materiality of Communication." In *Materialities of Communication*. Edited by Hans Ulrich Gumbrecht and K. Ludwig Pfeiffer. Translated by William Whobrey. 1–12. Stanford, CA: Stanford University Press, 1994.
Pinkard, Terry. *Hegel: A Biography*. Cambridge: Cambridge University Press, 2000.
Preisendanz, Wolfgang. *Humor als dichterische Einbildungskraft. Studien zur Erzählkunst des poetischen Realismus*. Munich: Wilhelm Fink Verlag, 1976.
Prendergast, Christopher. *The Order of Mimesis. Balzac, Stendhal, Nerval, Flaubert*. London: Cambridge University Press, 1986.
Quintilian. *The Institutio Oratoria of Quintilian*. Translated by H. E. Butler. Cambridge, MA: Harvard University Press (Loeb Classical Library), 1920.
Rank, Otto. *The Double: a Psychoanalytical Study*. London: Karnac, 1989.
Ray, Gene. "Reading the Lisbon Earthquake: Adorno, Lyotard, and the Contemporary Sublime." *The Yale Journal of Criticism* 17 (1) (2004): 1–18.
Reinhardt, Karl. *Tradition und Geist. Gesammelte Essays zur Dichtung*. Göttingen: Vandenhoeck & Ruprecht, 1960.
Riley, Matthew. *Musical Listening in the German Enlightenment: Attention, Wonder, and Astonishment*. Aldershot: Ashgate, 2004.
Rodowick, David N. "An Elegy for Theory." *October* 22 (Fall 2007): 91–109.
Rosenkranz, Karl. *Aesthetik des Hässlichen*. Stuttgart-Bad Cannstatt: Friedrich Frommann, 1968.
Rosenzweig, Franz. *Der Mensch und sein Welt. Gesammelte Schriften III. Zweistromland: Kleinere Schriften zu Glauben und Denken*. Edited by Reinhold and Annemarie Meyer. Dordrecht: Nijhoff, 1984.
Rosenzweig, Franz. *Der Stern der Erlösung*. Frankfurt am Main: Suhrkamp, 1988.
Rousseau, Jean-Jacques. *Émile; or, On Education*. Translated by Allan Bloom. New York: Basic Books, 1979.
Rousseau, Jean-Jacques. *Rousseau, Judge of Jean-Jacques: Dialogues*. Translated by Judith R. Bush, Christopher Kelly, and Roger D. Masters. Hanover: University Press of New England, 1990.

Rousseau, Jean-Jacques. *Reveries of a Solitary Walker.* Translated by Charles Butterworth. Indianapolis: Hackett, 1992.
Rousseau, Jean-Jacques. *The Confessions and Correspondence, Including the Letters to Malesherbes.* Translated by Christopher Kelly. Hanover, NH: University Press of New England, 1995.
St. Ambrose. *Seven Exegetical Works.* Translated by Michael P. McHugh, Vol. 65 of *The Fathers of the Church.* Washington, DC: Catholic University of America Press, 1972.
Sayre, Robert and Michael Löwy. "Figures of Romantic Anti-Capitalism." *New German Critique* 32 (1984): 42–92.
Schelling, F. W. J. *System of Transcendental Idealism.* Translated by Albert Hofstadter. In *Philosophies of Art and Beauty: Selected Readings in Aesthetics from Plato to Heidegger.* Edited by Albert Hofstadter and Richard Kuhns. 347–77. Chicago: The University of Chicago Press, 1976.
Schelling, F. W. J. *Ausgewählte Schriften.* Edited by Manfred Frank. 7 vols. Frankfurt am Main: Suhrkamp, 1985.
Schelling, F. W. J. *The Philosophy of Art.* Translated and edited by Douglas W. Stott. Minneapolis: University of Minnesota Press, 1989.
Schiller, Friedrich. *Über die ästhetische Erziehung des Menschen in einer Reihe von Briefen. Werke,* Vol. 12. Stuttgart and Tübingen: Gottaschen Buchhandlung, 1838.
Schiller, Friedrich. *Letters on the Aesthetic Education of Man.* Edited and translated by Reginald Snell. New Haven, CT: Yale University Press, 1954.
Schiller, Friedrich. *Philosophical Fragments.* Translated by Peter Firchow. Minneapolis: University of Minnesota Press, 1991.
Schiller, Friedrich. *Essays.* Edited by Walter Hinderer and Daniel O. Dahlstrom. New York: Continuum, 1993.
Schiller, Friedrich. *Letters on the Aesthetic Education of Man.* In *Essays.* Edited by Walter Hinderer and Daniel O. Dahlstrom. 86–178. New York: Continuum, 1993.
Schiller, Friedrich. "On Incomprehensibility." In *Theory as Practice: A Critical Anthology of Early German Romantic Writings,* edited by Jochen Schulte-Sasse et al. 118–28. Minneapolis: University of Minnesota Press, 1997.
Schiller, Friedrich. *On the Study of Greek Poetry.* Edited and translated by Stuart Barnett. Albany: State University of New York Press, 2001.
Schiller, Friedrich. *"Kallias or Concerning Beauty:* Letters to Gottfried Körner." Translated by Stefan Bird-Pollan. In *Classic and Romantic German Aesthetics.* Edited by J. M. Bernstein. 145–83. Cambridge: Cambridge University Press, 2003.
Schlegel, Friedrich. *Kritische Friedrich-Schlegel-Ausgabe.* Edited by Ernst Behler et al. Paderborn: Schoeningh, 1958.
Schopenhauer, Arthur. *Die Welt als Wille und Vorstellung.* 2 vols. *Sämtliche Werke.* Wiesbaden: F. U. Brodhaus, 1966.
Schopenhauer, Arthur. *The World as Will and Representation.* 2 vols. Translated by E. F. J. Paynes. New York: Dover, 1969.
Schopenhauer, Arthur. *The World as Will and Representation.* Translated and edited by Judith Norman, Alistair Welchman, and Chistopher Janaway. Cambridge: Cambridge University Press, 2010.
Schulte-Sasse, Jochen. "General Introduction: Romanticism's Paradoxical Articulation of Desire." In *Theory as Practice: A Critical Anthology of Early German Romantic Writings.* Edited by Jochen Schulte-Sasse et al. 1–43. Minneapolis: University of Minnesota Press, 1997.

Scruton, Roger. "Absolute Music." *The New Grove Dictionary of Music*, rev. ed., Vol. 1, 36–7. London: Macmillan, 2001.
Sedlar, Jean W. *India in the Mind of Germany*. Washington, DC: University Press of America, 1982.
Shaftesbury, Anthony Ashley Cooper, Third Earl of. "Sensus Communis; an Essay on the Freedom of Wit and Humor." In *Characteristicks of Men, Manners, Opinions, Times*. Edited by Douglas den Uyl. 37–94. Indianapolis: Liberty Fund, 2001.
Simpson, Leonard, Esq, ed. and trans. *Correspondence of Schiller with Körner*, 3 vols (Vol. 2). London: Richard Bentley New Burlington Street, 1849.
Sloterdijk, Peter. "Rules for the Human Zoo: A Response to the *Letter on Humanism*." Translated by Mary Varney Rorty. *Environment and Planning D: Society and Space* 27 (2009): 12–28.
Smith, Adam. *The Wealth of Nations*. Edited by Edwin Cannan. New York: The Modern Library, Random House, 2000.
Soni, Vivasvan. "Introduction: The Crisis of Judgment." *The Eighteenth-Century: Theory and Interpretation* 51 (3) (2010): 261–88.
Spinoza, Baruch [Benedict de]. *The Collected Works of Spinoza*. Vol. 1. Edited and translated by Edwin Curley. Princeton, NJ: Princeton University Press, 1985.
Spitzer, Leo. *Classical and Christian Ideas of World Harmony. Prolegomena to an Interpretation of the Word "Stimmung"*. Baltimore, MD: Johns Hopkins University Press, 1963.
Sprung, Mervyn. "Nietzsche's Trans-European Eye." In *Nietzsche and Asian Thought*. Edited by Graham Parkes. 76–90. Chicago. University of Chicago Press, 1991.
Steiner, F. George. "Contributions to a Dictionary of Critical Terms: 'Egoism' and Egotism'." *Essays in Criticism* II (4) (October 1952): 444–52.
Steiner, F. George. *Real Presences*. Chicago: Chicago University Press, 1989.
Stiegler, Berndt. *Montagen des Realen. Photographie als Reflexionsmedium und Kulturtechnik*. Paderborn: Fink, 2009.
Sulzer, Johann Georg. *Allgemeine Theorie der Schönen Künste*. 2nd ed. [by Friedrich Blankenburg]. 4 vols. plus index vol. Leipzig: Weidmann, 1794. Facsimile reprint with Introduction by Giorgio Tonelli. Hildesheim: Georg Olms Verlag, 1994.
Szondi, Peter. *Essay on the Tragic*.Translated by Paul Fleming. Stanford, CA: Stanford University Press, 2002.
Tambling, Jeremy. *Allegory*. London: Routledge, 2009.
Tholen, Georg Christoph. "Medium, Medien." In *Grundbegriffe der Medientheorie*. Edited by Alexander Roestler and Bernd Stiegler. 150–72. Stuttgart: Uni-Taschenbücher, 2005.
Turvey, Malcolm. *Doubting Vision: Film and the Revelationist Tradition*. Oxford: Oxford University Press, 2008.
Ulmer, Gregory. "The Object of Post-Criticism." In *The Anti-Aesthetic. Essays on Postmodern Culture*. Edited by Hal Foster. 83–111. Port Townsend, WA: Bay, 1983.
Vedral, Vlatko. "Living in a Quantum World." *Scientific American* 304 (6) (June 2011) 38–43.
Von der Luft, Eric. "Sources of Nietzsche's 'God is Dead!' and Its Meaning for Heidegger." *Journal of the History of Ideas* 45 (2) (April–June 1984): 263–76.
Wackenroder, Wilhelm Heinrich. *Sämtliche Werke und Briefe. Historisch-Kritische Ausgabe*. Edited by Silvio Vietta and Richard Littlejohns. 2 vols. Heidelberg: Winter, 1991.

Weineck, Silke-Maria. *The Abyss Above. Philosophy and Poetic Madness in Plato, Hoelderlin and Nietzsche*. Albany: State University of New York, 2002.

Weitz, Morris. "The Role of Theory in Aesthetics." *The Journal of Aesthetics and Art Criticism* 15 (1) (September 1956): 27–35.

Wellbery, David E. *Lessing's Laocoön. Semiotics and Aesthetics in the Age of Reason*. New York: Cambridge University Press, 1984.

Wellbery, David E. "Stimmung." In *Historisches Wörterbuch Ästhetischer Grundbegriffe*. Edited by Karlheinz Barck et al., Vol. 5, 703–33. Stuttgart: Metzler, 2003.

Wiesing, Lambert. *Sehen lassen—Die Praxis des Zeigens*. Berlin: Suhrkamp, 2013.

Wilamowitz-Moellendorff, Ulrich von. *Einleitung in die griechische Tragödie*. Berlin: Weidmann, 1907.

Winckelmann, Johann Joachim. "Thoughts on the Imitation of the Painting and Sculpture of the Greeks." In *German Aesthetic and Literary Criticism: Winckelmann, Lessing, Hamann, Herder, Schiller, Goethe*. Edited and translated by H. B. Nisbet. 32–54. Cambridge: Cambridge University Press, 1985.

Wittgenstein, Ludwig. *Tractatus Logico-Philosophicus*. London: Routledge, 2001.

Wolff, Christian. *Vernünftige Gedancken von Gott, der Welt, und der Seele des Menschen*. Neue Auflage (original edition, 1720). Halle: Renger, 1751.

Young, Julian. *Heidegger's Philosophy of Art*. Cambridge: Cambridge University Press, 2001.

Young, Julian. *Schopenhauer*. Abingdon: Routledge, 2005.

Zelle, Carsten. "*Angenehmes Grauen*": *Literaturhistorische Beiträge zur Ästhetik des Schrecklichen im achtzehnten Jahrhundert*. Hamburg: Meiner, 1987.

Zerilli, Linda M. G. "'We Feel Our Freedom': Imagination and Judgment in the Thought of Hannah Arendt." *Political Theory* 33 (2) (2005): 158–88.

Žmegač, Viktor. "Montage/Collage." In *Moderne Literatur in Grundbegriffen*. Edited by Dieter Borchmeyer and Viktor Žmegač. Tübingen: Niemeyer, 1994.

Notes on Contributors

Ian Balfour is Professor of English at York University. His publications include *The Rhetoric of Romantic Prophecy* (Stanford, 2002) and a collection called *Late Derrida* (SAQ).

Karyn Ball is Professor of English and Film Studies at the University of Alberta, specializing in literary and cultural theory. She is author of *Disciplining the Holocaust* (SUNY, 2009), and her articles have appeared in journals such as *Cultural Critique*, *Women in German Yearbook*, *Differences*, *English Studies in Canada*, *New Literary History*, *Alif*, *Holocaust Studies: A Journal of Culture and History*, and *Angelaki*.

Michel Chaouli teaches German and Comparative Literature at Indiana University, Bloomington. He is the author of *The Laboratory of Poetry: Chemistry and Poetics in the Work of Friedrich Schlegel* (John Hopkins University Press, 2002), *Thinking With Kant's Critique of Judgment* (Harvard University Press, 2016), as well as articles on a wide range of literary and philosophical topics, which can be found at bit.ly/chaouli.

Rey Chow is Anne Firor Scott Professor of Literature and the current director of the Program in Literature at Duke University. The books she has authored include, most recently, *Entanglements, or Transmedial Thinking about Capture* (Duke University Press, 2012) and *Not Like a Native Speaker: On Languaging as a Postcolonial Experience* (Columbia University Press, 2014). Her writings, widely anthologized, have appeared in more than ten languages. She serves on the boards of about fifty academic journals, book series, and research centers around the world.

Stanley Corngold is Professor (emeritus) of German and Comparative Literature at Princeton University. He is a Fellow of the American Academy of Arts and Sciences.

Notes on Contributors

Peter Fenves is the Joan and Serepta Harrison Professor of German, Comparative Literary Studies, and Jewish Studies at Northwestern University. He is the author of several books, most recently *Late Kant: Towards Another Law of the Earth* (Routledge, 2003) and *The Messianic Reduction: Walter Benjamin and the Shape of Time* (Standford University Press, 2011).

Eva Geulen is a scholar of German literature and philosophy and has taught at various institutions in the United States and in Germany. As of 2015 she is Professor of Cultural Studies at the Humboldt University in Berlin and Director of the Center for Literary and Cultural Research (ZfL) in Berlin.

Darío González is a lecturer in philosophy and aesthetics at the University of Copenhagen, Department of Media, Cognition and Communication, and Department of Art and Cultural Studies. He is also an affiliated researcher at the Søren Kierkegaard Research Centre. He is the co-editor of *Escritos de Søren Kierkegaard* (Trotta, 2000–10).

Fabian Goppelsröder studied philosophy and history in Berlin and Paris and received his PhD in Comparative Literature from Stanford University. Currently he is a Feodor-Lynen-Fellow in the Department of Germanic Languages at the University of Chicago.

Paul Guyer is the Jonathan Nelson Professor of Humanities and Philosophy at Brown University and Florence R. C. Murray Professor in the Humanities Emeritus at the University of Pennsylvania. He is the author, editor, and translator of numerous works on and by Kant, and published *A History of Modern Aesthetics* in three volumes in 2014 (Cambridge University Press).

Mirko M. Hall is Associate Professor of German Studies and Chair of Languages, Cultures, and Literatures at Converse College. He is the author of *Musical Revolutions in German Culture: Musicking against the Grain, 1800–1980* (Palgrave Macmillan, 2014) and co-editor of the forthcoming volume *Beyond No Future: Cultures of German Punk* (Bloomsbury, 2016).

Kai Hammermeister, formerly a professor of German literature and philosophy, now works as a Lacanian psychoanalyst in Berlin.

Kenneth Haynes teaches Comparative Literature at Brown University, where he specializes in the study of classical reception. He is the author of *English Literature and Ancient Languages* (Oxford, 2003) as well as translator and editor of *Johann Georg Hamann: Writings on Language and Philosophy* (Cambridge, 2007).

Andrew Lyndon Knighton is Professor of English at California State University, Los Angeles, where he has also served as the Bailey Endowed Chair of American Communities. He is the author of *Idle Threats: Men and the Limits of Productivity in Nineteenth-Century America* (New York University Press, 2012).

A. Kiarina Kordela is Professor of German and Director of the Critical Theory Program at Macalester College, and honorary adjunct professor at the University of Western Sydney, Australia. She is the author of *$urplus: Spinoza, Lacan* (SUNY, 2007) and of *Being, Time, Bios: Capitalism and Ontology* (SUNY, 2013), and the co-editor of *Freedom and Confinement in Modernity: Kafka's Cages* (Palgrave-Macmillan, 2011) and of a two-volume collection titled *Spinoza's Authority: Resistance and Power* (Bloomsbury, 2016).

Richard Leppert, a musicologist, is Regents Professor in the Department of Cultural Studies and Comparative Literature, University of Minnesota, Minneapolis. His research and writing is concentrated on Western European and American cultural history from the seventeenth century to the present.

Jürgen Link is Professor Emeritus at the University of Dortmund. He is the author of *Versuch über den Normalismus: Wie Normalität produziert wird* (Verlag für Sozialwissenschaften, 1996) and was a long-time editor of the journal *kultuRRevolution. zeitschrift für angewandte diskurstheorie*.

David Martyn is Professor in the Department of German and Russian Studies at Macalester College. He is the author of *Sublime Failures: The Ethics of Kant and Sade* (Wayne State, 2003) as well as editor of a critical edition of Moses Mendelssohn's *Jerusalem*.

Patrizia McBride is Professor of German Studies at Cornell University. Her interests include modernism and avant-garde studies; narrative theory; visual culture and media studies; the relationship between literature, philosophy, and political theory.

J. D. Mininger is Professor of Philosophy at Vytautas Magnus University (Kaunas, Lithuania), Associate Dean at LCC International University (Klaipeda, Lithuania), and an adjunct professor at the University of Bologna. His publications include the collection *Politics Otherwise: Shakespeare as Social and Political Critique* (Rodopi, 2012). He is managing editor of the Value Inquiry Book Series (Brill/Rodopi), and co-editor of the sub-series *Philosophy, Literature, and Politics*.

Johannes von Moltke is Professor in the Departments of Germanic Languages and Literatures and Screen Arts and Cultures at the University of Michigan. He is the author, most recently, of *The Curious Humanist: Siegfried Kracauer in America* (University of California Press, 2016).

Jason Michael Peck teaches in the Department of Modern Languages and Literature at the University of Rochester. He is the author of the forthcoming book *The Poetics of Debt: Political Theologies From The Merchant of Venice to the Occupy Movement* (Brill, 2017).

Sanna Pederson, who specializes in German music history and culture in the nineteenth century, has been the Mavis C. Pitman Professor of Music at the University of Oklahoma since 2001.

Thomas Pepper teaches in the Department of Cultural Studies and Comparative Literature at the University of Minnesota. He is the author of *Singularities: Extremes of Theory in the Twentieth Century* (Cambridge, 1997).

Jochen Schulte-Sasse (1940–2012) was Professor Emeritus at the University of Minnesota, where he taught in the Departments of Cultural Studies and Comparative Literature, and German, Scandinavian, and Dutch. He was a founding co-editor of the influential Theory and History of Literature series, published by the University of Minnesota Press (1981–98), and a co-editor of the journal *Cultural Critique*.

Christian Sieg holds a research position at the "Religion and Politics" Cluster of Excellence and teaches in the Department of German Studies at the Westfälische Wilhelms-Universität Münster. His recent publications include *The Ordinary in the Novel of German Modernism* (Aisthesis, 2011) and the collection *Autorschaften im Spannungsfeld von Religion und Politik* (Ergon, 2014).

Vivasvan Soni is Associate Professor of English at Northwestern University. He is the author of *Mourning Happiness: Narrative and the Politics of Modernity* (Cornell, 2010), which won the MLA Prize for a First Book.

James A. Steintrager is Professor of English, Comparative Literature, and European Languages and Studies at the University of

California-Irvine, where he is also director of UCI Critical Theory. His most recent book is *The Autonomy of Pleasure: Libertines, License, and Sexual Revolution* (Columbia University Press, 2016).

Silke-Maria Weineck is Chair of Comparative Literature and Professor of German Studies and Comparative Literature at the University of Michigan. She is the author *of The Abyss Above: Philosophy and Poetic Madness in Plato, Hölderlin, and Nietzsche* (SUNY Press, 2002) and *The Tragedy of Fatherhood: King Laius and the Politics of Paternity in the West* (Bloomsbury, 2014).

Index

absolute, the 11–12, 84–5, 175
Adorno, Theodor W. 74, 98–9, 125, 179, 198, 207, 220–2, 236–43
   Aesthetic Theory 1, 41, 48, 117, 225–31, 233–5
   Commitment 238–9, 241
   Dialectic of Enlightenment 48, 99, 233, 243
   "enigmaticalness" 241–3
   and Horkheimer 170, 233
   Kierkegaard: Construction of the Aesthetic 105
   Minima Moralia 237
aesthetic/s
   Baumgarten on 1–2, 4, 14, 26, 77
   of cinema 196–7
   cognition 23, 77
   as a discipline 42, 76–7, 83, 92–3, 136–8, 176
   enjoyment 35
   experience 19, 21, 25, 36, 149, 182, 237, 242
   idea 29, 72 *see also* Kant, *Critique of the Power of Judgment*
   ideology 106–8, 228
   illusion 46
   intoxication 176
   political 236–43
   theory 17, 153, 176, 203, 243
Agamben, Giorgio 180
allegory 100–8, 110, 135
alphabetization 172 *see also* Kittler

Ambrose, Saint 6
anti-aesthetic/s 95–7
anxiety 116, 118, 181, 192, 194, 227, 233
Apollonian 32, 130–2 *see also* Nietzsche, *The Birth of Tragedy*
Aristophanes 63
Aristotle 17, 43, 45, 129, 220
Arnheim, Rudolf 196
attention (*Aufmerksamkeit*) 69
Auerbach, Erich: *Mimesis: The Representation of Reality in Western Literature* 49–50
autonomous art 69, 198, 229, 238–9
autonomy 1, 14, 19, 21, 49, 75
avant-garde 208, 215–16, 237

Babbitt, Irving 52
Balázs, Béla 202–3
baroque culture 133
Barthes, Roland 143
Baumgarten, Alexander Gottlieb 25, 69, 76–7, 174
   Aesthetica 15, 26, 45, 136
   Reflections on Poetry 1, 14, 18, 78
Bazin, André 203
beauty/beautiful 15, 25–33, 35, 47, 79–81, 174–5, 177, 219, 221
   adherent 29
   Adorno on 33
   artistic 27, 31

judgment of 21–3 *see also* judgment
Kant on 28–30, 54
of nature (*das Naturschöne*) 202–3
"purposiveness without a purpose" 22, 113, 200 *see also* judgment; Kant
and ugliness 219–26
Beethoven, Ludwig van 68, 72, 74, 84
Being 23, 152–3, 167, 177
Beiser, Frederick C. 77, 101
Belting, Hans 138
Benjamin, Walter 109, 205–7, 231, 236–7
  Arcades Project, The 103–5
  "aura" 198, 232, 237
  On Some Motifs in Baudelaire 231–2
  Origin of German Tragic Drama, The 96, 103–5, 129, 132–5
  "tragic time" 3
  Work of Art in the Age of Its Mechanical Reproducibility, The 98, 117, 169–70, 197–8, 207
Bloch, Ernst 159, 207
Blumenberg, Hans 119, 121, 126
Boehm, Gottfriend 138, 140, 143
Bohr, Niels 119
boredom 195
Brahms, Johannes 85
Brecht, Bertolt 127, 169, 236–7, 239–40, 242
Breitinger, Johann Jakob 44–5
Brentano, Clemens 73
Bruckner, Anton 89–90
Buddhism 146–9
Bürger, Peter 208, 237
Burke, Edmund 35
Burke, Kenneth 60

Calderón de la Barca, Pedro 133

Cohen, Hermann 156–8
Coleridge, Samuel Taylor 5, 13
committed art/commitment 236–43
commodity fetish 104–5
constellation 103
culture industry 98–100 *see also* Adorno

Dadaism 205
Dahlhaus, Carl 86, 89–90
Danto, Arthur 91–2
Daoism 152
death drive 167–9, 185–6
Deleuze, Gilles 114
Derrida, Jacques 41, 166, 171
desire 106–8, 118
digital culture/digitization 138, 172, 209
Dionysian 32, 130–2 *see also* Nietzsche, *The Birth of Tragedy*
Döblin, Alfred 206–7
double/Doppelgänger 183–6
Duchamp, Marcel 91

earth 153, 178 *see also* Heidegger
Eggebrecht, Hans Heinrich 90
empiricism 17
Empson, William 181
end of art 91–9
  Hegel on 32, 92–4
Enlightenment 12, 14, 68–71, 145
ethics 76–83
Euripides 131

feeling 51–9, 190–1
  of intelligibility 57
Feuerbach, Ludwig 87, 165
Fichte, Johann Gottlieb 9, 11, 145
figure *see* trope
film 170, 196–203, 205
Forkel, Johann Nicolaus 70–1
form 220–1, 225–6

formalization/formalism 109, 112–14, 201–2, 238
Foucault, Michel 13, 171, 212–13
Frank, Manfred 107, 180
freedom 36–9, 80–3, 164, 225–6, 230
free play of the faculties 21, 28, 56
Freud, Sigmund, 123, 167, 169, 181–7, 231–2

Gadamer, Hans-Georg 101, 178–9
genius 5, 31, 44, 46–9, 102, 158–9
"God is dead" 119–26
Goethe, Johann Wolfgang von 203
  Elective Affinities 62
  Faust 51, 55
  On Truth and Verisimilitude in Art 48
  Simple Imitation, Manner, Style 47–8
  Sufferings of Young Werther, The 54–9
Gogh, Vincent van 177
good (the) 79–81, 174
Gottsched, Johann Christoph 44, 76–7, 174
Gräfle, Albert 68
Greenberg, Clement 221

Habermas, Jürgen 170
Halm, August 89
Hammermeister, Kai 3
Hanslick, Eduard 84–5, 220
Hegel, Georg Wilhelm Friedrich 1, 23, 30, 66, 82, 84, 118–19, 129, 145, 157, 167, 175, 178, 223, 229
  Hegel's Aesthetics: Lectures on Fine Art 11–12, 31, 92–3, 191, 223
  Phenomenology of Spirit 93–4, 165
  Science of Logic 146
Heidegger, Martin 109, 123, 166–7, 175–80, 231
  Basic Concepts of Metaphysic, The: World, Finitude, Solitude 195
  Being and Time 96, 139, 152, 193–4
  "Contributions" 96, 195
  on language 167, 177
  Origin of the Work of Art, The 116–17, 153, 176–8
Heine, Heinrich 94–5, 119
Henrich, Dieter 22, 94
Herder, Johann Gottfried 39–40, 164
hermeticism 230, 239
history
  Benjamin on 133–5, 161–2, 169
  cyclical theory of 157
  end of 158
  Hegel on 23–24
  historical *a priori* 171–2
  historical life 134
  historical time 122
  world 156–7
Hoffman, Ernst Theodor Amadeus 72, 86, 235
Hoffmannsthal, Hugo von 192
Hölderlin, Friedrich 23, 55, 96, 115, 157
Hullot-Kentor, Robert 105
Hume, David 17–18, 111
Husserl, Edmund 166
Hutcheson, Francis 18–19, 22

ideal-content 109–12
ideal-spectator 125–6
idealism (German) 30, 175, 198
imagination 5–13, 28–9, 37
  poetic 7
  productive 8–9
  reflective 10
imitation *see* mimesis
immeasurable/immense (the) 36
infinite approximation 107
intuition 10–12, 22, 31
  intellectual 13
irony 60–7, 115, 229
  as permanent parabasis 65–6 *see also* Schlegel

Romantic irony 94
Socratic irony (or self-irony)
  62–4
verbal irony 62

Jacobi, Friedrich Heinrich 145
Jameson, Frederic 240
Judaism 156–7, 159
judgment 14–24, 174
  aesthetic 9, 18, 20–2, 54, 56–7, 79, 174, 191
  autonomous 14, 20, 22
  of the beautiful 21–3 *see also* beauty/beautiful
  determining 20
  reflective/reflecting 9, 20
  synthetic 19
  of taste 21–2, 174
Jünger, Ernst 231, 233

Kant, Immanuel 16–17, 19, 31, 34, 52–4, 167, 179, 199–200, 202
  Critique of the Power of Judgment / Critique of Judgment 1, 8–9, 15, 20–3, 28–30, 36–8, 46–8, 54, 56, 79–80, 112–14, 158–9, 164, 174, 181–2, 189–90, 202, 222
  Critique of Practical Reason 54
  Critique of Pure Reason 8, 110–11, 122, 164, 228
  Observations on the Feeling of the Beautiful and the Sublime 53
  Toward Eternal Peace (Zum ewigen Frieden) 157
Kierkegaard, Søren 192
Kittler, Friedrich 168, 172
Kracauer, Siegfried 97–8, 197, 199, 202–3
Krug, Wilhelm Traugott 155
Kurth, Ernst 89
Kuspit, Donald 91

Lacan, Jacques 115, 171, 187

Lactantius 6
Leibniz, Gottfried Wilhelm 25, 174
Lessing, Gotthold Ephraim 123, 199, 220, 223
  Laocoön 45, 168
Lessing, Otto Eduard 52
Levinas, Emmanuel 139
listening 68–75
  structural listening 74
Locke, John 15–16, 24,
Longinus (Pseudo-; Boileau's) 34–7
love 58
  heart 58
  self-love 56
Luhmann, Niklas 170–1
Lukács, György (Georg) 169, 196–7, 199, 236, 238, 240, 242
Lyotard, Jean-François 41, 91

Mach, Ernst 183–5
Man, Paul de 100, 105–6
Mandeville, Bernard 24
Marcuse, Herbert 167
Marlowe, Christopher 127
Marquard, Odo 93
Marx, Karl 111, 115, 165, 167
materiality
  of communication 168
  Marx on 169
mediation 163–73, 208, 239
  in relation to immediacy 167
medium 163–73, 196, 200, 202–3, 204
  as in-between 164–8
  as material carrier 168–73
Mendelssohn, Moses 27, 37, 174
Mersch, Dieter 144
messianism 155–62
  Benjamin on 161–2 *see also* Benjamin
  epistemological 160
  messianic critique 157–8, 160–2
  messianic hope 159 *see also* Bloch

mimesis 43–50, 177, 187
  Adorno on 48–9, 242
  Aristotle on 43–4
  mimetic cognition 49
Mirandola, Pico della 6
Mitchell, W. J. T. 138
montage/collage 204–9
mood/attunement 188–95
Moritz, Karl Philip 47
Muecke, Douglis Colin 61
Müller, Heiner 127
Münsterberg, Hugo 199–201
music
  absolute music 72–3, 84–90
  instrumental 71–3, 84
  program 87–8
  sonata form 74
  and ugliness 219–20
mystical 142 *see also* Wittgenstein
myth 121

Nancy, Jean-Luc 41
naturalism 214–15
nature, imitation of 43–5, 48
negation 165
neo-Kantianism *see* Hermann
  Cohen
new media 97–8, 172, 209
Nietzsche, Friedrich 33, 88, 176,
  227
  Birth of Tragedy, The 1, 32, 95–6,
    116, 124–5, 129–32, 150–1,
    175
  Gay Science, The 120–5
  Genealogy of Morals, The 163
  Twilight of the Idols, The 123
normality 210–18
  antinormalistic polemics 215–16
  as different from normativity
    210–11
  flexible normalism 212, 216–18
  normalism 211
  normalistic narrative 213–14
  protonormalism 211–12

normalizing society 213 *see also*
  Foucault
nostalgia 194–5
nothingness 145–54
  Heidegger on 152–3
  nihilism 145, 162
  nirvana 145
Novalis (Georg Philipp Friedrich
  von Hardenberg) 12, 73

"Oldest System Program of
  German Idealism" 82–3
  see also Hegel; Hölderlin;
  Schelling

paradox 120, 131, 166, 168, 170–1,
  173
pastiche 204
perception 18–19
perfection 25–7, 36, 78–9
performative self-referentiality 109,
  116–18
philosophical hermeneutics 178–9
picture theory/*Bildwissenschaften*,
  picture as fact 141 *see
  also* showing [*Zeigen*];
  Wittgenstein
Plato 76, 81, 129, 174, 186–7, 220
poetry 44–6, 66, 178, 192, 206–7
praxis 242–3
Preisendanz, Wolfgang 94
Prendergast, Christopher 50

Quintilian 61–2

Rank, Otto 184
rationalism 17
Ray, Gene 234
realist novel 238 *see also* Lukács
reason 10, 12
redemption 159, 192 *see also*
  messianism; Rosenzweig
reflection 7
  aesthetic 13, 107

Riegl, Alois 192
Roh, Franz 206
Romanticism/Romantics 86–7, 106, 175, 180, 198, 225
   early Romantics 7, 11–13, 66, 68, 73, 101, 107, 157, 222
   romantic anti-capitalism 231
Rorty, Richard 180
Rosenkranz, Karl 192, 225
Rosenzweig, Franz 159–61
Rousseau, Jean-Jacques 14–15, 19, 52–4

Sartre, Jean-Paul 236, 238–42
Saussure, Ferdinand de 109
saying [*Sagen*] 136–44 *see also* showing [*Zeigen*]
   Wittgenstein on 140–4
Schelling, Friedrich Wilhelm Joseph von 114, 129, 146, 157, 175, 177, 229
   Philosophy of Art 12, 76
Schiller, Friedrich 1, 7, 24, 30, 190
   aesthetic education of man 39
   aesthetic state 80–2
Schlegel, Johann Elias 45
Schlegel, Karl Wilhelm Friedrich 12, 60, 72, 74, 94, 115, 222–3, 228
   on irony 64–6
Schmitt, Carl 129, 134, 231
Schopenhauer, Arthur 30–3, 88, 129
   World as Will and Representation, The 31, 145, 147–9, 165–6
Schulte-Sasse, Jochen 107, 115, 227–8
self-interest 17, 19, 112, 118
sensation *see* feeling
sensibility/sensible 8, 83, 111, 164
   representation 37
   sensual cognition 78
sentimentalism (*Empfindsamkeit*) 58
Shaftesbury, Anthony Ashley Cooper, the Third Earl of 24

Shakespeare, William 133–4, 224
shock 205, 231
showing [*Zeigen*] 136–44 *see also* saying [*Sagen*]
   Heidegger on 139
   Wittgenstein on 140–4
shudder 36, 227–35
signs 46
Simmel, Georg 193
Sloterdijk, Peter 172
Smith, Adam 24, 111–12
Socrates 62–3, 150, 186
Sophocles 131
Spinoza, Baruch [Benedict de] 114
Spitzer, Leo 188
Steiner, George 55, 126
Stiegler, Bernd 209
structuralism 109, 114–16
"Sturm und Drang" 58–9
subjectivity/subject 5–6, 13, 69, 74–5, 114–15, 131, 149
sublime (the) 34–42, 149, 181, 227, 235
   Adorno on 41, 234 *see also Aesthetic Theory*
   dynamical 37, 234
   Hegel on 40
   mathematical 37, 234
   sublimity of action 38–9 *see also* Schiller
   ugliness 222
Sulzer, Johann Georg 27–9, 31, 70
symbol/symbolism 101–2
Szondi, Peter 129

taste *see* judgment
theater 48, 129, 196, 199, 239–40
Tholen, Georg Cristoph 172
Tieck, Ludwig 73, 86
tragedy 127–35, 149
   "proletarian" 128
   tragic hero 133
transcendental signifier 124
Trauerspiel see Walter Benjamin

trope 61–2, 100–3, 106
truth 174–80, 222
　aesthetic 180
　as disclosure and concealment 153, 177–8, 193–4
　truth-content of the artwork 240–1

ugly 219–26
　the repulsive 225 *see also* Rosenkranz
uncanny 181–7, 194, 227, 235
unconscious 113, 115, 118, 181, 184, 187, 235
understanding 28–9
unrepresentable 41

value 109–18
　aesthetic 109–10, 113–17, 201
　economic 109–12
　ethical 109, 111–13
　linguistic 109
　surplus 118
visual *logos* 144 *see also* Mersch

Wackenroder, Heinrich Wilhelm 73–4, 86
Wagner, Richard 84, 88, 132
Wagnerism 89
Waldenfels, Bernhard 139
Wellbery, David E. 46, 189–90
will 147–9 *see also* Schopenhauer
will-to-power 97, 125, 151, 176, 227, 233
Winckelmann, Johann Joachim 101, 110, 174
wit 15, 51
Wittgenstein, Ludwig 140–4
Wolff, Christian 25, 174

www.ingramcontent.com/pod-product-compliance
Lightning Source LLC
Chambersburg PA
CBHW052218300426
44115CB00011B/1742